THE LANDSCAPE
OF CONTEMPORARY
INFRASTRUCTURE

THE LANDSCAPE OF CONTEMPORARY INFRASTRUCTURE

Kelly Shannon Marcel Smets

NAi Publishers, Rotterdam

CONTENTS

INTRODUCTION

PURPOSE
AND CONCEPTION

INFRASTRUCTURE AS PUBLIC ENDEAVOR

The growing and unmistakable interest in infrastructure calls for a sound overview of recent exemplary design. Across the globe, public authorities view infrastructure – particularly transport infrastructure – as their primary field of investment. In a world where urbanization is increasingly produced by private capital, infrastructure appears as the backbone onto which these building initiatives can be grafted. As such, infrastructural design emerges as one of the last resorts that allow public authorities to give structure to haphazard settlement and reclaim the discipline of urbanism. Furthermore, the importance of mobility and transport is universally recognized. Accessibility lies at the root of development and the infrastructure needed to secure it determines the quality of the environment, both at the global level (by giving access to places and making them part of the world economy), and at the local level (by enhancing the dwelling quality of the public realm).

As societies become increasingly urbanized, decision-making and spatial feasibility make infrastructure more and more complex. The radical transformation and creation of landscapes through infrastructural development is a global phenomenon. Large-scale, capital-intensive infrastructural projects are completely transforming urban and rural territories alike. Urban conurbations and settlements are repositioned on the basis of new economies, proximities, and hierarchies, while landscapes and ecologies are radically altered. Yet growing population density and social improvement have sharpened the resistance to the possibly disruptive interventions of airports, highways, railroads, and even waterways in natural landscapes and/or built environments. A well-oiled community design process of forums, task forces, and advisory committees has allowed citizens and action groups opposed to the hindrances provoked by infrastructure to become more relevant, and their highly publicized campaigns generally make politicians think twice before committing to projects. The involvement of so many stakeholders, and also the shortage of space and the growing intermodal character of transport solutions, definitely augments the difficulty and complexity of the design problem. Today, the creation of infrastructure can no longer simply be considered as the accumulation of a large object in isolation from its surroundings. Landscape and infrastructure merge and movement corridors are (re)worked as new vessels of collective life. An entire new spectrum of the public realm becomes a terrain for investigation. In order to function, fit and be acceptable, infrastructure needs to enhance the quality of the landscape. Hence, conceiving infrastructure blends with generating architecture, building landscapes, and producing urban settings and living environments. It engages social and imaginative dimensions as much as engineering. In that respect, designing transport infrastructure today comes down to making it part of an integrated project. Once married with architecture, mobility, and landscape, infrastructure can more meaningfully integrate territories, reduce marginalization and segregation, and stimulate new forms of interaction. It can then truly become "landscape."

INFRASTRUCTURE AS AN INTEGRATED DESIGN PROJECT

Approaching infrastructural design as an integrated project drastically changes the position, contribution, and responsibility of the professional disciplines involved in its creation. Unlike in previous generations when large engineering offices were engaged for the entire management of the building process of infrastructure – from preliminary design to the control of execution drawings, launch of the tender, and follow-up of the contractor/developer – there is now a growing tendency to have multiple disciplines involved from the outset. Generally speaking, the urban designer or landscape architect is no longer simply there to beautify a project that is principally based on technical considerations, but is often a primary designer of infrastructure together with engineers. To arrive at a satisfactory proposal, the work is usually undertaken in close collaboration with specialized firms in construction or traffic management, but the emphasis on architecture and landscape resulting from a new distribution of tasks is evident. A cyclical process whereby the renewed interest in spatial quality on the side of public clients has strengthened the position of urban and landscape design, and has produced projects that in turn inspire other public bodies to heighten their ambition for a quality infrastructure, has thus been set in motion. Such a process prompts the new models of contemporary practice.

This book is modeled on the interplay between the two roles of practice: the one of receiver, and the one of inspirer. It documents and gives critical commentary on noteworthy projects and offers a catalog of references and comparable cases. The growing complexity of today's infrastructural projects pushes practitioners to seek sensible solutions that can be informed by analogous problems elsewhere. In the pioneering field of integrated landscape design, the professions of the built environment are constantly searching for models. At the same time, due to the impact of local specificity, it is clear that such models should not be considered as rules, norms, or laws. They have no universal validity and can never be identically applied from one situation to another. No matter how spatially attractive a concept or scheme may look, it is never more than the outcome of a particular design process influenced by local interests and circumstances. For that reason, the real value of the model rather resides in the mindset and the reasoning that led to the configuration of the intervention. This book distils such attitudes rather than simply compiling an inventory of blueprints.

Therefore, the ambition of this book is larger than the overview it apparently suggests. The book develops pertinent themes in the landscape of contemporary infrastructure, illustrated by exemplary built projects across the globe. It endeavors to show that infrastructural development is not merely a technical matter to be left to traffic planners, engineers, and politicians, but a crosscutting field that involves multiple sectors and where the role of designers is essential. Fundamentally, the outline of projects aims for reflection on an archetype of classification rather than a documentation based on a selection of cases. The reasoning behind the register is more important, and hopefully more durable, than the register itself. The rationale for this choice is rather evident: at a time when computer-refined search engines and availability of information are so prevalent, the mere compilation of cases has become rather senseless. Such a catalog risks becoming quickly outdated and will necessarily be incomplete. A taxonomy of design attitudes, by contrast, should remain valid over time. Hopefully, it can keep on functioning as a directory, an outline that helps others to integrate new cases and refine the meaning of design approaches that are put forward with this book.

A BOOK STRUCTURE BASED ON FOUR ENTRIES

The taxonomy of design attitudes that forms the backbone of this book is based on four fundamental ways in which transport infrastructure affects the spatial environment and how it is perceived. These four basic entry points also determine the composition of the four chapters. The first chapter argues that mobility constitutes the footprint of urbanization and explores the role of transportation networks in structuring urbanization. It analyzes the ways in which the transformation of accessibility shapes the spatial organization of the territory and investigates how the spatial form of the transport network either emphasizes the global character that the network enhances or strengthens the local identity of the places it crosses.

The second chapter focuses on the physical presence that infrastructure inevitably imposes on its environs. It discusses the different approaches toward the integration of these large objects into the surrounding landscape, both from the point of view of avoiding the hindrances they create and the opportunity they contain for investing in the overall refurbishment of the areas.

The third chapter fundamentally considers the ways in which the motion generated by transport infrastructure affects the perception of the surrounding landscape. It shows the diverse methods that designers make use of to stress this idea of movement in the layout of their infrastructure, often with the intention of increasing the legibility of the environs it traverses.

Finally, the fourth chapter reflects on the role of infrastructure as public space. Considering its sheer number of users – comparable to major sports events – and its easy accessibility in practical and social terms, transport infrastructure has clearly become the prime public space of the present day, particularly in countries where the classical public urban realm (market place, road, and roadside parking) has been replaced by a collective private realm (shopping mall, parking building, etc.). But it belongs to the specific nature of transport accommodation that it entails a common experience not only of place but also of voyage. Therefore, designers portraying these spaces typically highlight the various types of behavior displayed by people on the move. Design attitudes toward transport infrastructure are, in this respect, also revealing for the mindset of society in general toward the significance of public space.

Based on these four entry points – mobility, physical presence, movement, and public character – the structure of the consecutive chapters is largely the same. Each chapter starts with an introductory essay, clarifying the meaning of the central theme and referencing other authors and historical precedents. There then follows a categorization of the design approaches itemizing the conceptual stances that designers of present-day infrastructure adopt in relation to the central topic of the chapter. Each category is explained in a short commentary and then exemplified by an overview of projects for several transport modes. The taxonomy is made more clear-cut and accessible through the identification and ample documentation of "majors" – projects of a highly exemplary nature. However, the making of such a choice inevitably implies that analogous projects would, often undeservedly, be excluded. For this reason, there is the inclusion of "minors" – projects that also highlight a particular approach. They are referred to in the opening text to elucidate the design attitude they bear witness to. The cumulative examples – of multiple modes of transport – reveal an approach to designing infrastructure and a relationship to landscapes that is archetypal. As with any taxonomy, categories only gain substance when they include a relevant number of cases. It is evident, for that matter, that all our categories in this book include many fine projects, and that the choice between "majors" and "minors" is motivated more by an assessment of archetypal qualification than by an appraisal of conceptual or spatial quality. Moreover, it must be repeated, this categorization is intended as a tool to highlight approaches. It is a conceptual, artificial operation, and several projects could clearly fit into more than one category.

THE ARCHETYPAL VALUE OF EXEMPLARY PROJECTS

Even though this publication is primarily intended to put forward a useful, multifaceted systematization of design approaches rather than an overview of projects, the choosing of cases to illustrate these attitudes remains critical. For this reason, the selection was premised on clear criteria and guidelines. Firstly, projects were to have already been implemented, or be in the course of realization. Costly works of infrastructure prove their social acceptance, economic viability, and political and financial feasibility by implementation. This ultimate criterion of societal approval helped to circumvent the debate on the many – sometimes enlightened – concepts that have been proposed in recent times to improve the institutionalized mindsets of transport and traffic management. This general rule of implementation was abandoned only in the case of a few "minors," for projects whose realization was still under discussion. A second criterion for selection was the current relevance of the projects. This term is hard to define precisely, but it refers to the expectation among practitioners for fresh and up-to-date projects. More classical and canonical projects that bear tremendous interest for practice, but which belong to another era, have been discussed as historical precedents. As a consequence, the selected reference projects are not more than 15 years old, unless a project exceptionally bears witness to such archetypal value that it outshines more recent examples of the same attitude. Of course, such assessment inevitably remains subjective. The main criterion for selecting case studies resides in their archetypal meaning. The projects you will discover do not in themselves reflect the preference of the authors, but are considered significant and representative. In order to be evocative of a global trend, the overwhelming number of projects from Europe or North America is complemented, as much as possible, by lesser-known examples from other continents.

Finally, a word must be said concerning the state of the art of this research. Contemporary discourse on the built environment is awash with "infrastructure" and "landscape" and their far-reaching conceptual scope. In Europe and North America, recent exhibitions, symposia, workshops, and articles have focused on new opportunities afforded by infrastructural development. Rotterdam's first biennale (2000) focused on mobility; the Paris-based Cities on the Move Institute presented the exhibition manifestoes and catalogues *Architecture on the Move: Cities and Mobilities* (2003) and *The Street Belongs to All of Us* (2007). Recent publications such as *The Mesh Book: Landscape/Infrastructure* by Julian Taxworthy and Jessica Blood and *Metropolitan Networks* by Jordi Julià Sort pay attention to the theme. *Zoomscape: Architecture in Motion and Media* by Mitchell Schwarzer and *On the Move: Mobility in the Modern Western World* by Tim Cresswell delve into key changes in modern history related to mobility and perception of the environment. *The Architecture of Parking* by Simon Henley sketches an overview of recent typologies in parking accommodation, *Les mégastructures du transport* by Corinne Tiry compares and analyzes important cases of multimodal transport worldwide, and *La métropole des infrastructures* by Claude Prelorenzo and Dominique Rouillard (eds) gathers together a collection of essays on the meaning of design in infrastructure. Harvard University Graduate School of Design hosted a conference and exhibit entitled "Inhabiting Infrastructure" (2004). And prominent magazines such as *Lotus* (with a principle article written by Smets),

L'Arca, *A+T*, *Techniques & Architecture*, and *Topos* have all dedicated thematic issues to the subject. Furthermore, many individual projects have been documented, both in articles in professional magazines and in monographic publications devoted to their author. Yet despite this overwhelming interest in the subject, this publication reveals itself as one of the first extensive, global overviews and systematic assessments of contemporary infrastructure projects.

This book builds upon and differentiates itself from the previous research and, at the same time, hopes to initiate future research into the fascinating subject. In the coming decades, the universal concern with sustainability and the predicted consequences of climate change will most likely lead to major breakthroughs in rethinking the interplay between infrastructure and landscape. The general level of awareness of environmental effects has renewed both public interest in and political commitment to alternative solutions to tried-and-true modes and models of mobility. Furthermore, technological innovations in transport vehicles – including electric cars, fully automated trains, and larger aircraft – and new materials will certainly keep on challenging the many professionals involved in designing infrastructure. The authors are perfectly aware of the impact these trends might exert on future concepts, but have preferred to incorporate the signs that point today in that direction into the discussion of design attitudes that forms the general frame of this book.

This comprehensive publication addresses itself to urban designers, architects, landscape architects, civil engineers, traffic planners, and policy-makers. It points toward the blurring of traditional disciplinary boundaries and opens up a plethora of new avenues in the creation of new landscapes and infrastructures. It may indeed be anticipated that the creation of successful 21st-century infrastructural projects will rely on creative public-private partnerships and the continued integration of civil engineering, urban design, landscape architecture, and architecture. That is why this book reveals the richness of projects that innovatively combine design and engineering, and simultaneously construct infrastructure and fascinating landscapes.

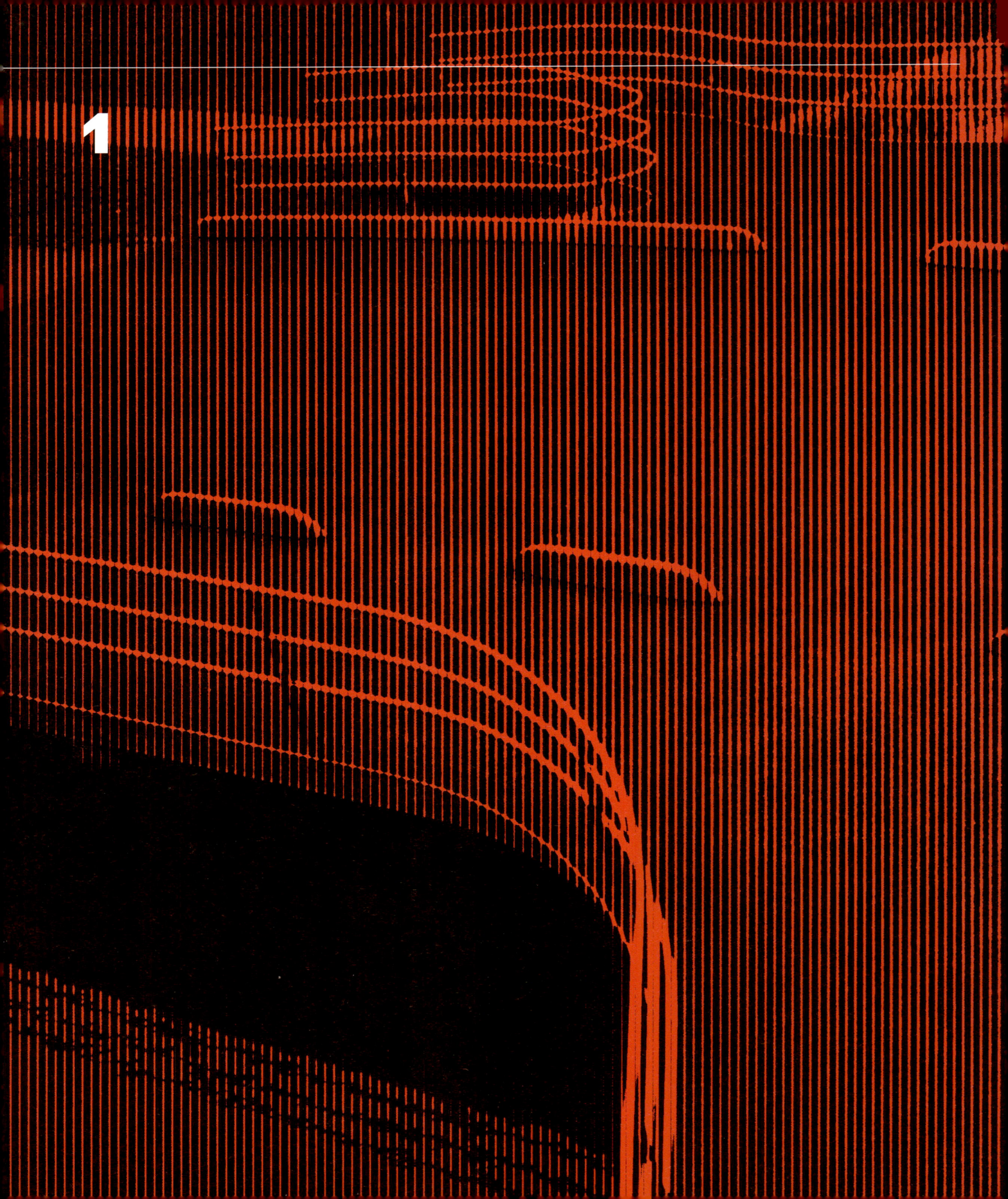

1

IMPRINTS OF MOBILITY ON THE LANDSCAPE

INTRODUCTION
SHAPING MOBILITY THROUGH INFRASTRUCTURE

Mobility has become a condition for modern life. Since World War II, the world has evidenced the growing division between production and consumption. In the global economic system, the activities of conceiving, manufacturing, marketing, and financing have increasingly separated and become geographically dispersed. The resulting growth of services and the shift of production to an assemblage of just-in-time components have given rise to new spatial and temporal relations. Consequently, contemporary society has become heavily dependent upon mobility for its economic life. In today's worldwide economy, the development potential of a city or region increasingly relies on the quality of its connections to the various transportation networks. A large body of literature exists on the *Rise of the Network Society*, documenting and critically interpreting the phenomenon that Manuel Castells terms the "space of flows." This book does not enter into such a debate. Instead, it is more interested in the tangible consequences that these new patterns of international exchange generate for local development and policy.

It is clear that local leaders often attempt to alleviate regional disparity by effective standardization and construction of new infrastructural systems. From this viewpoint, investment in infrastructure is intended as a lever for stimulating local welfare. The preferred form of transport is generally inspired by technical innovation, but it ultimately depends upon the transport mode that best serves society's purposes. As a rule, ships and trains, the favored vehicles of early industrialization, have been supplanted by air and road transportation in the 20th century. Conversely, in the 21st century, scarcity of resources, saturation of existent networks, and predicted impacts on climatic change drive the search for the most effective modal split. To cater for the territorial extension of economic exchange, the size and density of infrastructural networks have systematically expanded. On the one hand, this trend is evidenced by the ever-growing density of highways in North America and Europe, the large-scale system of super-airports (particularly in the emerging economies of Asia), and the drive of many nations to build and/or expand their high-speed rail networks, ports, and waterways. On the other hand, to guarantee fluidity, societies make heavy investments to enhance the capacity of existing infrastructure systems.

By definition, infrastructure sustains a condition of continuous flux: it generates an urban dynamic and stimulates movement to the limits of its own capacity or the endurance of the settlement it

has helped to create. A static object that frames flows, it incessantly needs to renew itself and search for alternatives. When the maximum physical and/or environmental carrying capacity is reached, two basic alternatives are available: to expand by doubling the existing capacity in another location, or to transfer the extra traffic demand to another transportation mode. Examples of the former can be found on many scale levels: the bypass built to lower traffic through towns, the encouragement of alternative routing to decongest highways, or the creation of second or third airports to meet air-traffic demands in larger metropolitan areas. The second case is most clearly illustrated by the recent introduction of high-speed trains as alternatives to both airways and highways. Independent tramways, upgraded sections of existing metro/rail connections, and cycle paths are also established as alternatives to urban thoroughfares. To redirect freight traffic from congested highways, great investments are made to expand the overall capacity of strategic waterways. Eventually, new forms of individual and collective transport emerge in response to traffic distribution, environmental constraints, and citizen actions.

Finally, the expansion, multiplication, and constant search to improve the performance of networks also increases the number of transfer points. In this sense, one can argue that the two main features that make mobility so visible are the transportation lines and the multi-modal interchanges. The former are easily discernible by the physical presence of the road, track, or path. They can also be materially hidden and only made perceptible by the occasional view or sound, as is the case with airplanes and subways. The latter involve many variants: exchanges between train, airplane, ship, bus, subway or tram, but mostly car, bike, and pedestrian for local transport. Hence the importance of parking as an intermodal amenity. To make the transfer possible, one or other form of infrastructure is required. For that reason, the network is most strongly expressed at its nodes. The perception of nodes prevails over the awareness of the lines, not only because of their intrinsic architectural dominance, but also because of their particular nature as meeting place and point of public interaction.

THE INVISIBLE SOURCE OF MUSHROOMING DEVELOPMENT
By providing accessibility to the wider world and acting as an interface between people and goods of different origins, transportation networks have always been a source of interchange. For that reason, urbanization has always developed around traffic nodes. In former times, cities grew at the crossings of rivers and

roads or the stopping places of carriages and caravans. In industrial times, railroads generated urbanization around train stations and cars created ribbon development. Today we are witnessing the growth of "edge cities" around highway exits, airports accesses, and fast-rail connections in the richer part of the world, while elsewhere informal trading and spontaneous settlements spring up around bus stations, along congested thoroughfares, and in derelict parking lots. Most of the time, these developments occur haphazardly, according to the rules of real estate profit, after the infrastructure has been put in place.

After World War II, mobility grew to become a requirement of modern life. The traditional equation between accessibility and transaction became a primary motor for spatial development. People traveling the network were equally vendors and customers, which made the appeal of centrally located areas increase with the number and intensity of connections they were served by. The denser the network, the more expanded the area of high accessibility and the wider the realm of potential development. Without necessarily being visible as a physical entity, the network thus produced a concentration of building mass and accumulation of activity. This mechanism is clearly illustrated by the densification process around airports all over the world. Airports are, in effect, nodes of invisible, computer-steered air routes. Similar invisible threads are the metro or underground rail lines that pop up every so often in the agglomerated cityscape and generate real estate

development whose density is a reflection of the important of the stations. These built landscapes, engendered by accessibility, are products of the market-driven economy. They spring from a process of urbanization in which the overall built form is shaped by successive incremental interventions that respond to the real estate value of their location. In this sense, there is a general shift from a single concentration of high-rise development in the easily reached downtown to a rhizoid spread of edge cities along the major infrastructural axes. Such a shift in urban form visibly marks the progression from the accessibility of the well-served central business district, to the more dispersed availability of well-connected hubs.

Throughout history, providers of infrastructure have tried to benefit from the conjunction of transport and development. Indeed, transportation lines help to intensify land use. As a consequence, they raise land prices and this surplus value can be used to repay the investment required for the provision of the line. This reimbursement of invested funds can take the form of either direct remuneration – by selling off or renting out the speculative development – or indirect compensation, for example by the generation of new tax revenue. In either case, the implementation of infrastructure becomes part of a consistent public or corporate planning strategy. The primary example of the first mode of operation is Arturo Soria y Mata's proposal for the Ciudad Lineal in Madrid, a linear settlement set up by the tram company and organized as a narrow spine that connects the city periphery with the existing urban cen-

1 LINEAR CITY

The transversal section of Arturo Soria y Mata's Ciudad Lineal. The tramline was to generate a development capacity that would in turn cover the cost of its construction.

ters along the tramway line [1]. The London Underground, propagating suburban development in the interwar period, is an example of how an indirect return on investment was realized [2].

Until today, the concern for compensating for the cost of infrastructure by either profiting from real estate development or augmenting the number of passengers remains a major incentive for integrating transport planning with urban development. An archetype of governmental action in this respect is the office and trade fair district La Défense in Paris (begun in 1951). Close to the Périphérique ringroad, it was conceived as an entity of its own that terminated Paris's historical axis on its western side and met the need for office space in the modernizing city without drastically altering its historic core. The mainly pedestrian-access business district was centered on an oval freeway loop and on top of a web of public transport lines. A precise determination and separation of flows was the outcome of a complex hierarchy of circulation routes [3]. A ringroad reserved for local traffic directly serves the eleven sectors of La Défense and the main parking garages. Expressways for long-distance traffic are grouped in the center, along with the entry points to public transport stations (suburban express line from 1970 and metro from 1992). As the maze of underground infrastructure has continued to expand, the most recent interventions focus on improving the legibility and spatial communication among the interventions.

Then again, in Japan – a land-scarce country – almost all suburban rail lines have been privately built. Typically initiated by large consortia, the railroads also exploit the land they render accessible. Train stations thus become mini-cities. They attract urban activities and built landscapes spring up around them that reflect the land-value appreciation that accrues from increasing the accessibility. The rhizoid nature of mushrooming development is thus determined by the general transportation scheme, which guides subsequent interventions to benefit from land-value exploitation. Tokyu is Japan's largest rail-based conglomerate. It explicitly anchors terminuses to high-rise commercial centers (containing the rail company's own department stores) and even a number university campuses to intermediate stations (along Shibuya and Sakuragicho in downtown Yokohama) to generate off-peak and reverse-direction rail traffic. Between 1960 and 1985, Tokyu transformed a vast, hilly, and scarcely inhabited area west of Tokyo into a planned community of 5000 hectares and nearly half a million residents (Tama Garden City). Another rail company, Keisei Corporation, developed Tokyo Disneyland. Most private rail companies in Japan have pursued other commercial ventures, including the construction and operation of hotels, department stores, sports stadiums, amusement parks, and other ancillary businesses.

Hong Kong, another land-scarce Asian urban agglomerate, with incredibly high density and steep topography, is widely regarded

2 **GARDEN CITY**
London Underground, Northern Line. Poster propagating the wellbeing of garden suburb extension.

3 **CIRCULATION SCHEME**
for La Défense, combining motorized traffic and public transport.

UNDERGROUND

THE SOONEST REACHED AT ANY TIME
GOLDERS GREEN
(HENDON AND FINCHLEY)
A PLACE OF DELIGHTFUL PROSPECTS

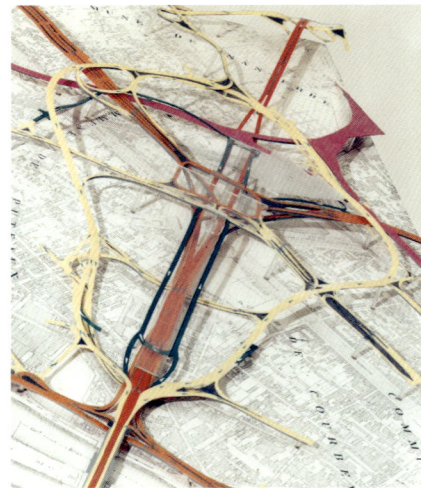

as having one of today's most successfully integrated public-transport systems in the world. The city's secret to that success has been to pay for the expensive public transit by marrying it with private real-estate development. Its network of trains, buses, ferries, and trams unites with an extensive system of pedestrian pathways and escalators that weave through retail developments and transportation hubs. To facilitate the development in the huge reclamation projects through which the city continues to expand, public transportation remains the key instrument. A case in point is the recent Kowloon Station by Terry Farrell where a new precinct of one million square meters was laid out around three large raised pedestrian landscape squares surrounded by highrise buildings [4]. The public platform is like an iceberg, with the bulk of sectionally layered transit underground. The station is an interchange between three separate rail lines, including the line from Hong Kong Central to Chek Lap Kok Airport. Airport check-in, coach, bus, and car transport are all on different levels and linked by a mezzanine concourse. Farrell's intervention also includes the urban design framework for air-rights development over and around the station.

In the colder parts of North America, underground pedestrian networks have a similar effect of giving structure to the built landscape above by regulating its accessibility and increasing land value accordingly. In Montreal, the city's multistory underground pedestrian passages form a complex, approximately 30 kilometers long, that provides facilities for business, shopping, rendezvous, and entertainment.[1] It is accessible by a number of integrated metro stations and offers a warm, dry atmosphere even during the raw Canadian winter [5]. The subterranean labyrinth intermingles and merges with the ground level, increasing the density of the urban core in a three-dimensional continuity. The web of permanently conditioned halls, corridors, arches, catacombs, and block-size spaces reveals a collective space in its own right. The networked pedestrian zone caters to the North American tradition of speculative planning in which profit-oriented logic favors gigantism and multifunctionalism to increase the influx of visitors and financial gain. Montreal's regulations allow developers to build private underground passages across public rights of way and the city is permitted to tunnel under private property (whereby a connection to the metro can be built at the expense of the private property owner). Such policies enable the municipality to have private capital finance projects of collective interest. Consequently, they enable Montreal's central city real estate market to be affected by its hidden infrastructural web of sprawling corridors.

In other harsh climatic circumstances – in Asian cities such as Singapore and Hong Kong, and UAE cities such as Abu Dhabi and Dubai – interconnected systems of commerce and marketing are ensconced in the embrace of central air-conditioning, creating hermetically sealed, pedestrian corridors of another type than in Canada. They form a labyrinth of multilevel shopping malls that

4 **CONTEMPORARY HUB**
Terry Farrell's Kowloon Station is an air-rights scheme that encompasses the land values created by widespread accessibility.

work like a constellation of capital-generating and socially segregated islands. They are more part of ongoing development than a generator of later growth. Nonetheless, their logical trajectories pave the way for yet more extensions to the corridor networks that turn into urban infrastructure parallel to the systems of transport mobility.

THE NETWORK AS IMPETUS FOR IMPROVEMENT

The landing of a transportation network typically acts as a boost for development. Yet it frequently sets off a reaction among established interests against the modifications initiated. To capitalize on both effects, investments in networks are often accompanied by comprehensive (re)development. Such recovery stems from a need for compensation. It seeks to balance investment in infrastructure by upgrading the urban environment and recuperating the surplus value created by public money for public benefit. It makes the chosen policy acceptable to the public by revealing the overall payback it produces for urban improvement. More often, such strategic planning is prompted by public authorities. Its general ambition is to turn a potential drawback into an asset, correct the standard effect of land exploitation, and use the arrival of the network/infrastructure as an opportunity for a project to enhance the public realm by providing a convincing mixture of activities, open spaces, and amenities. Depending on the willingness to add public funds, it usually corroborates or reverses the capsular nature of transport infrastructure.

When recovery is primarily viewed as a way to make the infrastructural investment politically feasible, it frequently takes on the form of an urban fragment, most often devoted to an overriding form or repetitive morphology, and to an area linked and identified with the transfer point – "airport-city," "train station district," "edge-city office park," and so on. These comprehensive developments occur primarily in the vicinity of airports, high-speed train stations, and highway interchanges. Their specific conception varies with the particular assignment, but they are mostly treated as cocoons. The transportation amenity is considered not only a source but also a part of the development. Connections and relationships are principally viewed in that respect. They hardly take into consideration other clues offered by the surrounding environment. They regularly construct new landscapes that detach themselves from the existing and mark their homogeneity by such a difference. However, when conversion is viewed as part of a larger operation of urban improvement, it generally spreads over a larger area. Instead of focusing on the immediate vicinity of multimodal transfer points, it touches on the many entry and exit stations of the transport line. By doing so, its territorial impact and effectiveness in transforming the perception of whole city districts widens. When localized along the network, amenities are indeed made accessible to the entire urban population. Infrastructure is thus intentionally set up by public authorities as a meeting place for different layers of society to interact and as a backbone of general civic improvement.

5 **UNDERGROUND NETWORKS**

Montreal's network of acclimatized subterranean passages is a public realm that generates the multi-faceted urban programming of the urban core.

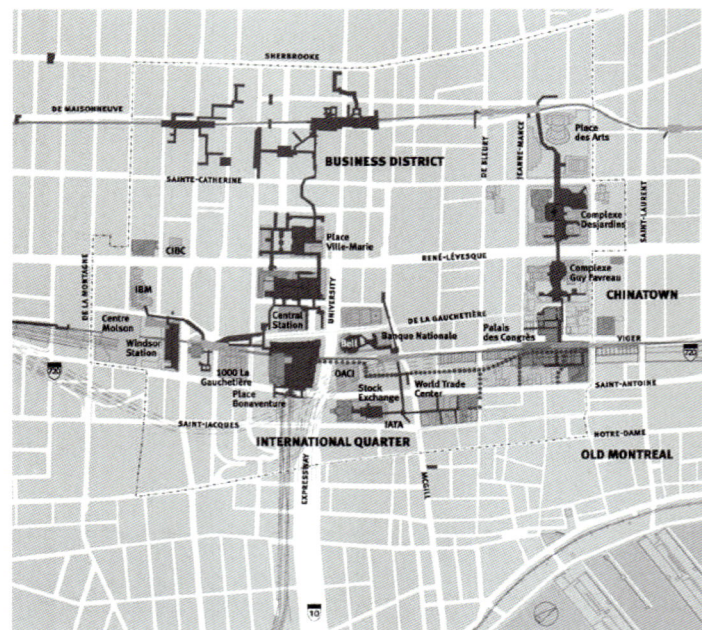

A canonical urban regeneration project in Europe, Canary Wharf, located in the London Borough of Tower Hamlets on the old West India Docks, has become a large business and shopping area while simultaneously rivaling London's traditional financial district. Nearly 100,000 people, the majority of whom are commuters, are employed in the former docklands. Much of the success credited to this icon of urban renaissance is credited to the routing of London's newest tube, the Jubilee Line Extension (JLE), to the area (effectively replacing the inadequate Docklands Light Railway). The Jubilee Line (from Green Park to Stratford) connects to all other Underground lines and its existing and extension lines link to new development areas such as the Millennium Dome, South Bank, and Thames Gateway. The JLE is a huge and expensive undertaking coordinated by Roland Paoletti, who made a name for himself in the 1980s with construction of the metro in Hong Kong. Old stations along the line were transformed and nine of the new stations along the extension were designed by well-known firms; Westminster (Hopkins Architects), Southwark (MJP Architects), Canary Wharf (Foster + Partners), and North Greenwich (Alsop & Störmer Architects). These endeavors revived the Underground as an important civic space and constituted a statement of the importance of London Public Transport not made since Charles Holden's designs of the 1930s [6-7].

In Stuttgart, an ambitious reconstruction project is representative of a series of such projects throughout Germany in particular, and Europe in general. The complete reconstruction of the existing main station area is justified as the German rail system adapts itself to high-speed travel. In the program dubbed Stuttgart 21, Deutsche Bahn will lay new tracks in a tunnel 12 meters below street level and convert the existing terminus into a through station. The through station's green roof is conceived as a pedestrian plaza, with facilities below at track level and a 70-meter-wide green Avenue 21 to structure the new urban district [8]. Similar projects have been discussed and are on the boards for Frankfurt and Munich.

Meanwhile, in many French cities – among them Strasbourg, Nantes, Montpellier and Grenoble – the construction or reinstatement of tram systems has been at the heart of many regeneration projects. For example, in the coastal city of Nice, sandwiched between the mountains and the Mediterranean Sea, an ambitious urban renewal program was coupled with the development of a system that mandates 60% of the residents in the metropolitan area and 80% of the total jobs to be within 500 meters of a tram line. Due to restrictions of topography and a lack of space for large infrastructural interventions, the new transport network has been cleverly developed in the residual spaces between highways, off-ramps, and imposing housing blocks. The system will eventually count three lines. For the moment, a large part of the first line's budget was invested in stormwater drainage works, rebuilding of the city's central Place Masséna, public lighting, and tree planting [9].

6-7 INFRASTRUCTURE AS REGENERATION

The civic quality of the London Underground was employed as a tool for regenerating the environment it serves – exemplified by Canary Wharf Station (Norman Foster/ Foster+Partners) and Westminster Station (Michael Hopkins/Hopkins Architects).

Canary Wharf Station

Westminster Station

In the city core, the project included large areas restricted to tram and pedestrian access. In outlying neighborhoods there are sections of grassed tracks. The depot, by Marc Barani, incorporates a park-and-ride facility for 700 cars and, in a highly composite design, spirals over the tracks on the sloping terrain of Las Palmas.

Finally, in extreme conditions, high in the Andes Mountains, Bogotá has also used infrastructure development as a massive driver for urban renewal. Its clear policy of enhanced accessibility serves as an instrument for supporting local cultural activities, promoting social inclusion and government credibility. Because of this recovery, Bogotá, a city once renowned for drug trafficking, urban guerrillas, and grinding poverty, has, in the last few years, been trust into the international limelight for its refurbished and newly constructed public space. A bus rapid transit system (TransMilenio) and extensive network of cycle paths (the largest in Latin America) spatially structures the upgraded public space and effectively integrates transport in an enlarged civic realm. Since 1996, the spearheaded programs in this city of nearly eight million to increase public-sector mobility have focused not only on the improvement and expansion of the municipal park system, but also on the municipal library system. Called "The Defense of Public Space," the initiative was established to recover illegally occupied space for pedestrians, and substantially renovate it through improvements in sidewalks, traffic signals, lighting, and trees.

These cases are particularly highlighted to demonstrate the configurative capacity of transportation networks. By the way in which it spatially organizes accessibility, transport infrastructure differentiates places in the overall structure of the city. It creates a surplus value that pays back for either the cost of installing the transport system or the investments made to intensify urban activity along its route. In both cases, the spatial layout of the transportation network becomes a vital instrument for intentionally organizing (through urbanism) or unintentionally witnessing (through urbanization) the development of the collective realm. Following such reasoning, the following sections of this chapter address the formative power of the network: first, the replication of the standardized solution to stress the overall identity of the network; and second, the elaboration of distinctive design solutions to stress the *genius loci* of the localities that the network serves.

1 Reyner Banham, "Megacity Montreal," in *Megastructure: Urban Futures of the Recent Past* (New York and London: Harper and Row, 1967), 105-129.

8 **RAIL RENOVATION**
The Stuttgart 21 renovation project in Germany is a canonical example of urban improvement linked to the modernization of railroads in Europe.

9 **TRAMWAY IMPETUS**
The tramway in Nice, France, creates a succession of profiles that blend together in a network that structures the town's central places.

STANDARD PROFILES AS A MEANS OF IDENTIFICATION

Historically, networks have often been identified by their standard appearance. This long tradition extends from the canals du Midi and de Bourgogne to the national highways initiated by Maria Theresia and Napoleon, the rail networks of the 19th century, and the highway systems of the 20th century. In all these cases, the standard had to do with an autonomous layer, which permitted the control of quality and efficiency by imposing a norm. Many standards grew out of practice. They initially came about through technical specifications, material characteristics, and uniform engineering. Over time, improved efficiency required levels of compatibility, interchangeability, and commonality – eventually leading to the adoption of uniform procedures, dimensions, and components. This tendency towards standardization also gave visual clues that elements along the network belong to the same system. The effect was one of imposing a new order on an existing landscape, and by doing so making modernization evident. According to academic Kathy Poole, "Through roughly 150 years of industrialization we have come to believe that the politics of efficiency are beyond question and that standardization is the ultimate expression of democracy."[1] Contemporary practice still draws upon this approach. The archetype serves to guarantee overall quality, and by doing so inevitably highlights the prevalence of the global dimension of the network on the local character it touches.

Even though design specifics are usually regulated by country, universal norms to ensure safety and efficiency draw railroad and highway settings universally closer. This is particularly evident in the language of highways, where the profiles of soft shoulders, taluses, guard rails, and faintly lit tunnels become a road-building bible of sorts, developed from the standardization of highway geometry. A sovereign catalogue of independent parts – from curve radii to interchanges, cloverleaf turnoffs, and overpasses – is thus imposed on the authentic landscape. Typical transversal sections continue to transmit a certain hierarchy in the road network, but making distinctions within the same category is generally not an easy task. However, a number of success stories in France and Germany prove that the conscious design of ramps, tollgates, and bridges can lead to well-designed roads, which reveal a sensitivity towards integrating the standard profile into the landscape or marking particularity through the very design of the prototypical elements. Both the A29 and A77 in France have developed a highway language of repetitive elements that aesthetically distinguishes them amongst the ever-growing highway trajectories [1-2]. The entire repertoire of operational elements of the A29 and the tollgates of the A77 attest to the possibility to overcome the banal standards and create an identity that does not cancel out a strong relationship to the landscape, in the first case, or a strong brand (so to speak), in the second case. Meanwhile, Thomas Herzog has developed a new prototype service station for Europe's fastest and most extensive highway network, the German Autobahn. His incongruous

1 USER PROFICIENCY

The A29 forms part of the highway of the Estuaries, situated on the west coast of France and linking some of the major ports of northern and southern Europe. The designers of the route were cognizant of its fragile environment and sought minimal land occupation and maximum recycling of site rubble, and foresaw an identifiable family of 32 bridges, six of them specially designed for mammals. The route exploits the regional features of the landscape. It invests in innovative architectural treatment to mark novelty, demonstrate a general attitude of care, and contrast with the authentic scenery.

2 HI-TECH TOLLGATES

Dubosc & Landowski Architects and Arcora Engineers designed five new tollgate stations and technical service buildings for the Dordives/Cosnes-sur-Loire Section of the A77 highway in France. The unusually powerful forms of the structures are all different, yet clearly part of one architectural family. The structure is of an apparent simplicity of white-painted, tubular-metal rigged arches, space frames, and soaring white masts that clearly distinguish the segment of the highway. The tollgates all convey a strong signal and, at the same time, are discreetly integrated into the environment and designed to be as light and transparent as possible.

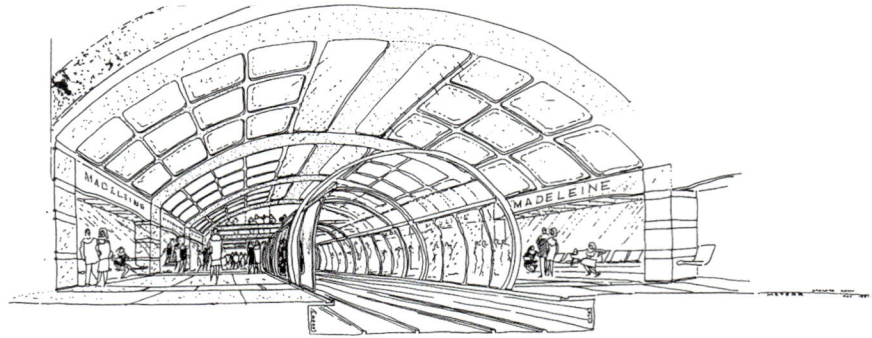

3 METRO IDENTITY

Line 14, François Mitterrand's "métro of the 21st century," was the first metro line built in Paris since 1935. Its general design concept by Bernard Kohn and Jean-Pierre Vaysse boasts state-of-the-art technology — including daylight illuminated staircases, prestigious no-corridor architecture, platform protection, glazed gates, and brightly lit underground spaces with minimal advertising and unauthorized trade. The Météor train is the world's first fully automated underground train, built by Alstom and Matra on the basis of a project by train designer Roger Tallon of Euro RSCG Design. In addition to the standard elements of the line's seven stations, the sleek train carriages themselves — 90 meters long, without compartments and with viewing glass in the forward and rear ends — are a strong part of the new line's identity.

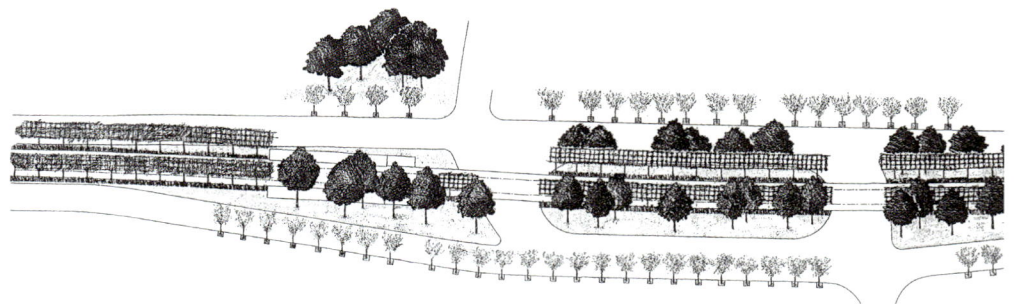

4 FORMAL CONTINUITY

Paul Chemetov with Alexandre Chemetoff and his Bureau des Paysages created a civic space in a peripheral, semi-industrial area of Paris characterized by rundown housing blocks and the absence of urban planning. The spine of this new public realm is a tramline between the districts of Bobigny and Saint-Denis, which previously lived with their backs to each other. The tramline — built along a road that traditionally served as the Paris orbital (RN-86) — was developed as a grand boulevard and introduced urban elements that were typical of traditional city centers: granite paving, rows of trees, cast-iron street furniture. The suburban neighborhoods were qualitatively upgraded by the formal continuity, irrespective of the difference in the characteristics and level of development of the areas the tramline crosses.

5 **BLOOMING BUS ROUTE**
The 22-kilometer-long section (from Amsterdam Schiphol Airport via Hoofd-dorp to Haarlem) and 14 elevated stops (by Maurice Nio) of the Zuidtangent High-Speed Bus lane in the Netherlands has been carefully designed to create a clear identity and continuity along the various urban and rural landscapes it traverses. The recurring elements — including 75-meter long, zebra-patterned concrete platforms, coverings, fencing, viaducts, windscreens, sound barriers, and tunnels — form a kit of parts in which subtle variations are possible. All bus-shelter facilities are black and white, apart from the colored glass roofs adorned with images of brightly colored flower blooms (alluding to the Floriade, the world's largest horticulture exhibition held here every 10 years). The names of the bus stops imprinted on the long glass wind-panels appear like a graphic work of art.

idea of a log cabin beside a race track is convincingly incorporated in a highly sophisticated "Meccano" of pieces that safeguards the intended architectural distinctiveness, yet makes it possible to adapt the basic package to local circumstances. His prototype, realized in the Lechwiesen Service Station along the Munich-Lindau highway, has reformulated the possibilities of imposed standards by integrating a strong environmental concern into a clear-cut, minimalist, and easily recognizable design.

New modes of public transport are clearly intended to express the *zeitgeist*. The newest generation of underground or metro lines, for example, stand for rapidity and resourcefulness. They have developed into symbolic icons of a proficient future and their standardization (and even automatization) has allowed emblematic design experimentation. The standard stations by Bernard Kohn and Jean-Pierre Vaysse of Line 14 (the Météor) of the Paris metro bring daylight, volume, and space into the natural darkness of the underground and portray the proficiency of automatic transport in the appearance of the trains [3]. Norman Foster's Bilbao Metro in Spain shows a 20th-century fin-de-siècle equivalent to Guimard's famous art nouveau entrances to the Paris Metro of a century ago. Both ventures used advanced technologies to offer an urbane sense of welcome, comfort, and arrival. This high-tech branding of new transport routes has an impact beyond aesthetics. It represents a new consideration and social value of the public realm. Beyond these exemplary yet perhaps somewhat exceptional metro projects, it is reassuring, and to some degree more impressive, to see that there are projects in less glamorous urban contexts that are able to transcend their function of transport. They evidently become agents of social restructuring in either deeply divided, rundown suburban territories or cities where public transport was never an integral component. The tangential tramline between the Paris suburbs of Bobigny and Saint-Denis links two neighborhoods separated by earlier infrastructure and gives a civic dignity to the new intervention [4]. In Houston the standardization of the road section and stops along the light-rail route marks a consistent continuity through dilapidated areas. The design quality of this new public transport mode is intentionally planned as an impetus to urban (re)development.

Not to be left out of this survey are bus routes, which in recent years have witnessed a revival as a sensible and efficient public transport system. The impact of Curitiba Brazil's bus network has been so strong not only in Latin America but also in Europe. The high-speed Zuidtangent in the Netherlands is among the first on the continent to marry speed and standardization with the appeal of a new transport line within confines that are more and more spatially restricted [5]. And finally, representative of quite another application is the magnificent bridge project for the Leidsche Rijn new town extension in the Netherlands. Maxwan developed a kit of parts that they call "orgware" for a family of iconic vehicular and pedestrian bridges. They clearly belong to a series, but also maintain their uniqueness in response to their differentiation of function and context.

1 Kathy Poole, "Civitas Oecologies: Civic Infrastructure in the Ecological City," in eds Theresa Genovese, Linda Eastley, and Deanne Snyder, *Harvard Architecture Review* (New York: Princeton Architectural Press, 1998), 131.

Service Station Prototype

LECHWIESEN SERVICE STATION

Munich-Lindau Highway, Germany

Architect: Herzog + Partner

Landscape Architect: Latz + Partner

Date: 1992–1996

Highway service stations, design, and environmentalism are strange bedfellows. Yet two mirror-image prototype service stations in Lechwiesen are not only an elegant and economical alternative to the general dreariness of highway service stations, but also cutting-edge structures with regard to an informed concern for energy conservation, use of materials, and integration with the landscape. The stations are composed of three main elements: a series of roofs suspended from steel pylons through which traffic passes to park and which covers the tanking area; a visitor area (restaurants, cashiers, toilets, covered terrace, and play area) connected to the parking and tanking areas via a passerelle; and a reinforced concrete functional block (containing kitchen, stores and cool rooms, staff and administra-

tion areas, and toilets and showers for truck drivers). The clearly stratified plan places nosier/dirtier functions nearest the road and recreational areas furthest away.

The complex was interpreted as a "pavilion in the woods" and the designed component of the landscape consists of avenues of trees and banks of hedges that knit the flexible spaces between the structures to the surrounding agricultural and woodland landscape and screen the motorway from its users. In its architectural expression, the complex too resonates a woodiness, since timber is the dominant material. The roof is particularly notable as a four-layer grid of vertically stacked timber planks nailed together to form continuous beams. The ecological design is exemplified by the manner in which

the forms were designed to naturally shed water (reducing lengths of rainwater pipes and gutters) and optimize natural ventilation (minimizing the necessity of mechanical air flows). In addition, waste and soil water is biologically purified in a soakaway plant on site.

The structures are prototypes for a new generation of service stations in which energy conservation and environmental responsiveness are first and foremost. At the same time, their imagery retreats from high-tech towards a more low-tech, human-touch expression. Replication of the prototype is feasible; a set of serial components with refined elements and details was designed to be simple enough to be prefabricated and easily assembled whatever the configuration of the site.

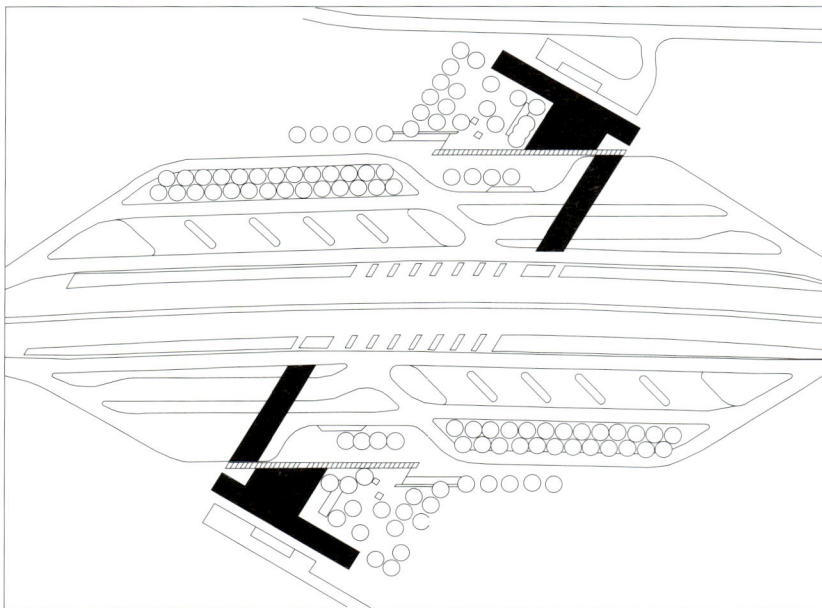

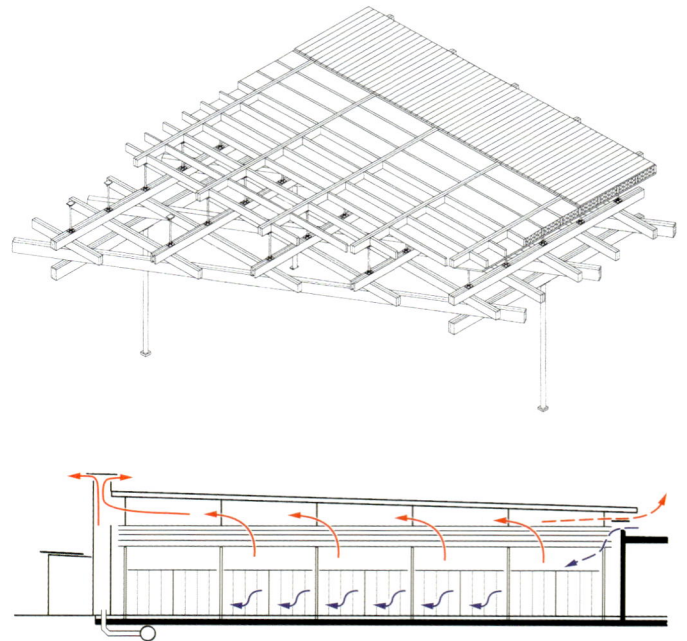

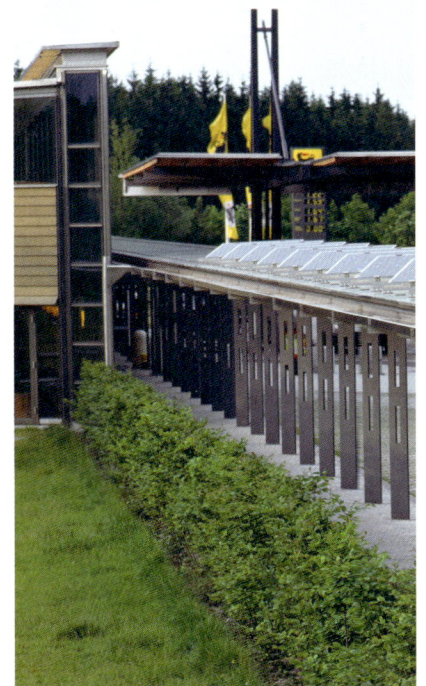

"Fosterites"

BILBAO METRO

Bilbao, Spain

Architect: Foster + Partners

Engineer: Ove Arup & Partners

Date: 1988–1995 (Line 1) and 1997–2004 (Line 2)

The striking curved glass "Fosterites," as locals call them, that rise from the sidewalk throughout Bilbao's streetscape poetically announce the hidden metro network below. The standard profile was efficiently engineered, evoking the sloped profile of the subterranean tunnels, and the prefabricated elements have become urban icons unique to the city. The eight, inner-city street-level entrances to Line 1 act as beacons for pedestrians. They are illuminated by night and admit natural light by day.

Regeneration of the industrial capital of the Basque autonomous region has been internationally lauded as an urban renaissance. Beyond the crowning glory of the signature

Guggenheim by Frank Gehry, the investment in infrastructure is widely applauded and the metro system is its most visibly evident component. The Bilbao metro links the greater region's one million inhabitants — from coastal villages, the industrial zone, the city center, and the suburbs — by a pair of interconnecting lines along the banks of the Nervión River. Travel is celebrated and an image of smooth, sleek neomodernity prevails. The expression of the tunnel bores reveals their construction technique, and their prefabricated, anti-vandal-coated, concrete panels (1.2 by 2.4 meters) contrast with the polished, maintenance-free stainless-steel and glass architecture of the expansive 16-meter-wide station caverns

(offering flexibility for future expansion). The space-age entry points lead via escalators or glass elevators to spaces large enough to accommodate mezzanines and staircases above the trains. Passengers are then conducted down to the platforms on each side by stairs that elegantly curve against the cavern walls. Benches, ticket booths, and entry control points all feature the same architectural language, offering cohesive legibility and identity to the station's interior. When complete, the system will have a total of 41 stations along two lines. Escalators proved impossible in the deep-cut stations of Line 2; instead, banks of large-capacity elevators are grouped in threes and configured as recognizable city markers.

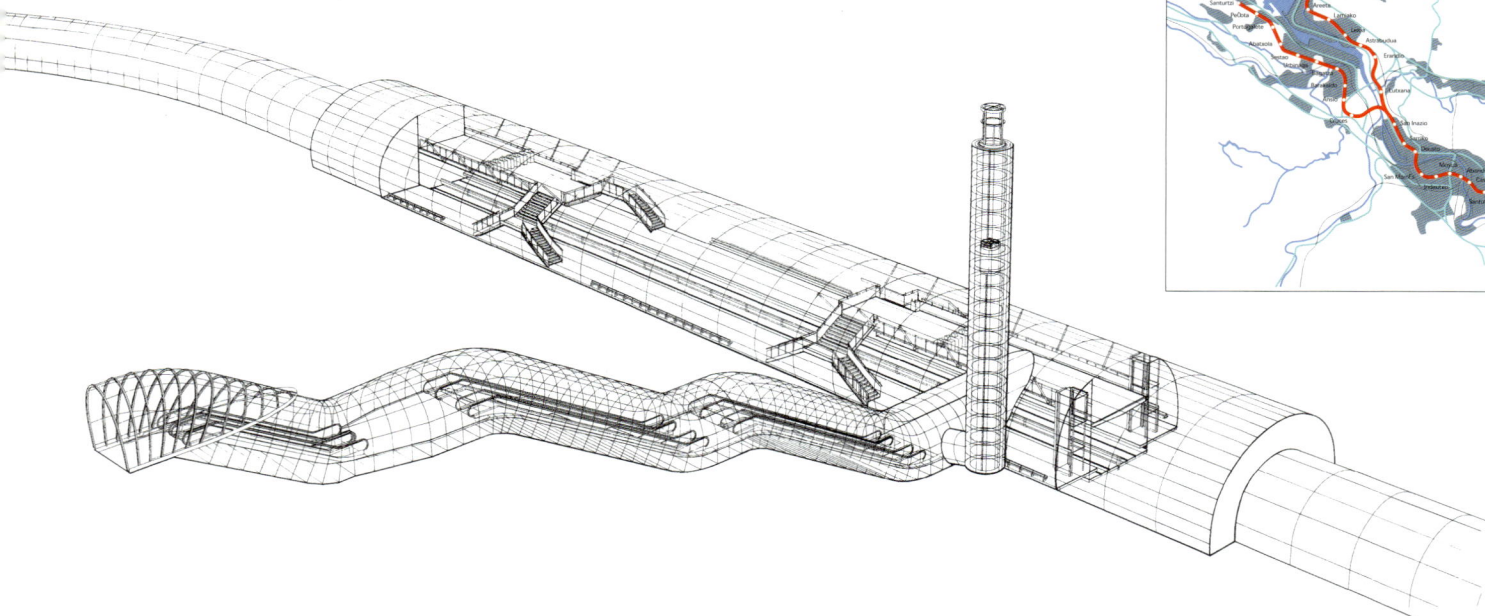

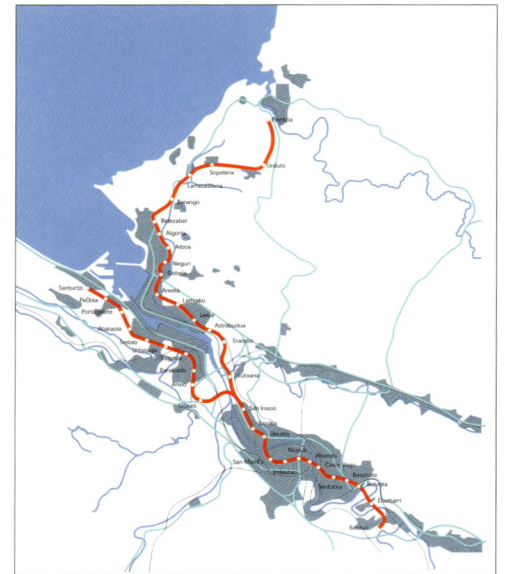

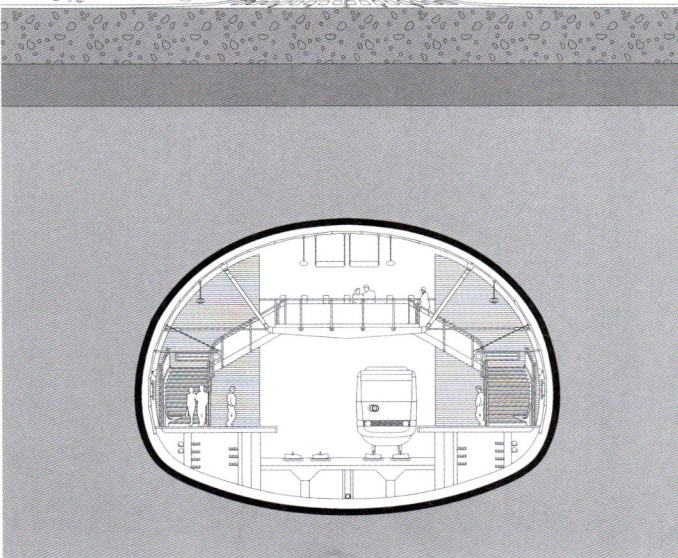

"Art on the Go"

HOUSTON METRORAIL

Houston, Texas, USA

Architect: HOK (Hellmuth, Obata + Kassabaum)

Date: 2001–2004

Houston, Texas, is renowned not only for its extremely car-dependent culture, but also for its "wild west" urbanism. It is a city planned without the tools of zoning and growth boundaries. Therefore, the intelligence of the Metropolitan Transit Authority's decision to invest in METRORail, a light rail network, was twofold. Evidently, it would provide the city with a new means of public transport and, at the same time, act as a lever to encourage higher density pedestrian-oriented development in the urban core. The first, 12-kilometer-long Red Line (also known as the Main Street Line) opened in 2004 and runs from downtown Houston southward to the Texas Medical Center and the Reliant Park sports complex. It passes the Museum District and terminates a short distance south of the Interstate 610 loop expressway, following the spine of Houston's main activity clus-

ters. The consistent landscaping of the transversal road section in which the tram line passes has become an easily recognizable reference for the urban intensification program that is intended to accompany the public transport investment. In July 2009, officials held a groundbreaking ceremony for two new lines, which will connect the north and southeast parts of the city with downtown Houston. They form part of the new federal investment program in infrastructure.

The 16 stations of the first line were designed by HOK Architects and developed as prototypes – giving a system-wide image to the line while allowing site adaptation through the use of colors, platform paving materials and patterns, column cladding, and variations in the glazing of the canopy's roof. The canopy's design consists of paired steel

channels as columns and cantilevered beams that support a translucent glass roof canopy that covers one-third of the 76-meter-long platforms. The Cultural Art Council of Houston and Harris County sponsored an "Art on the Go" program in which the platform paving, glass canopy, column cladding, railings, and walls became the surfaces of the artists' canvases. The identity of each station became clear, while the overall vocabulary was strong enough to brand the system as one. In Downtown, Midtown, and the Texas Medical Center, the light-rail stations are split-center platforms located in the middle of the street with tracks on both sides of the platforms. Landscaped esplanades recalling similar historic esplanades in Houston are located between the platforms continuously down the streets. Three stations serve as bus-to-rail transfer stations, and one station is located next to a 1000-car park-and-ride facility.

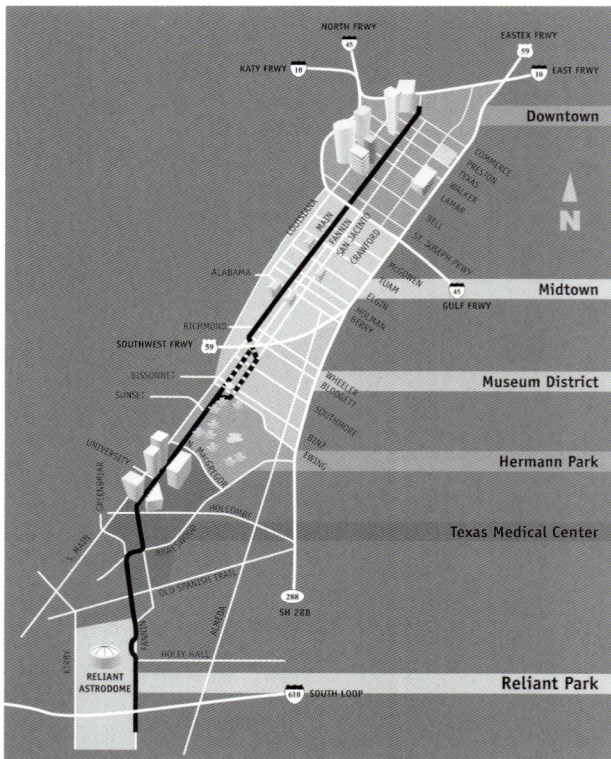

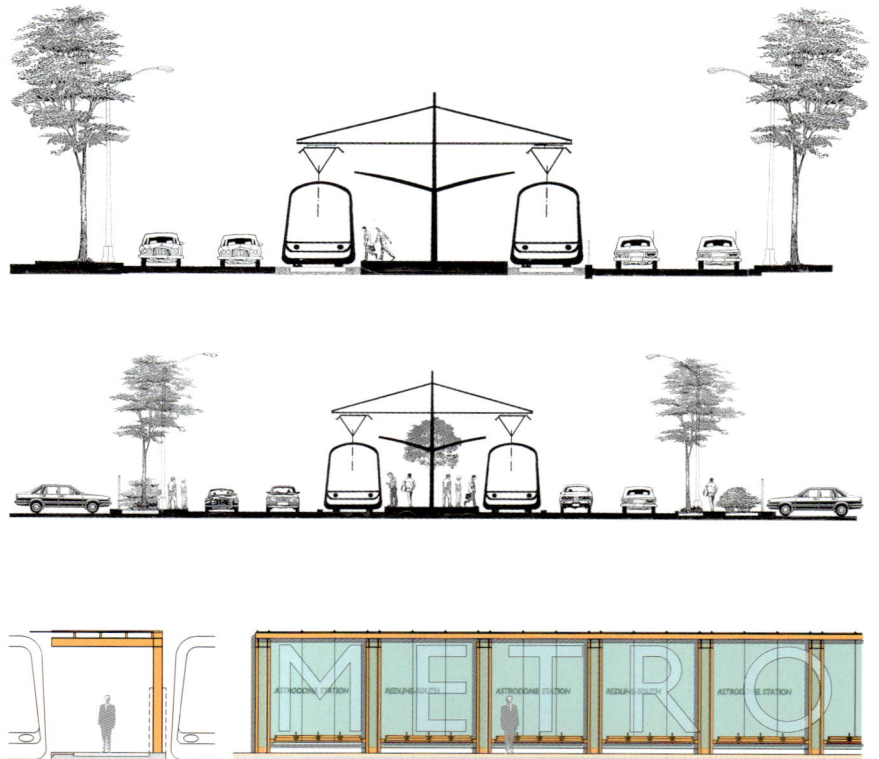

Red Tube Icons

CURITIBA BUS SYSTEM

Curitiba, Brazil

Architect: Jaime Lerner (architect and mayor)

Date: 1966–1990

The cylindrical, clear-walled tube-like stations of the Curitiba Bus Rapid Transit (BRT) system represent the city's forward-looking and cost-conscious approach to comprehensive urban development. Urban growth, poverty alleviation, and urban transport have been folded into an efficient and highly visible system that radically transformed the city. Curitiba, with a greater metropolitan population of 2.2 million, has one of the most heavily used yet low-cost transit systems in the world. Buses run in dedicated lanes where their movements are unimpeded by traffic signals and congestion, while fare collection prior to boarding results in quick passenger loading and unloading. The iconic stations are equipped with turnstiles, steps, and wheelchair eleva-

tors. Passengers pay their fares as they enter the stations and wait for buses on raised platforms. Instead of steps, buses have extra-wide doors and ramps that extend out to the station platform when the doors open. The clear-walled tube stations serve the dual purpose of providing shelter from the elements and facilitating the simultaneous loading and unloading of passengers, including wheelchairs, efficiently. Moreover, located within these terminals are conveniences such as public telephones, post offices, newspaper stands, and small retail facilities.

The integrated public transport is part of a larger vision that is all the brainchild of Jaime Lerner, a planner who was Curitiba's mayor

for three alternating terms over a 20-year span. When he first took office in the 1970s, Brasilia was still shining in its modernist glory and the French planner Agache sought to widen Curitiba's roads and radically transform the city on behalf of the private car. By contrast, Lerner sought to guide growth linearly along specified corridors and pedestrianize the historic center. Five main arteries lead into the city center from the periphery and are the backbone of new urbanization and the supporting BRT system. The main lines are fed by conventional buses on circumferential routes around the central city and on inter-district routes that in turn are fed by minibuses routed through residential neighborhoods.

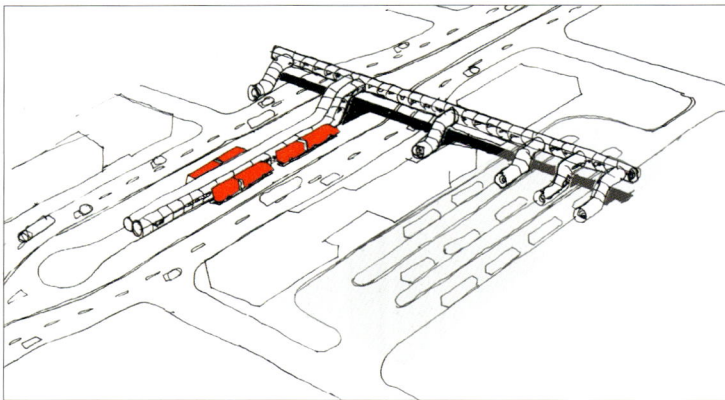

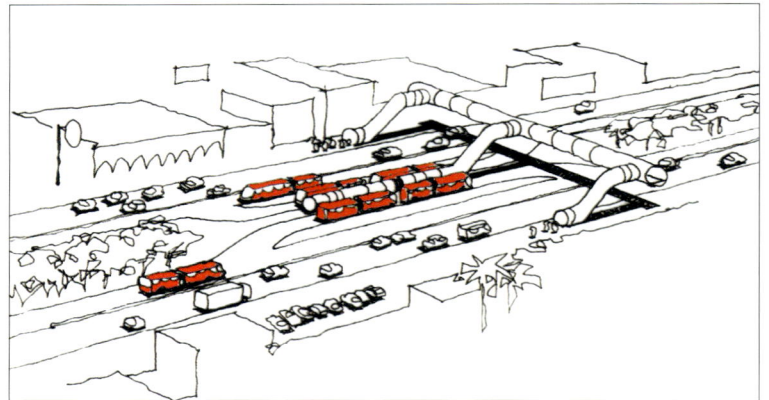

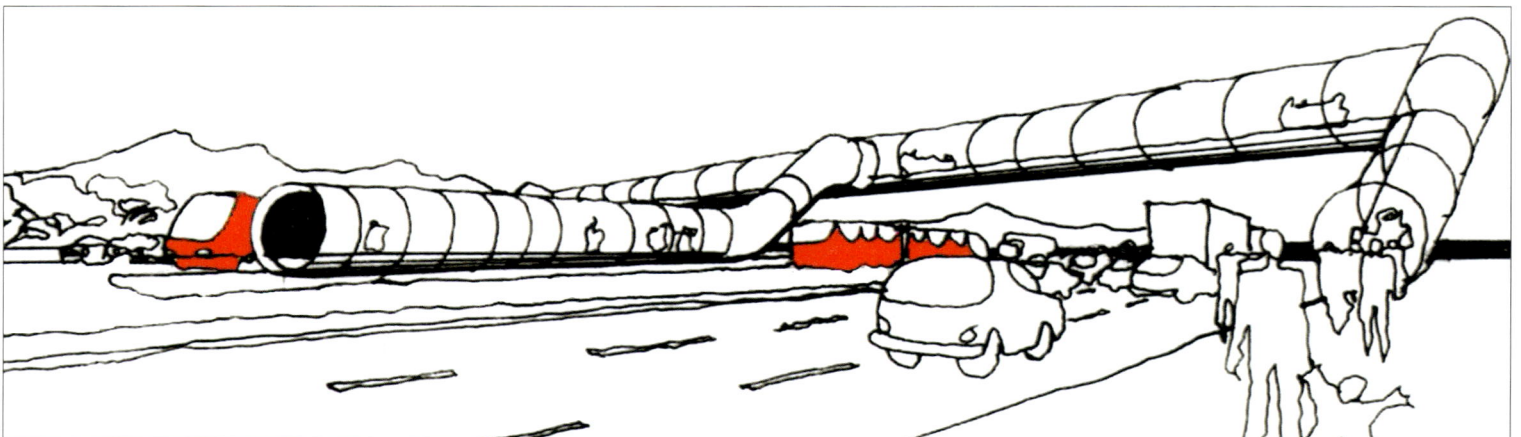

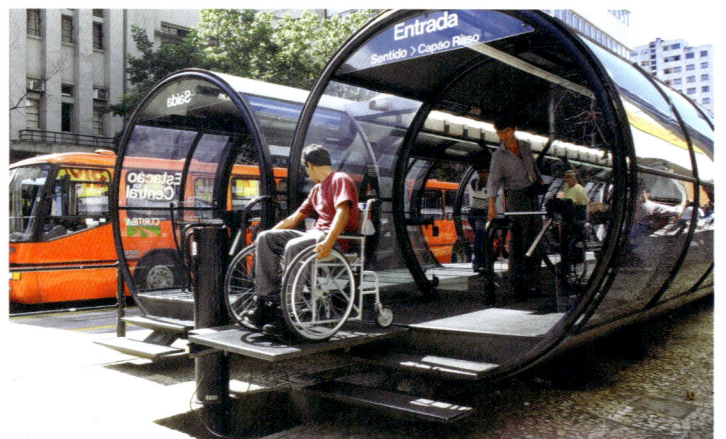

Dutch "Orgware"

LEIDSCHE RIJN BRIDGES

Utrecht, the Netherlands

Architect: Maxwan Architects and Urbanists

Date: 1997–2005

A modesty tempered by pragmatism — Neufert traffic norms of turning radii for cars — led Maxwan to create a series of iconic bridges in the Leidsche Rijn project. The canals running through the new housing district are both narrow and non-navigable, and therefore the short-span bridges are all stationary with nonliftable components. The bridges were thus conceived as fragments of road that happened to be above water. Since a good road implies efficiency and luxury of connection, bridges made the smoothest links possible, resulting in an elegantly choreographed vehicular and pedestrian ballet. The powerful expression is due to the subtle massaging of traffic flows. Depending upon the particular context of each bridge, the expression varies. In some places two bridges join together and separate according to traffic requirements.

Maxwan was involved not just in the design of the bridges, but also in the entire master plan for Leidsche Rijn, a new extension to the city of Utrecht that will have 30,000 housing units by the year 2015. Working with Crimson, the architects based their approach on the fact that 70% of the project is to be financed by the private sector. They developed their plan and tools — bridges and also housing and other amenities — from within, based on the notion of "orgware" (organizational ware). Orgware is a term taken from economics that describes the set of political, legislative, and administrative factors that dictate both the implementation of ideas (software) and the construction of physical elements (hardware). The concepts translate to a form of "soft urbanism" that is realistic, opportunistic, and flexible, and that responds to the floating logic of the market. The bridges, which will eventually total 100 in number, were designed as sixteen families and result in incredible diversity due to the specificities of traffic connections. The norms of civil engineering, combined with the imagination of Maxwan, led to the development of a new look for public space and playful mobility connectors.

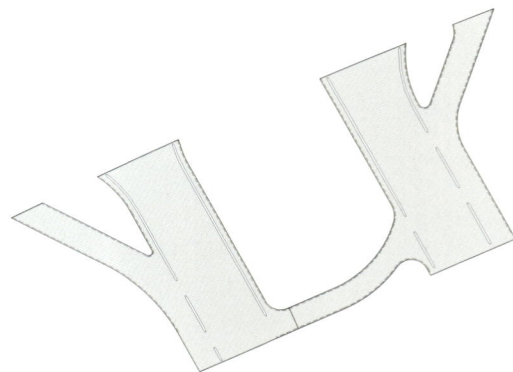

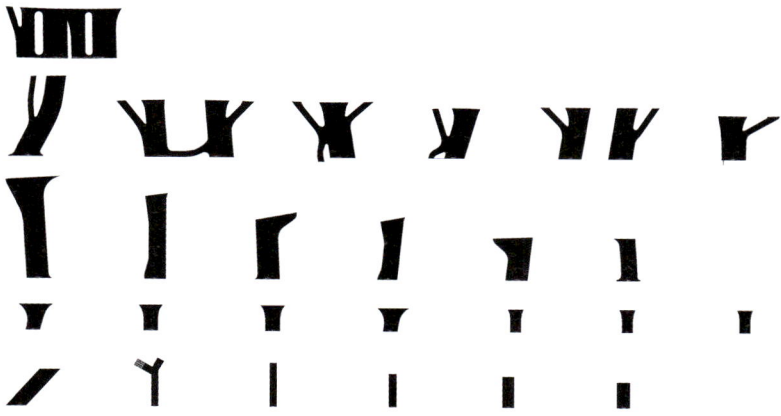

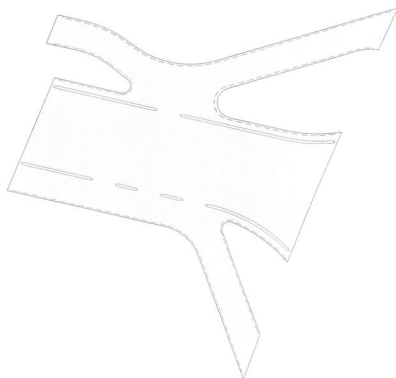

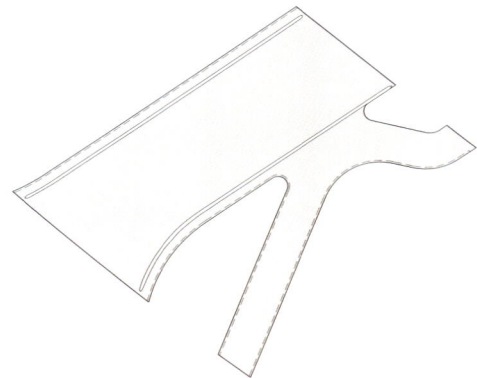

THE NETWORK AS A GATEWAY TO REGIONAL CHARACTER

When superposed on the existing landscape, the network usually spawns development that inevitably combines both global and local features. The merging of these two characteristics is exactly what makes the specificity of the place. When the network engages with a place, it straddles the threshold between two cultures and initiates exchanges of various sorts. More often than not, the network brings new activities (and new customers), which in turn enrich local economies. At the same time, the experience of the local (in cultural or economic terms) is what attracts the traveler to visit. To advertise this local character, it is often emblematized at the entry point, at the threshold between the two cultures. This idea of merger is most clearly identified by the effort to optimize local features in the landscape treatment and integrate regional elements into the architectural definition of today's highly global transport networks. In such a way, local distinction and representation are a means of homecoming and find their way into the iconic image of clear and recognizable airports, high-speed train stations, and service stations along highways. The consciousness of a particular character is considered a more complete sensation, an awareness of local culture at the safe distance of immediate connection to the network.

The gateway aspect of many components of infrastructure is extremely obvious. Airports are first points of entry to regions and cities and often conceived as monumental emblems. An excellent example can be found in Singapore, which sought, in the expansion of Changi Airport in 2000, to create a gateway befitting its image as a "City on a Garden." A huge vertical wall featuring a woven tapestry of living plants – evoking a southeast Asian equatorial rainforest – creates a powerful identity inside the terminal and introduces guests to the city's renowned relation of infrastructure and vegetation, as strongly expressed by the greening of its road profiles [1]. In California's Los Angeles International Airport, a magnificent lighting plan celebrates not only the threshold between road and airport, but vehicular circulation and the lifestyle it permits. The arrangement of gigantic pylons works as a symbolic gesture for the city – serving as a beacon, framing views, garnering attention, and reducing confusion with regards to navigating the interchange. The lighting resembles runway lights during take-off and landing and effectively serves as a means of breathing life into vast environments of asphalt and concrete [2]. In Denver, the airport complex itself functions as a gateway to the city and the Rocky Mountain region at large. The large tensile roof-peak structure mimics the mountains. An even more expressive and sophisticated allusion to the local context emerges in the San Pablo Terminal of Seville, Spain, by Rafael Moneo. The complex (terminal and parking area) eloquently references the city it serves. It renders homage to the Great Mosque of Córdoba and interprets its Spanish-Moorish architecture in the forms, colors, detailing, and spirit of the airport [3]. Similarly, the new Siem Reap International Airport in Cambodia by Arche-

1 **GREEN TAPESTRY GATEWAY**

Landscape architect Tierra's "Green Tapestry" at Terminal 3 of Changi Airport on the island nation of Singapore is a monumental wall (300 meters long, 15 meters high) of tropical plants suspended below the roof's dramatic butterfly-winged skylights. The massive wall of vines, creepers, and epiphytes not only divides the mega-building in plan into landside/airside sections but also connects the vertical space of the check-in and arrival areas, which are separated by a glass security screen. Four cascading water walls (18 meters high and 6 meters wide) made from shredded glass panels laminated to stainless steel plates are interspersed in the living wall of green.

2 LAX DANCE OF LIGHT

The animated pylon lighting intervention (by IMA Design Group and Ted Tokio Tanaka Architects) at the crossing of Sepulveda and Century Boulevards – primary arterial entries to Los Angeles International Airport (LAX) – celebrates the city's car culture as the welcoming gesture of Los Angeles. The monumentalized interchange is marked by a circle of 14 pylons (36.5 meters high, 3.6 meters in diameter, and 18 meters apart) on a 61-meter radius, with an additional 16 pylons on Century Boulevard (descending in height and diameter as they move away from the airport). The pylons are steel structural frames clad with curved glass panels that visually orchestrate the site with computerized lighting effects.

3 HOMAGE TO LOCAL TRADITION

The San Pablo Airport in Seville (1992) by Rafael Moneo is a complex embedded in the geometry of the highway. Yet even in the parking lots, references to the particular typology of the historic city are made. The lots are conceived as an alternating system of patios with shades and open areas with orange trees. The introvert two-story airport building is structured by large concourses with a double series of expansive cupolas, painted a deep blue and resting on columns with unique capitals. The concrete block facing of the exterior is made with local sand, accounting for the yellow *albero* tinge. The roof coverings utilize traditional blue glazed tiles that reflect the intensity of the Sevillian sun.

4 **GARDEN ARCHITECTURE**
Siem Reap-Angkor International Airport was developed and designed by Archetype Group and officially opened in 2006. Located in the home of Angkor Wat (Cambodia), its long sweeping elevations and galleries play with the Angkorean heritage. The playful roofs are anchored in more recent traditional Khmer architecture. The assortment of internal gardens creates an openness rarely seen in modern airports. A glistering wall of glass blocks turns into a shadow theater while passengers await their luggage. The impressive ceiling height (13 meters) here and there strategically compresses to lead the action forward. Modern interpretations of ancient gates are vivid and ever present. Huge, punched window openings provide seating possibilities as well as relaxing views to water features and lush greenery.

5 **DISCREET GATEWAYS**
The Porto Metro system links six municipalities within the metropolitan area. The new network has been developed by Porto-based architect Eduardo Souto de Moura as an opportunity to transform the town and highlight or upgrade the existing qualities of urban fabric. Where possible, entrances to the metro have been integrated in gardens and the common language of materials and forms not only creates immediate recognition but also exudes an identity related to the specific urban culture of Porto and not to an anonymously imported or generic kit of parts. Extensive use of granite, limestone, and azulejo tiles creates continuity between the stations and the buildings in their vicinity, whereas urban shelters consist of freestanding glass structures that can be adapted to the different characters of locations.

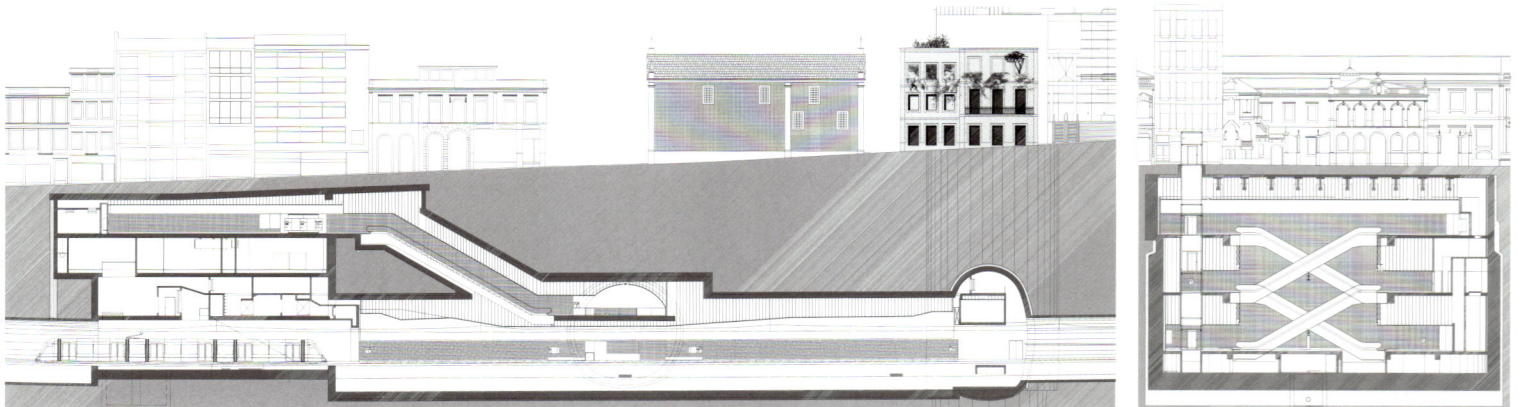

6 SURREAL JUXTAPOSITIONS

In 1992 a house in the small western Japanese town of Mihonoseki was flattened by an 8-kilogram meteor. The bizarre accident has proven a savior of sorts for the town, whose population had been falling. It is now a bustling tourist destination, and the ferry terminal and meteor museum designed by Shin Takamatsu is a strongly gestural building. The centerpiece, a squashed ovoid form, derives from the actual shape of the meteor and symbolic location on the theatrically buckling roof is a reminder of the circumstances surrounding its extraordinary arrival in the town. The additional programs of a civic meeting hall and therapeutic saltwater pool gave Takamatsu additional forms in composing the gateway as a gigantic sculpture.

type Group alludes to the mystical vanished empire of the Khmers (Angkor) and more recent traditions of local architecture as well. A modern interpretation of ancient gates, internal gardens with lush greenery and water features, and playful roofs marks the small airport with a very particular and local identity [4].

The network of metro, tram, and train infrastructure has also been subject to the idea of relaying local characteristics of the sites they occupy. The Portuguese architect Eduardo Souto de Moura used the opportunity of Porto's new tram and underground network to reshape the city and to make the stations part of a larger urban project, designed by one of the city's well-known architects. The network itself, with its modest and exquisitely detailed stations and accompanying structures, becomes an entry to a renovated and recognizable part of the town [5]. In the south of France, landscape architects Michel Desvigne and Christine Dalnoky have highlighted not the urban context but the cultivated and natural landscape to give the three stations along the TGV Méditerranée line a distinct identity that clearly elevates them above the generic technical requirements of engineering logic. On the whole, the TGV line is constructed as a fold in the territory, whereas the stations integrate the new infrastructure, not by hiding or denying its presence, but by inserting it within the overall logic of landscape constitution that existed prior to the intervention. Each station thus emanates from local circumstances, typifying its region upon arrival. Another construction that highlights the qualities of the existing landscape is the service station-cum-park along the A16 highway in the north of France. Architect Bruno Mader and landscape architect Pascale Hannetel have created a vital oasis to relieve the tunnel-like monotony of travel by providing a radical change of scenery and presenting the service station as an outlook and entry point to the discovery of the natural reserve behind. The project is an elegant, informed, and creative synthesis that encapsulates the Bay of Somme's regional attributes.

In many instances, bridges provide clear gateways to locations that seek to enhance their own character. In Amsterdam, the Netherlands, Grimshaw Architects created a specific vocabulary for the bridges connecting the city to the new reclaimed IJburg development in the IJsselmeer. The white-painted steel structures have an appearance of lightness and modernity, and a nautical aura. They form elegant transitions from the old to the reclaimed land. In Toronto, Canada, Montgomery Sisam Architects have had a longer heritage to refer to in their pedestrian/bicycle bridge over the Humber River. The "thunderbird" was a sacred symbol of the aboriginal Eastern Woodland First Peoples and the architects have used an abstraction of it for the structural-steel bracing – thus linking not only the two sides of the river to each other but also the sociocultural past of the region with the contemporary era. Finally, a quite exceptional circumstance is expressed in an almost surrealistic building (and incident) in western Japan. A meteor crash prompted Shin Takamatsu to design a museum and ferry terminal with a purist-pictorial approach – creating a symbolic gateway commemorating the event through a juxtaposition of elementary and complex forms. At the same time, the building is extremely rooted to its particular historical context, despite the structure's extreme freedom of plan [6].

White-Tipped Peaks

DENVER INTERNATIONAL AIRPORT

Denver, Colorado, USA

Architects: Fentress Architects

Engineers: S.A. Miro, Inc., Martin/Martin, Severud Associates Consulting Engineers

Date: 1989–1995

The large Denver International Airport is located 40 kilometers east of the "mile high" state capital in Colorado on the plain at the foothills of the Rocky Mountains. It is both a powerful expression of the notion of gateway to the region and an aerodynamic symbol of visual drama. As a picturesque analogy, its white fabric roof formed into peaks is a conscious echo of the snow-capped skyline of the mountains that form a dramatic backdrop to the plateau. It also evokes the intertwined tent structures of the former Indian settlements that originally populated these western plains. The Teflon-coated, fiberglass tensile roof structure makes the building legible to all users and unites all the common functions of the complex. The soaring peaks are created by 34 steel masts, placed in pairs 50 meters apart with 20-meter intervals between each pair. Two layers of fabric (the outer as the primary tensile structure and the inner as an acoustic barrier) are draped between the peaks and are tensioned by cables, following the ridges and the valleys, with ridge cables taking downward thrusts of snow and self-weight and the valley ones resisting upward forces from the wind.

The 275-meter-long terminal is flooded with natural light through triangular clerestory windows, huge glass endwalls stiffened by horizontal bowstring trusses, and indirect light penetrating through the fabric itself. The lofty open spaces of the airport function as a symbol for the city and smaller tents form a canopy over passenger set-down at the vehicular departure areas. Denver International Airport has had some of the worst publicity of large projects in the USA. It was initially argued that the growth of the city was stunted by the image and capacity of its old Stapleton Airport. The push for the project became extremely political and it was beset by massive delays and cost overruns. One of the major justifications for the fabric roof was the speed of erection it offered. Pragmatics ultimately led to this strong symbolism and iconic image for Denver.

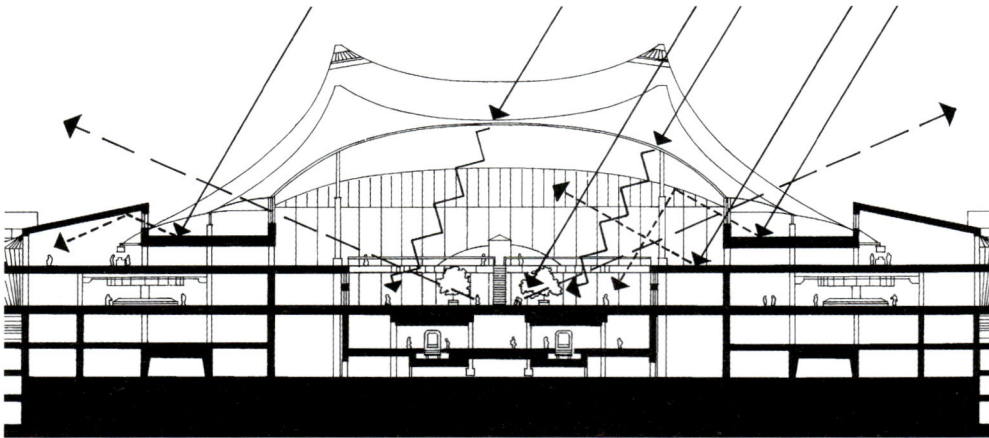

→ Direct Light
⌁ Diffused Light
----▶ Refracted light
-- -- ▶ Direct View of Sky

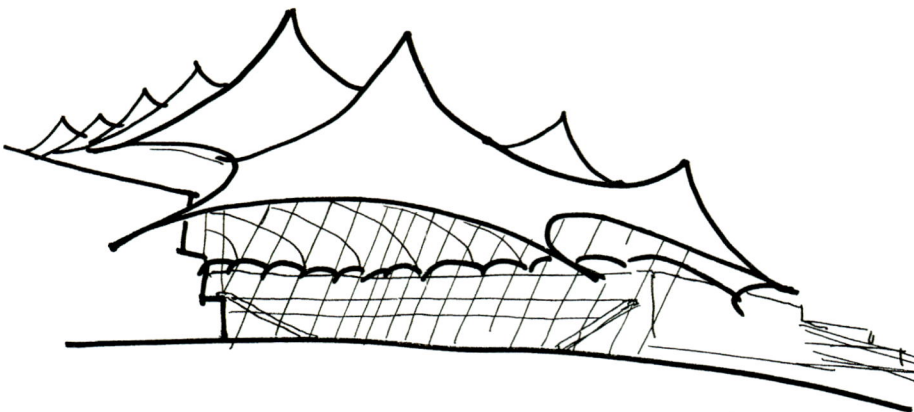

Agriculturally Embedded

TGV MÉDITERRANÉE

Aix-en-Provence, Avignon and Valence, France

Architect: AREP Group

Landscape Architect: Michel Desvigne and Christine Dalnoky

Date: 1994–2002

The new stations along the TGV Méditerranée line have been treated as opportunities for upgrading not only urban areas but also the larger territorial environment. Michel Desvigne and Christine Dalnoky's interventions in three stations – Aix-en-Provence, Avignon, and Valence – have restored legibility to the landscape and underlined the agricultural heritage of southern France. In all three sites the stations are concealed. The line is lowered in a trench, hiding it from view and lowering the general appearance and roof of the stations. In conjunction with this design decision, the landscaping around the stations has been directed by what James Corner called "a farmer's pragmatism and a landscaper's eye."[1] The territory is reconstituted and reinterpreted as an agricultural setting. New plantings are based on the same logic as that of the cultivation areas, echoing the pattern of surrounding fields and orchards and endowing the stops with a vocabulary in line with the identity of the region. Spatially defined planted areas such as wind-protection plantations, fruit groves, and avenues are quoted from the everyday cultivated landscape. In contrast with the low trees of the parking areas, tall trees mark access points to the stations. The station buildings themselves are modestly integrated into the landscape yet reveal a sense of civic monumentality from within.

In Aix-en-Provence the presence of the station in the landscape is highlighted by rows of nettle trees lining the platforms. A garden of oleanders stretches between the trees and the platform. The parking lots (for 700 cars but expandable to 1100) are planted with oaks. In Avignon, the station and parking areas are developed on terraces. The station itself is enclosed by two double rows of plane trees and adorned by a bed of tulips.

Parking is under orchards and lines of trees shelter the complex from winds. Finally, in Valence, the crevice in the landscape contains an architectural fold that gives scale to the station, seamlessly adapts to the landscape, and is still able to convey a grand space from within. The large structure is camouflaged by way of sectional manipulation and planting. The north-south axis of the parking areas serves as the layout grid for the future 250-hectare ZAC (concerted development zone) planned by the local municipality. As the project in Valence reveals, the stations of the Méditerranée line were all designed to generate and support new growth around the stations while maintaining the identity and configuration of their surrounding landscapes as a cohesive setting.

[1] James Corner, "Agriculture, Texture, and the Unfinished," in *Intermediate Landscapes: The Landscape of Michel Desvigne* (Basel: Birkhäuser, 2009), 7.

Avignon

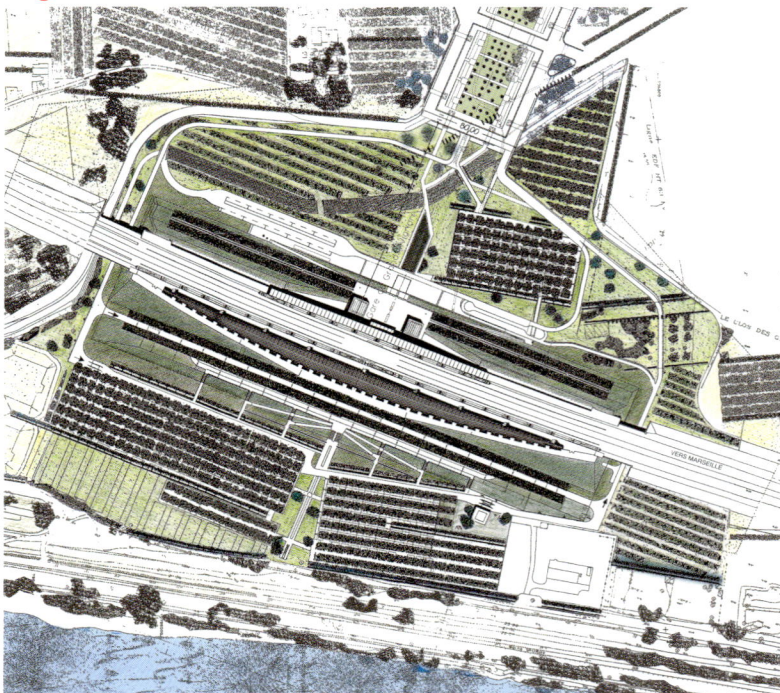

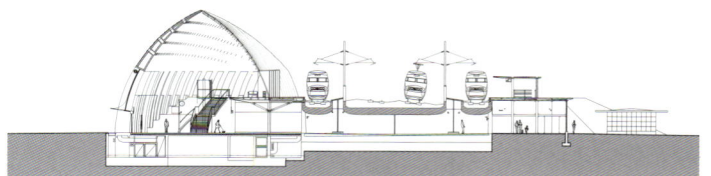

Valence

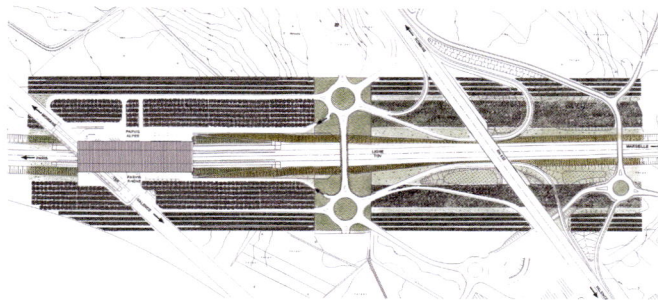

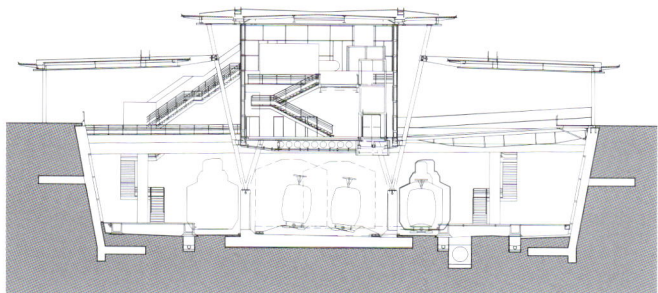

Aix-en-Provence

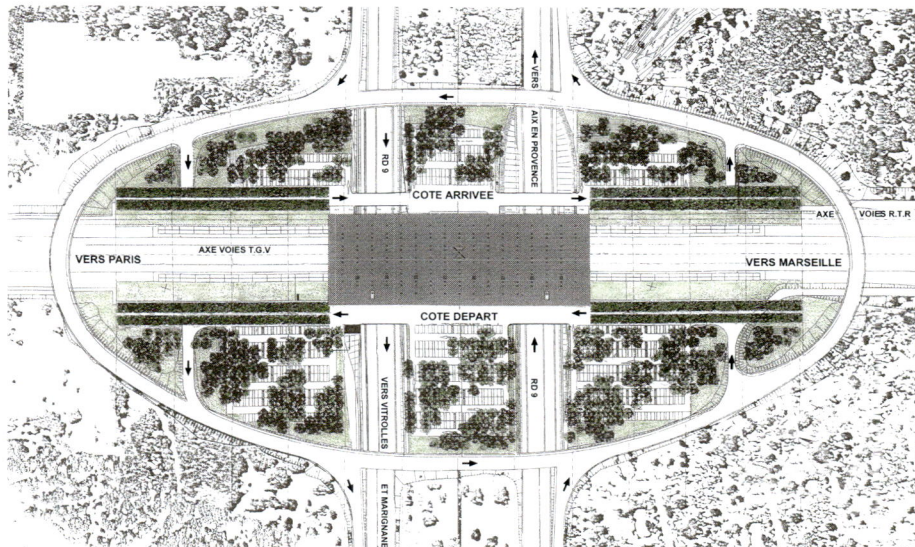

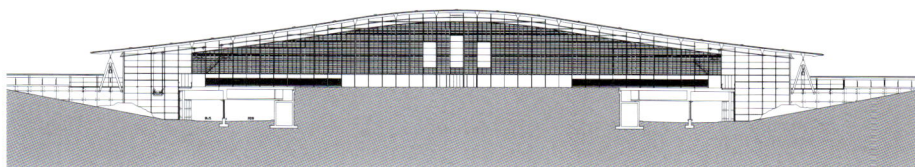

Delta Viewing Platform

A16 SERVICE STATION

Bay of Somme, France

Architect: Bruno Mader

Landscape Architect: Agence HYL (Pascale Hannetel)

Date: 1995–1998

The Bay of Somme, in northern France, is recognized as a spectacularly beautiful natural setting where expanses of open water, marshes, dunes, and saltwater meadows seemingly merge land and sea. It is one of France's major sites for migrating birds and the bay's particularly wide mouth into the English Channel offers vistas that change dramatically with the tides and the seasons. The rest stop and service station by architect Bruno Mader and landscape architect Pascale Hannetel is not only an environmentally-friendly complex in the fragile delta landscape but also a park that frames the beauty of the territory and gives accessibility to visitors. A comprehensive foundation of earthworks, using 2–2.5 meters of soil from the excavations of the highway, created a platform, which includes canals and wetlands, to support the structures. Steep slopes separate the A16 highway and the park, and the only visual contact between the two is provided by the canals, which are level with the motorway.

The service area is located at one end of the 20-hectare site to avoid interrupting panoramic views, while the parking lots, bordered by canals, are grouped together at a lower level to allow visual continuity between the site and the landscape. Three transversal canals structure the site and collect and treat surface water (with hydrocarbon filters and reed beds in the pool) from the service area and the adjacent highway. One of them forms a pool that extends alongside the pontoon adjacent to the long horizontal service building and around the circular belvedere. The service station is aligned with an avenue of four rows of ash trees, mirroring the geometry of the interior's structural timber columns. A large yet super-thin roof-plate shelters the various service areas. The glulammed larch columns pierce through the roof plane, recalling the region's rows of timber posts of the coastal mussel and oyster beds. Opposite the fuel pumps, the shop, toilets, and cafeteria are housed in three concrete blocks (the panels of which are textured with pebbles from the region's Le Hourdel beach), the gaps between them framing a series of views over the plains of Picardy beyond. The café, boutiques selling regional products, and an exhibition area are housed in a large, light, glazed building overlooking the adjacent marsh. Steps lead down to a pedestrian walkway, extended by the terrace alongside the canal and ending at the circular belvedere, the ground floor of which is a diorama of the plant and animal life of the region. By night, lighting built into the floor and walls marks the way across the pools, which are illuminated from lights placed beneath the walkways and pontoons.

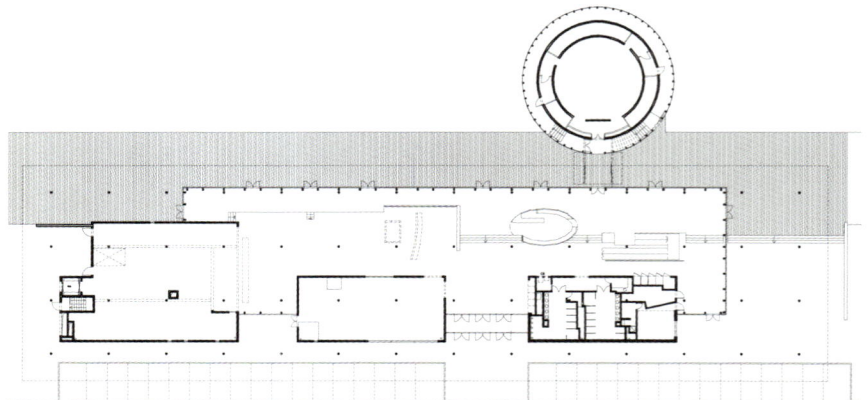

Sinuous Threads

IJBURG BRIDGES

Amsterdam, the Netherlands

Architect: Grimshaw Architects

Engineer: IBA (Ingenieursbureau Amsterdam)

Date: 1997–2001 (bridges 1 & 2) 2004–ongoing (bridges 3 & 4)

IJburg is the latest expansion of Amsterdam into the IJsselmeer, a vast freshwater lake east of the city. The new development is built on an archipelago of seven artificial islands between Amsterdam and Almere. Grimshaw has been responsible for designing the bridges that connect the islands to the mainland and serve as both literal and symbolic gateways to the new development. Completed in 2001, the first two bridges – connected like umbilical cords to Amsterdam's existing infrastructure – accommodate two tramlines, two cycle paths and pedestrian footpaths, as well as several lanes of traffic, mains drainage, and other public utility services. The expressive form of the main bridge (250 meters long and 30 meters wide) clearly conveys its status. The white-painted steel of its undulating wave-like form, with two arches linked by a counter-arch, stands boldly in the context and elegantly reinterprets a standard arched bridge. The main, outward arches slope inward yet work conventionally, while the counter-arch, visually continuous with the other two, functions as a bowstring truss. It is in compression but looks as though it were in tension. The carriageways were developed as two separate decks divided by a sizable gap with views of the water below to ensure that travelers experience their passage as a bridge and not a causeway.

A second smaller bridge between two islands adopts the same language but with a different configuration. The system has sufficient flexibility to work for all vehicular bridges among the new islands, with double-span variants used where old land meets new. A second set of bridges commissioned in 2004 is being developed as part of the same family of structures. The new bridges are designed to convey even further lightness and movement. To enhance the sense of motion, the lower tube runs continuously across the canal, only lightly touching the streamlined concrete feet. The bridges are much more than mere connective conduits for cars, trams, bicycles, and pedestrians: they are intended to become the identity markers for the new development. They are designed to brand the area with their elegant engineering and expressive forms.

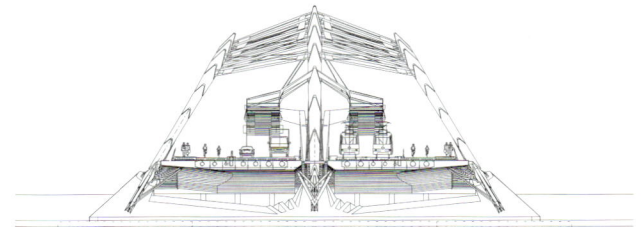

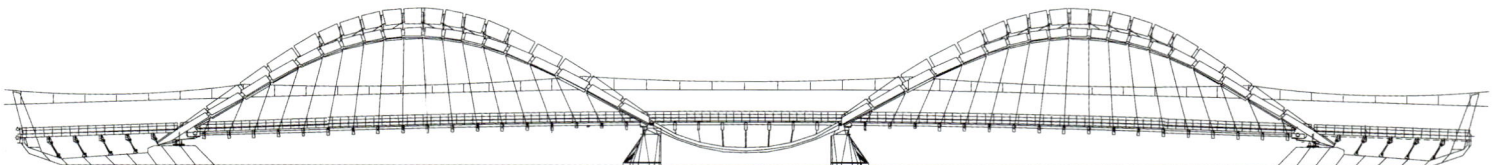

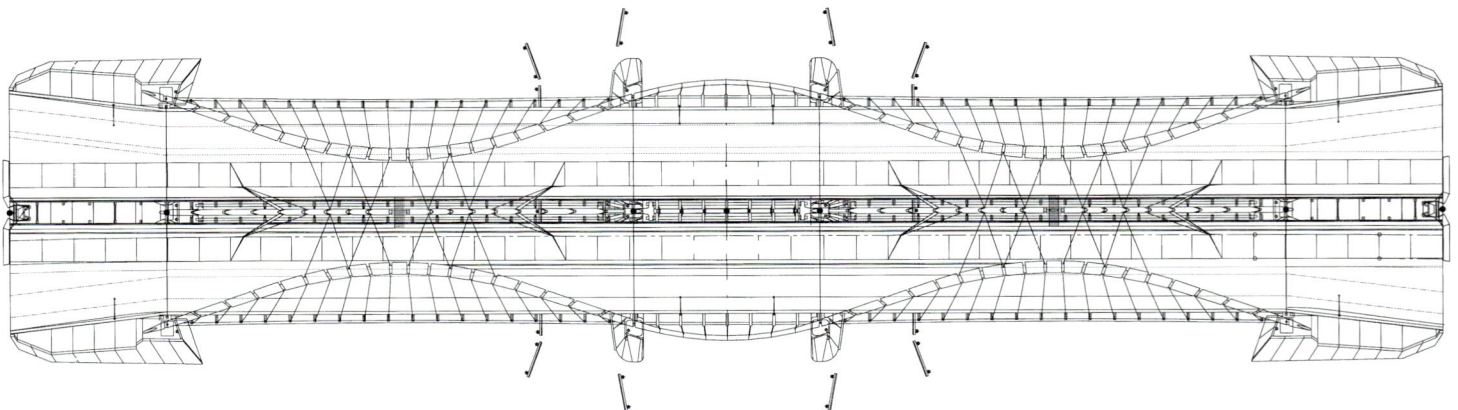

Thunderbird Icon

HUMBER RIVER BRIDGE

Toronto, Canada

Architect: Montgomery Sisam Architects

Landscape Architect: Ferris + Associates

Engineer: Delcan Corporation, Artist: Environmental Artworks

Date: 1996

The Humber Bridge not only provides a vital link in the continuous 325-kilometer-long scenic waterfront trail system along Toronto's north shore of Lake Ontario, but also symbolically connects back to the area's social and cultural history. The innovative engineering of soaring double-tubular arches of the 139-meter-long pedestrian and bicycle bridge includes steel cross-bracing that is based on an abstracted thunderbird, an aboriginal icon of the Ojibways (Eastern Woodland First Peoples) who occupied the site for almost two hundred years. The bridge forms a gateway between Toronto and Etobicoke at the mouth of the Humber River and along an old aboriginal trading route. Under the bridge, bronze turtles, canoes, and other native icons embedded in concrete walls and with interpretive plaques trace the prehistory of the river system. In this way, the Humber Bridge essentially connects a series of worlds: the aboriginal and the present, the authentic and the artificial, the natural and the man-made. Because of its judicious implantation, it opens up fascinating vistas on all of these aspects and thus renders an impression of doorstep and passage.

The project is the first step in a multi-year plan by Metro Toronto Transportation to replace a series of existing structures. With architectural expression and engineering design joining forces to achieve its unique configuration, the new bridge was built using 1200-millimeter-diameter high-strength steel pipe bent into twin arches that rise 21.3 meters above grade. The spacing between the arches is wide at the base but narrow at the top, imparting a futurist basket-handle appearance to the superstructure. A total of 44 stainless steel hangers 50 millimeters in diameter were strung from the arches to support the 22 floor beams to form the bridge deck, creating what architect David Sisam calls a "room-like quality" for visitors crossing the bridge.

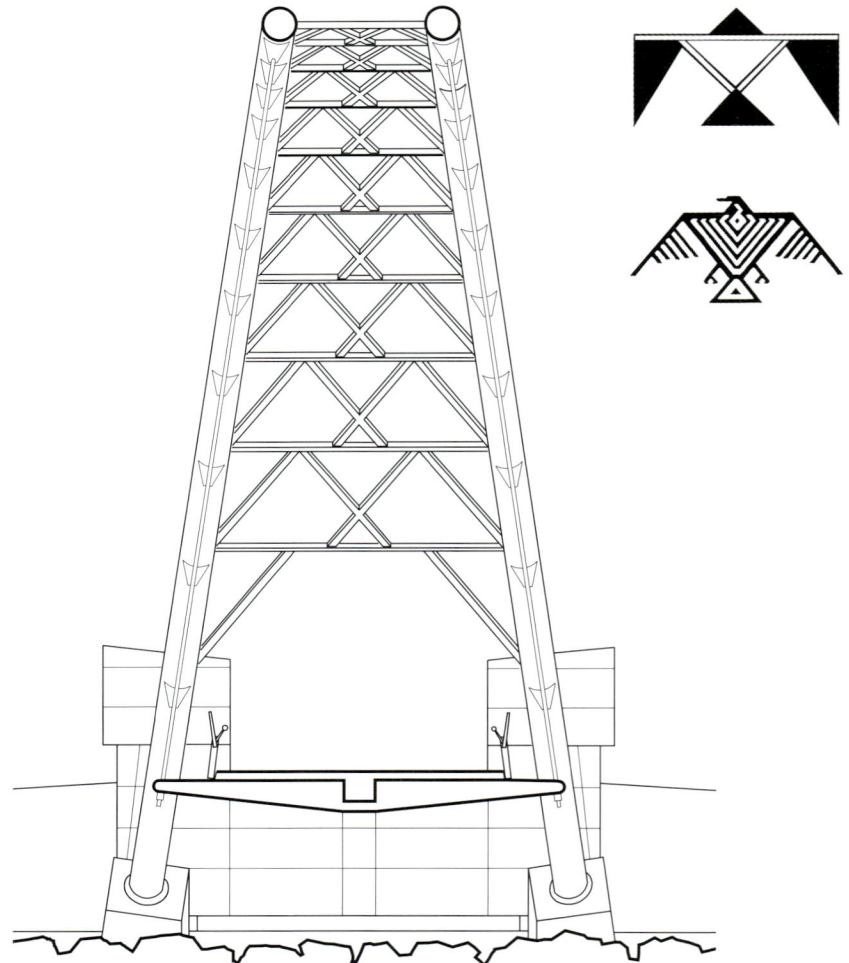

2

PHYSICAL PRESENCE
IN THE LANDSCAPE

INTRODUCTION
FROM URBANISM TO ENGINEERING AND BACK

The most elementary way in which infrastructure affects or creates landscape is by its material presence. Often, its mere physical form imposes itself through dimensions. The territorial dimension of infrastructure – its sheer bigness and muscularity – categorically ensures it is visually impressive within the landscape. In several cases, the juxtaposition of infrastructure and natural landscapes enhances the sense of distinction. Leo Marx has aptly referred to the sublime qualities of the machine in the garden – the contrast between the ideal Arcadia and the corrupting influences of civilization.[1] Inevitably and unavoidably, infrastructure fundamentally changes the original situation of a territory. While establishing a connection, it produces a rupture. In urbanized settings, infrastructure often isolates by constructing barriers. In natural surroundings, the intrusion of the machine into the natural, bucolic landscape challenges the ecological balance and the beauty of the scenery. Its production of noise, pollution, and other nuisances turns it into a fiend rather than a friend. For these reasons, making infrastructure inexorably poses the question of integration into the surrounding environment.

Initially, infrastructure was part and parcel of regional and urban structuring. It obeyed conditions imposed by the environment – topography, flood, soil resistance – and gave way to building form around it. Infrastructural systems acted as ordering devices. They were conceived as integrated man-made landscapes. Up to the 19th century, morphological cohesion between infrastructure and urbanity was engraved in traditional and newly developed road typologies. Vehicular movement was intelligently married to pedestrian circulation and augmented by auxiliary programs to act as an instrument that guided rapidly developing parts of the city. Baron Haussmann's famous network of boulevards in Paris was both brutally imposed on the urban fabric and embedded in it, since it extended to include a system of parks, squares, and monuments. Within a vision of urban integrity, the boulevards were tactically located to take advantage of existing monuments and amenities, topographical conditions, and real estate opportunities. Sectional richness was explicitly designed and the landscape, street furniture, building edges, and utilities below the surface were all built concurrently; they formed a new system of transport, promenade, utilities, and power [1]. Similarly, Frederick

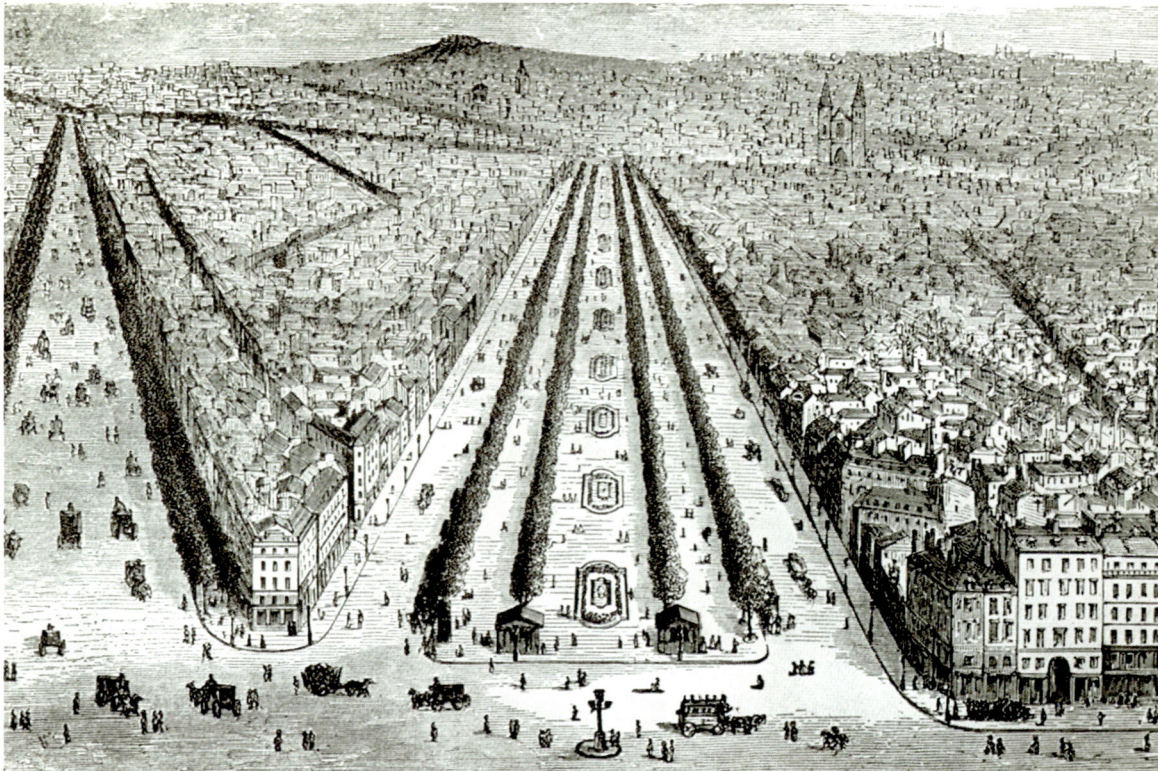

1 **METROPOLITAN BOULEVARDS**
Baron Haussmann's boulevards were simultaneously autonomous and cleverly embedded in the fabric of the city.

2 **EMERALD NECKLACE**
Frederick Law Olmsted transformed a pragmatic objective (control of the natural ecology of tidal wetlands) into a rich, multi-layered system of "circulation and respiration" of urban infrastructure.

Law Olmsted's projects in Boston and New York are canonical for their intertwining of transportation infrastructure, flood, and drainage engineering, and for the creation of a scenic landscape [2]. His projects are simultaneously tidal mitigation systems, automobile parkways, real estate development projects, public parks, and sites for urban gardens – all related to an even larger metropolitan system of parks and parkways. As evidenced by these paradigmatic projects of the 19th and early 20th centuries, infrastructure was both an icon of technological modernization and the harbinger of an immanent improvement in quality of life. Projects traversed scales; they were particular and comprehensive in scope, and local and metropolitan in impact. Urban planning, civil and sanitary engineering, and landscape architecture folded into one another, as did concerns for mobility, health, recreation, and scenery. Many important urbanists of the 19th and early 20th centuries combined such concerns. In the case of Raymond Unwin's close, and Soria y Mata's and Le Corbusier's linear cities, the new form of the road or transport system also represented the backbone of a new settlement structure. In such a way, the infrastructural project in cities remained deeply rooted to urbanism.

However, in the same modern era, infrastructure between cities became progressively disconnected from its environs as it was turned into a transport system of its own. The modern network – an amorphous connective web of roads, highways, railroads, ports, and so on that crisscrosses the land with relative indifference to

geography – has been set up predominantly by engineers, in accordance with an autonomous logic of performance and technical requirements. A mesh of interconnections has overlaid both urban and rural logics, resulting in a new territoriality. In the countryside, the image of a bucolic landscape has vanished, and the sites of primitive hardship are transformed into manufactured landscapes of pragmatism by market economics and engineering reasoning. By the mid-20th century, bureaucratic and technocratic production modes had moved infrastructure toward being a component of traffic management rather than of urbanism. Utilitarian terms, efficient circulation, and the technological panacea – asphalt – resulted in the specialization of road design. Highly standardized freeways and expressways with almost no relation to the immediate environment became commonplace. In Nazi Germany and Eisenhower's America, roads came to be considered strategic organizational devices which were underpinned by military defense purposes [3]. They were also used in propaganda drives as massive public-works projects that would diminish unemployment. The autobahn was boasted as an investment that would not only improve infrastructure but also promote national unity, strengthen centralized rule, and facilitate the easy movement of military forces.

It soon developed into a European model, while the New Jersey Turnpike (completed in 1951) became a road-building bible with its rationalizing highway geometries, system of rest stops, toll

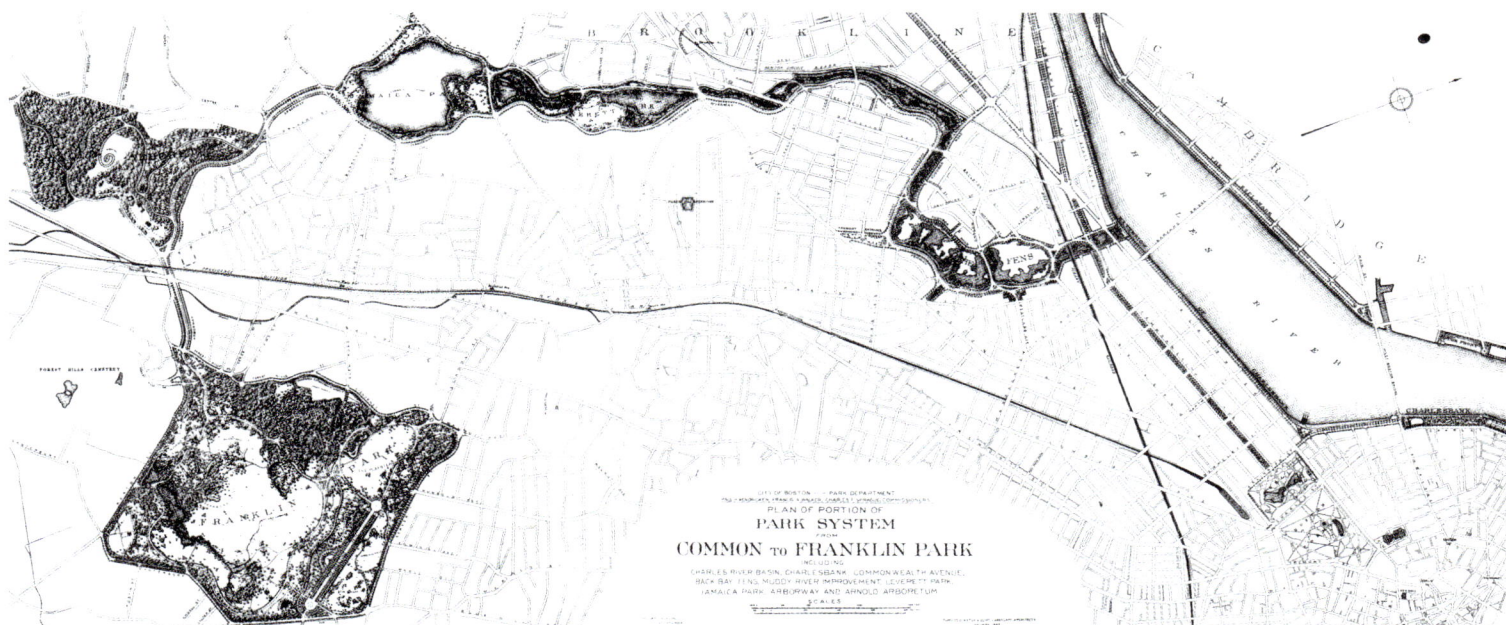

PLAN OF PORTION OF
PARK SYSTEM
FROM
COMMON TO FRANKLIN PARK

booths, and gas stations replicated nearly worldwide, and it established the basis of a novel road-based culture [4].[2] Roads were neither perceived nor designed as instruments of urban and territorial structuring, but became generic infrastructure – corridors for the transit of autos, sealed from containment by the environment, with unchanging sections whatever the location.

The devastation that the new attitude was wreaking on urbanism did not go unopposed. As early as 1951-3, Louis Kahn conceived alternative traffic circulation in Philadelphia [5]. Kahn compared infrastructure to natural ecologies whereby the fluid streams of traffic are likened to rivers and an entire conceptual repertoire is developed. "Expressways are like rivers. These rivers frame the area to be served. Rivers have Harbors. Harbors are the municipal parking towers; from the Harbors branch a system of Canals that serve the interior… from the Canals branch cul-de-sac Docks; the Docks serve as entrance halls to the buildings."[3] Others, such as Doxiadis and Candilis-Josic-Woods, viewed traffic as the spine of urban life in their numerous models for city expansion. Robert Moses's New York parkways were inscribed in the metropolitan conception of a city that melded landscape, infrastructure, and urbanization. Throughout the 1950s and 1960s, landscape architect Lawrence Halprin worked with the California Department of Transportation and the Federal Highway Administration to create choreographed compositions of parks and sculpted freeways. By the late 1960s and early 1970s, the concept of ecology emerged

and with it two influential books: Ian McHarg's *Design with Nature* (1969) and Reyner Banham's *Los Angeles: The Architecture of Four Ecologies* (1971). McHarg developed the notion of "green infrastructure" and advocated that "form must not follow function, but must also respect the natural environment in which it is placed." Banham, on the other hand, juxtaposed natural ecologies with artificial ecologies. In his comprehensive appreciation of Los Angeles, Banham's more visionary use of ecology included the instability of natural processes and man-made flows as forces that have a deterministic influence on an environment's spatial patterns. In Europe, Buchanan's *Traffic in Towns* (1963) shaped the reaction against inconsiderate urban renewal. It gave way to the notion that traffic, like any other urban activity, had to be molded in accordance with the physical characteristics to fortify the qualities of the environment to which it gave access.

In the past decades, there has been growing criticism of the territorial upheavals wrought by infrastructure. Due to extending urbanization and sprawl, the hindrance caused by the systematic intensification of infrastructure increases in accordance with the growing demands for transport. Obviously, one is always poking into someone's backyard, even in the remotest places. The more works of infrastructure planned, the more opposition there is from those who decry the disappearance of a patrimonial and usually conservative conception of the landscape. From critics, a preservationist attitude reigns. The landscape is viewed as a pub-

3 **"UNITED GERMANY" VIA INFRASTRUCTURE**
The world's first limited-access (cars and motorbikes only), high-speed road network was the German autobahn.

4 **FIRST ASPHALT SUPERHIGHWAY IN THE UNITED STATES**
The New Jersey Turnpike's norms for toll plazas, road shoulders, cloverleaf interchanges, and size of driving lanes became a universal standard for highway design.

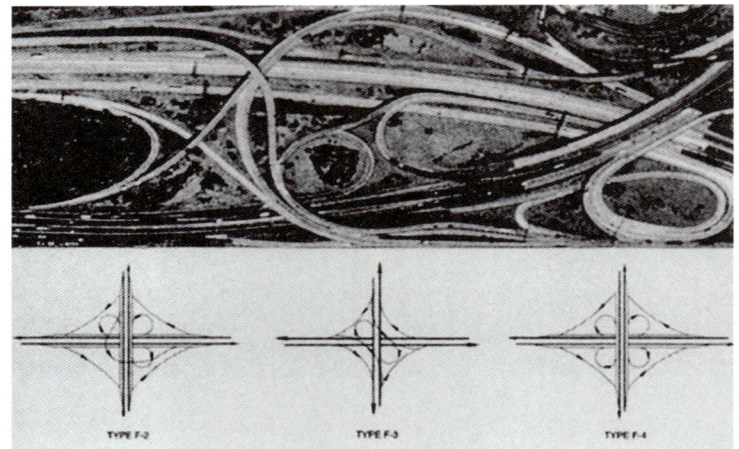

lic space that has to be safeguarded (if not already spoiled) and recovered (if heretofore invaded by infrastructure). The decision-making process of implementing new infrastructure thus becomes increasingly difficult. On the one hand, citizens are increasingly adept at defending their interests. Actions of local residents are often blown out of proportion, and the NIMBY ("not in my back-yard") phenomenon can no longer be shrugged off. On the other hand, the design of infrastructure itself has become increasingly complex. As a rule, it must serve a multimodal purpose. In addition, it is simultaneously under the pressure of adhering to international norms and adapting to specific local contexts – both in spatial and sociocultural terms.

Since the 1990s, concerted efforts have been made to move away from an infrastructure that was predominantly determined by engineering requirements. The civilizing of freeways exemplarily achieved in Barcelona, France's various TGV and tramway projects, and the global exuberance of expression and mixed-use of stations (train, ferry, bus, airplane) are all actively delivering the creation of infrastructure back to the field of urbanism. In the most fruitful projects of today, the engineer has turned into the director of a team of multifaceted competence – working alongside landscape architects and urban designers. At the same time, enlarged mobility of people and goods is increasing demands on multimodal infrastructure. Extreme sophistication and extra-large capacities must be dealt with in the newest generation of

hubs, logistical centers, super-airports, and container terminals. The technical requirements of such programs are highly demanding and involve serious design investigation to exceed the merely engineered solution and become part of contemporary urbanity. Finally, the intellectual promise of the emergent field of landscape urbanism is one of great optimism, which stems from the melding of disciplines and the enhanced relationships between natural systems and public infrastructure. New urban design strategies thus evolve from developing networks of landscape infrastructure related to ecological systems. A thoughtful synthesis of transport infrastructure's civil engineering requirements needs to be reasserted as a language of aesthetic expressiveness – where public works effectively engage urbanism.

1 Leo Marx, *The Machine in the Garden: Technology and the Pastoral Ideal in America*. (New York: Oxford University Press, 1964).
2 Pierre Berlanger, "Synthetic Surfaces," in *The Landscape Urbanism Reader*, ed. Charles Waldheim, (New York: Princeton Architectural Press, 2006), 239-265.
3 Louis Kahn as quoted by James Corner, "Terra Fluxus," in *The Landscape Urbanism Reader*, ed. Charles Waldheim, (New York: Princeton Architectural Press, 2006), 30.

5 **"EXPRESSWAYS ARE LIKE RIVERS"**
Louis Kahn's 1950s traffic studies for Philadelphia liken mobility to natural processes. His abstract notational system corresponds to different tempos of traffic.

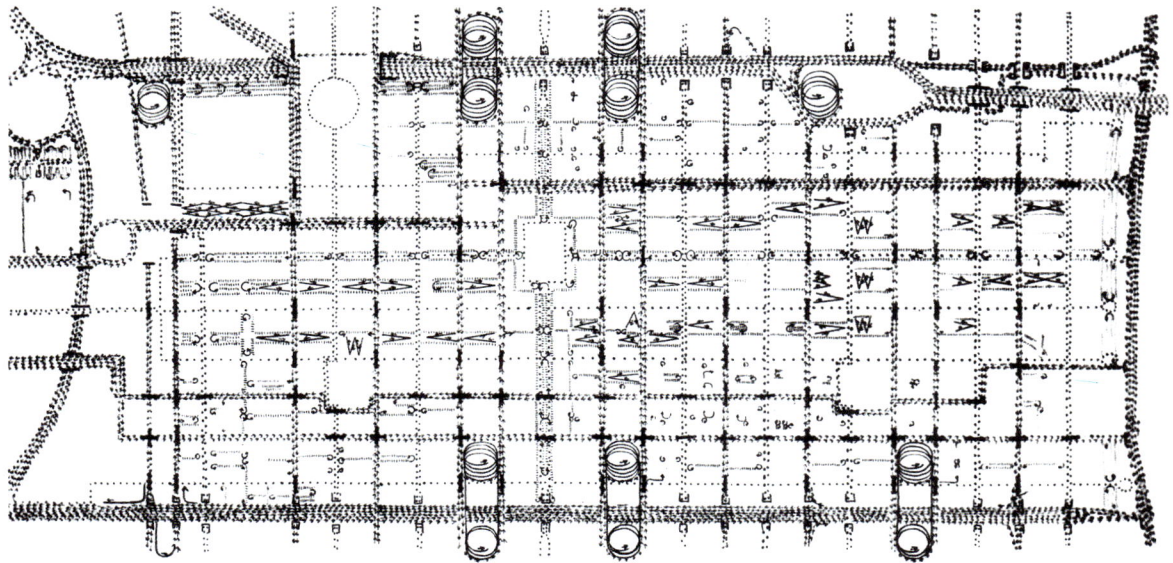

THE ARTIFICE OF HIDING

A growing environmental awareness, coupled with the NIMBY syndrome, has resulted in a spectrum of projects that go to great lengths to deal with the compromising effects of infrastructure upon the landscape. Considerable expense has been made to bury or hide both existing and new infrastructure. There clearly exists a societal consensus to hide the visibly undesirable. Concealment through topographical manipulations and clever design in section is often a mechanism employed to render infrastructure inconspicuous. Hiding seeks to obscure or obliterate an infrastructural intervention. By doing so, it creates a paradoxical situation, namely the illusion of an acceptable landscape when that is actually destroyed by the heavily engineered infrastructure underneath. Languages of invisibility recast infrastructure and utilize its disturbance to create or suggest landscape and community linkages. A double world is thus constructed: the underworld of traffic and train movement, stench, noise, and parking versus the upper world of beauty, delight, recreation, and social interaction. Often, this division also corresponds to a division in professional involvement: landscape architects are frequently called in to embellish the space regained by covering railroads or throughways, or to furbish the squares on top of underground parking garages.

Within the artifice of hiding, two broader categories can be distinguished. The first deals with urban areas, the second with the open landscape. In urban settings, burying highways, railroads, and parking garages not only solves a visual problem but also, in many instances, creates valuable real estate and enlarged public realms. Regularly, inspiration for the new surface treatment is sought in the surrounding urban morphology. It establishes a focal point for the adjacent district, while confirming the separation between the realms of traffic and pedestrians. A number of projects have attempted to rectify previous urban highway intrusions that hacked their way through neighborhoods in the 1950s and 1960s. They include significant highlights such as Jardins Wilson in Paris and less convincing projects such as the Big Dig in Boston [1]. Maxwan's concept for covering the A2 expressway near Utrecht, the Netherlands, promises the continuity of the urban fabric over the infrastructure for the Leidsche Rijn extension of 30,000 new dwellings and accompanying office and commercial spaces [2]. The notion of covering over railroad lines and yards gains legitimacy in several European cities as a dominant way of both stitching together formerly separated urban districts and gaining a new point of urban and economic activity. Finally, there is a growing trend to bury perhaps the modern city's principal eyesore: car-park facilities. In many cases, such sites are reclaimed from areas that were blights on the district and turned into recreational and gathering amenities above with access and car-park facilities below.

2 **SECTIONAL MANIPULATION** The Leidsche Rijn A2 Expressway covering project near Utrecht by Maxwan aims for continuity of the urban fabric over the massive highway infrastructure for an extension district consisting of 30,000 new dwellings and accompanying office and commercial spaces. A civic presence was programmed atop a long dike tunnel through a series of sectional manipulations. Technical regulations to limit the risk of explosion compromised the initial intention, resulting in an adapted concept of two shorter tunnels and a concentration of urban continuity along two paths.

1 BURYING UNDERGROUND

The Boston Central Artery/ Tunnel project (more commonly known as the Big Dig) replaced the city's controversial "green monster" – a 7.8-mile-long (12.55 kilometers), six-lane elevated highway – with a massive tunnel containing an 8-10 lane expressway. Unfortunately, the tunnel was exclusively engineered to function as a state-of-the-art piece of transport infrastructure. The opportunity to become a component of Olmsted's Emerald Necklace was missed when the large swathe was divided into parcels to become repositories for markets, monuments, and cultural festivals. This refurbishment incorporates the predictable mix of grassy lawns, paved areas, performance spaces, and water features that forms the blueprint for downtown beautification today.

Before

After

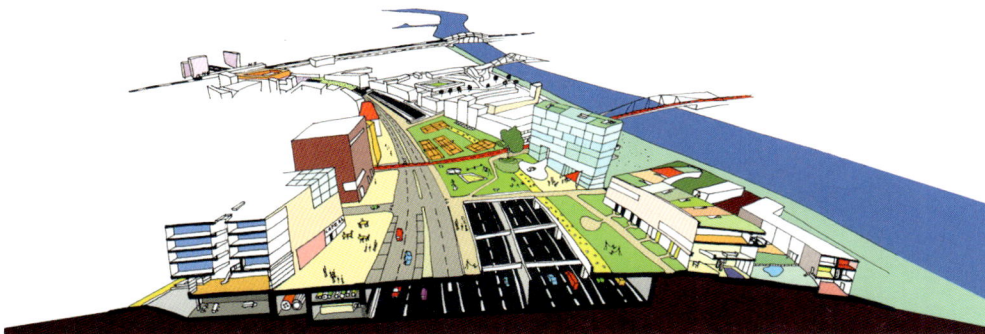

3 **ECOLOGICAL BRIDGES**
The A5 national road that links Yverdon-les-Bains to Solothurn in Switzerland crosses landscapes of various natural and ecological value. The road features 22 tunnels that vary in length from 180 to 2850 meters. The last realized section (2002), between Solothurn and Biel, is 6420 meters long and runs through a vast and open landscape of grassland with a water table near ground level and is subject to occasional flooding. In response, Metron Landschaft designed different open sections and tunnels, the longest of which is the 1820-meter-long Witi tunnel underneath Witi de Granges, an important international bird reserve and recreational area. Not only is the road hidden, but the design favors the circulation of wild animals and reduces traffic noise.

In the more open countryside, hiding takes on another role. Earthworks and the creative insertion of neighborhood-related programs are employed to mask otherwise brutal infrastructural impositions on the landscape. As the use of cars continues to grow worldwide, the construction of highways remains a central task for ministries and transport departments. Often, their routes are highly contested and provoke heated political debates. In several countries the image problem of new highway or rail connections – particularly in the countryside where an idyllic construct still reigns – has resulted in great expenditure related to public litigation. As environmental issues gain political ground and sustainability more forcibly enters the public consciousness, there will undoubtedly be more such positive mitigation and remuneration in large-scale infrastructure projects. Ecological bridges, such as the A5 national road that links Yverdon-les-Bains to Biel and Solothurn in Switzerland, are becoming more and more commonplace [3]. In Denmark, the large Ørestad project brought with it a new interlinked network of connections. The route of the new highway and railroad bisected the town of Tårnby, and the problematic situation was turned into an opportunity to mark the crossing architecturally. The cut in the landscape has become part of the fabric; it is hidden by a large public balcony and gives way to a new formal setting. In particular, the construction of high-speed railroads through the countryside proves to be a sensitive issue. It has often led to projects that either mitigate incisions in the territory or evade conflicts by routing large portions of the line through tunnels. In the European context, several projects have cleverly adopted this tactic, some modest and others terribly expensive, like the construction of a seven-kilometer-long bored tunnel under the so-called Green Heart of the Netherlands [4]. In the last decades, finally, the ambition to transform parking areas into plots of planted settings has often resulted in stacked solutions of underground parking with gardened roofs. On occasion, the proliferation of the ubiquitous, nondescript, and generic urban periphery business parks has led to more inventive campus settings that include innovative parking complexes. The combination of private car parking and a public park, as in Google's North Charleston Campus (originally built for Silicon Graphics), is representative of such a hiding tactic.

4 BORING AT GREAT DEPTH

The Green Heart Tunnel, 14.5 meters in diameter, 7 kilometers in length, bored approximately 30 meters below "normal" water level, is located between the town of Leiderdorp and the village of Hazerswoude in the Netherlands. The tunnel is to accommodate high-speed trains. The gigantic expense, magnified by the fact that the tunnel is bored below the water table, was justified in the name of preserving the peaty grasslands of the Randstad's so-called Green Heart, one of the last undisturbed, undeveloped landscapes in the country.

Elegant Covering

JARDINS WILSON

Plaine Saint-Denis, France

Architect: Benôit Scribe; Yves Lion, Alan Levitt

Landscape Architect: Michel Corajoud

Date: 1994–1997 (design), 1997–1998 (construction)

Jardins Wilson is emblematic of the contemporary approach to hiding: the polluting, vehicular world below is simply covered over and bears no indication of the newly created, peaceful pedestrian world above. There is complete disconnection between the two. The project is also one of recovery. The covering of part of the A1 (Paris-Lille) highway, between Saint-Denis and Aubervilliers in the northern suburbs of Paris, partially returns the once important axis to its former glory. Before the brutal open trench infrastructure ripped through the fabric in 1965, Avenue du Président Wilson in Saint-Denis was an old royal road lined by majestic trees. The building of a platform over part of the scar followed a campaign waged by the inhabitants.

The 38-meter-wide and 1300-meter-long newly landscaped platform reconnects the urban fabric across the highway and creates an enlarged public realm. In the early stages of the rehabilitation process, the design of the surface was closely linked to technical decisions. The earth atop the concrete structure had to be minimized to limit its weight, yet rich enough to support a living environment. The once fragmented industrial area was restructured by a public spine – a combination of gardens with local surface traffic serving a rich mixture of residential, office, and commercial premises. The Jardins Wilson project was part of a city-wide policy to renovate the former industrial district of Plaine Saint-Denis by restructuring the area and improving public space. It was explicitly integrated within a set of transversal passages and connections between the canal and railroad that run parallel to it. The linear platform hiding the expressway thus creates a Mediterranean model of the

paseo (promenade) atop. The lawn is divided into three zones: two public squares, and parking areas that are book-ended by a cherry tree garden to the south and a willow garden to the north. Two service roads, each 14.5 meters wide, run alongside the central core of the covered sunken road and contain pedestrian passageways, planting with ornamental fruit trees, a continuous line of parking places, two lanes of traffic, and a border of silver linden trees and ivy. Ventilation shafts and the emergency kiosk exits designed by Yves Lion and Alan Levitt separate the various atmospheres and program areas of the park, while the architectural regularity contrasts with the random arrangement of trees and bushes.

Before

After

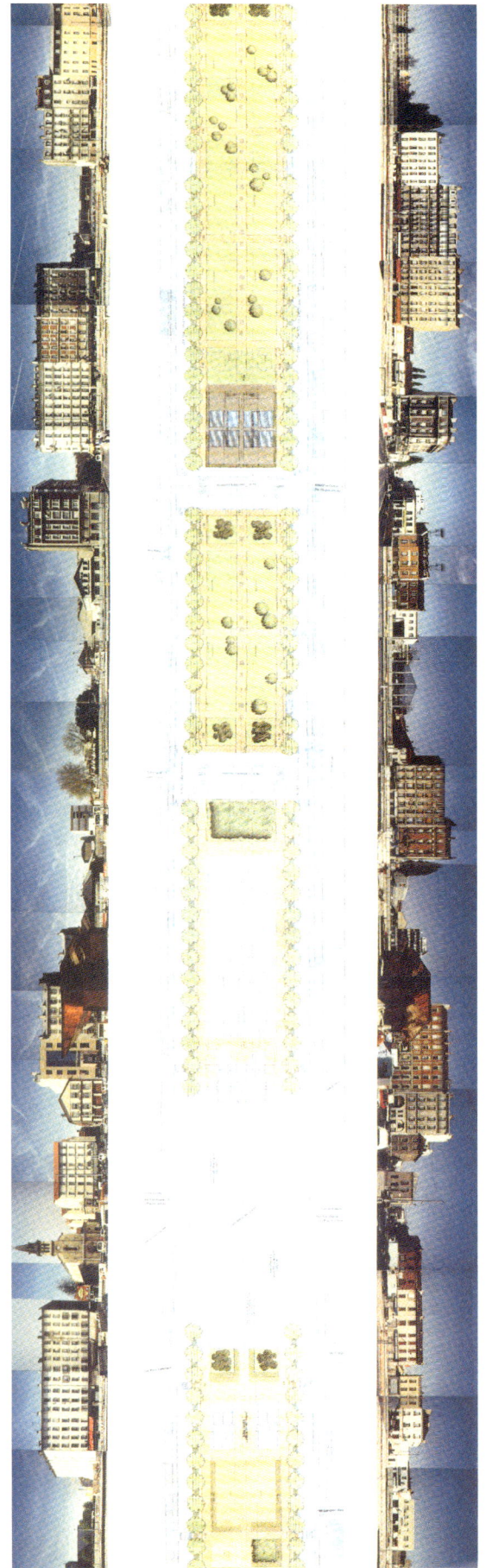

Pocket Park(ing)

PLACE DES CÉLESTINS

Lyon, France

Architect: Michel Targe

Landscape Architect: Michel Desvigne and Christine Dalnoky

Interior Architect: Wilmotte et Associés SA d'Architecture (Jean-Michel Wilmotte), Artist: Daniel Buren

Date: 1994–1995

The hiding of urban parking lots and garages has become commonplace in many European towns. In the city of Lyon, it formed a constitutive part of the city's exceptional policy of urban renewal, based on modest, pragmatic, yet tasteful projects. Under the guidance of Henry Chabert, head of the Department of Urban Planning, and Michel Noir, himself an architect and mayor of the city, Lyon embarked in the early 1990s on a progressive program to upgrade the city and its peripheral environs. This comprehensive planning venture included several projects, including the Plan Presqu'île (conservation and revitalization of the historic center), Plan Bleu (restructuring of the banks of the Rhône and Saône rivers), Plan Vert (renewal and creation of parks and public space), and Plan Lumière (theatrical nocturnal landscape). The hiding of parked cars – which had become omnipresent eyesores along quays, avenues, squares, and streets – thus became

part of the program that reorganized traffic circulation and bus routes. In the historic center, underground parking garages turned into a prerequisite for rendering squares accessible to pedestrians. In total, 12,000 underground parking places were produced along with the refurbishment of many squares. The underground parking component of its progressive mobility policy also included the development of park-and-ride facilities and an extensive light-rail network.

Located in the heart of the Presqu'île peninsula, Place des Célestins is the entry square to the 18th-century Célestins Theater and serves as an oasis in the midst of the dense fabric. The square was renovated in 1995, but still stands as an example in its genre. In fact, the design of both the civic space and the garage underneath merits attention. According to the landscape architects, the former was meant to have "the porousness

of a square and the intimacy of a garden." Its elementary geometry – white limestone paving at the perimeter and a two-step elevation change separate vehicles and the rectangular gardens of water and wood – is offset by a diversity of vegetation (rhododendrons, magnolias, etc.). In the parking garage, Michel Targe's helical architecture refers to the staircases of the traditional housing typology in Lyon. It forms a cylindrical composition that marries with the artwork of Daniel Buren. At the bottom of the wells, an inclined mirror, animated by a circular movement, reflects the arcades underlined by bands of black. The public space above and the garage below are linked in the center of the square by an urban endoscope – giving unexpected views of the parking ramp. Ultimately, the hiding trick here is revealed.

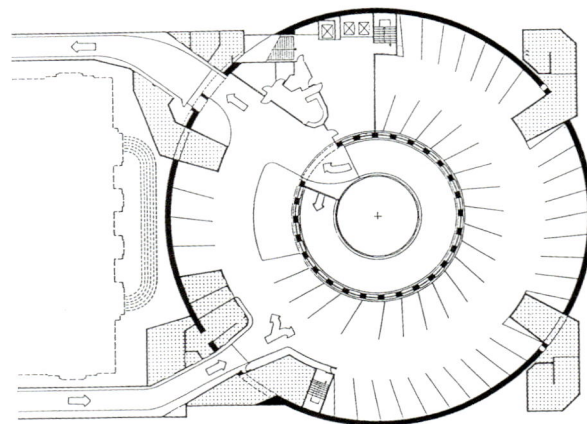

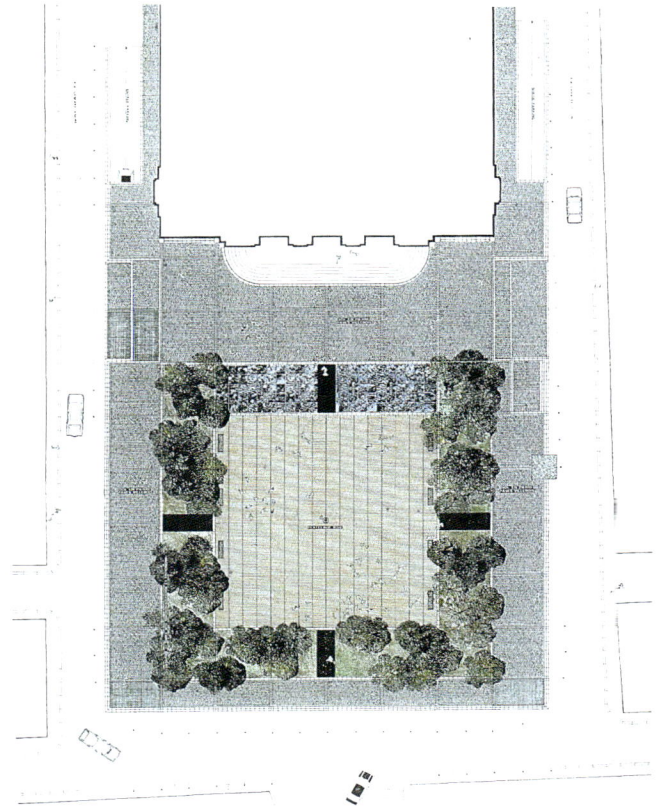

Earthwork Stitch

Tårnby, Denmark

Architect: KHR arkitekter AS

Date: 1994–1998

TÅRNBY STATION

Tårnby Station forms part of the landworks in connection with the 16-kilometer-long Øresund Fixed Link (constructed between 1995 and 2000), one of Europe's largest ever engineering projects and the longest cable-stayed bridge in the world. The Øresund Link was established to improve transport connections between Sweden and Denmark, and thereby to expand cultural and economic cooperation in the Øresund Region. The coast-to-coast connection between the outskirts of Copenhagen and Malmö was constructed as a combined road and railroad link, and the two countries agreed to pay for the necessary landworks and integrate the new transportation lines into the existing railroad and road networks. The Danish landworks consist of an approximately 12-kilometer-long electricity-powered railroad from the Øresund coast

to Copenhagen Central Station. The railroad has stations at Copenhagen Airport in Kastrup, in Tårnby, and in the Ørestad urban development area.

While the symbol of the larger Øresund project – the bridge – is about exposure and show, the accompanying nine-kilometer-long corridor for road and rail traffic across the island of Amager is about hiding. The engineered route of the twin corridors bisects the community of Tårnby. The challenge of how to effectively bury the cut in the fabric was gracefully met by the design of a 680-meter-long covering section over the road and tracks. Similar to the Jardins Wilson in Paris, the concrete structure is topped with earth, yet in this case developed as a longitudinal plaza with entry pavilions to the subterranean rail platforms

below. The remaining part is covered in an unpretentious green that unobtrusively links the old village settlement of Tårnby over the railroad track with the shopping area of its modern extension. The resulting artificial terrain is slightly hilly, yet flat enough to be easily bridged. The empty area operates as a traffic junction and the hub includes a bus transit stop that leads to the station seven meters underground. The station itself consists of three long, low buildings and a travel center, one story above grade. They offer access to platforms while providing openings that allow daylight to enter at railroad level. The scar inflicted by the infrastructure is adequately put to use. By turning it into a middle ground of its own right, the architects effectively connect two substantially different realms, that of the former village street and the new town shopping precinct.

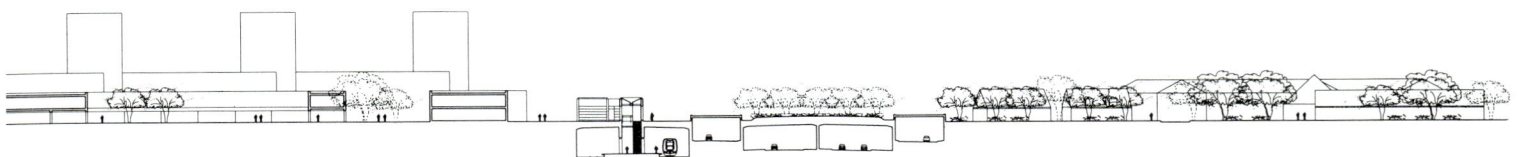

Green Garage

SILICON GRAPHICS NORTH CHARLESTON CAMPUS

Mountain View, California, USA

Architect: Studios Architecture

Landscape Architect: SWA Group

Date: 1994–1997

Studios Architecture has created an 1100-capacity parking garage for Silicon Graphics North Charleston Campus (bought by Google as its corporate headquarters in 2004) in Mountain View, California, that defies the stereotype of the office-park parking garage. Hiding has in this case transformed the large infrastructure into a pedestrian landscaped park. The Google headquarters is considered a benchmark for suburban corporate campus design in North America, as it was developed on an 11-hectare brownfield site a short distance from San Francisco Bay and includes both a research and development campus for a private company and a two-hectare public park.

The site was developed in public-private partnership with the city of Mountain View. The campus is noteworthy for two innovations. First, its strong identity owing to the blurred distinction between the private and public realms. Campus and park are treated as one landscape. Second, the large building footprints are clustered around podium-level courtyards and gardens, under which most of the 1700 parking places are buried. At the east and west ends, the landscape slopes up to the podium from natural grade, providing a seamless connection from the park on the east through the campus to the improved creek corridor on the west. There are three main gardens that structure

the campus and within each, at the building stair towers, the ground is cut away to create openings that naturally ventilate the garage without the need for mechanical equipment. The "green garage" has larger than usual floor-to-ceiling heights (11 feet, or 3353 centimeters) under a roof that functions as a park. The remaining parking at grade is also hidden by a new method. Groves of pole-mounted solar panels (9212 in total) are planted between rows of Saabs and SUVs, generating power and creating shade. The 16-megawatt solar system will be able to supply 30% of Google's energy needs.

ASSIMILATION THROUGH CAMOUFLAGE

The intentional obscuring of something from view has its roots in military techniques – known as CCD (camouflage, concealment, and deception) – where objects either look the same as the surroundings, cannot be seen, or look like something else. The combat philosophy of "blending with nature" and taking on the color of the surroundings is also recognizable in infrastructural projects situated in particularly dense urban contexts and environmentally vulnerable territories. A historical example of such camouflage is Rio de Janeiro's reclamation project for a waterfront highway in the 1950s. Flamenco Park (1954) by Roberto Burle Marx assimilates the busy expressway into a parkway. Cultural infrastructure and road infrastructure are spatially tied together. Marx's park simultaneously frames landscapes and orders flows. His camouflage technique can be most literally discerned in the threshold space of Copacabana where large surface paintings form both beach boardwalks and parking areas along the seaside boulevard [1].

The concept of imperceptibility and assimilation shares similarities with that of hiding and putting out of sight. When incorporation into the surrounding environment is fully achieved, the foreign body is no longer visible. Camouflage is thus a vital form of hiding – not by creating two worlds, but by having the alien landscape of traffic and circulation assume the form of its environs and therefore disappear. As such, the features of the existing landscape are underlined in this approach. Obviously, this result is never fully achieved. For that reason, it rather prevails as an ideal objective, and should be distinguished as a separate attitude. Fundamentally, two modes of assimilation through camouflage can differentiated, depending upon their emphasis on duplicating the formal appeal or structural features of the landscape. The latter gives way to an attitude of inclusion, whereby existing structures of the landscape are underlined and/or processes of authentic landscape formation are orchestrated. The former leads to replication, and has embedded within it the danger of yielding to the picturesque.

The strategy of inclusion aims to integrate a foreign object into a territory and make it seem as though it had always been there. In Norway, the existing condition of the surrounding woods has been carefully reprocessed in the setting of the new Oslo airport. Quite incredibly, the huge infrastructure appears, both from the air and at ground level, to be completely embedded in the nearby evergreen forest. A smaller program, but also one of intelligent assimilation, is the parking garage of Gare d'Issy-Val de Seine. The complex construction is literally embedded in the slope of an existing RER transport landscape and its roof will serve as the platform for a new tramway. The structure is simultaneously a retaining wall and a large parking facility. Likewise, in Nice, an as yet unbuilt project implants the port terminal into the urban topography, constructing an accessible terrace as public platform for the city and a terminal that can only be seen from the sea. In

1 BLISSFUL PLAYGROUND
Roberto Burle Marx's large painting-like mosaics between the built urban wall of Copacabana and the four-kilometer-long curving beachfront are renowned for turning tropical landscaping into an art. Completed in 1970, the dynamic, colorful, abstract stone mosaics range from cubist abstractions near the urban strip to a reinterpretation of a Portuguese wave pattern closer to the sea. The café-restaurant spillover onto the sidewalks and the areas for car parking and bikini-touting pedestrians on the seafront promenade are worked into a cohesive spatial entity that cleverly camouflages the pragmatics of a busy thoroughfare.

2 ARTIFICIAL TERRACE

The Nice port terminal, for passengers and cars, by Jacques Ferrier effectively folds the public ground plane into a three-dimensional camouflage composition. Conceived as a transversal building, the terminal is open to both the sea and the city; it reconnects the urban tissue with the water. The terrace of the terminal, with its kiosks and cafeteria, is the end point of an urban promenade, a belvedere on the sea. Planted with Mediterranean pines, the terrace partially covers the disembarkation ramp and extends towards the city side through a ramp. Infrastructure is camouflaged as an oversized and amazing esplanade.

2 EARTHWORK SCREENING

In the Channel Tunnel Rail Link in England (now called High Speed 1) CTRL Landscape Architects reuses the soil to create engineered earthworks that reduce both the visual and environmental effects along the route and grade the new railroad into its surroundings. The railroad's "fit" into the landscape lessens the impact of the section cut by continuing the character of the largely rural landscape, typically through the application of gentle slopes. The visual integration of the railroads by earthworks has been designed in conjunction with greenery in the form of extensive broad-leaved woodland and grassland.

4 OVERWHELMING TREE-PLANT

West 8 has cleverly masked Amsterdam's Schiphol Airport by the systematic planting of birches in the leftover spaces of its surroundings. Because of their thin and flexible branches, birch trees are not suitable for large bird perching. Their seeds are also unappealing for migratory flocks. The trees are initially planted in bright green clover patches that fertilize the soil and support beehives. After one year the clover gives way to grasses. Every planting season, 25,000 new trees are added. Over time, the plantation is envisioned to grow into an "unpretentious green counterpart to the buildings, billboards, and infrastructure."

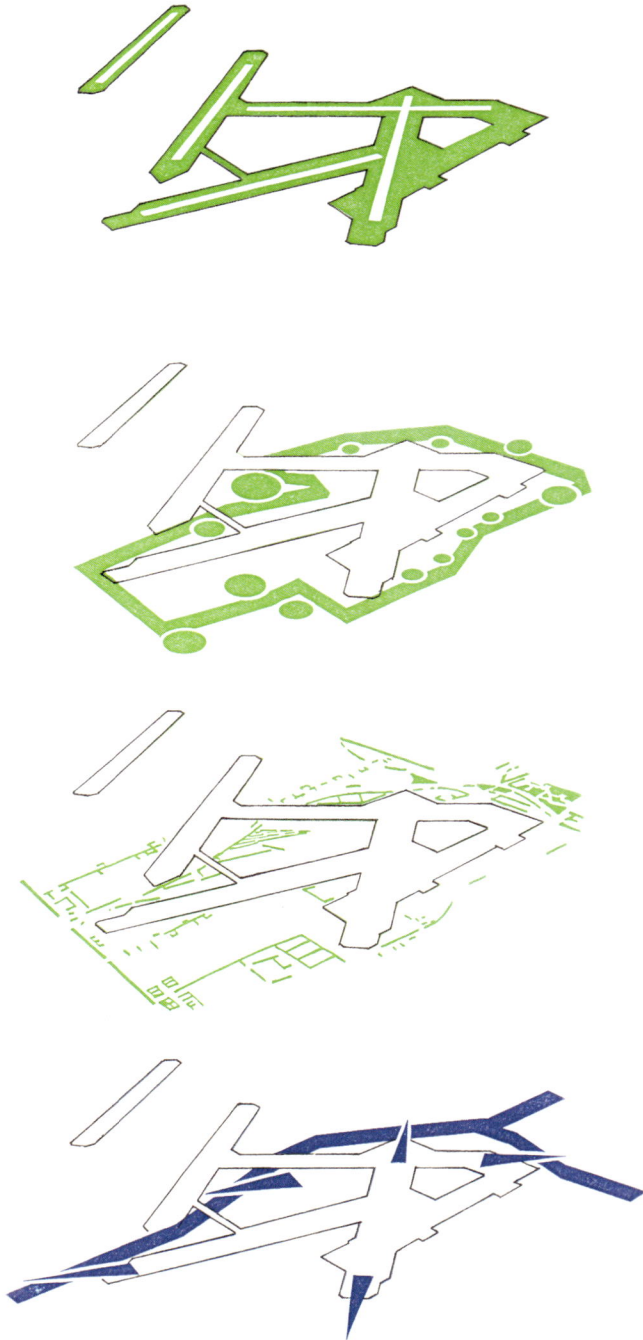

5 VERNACULAR SERVICE STATION

The Westmorland South service station on the M6 highway near Tebay, England, pays tribute to the Lake District landscape and the local vernacular. The station is sheltered from the motorway by earth bunds planted with native Scots pines and birch; the bunds are inset with informal hard-surfaced picnic areas. The main building, the petrol station, and the parking areas lie in a shallow hollow that limits their impact on the landscape, although all facilities are visible upon leaving the highway. The main building, with views over moorland to distant mountains, appears as a countryside lodge — with stone walls, a slate roof, and an interior of massive exposed timber trusses (salvaged from a Lancashire textile mill).

6 CIVIC CLOAKING

Zimmer Gunsul Frasca Architects has deceptively cloaked a multimodal transit station north of Seattle, in Everett, Washington, in an outer skin of civic monumentality reminiscent of earlier times. The exterior image corresponds with the ambition to portray the building as a civic gesture. Camouflage does not merely act by playing with decorum, but by infusing the building with programs unusual for a station. It contains university classrooms, a career-development center, community meeting spaces, and ample public art.

addition, the terminal constitutes a new dike that not only meets all technical requirements but is also conceived to fuse into the city's coastal promenade [2]. A more common form of deception in infrastructural projects is that of screening or concealing through the extensive use of earthworks and/or vegetation. The British side of the Channel Tunnel Rail Link (now called High Speed 1, or HS 1) rationalized the infrastructural disturbance of the railroad at the regional scale by recycling excavated soil for visually screening earthworks [3]. The plateau Kirchberg by Peter Latz has developed into a highly urbanized area while maintaining the image of a mountainous meadow and woodland garden. The major access route is lined by trees and artworks, transforming it from a functional highway into a domesticated avenue, alternated with large patches of autochthon bocage. In a similar vein, Adriaan Geuze cleverly uses trees to create a comprehensive landscape and disguise Schiphol Airport by integrating the leftover spaces into a massive collection of birch trees [4].

The second strategy is a more explicit form of deception, through the tactic of replication whereby infrastructure and building types are literally camouflaged. Integration, or not being seen, allows an otherwise visible object to remain indiscernible from the surrounding environment. Examples are numerous and span from the vegetal hiding of concrete infrastructure in the rich city-state of Singapore, where the tropical lushness is symbolically used to push forward the city's motto of "a tropical city of excellence," to more subtle examples such as Westmorland South, a service station on England's M6 motorway that looks like a nature lodge [5], and the train-bus station in Everett, Washington, which is programmatically combined with educational, shopping, and community facilities and has the stature of a civic building [6]. The vine-encased Ballet Valet parking garage in Miami's South Beach exemplifies a literal form of camouflage with hanging gardens and vernacular facades concealing a massive parking garage.

Wooded Airport

OSLO AIRPORT

Gardermoen, Norway

Architect: Aviaplan AS / Narud Stokke Wiig Architects & Planners

Landscape Architect: Bjørbekk & Lindheim

Date: 1993–1998

Camouflaging a work of infrastructure as enormous as an airport may sound like an oxymoron. Yet the new 13-square-kilometer Oslo airport to the northeast of the city at Gardermoen achieves such an unimaginable feat. It has been immersed into the landscape – a moor in the gently rolling forested landscape of Akershus county – through grouping structures in large open-air rooms bounded by seemingly untouched patches and belts of coniferous and deciduous trees. In Norway, the affinity of man-made interventions to the natural environment had been an unspoken, long-standing tradition. Consequently, for the new airport, traditions were not left to risk. The Norwegian parliament insisted that the airport "evoke Norway" and stipulated the creation of both

a high-tech airport and an example of Norwegian *byggeskikk* (vernacular). The parliamentary mandate was translated into a handbook of visual rules for designers, which included concepts such as "prudence, closeness to nature, an open and egalitarian society, and good usage of local resources." Aviaplan developed an overall landscape plan with clear guidelines for the continued development of the airport, including buildings as well as open and planted spaces. Their landscape structure plan governs all aspects of environment and scenery: vegetation, soils, intended or preserved characteristics of the Norwegian landscape, and aesthetic qualities such as light and color. The manual required documentation of existing features and preservation of their

quality wherever possible, and even imposed a fine of NOK 60,000 for each tree felled without a permit.

The airport is situated at the threshold between the dark evergreen forest in the northeast and the farming flatlands to the south. The terminal, made of warm wood and expansive glass facades, is screened by and looks toward the forest, while to the south ancillary buildings are grouped, and roads and a railroad nestle into a constructed mosaic of birch and maple trees. Low-maintenance flower meadows surround buildings and runways, and dry walls merge with the surroundings, articulating a quintessential yet state-of-the-art landscape of transportation.

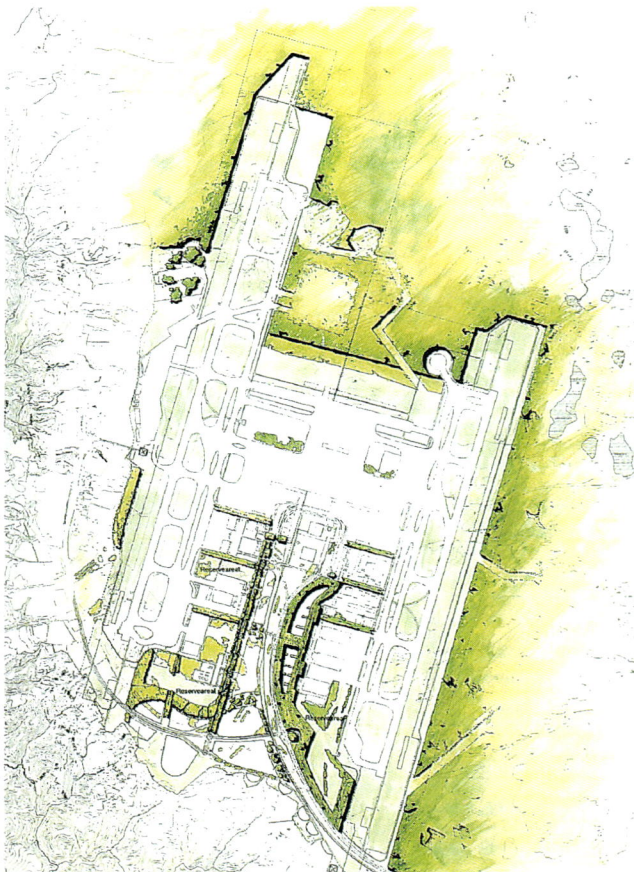

Parking as Retaining Wall

Issy-les-Moulineaux, France

Architect: Atelier de Midi architectes

Date: 1995

PARC DE LA GARE D'ISSY-VAL DE SEINE

The structure, situated at the extraordinary node of different modes of transport, is both a three-level 6650-square-meter parking garage for nearly 300 cars and a foundation of the future Val-de-Seine tramway – all inscribed into the excavated slope that carries the tracks of an RER line (which remained in operation during construction of the parking garage and tramway building). The bunker-like strength of the structure required complex construction techniques. The building has to resist three types of forces: the RER exerts transverse pressure on the east side; the tramway station transmits significant longitudinal loads, along the north-south axis of the parking garage in case of the sudden braking of a tram; and finally, due to a high water table, special attention was required to resist upward pressure from the water below.

Yet the representation of the structure is anything but bunker-like. Columns are trapezoidal and function as arcs, and the upper slab is poured concrete. The architecture of the project has been determined by the functional proximity to the station of Issy-Plaine and by the particular proportions of the volume to be managed. The parking building is 148 meters long and only 15.5 meters wide, with a 5.7-meter-high facade (corresponding to the two upper levels of the parking) oriented to the west. The long elevation is composed of translucent glass bricks framed by the columns and the horizontal beams that protrude slightly. The monotony of this motif is broken by the deep cut of the entrance and by the protruding vertical circulation elements. A long ramp at the north and staircases in the center and south ensure a direct relation between the three levels of parking and the tramway platforms. The building is embedded in the earthwork of the train-tramway structure, which functions as a retaining wall. Structure has been assimilated with program and transport has been assimilated with landscape.

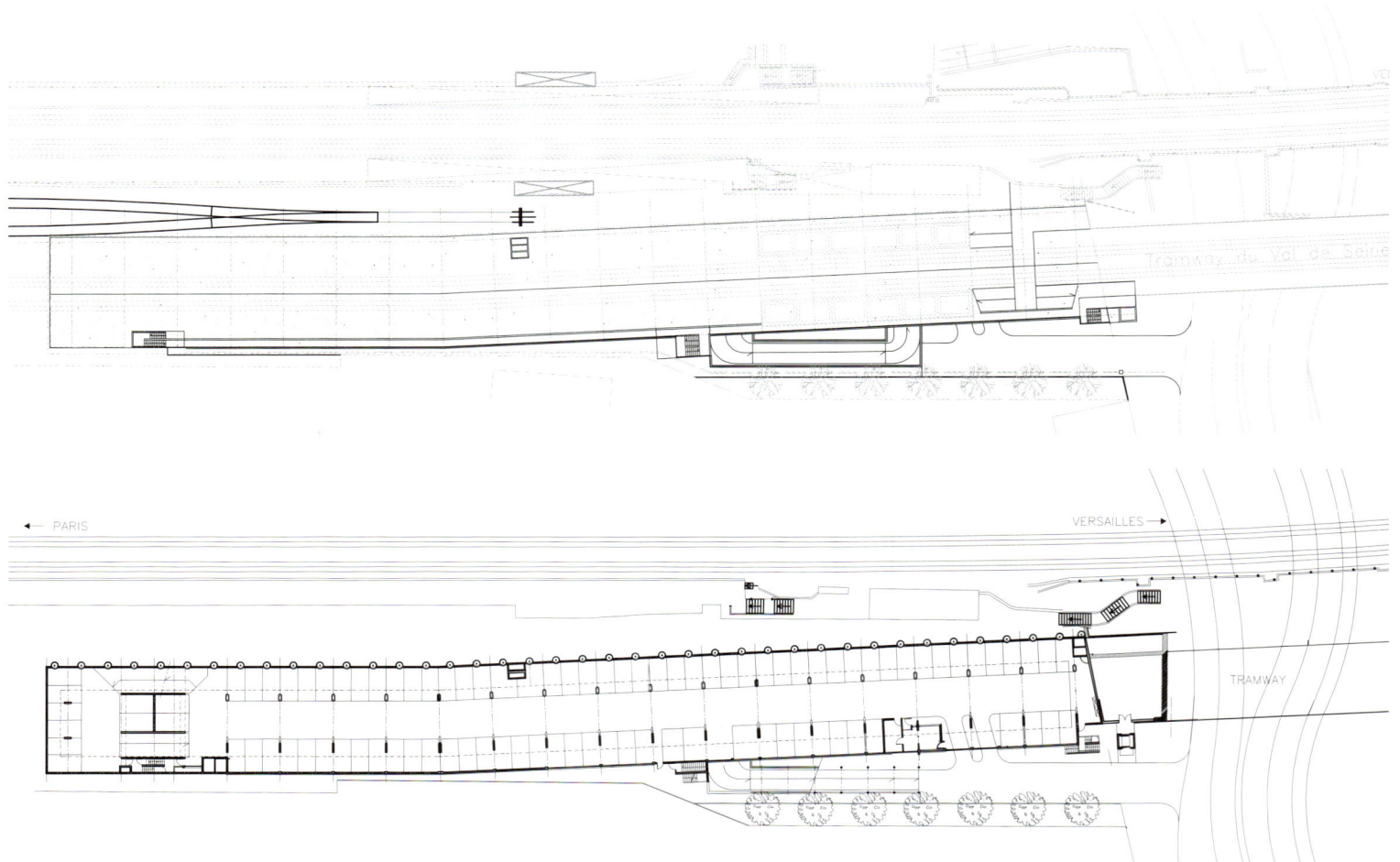

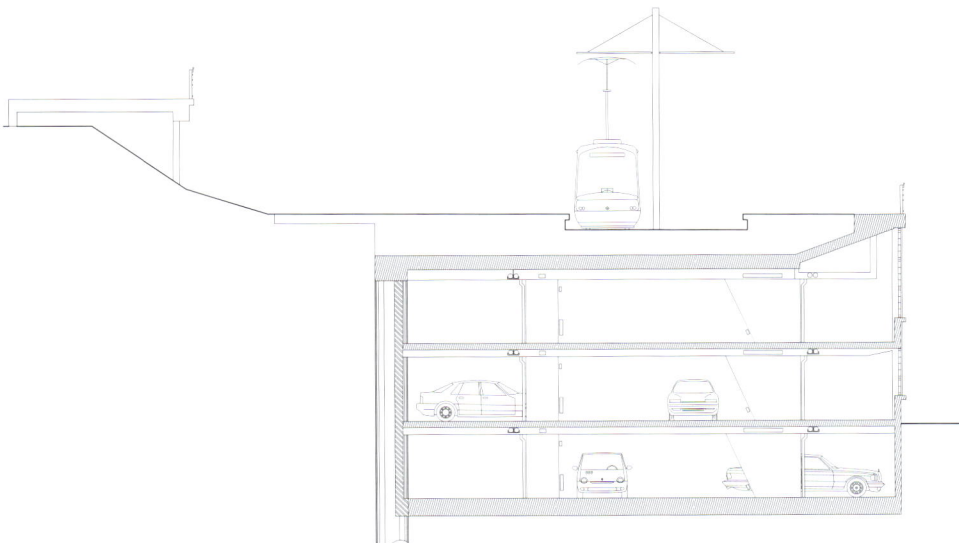

Restituting the Countryside

PLATEAU DE KIRCHBERG

Luxembourg

Landscape Architect: Latz + Partner (Peter Latz)

Date: 1993–2008

The Plateau de Kirchberg utilizes deception techniques at multiple scales. At the regional scale, the urbanization of the plateau has retroactively been camouflaged as an inhabited park, while large infrastructure works for road and rainwater treatment have been screened by landscaping. In the early 1950s, Luxembourg gambled on being the full-fledged capital of the newly established European Economic Community and subsequently began a program of building European institutions in a concentrated area on the sandstone plateau across the Alzette River, only half a kilometer to the east of the city center. The initiative resulted in a series of isolated office structures built in accordance with the principles of functionalism and the primary requirements of the car. As the 360-hectare area continued to urbanize, new concerns arose, and a renovation of the area was developed based primarily upon landscape restructuring.

One of the major initiatives was that of transforming the overscaled highway into a broad urban avenue, with trees both on its central median and along its outer edges. The 60-meter-wide, densely planted road section continues for a distance of 3.5 kilometers. It connects formerly separated quarters by facilitating the crossing and constituting a landscape in its own right, stretching from the eastern roundabout (embellished with 20-meter-high weathering steel sculpture by Richard Serra) to Rue Weicker in the west. The avenue demonstrates only one part of the new, more open concept for the precinct. Another aspect is the innovative ecological and aesthetic rainwater management scheme in association with a 65-hectare landscaped area of open greenery and woodland. The infrastructure for the rainwater, which formerly drained into the underground sewage and wastewater channels, is now integrated into the landscape through open ditches and retention pools are planted with attractive marshland plants. Rainwater management thus becomes an elementary component of the infrastructural landscape. Engineered, functional infrastructure is effectively camouflaged as a biotope network, and ecology is rendered visible as land art.

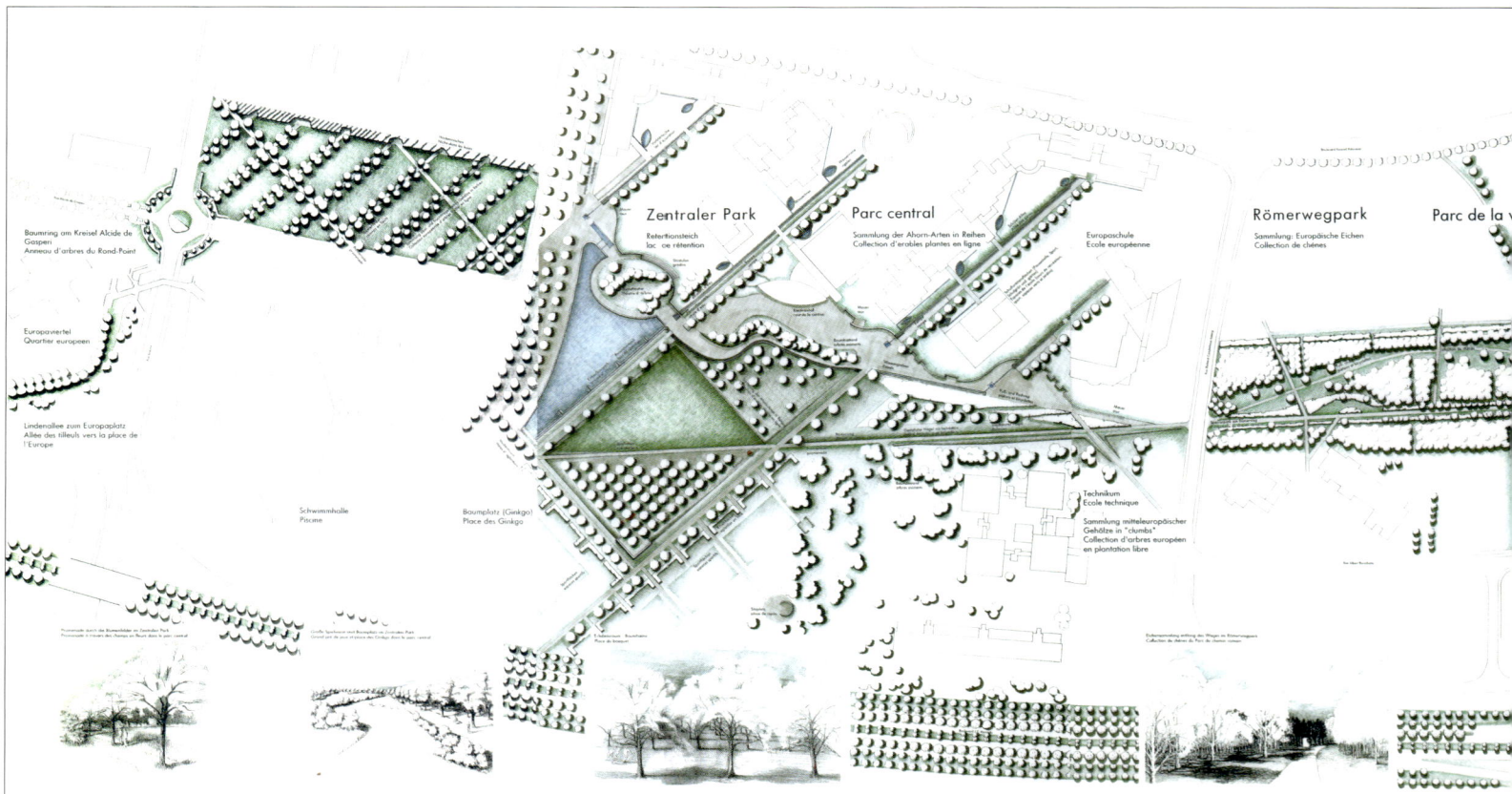

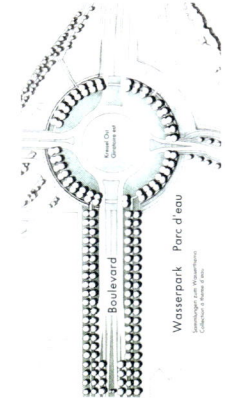

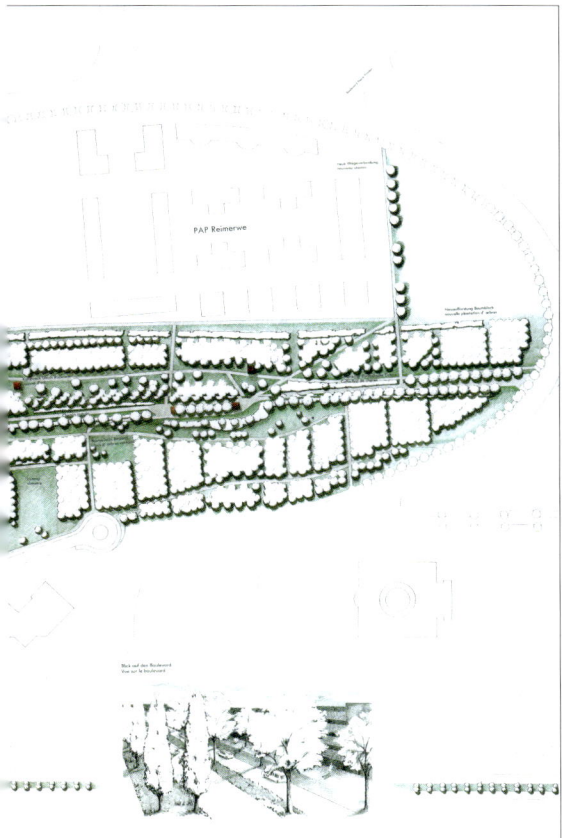

Parking Lattice

BALLET VALET PARKING GARAGE

Camouflage is a recognized design strategy for Arquitectonica, a firm known for its contribution to new urbanism. The post-modernist aesthetic is easily attacked, but it often proves more easily accepted than other contemporary interventions. This is visibly the objective of the Ballet Valet parking garage located in the famous 1920s art deco district of Miami's South Beach. The 19,140-square-meter facility boasts five parking levels for a total of 650 car spaces shielded by a vertical matrix of tropical greenery and a restored band of historic art deco facades on the ground floor (now boasting retail shops). The garage facade consists of grid-patterned fiberglass components in different shades of green and creates an armature for wavelike forms that are sheathed and overgrown with indigenous vines.

Apart from the successful camouflage-deception effect, the project has been instrumental in initiating a process of urban renewal in South Beach beyond the ocean-front strip. Since its renascence in the mid-1980s, the area – designated a historic district by the National Register of Historic Places – has witnessed redevelopment along Ocean Drive while areas in the immediate vicinity fell victim to further dilapidation. Through the creation of a public-private partnership in a complicated political environment – with a coalition of historic preservationists, advocates of antigrowth, and countless other special-interest groups – the project became a work of public infrastructure that successfully catalyzed new development. Located on the second block inland from the beach, the garage-cum-shopping facility guarantees a revenue source for the city, provides much needed parking for the district's visitors (more than 20,000 a day), and alleviates the density of the one-block-wide renewal effort along the shore by encouraging development inland. Since Ballet Valet opened, more than 30 properties in a three-block radius have been renovated and the site is the core of a new retail district.

FUSION INTO A NEW COMPOSITE

Fusion involves the combining of two distinct things, the merging of different elements into one. Fusion is a state of amalgamation, of joining together into a single entity. In science, composites are made of distinct components. Their primary elements are complementary substances that combine to produce structural or functional properties that are not present in any individual component. In an inclusive landscape project, inspiration is taken from the existing territory, but the initial situation is, in turn, amended by the infrastructure that becomes part of it. Absorption of a foreign element into a context always transforms that context. Any new addition inevitably changes the existing environment by its presence. Integration in this sense is not attained by trying to color the new intervention in accordance with its surroundings, but by reconfiguring the existing setting into a new composite landscape. In this approach, infrastructure is evidently rendered visible, but doesn't stand on its own. The new formal organization takes into account all technical demands, but gives way to an all-embracing and unique environment. It is developed as a specific solution from the programmatic requirements and the constraints of flux and traffic on the one hand, and the local morphology and topography on the other hand. As different elements and considerations merge or fuse into a new, original composition, they inevitably rely on urbanism.

As a strategy for refurbishing highways, this concept of fusion into a new composite is steadily gaining ground. In general, there are two broad ways in which this is done. The first reveals an act of acceptance of the infrastructure whereby tactics are employed to make the road part of a fuller, enriched, and more complex (urban) landscape. Numerous examples of this manner of ameliorating complicated highway infrastructure that disturb landscapes occur. A canonical project of this type is that by George Hargreaves in Louisville, Kentucky, whereby the underbelly of the elevated traffic artery was restructured to connect the city with the Ohio River through the creation of a new landscape. A series of tapering lawns, graded for flood protection, enlarge the public realm and turn an eyesore into a civic amenity. In a similar vein, several projects by Barcelona-based architects Batlle and Roig – including their well-publicized Parc de la Trinitat, which worked keenly with levels and access – transform peripheral infrastructure into urban entities [1]. Their more recent Park de la Riera in Sant Cugat del Vallès reconciles the once rural area with a highway by setting off the latter as a scenic platform of an in-between urban park created along the contours of the land at hand [2]. A second strategy is one of active change, of alleviating the effect of traffic by making the road part of a new and more complex section. This solution is evidenced by Reichen and Robert's project for the large-scale restoration of Faliron Bay on the Athens seafront. A 1960s expressway was moved and rebuilt in trench, and then flanked by buildings and linear parks to provide visual screens and abate noise. Traffic

1 **INTERCHANGE PARK**
Triggered by improvement works associated with the 1992 Olympics, the 1993 Nudo-de-la-Trinitat in northeast Barcelona by Enric Batlle and Joan Roig has become a much-referenced project of landscape urbanism. The fusion of a new composite from mobility and urban ecology is realized in a refreshing coexistence between city and road. Civil engineering, urbanism, and landscape are melded into one, with a huge park and sports complex poetically filling the spaghetti-like interchange. Powerful, broad, and sweeping gestures of water, allees, seating, sports courts, parking lots, meadow swaths, walks, and lighting all work to create a novel dialogue between high velocity travel and serene landscape.

2 **BLURRED THRESHOLDS**
Riera Park, the central park of Sant Cugat del Vallès, 20 kilometers north of Barcelona, restructures the main access to the city as a parkway of sorts. Batlle and Roig adapted the road network and the spatial premises for future construction in such a way that it respects and accentuates the morphology of the site. The park is structured by a *paseo* (promenade) along the banks of the Bomba River that follows the curve of the site and joins the park – dissected by cross-paths whose grid recreates the field division of the original farming settlement – to the road via steps. The subtle sectional interventions blur the distinctions between the realm of infrastructure and that of landscape.

3 **SUBURBAN CONNECTOR**
The Boulevard Intercommunal de Paris (RN170) by Patrick Duguet is a 3.4-kilometer-long clearway inserted into the urban fabric of Saint-Gratien in the Val d'Oise region, northwest of Paris. At the same time, it includes a 570-meter-long semicovered section along the Marais residence at Saint-Gratien on the rue d'Ermont, integrating acoustic screening, an urban park on top, and a promenade along the route. The project manipulates public space as a lever, as the strategic element in the alignment of the road. The road creates a recognizable yet diversified suburban landscape form that unifies the scattered territory and restructures the neighborhoods along its route. The multiple profiles of the boulevard manage simultaneously to create strong spatial connections and to respond to localized programmatic needs and topographical conditions.

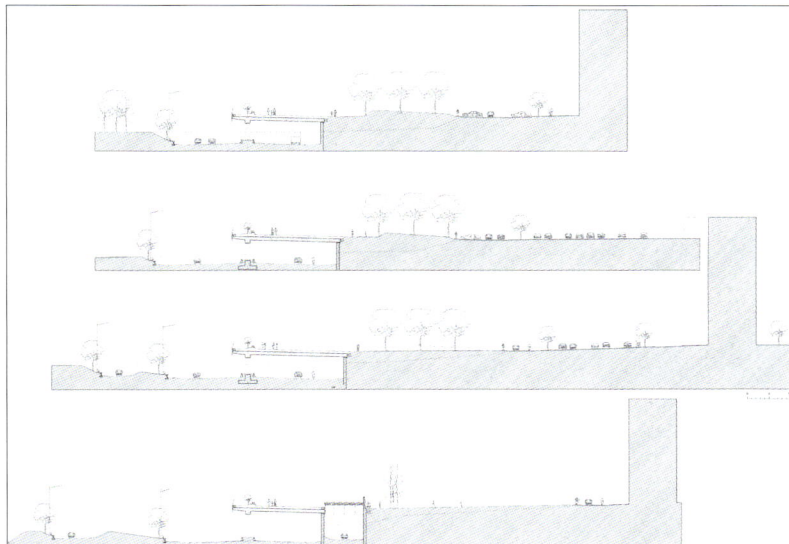

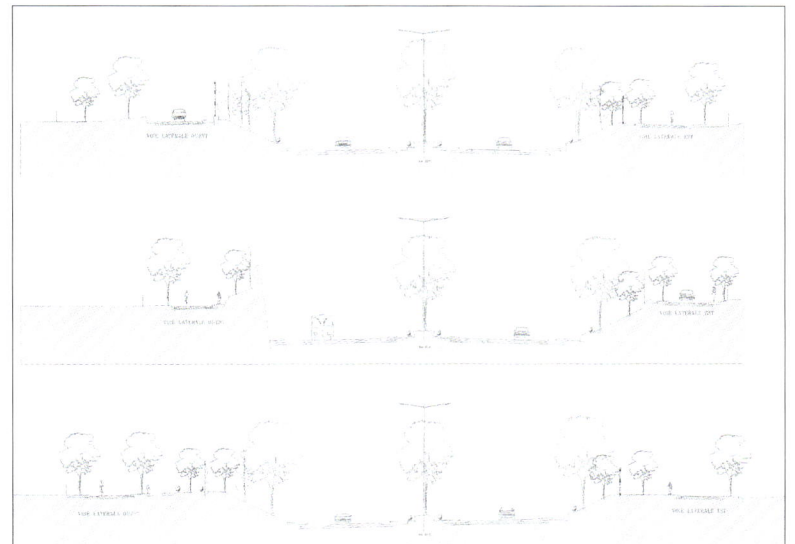

rerouting provided for a new boardwalk and introduced a memory of the sea to the neighborhoods in the form of large canals and esplanades. Of course, the two strategies may be combined within one project, as is the case in the Boulevard Intercommunal northwest of Paris by Patrick Duguet [3]. The intervention is neither insertion nor concealment, but intelligently utilizes public space as a lever and strategic element in the positioning of the road. Lateral public spaces and semicovered platforms respond to differing urban contexts along the route.

The ambition to blur distinctions between the natural landscape and the created infrastructure, which is evidenced by projects that manipulate the ground plane and create artificial topographies, is clearly another example of fusion into a new composite. The use of a seemingly multipurpose structure – it appears as an all-embracing, complex, and diversified topography – that is constructed as a singular built intervention, masks the differences between inside and outside, soil and roof, mass and void, transparent and opaque. Such fusion is a concept appropriate for much of the work of Zaha Hadid, and the Hoenheim Terminal in Strasbourg is a particularly eloquent example. Infrastructure, landscape, and architecture are folded onto one another and the static structure exudes an inquisitive force, an indeterminate energy, a kinetic motion. The provincial Twerenbold touring company bus terminal in Baden-Rütihof, Switzerland, less dramatically employs a similar tactic with a trapezoidal-planned extension to an existing structure. The twisted steel-framed roof boldly folds over the new passenger and coach areas [4]. A more literal approach to earthworks is evident in the parking concept by Sanfeliu, Martorell and Lamich for a peripheral Barcelona housing project. Their parking lot is viewed as new land form, where the regularity of car placement reproduces a landscape of regular waves in which the presence of the cars becomes part of a new unified treatment of the artificial soil.

Finally, at the scale of pedestrian infrastructure, the notion of fusion is elegantly expressed by the escalators linking the large parking lot to the historic city of Toledo. Martínez Lapeña and Torres merges topography and pedestrian movement in what appears as a cleft on a mountainside slope. In a less dramatic manner, Michael Van Valkenburgh successfully merges city and nature along the Allegheny Riverfront of Pittsburgh by appropriating the leftovers between a waterfront highway and the riverbank [5].

4   **TRAPEZOIDAL FOLD**
The Twerenbold Bus Terminal in Baden-Rütihof, Switzerland, by architects Knapkiewicz & Fickert is an elegant addition to an existing shed-like structure. The sheltered bus park and fully glazed reception-waiting area are protected by a thick roof that rises from the ground, returns on itself, and envelops part of the existing building. The twisted roof over the trapezoidal plan has enormous steel structure spans, which are clad with green PVC sheeting. The light effects and geometry games accentuate the literal and figural unfolding of the terminal from the existing fabric.

5 INTERCONNECTING RIVERFRONT

Two long yet narrow leftover swathes of land between the Allegheny River and the tangle of highway infrastructure have been skillfully reorganized by Michael Van Valkenburgh into a two-tiered riverfront park. The inclusive landscape project developed a lower park with native floodable species and an upper level (eight meters higher than the lower level) urban promenade with plants and materials typically found in Pittsburgh's public realm. The wild nature of the lower level fuses with the dynamic river while the upper park becomes an extension of the city's civic fabric. The project realized, 80 years later, the concept of an Allegheny riverfront park as developed in 1911 by Frederick Law Olmsted Jr.

Before

After

Domesticating the Highway

LOUISVILLE WATERFRONT PARK

Louisville, Kentucky, USA

Landscape Architect: Hargreaves Associates

Date: 1999–2009 (completion phase 3)

In Louisville, Kentucky, George Hargreaves successfully fused a complicated highway spaghetti structure and a public waterfront, remarrying the eastern edge of downtown with the Ohio River. A former brownfield site of scrapyards, sandpits, and industries cut off from the urban fabric by railroad lines has thus been transformed into an important public space for the city. The project combines explicit engineering requirements and environmental concerns. The design provides a series of river-related spaces for recreation, and also accommodates and slows flood waters and reestablishes lush riverside planting drawn from a palette of native species. The entire project is graded to provide flood protection, while simultaneously breaking down visual barriers between the city and the river.

The waterfront is made up of a series of varied, flexible, and programmable spaces: a working wharf, Festival Plaza, Overlook, and Lincoln Memorial. The centerpiece of the park is the sloping Great Lawn, which directly connects the city fabric to the river under the I-64 highway and serves as an informal amphitheater. The different park programs are located according to elevations, with some areas allowing temporary flooding. The park ebbs and flows with the river and its natural processes. The project includes molded landforms and earthworks, hallmarks of Hargreaves Associates work. The artificial topographies afford spectacular views of the river and city from elevated play meadows. The rising landforms enclose more intimate spaces, opening out to inlets and riparian habitats. Their form solves pragmatic issues that deal with the mechanics of manipulating natural processes, and to this extent they create didactic landscapes.

Transversal Articulation

FALIRON COAST

Athens, Greece

Urban and Infrastructural Designer: Reichen et Robert & Associés

Date: 1999–2004

Faliron Bay, the estuary of the Kifissos and Illissos rivers and the inlet that links the ancient town of Piraeus to the sea, has a six-kilometer-long coastline of strategic significance to Athens. In classical antiquity, it was the first harbor of Athens before it was replaced by Piraeus. In the 1870s Faliron developed as a seaside resort and in 1896, during the first modern Olympic Games, Faliron Bay was the venue for cycling and tennis events, while nearby sites were used for target shooting and swimming. In the 1970s the link between land and sea was interrupted by Poseidon Avenue, a coastal expressway that isolated the urban fabric from the coast, creating a monument of air, noise, and visual pollution. Because the expressway obstructed rainwater runoff into the sea, the severity and frequency of flooding increased. The estuary itself became degraded by the canalization of both rivers, while the dumping of demolition materials created a no man's land on the shoreline.

The 2004 Olympic Games brought about an opportunity to mend the area, since it was identified as one of three major concentration points for allocating sports stadiums. Redevelopment of brownfield sites for venues will have a second round of reconfiguring as, by 2010, adaptive reuse of event facilities will have been completed and the area will become a large marine education and entertainment center. The major success of the project is credited to Reichen et Robert's urban design strategy. Most important in that respect was the rerouting of Poseidon Avenue to the south, designed as a "rift" of successive sections of the natural and man-made landscape that required the creation of overhead passages from city to sea. While harboring through traffic, the highway thus becomes part of an encompassing landscape form that serves to limit the environmental impact of the motorized passage it engenders. Traffic rerouting also facilitated the return of sea to neighborhoods in the form of large canals – dealing with rainwater evacuation and providing refuge for small boats – and three new links between the coast and the hinterland were established. The main one is a 50-meter-wide esplanade, 800 meters long, that runs parallel to the historic Syngrou Avenue axis and ends under a shady grove of palm trees and café space at the water's edge. It acts as a bridge over the traffic intersection at the Delta. Public open space thus acts as an operational means to embrace the identity of the place and to encourage social and cultural integration.

Folded Space

HOENHEIM-NORD TERMINUS

Strasbourg, France

Architect: Zaha Hadid Architects

Date: 1999–2001

The city of Strasbourg prides itself on the development of a tramline that encourages commuters to leave their cars parked on the periphery and use public transport to access the city center. They have invited artists and architects to make designs at key points along the lines, elevating the usually utilitarian park-and-ride facilities into places of an enlarged and attractive public realm. Zaha Hadid, acclaimed for her fluid structures, fusing land and architectural interventions through the sculptural folding of surfaces, was commissioned to develop the tram station and a parking facility for 800 cars at the northern apex of Line B. As such, the Hoenheim Terminus station and parking complex is representative of the fusion into

a new composite attitude. Its synthesis between ground, walls, light, and space establishes a relation between dynamic and static elements at different scales. At the edge of Strasbourg, where transport lines (highway, bus, tram) converge, the terminus building appears as a series of superimpositions, of vectors and space grounded in motion. Sharp diagonals guide cars and passengers toward a minimally enclosed volume of the station. The ensemble appears as an elongated, folded ground plane, at once a parking lot surface, a roof canopy, and sheltering walls.

The expansive car surface slopes toward the station and initiates a series of simple yet

powerful and sculptural folds of the landscape. The surface itself was imagined as a magnetic field of slightly curving (in response to site boundaries) white lines on the black asphalt. Parking spaces have vertical lampposts that work reciprocally with the tilt of the land: where the slope of the ground is steeper the posts are higher, and their height decreases as the slope flattens out. The overall effect is one whereby the void becomes a generator of form and whereby the new ground plane is indistinguishable from a preexisting condition. Infrastructure fuses with landscape to produce a new artificial nature that articulates the transition of open landscape, public interior space, and the flows of mobility.

Car Waves

VERNEDA PARKING LOT

Barcelona, Spain

Architect: Carlos Sanfeliu Cortés, Bernat Martorell Pena, Luís Lamich Arocas

Date: 1999

The creation of an artificial landscape in a housing district consolidated in the 1960s with structures of little architectural value has seamlessly fused park and parking. The project has created parking as new landscape, using the regularity of car placement to produce a landscape of regular wave movements in which the place taken by the cars becomes secondary. The district of Verneda, situated in Barcelona's eastern quadrant, was marked by freestanding residential blocks, poor quality public space with ample *terrain vagues*, and a severe lack of surface parking. The simple yet intelligent solution by Sanfeliu, Martorell, and Lamich created a topographical play of volumes that was able to integrate a large-surface parking lot, with public open spaces of green areas and new terraces linked to restaurants occupying the base of the housing slabs.

A topographical complexity is created by lined parallel bands of terrain, mostly paved, that are differentiated from one another by their longitudinal sections. They organize and characterize different areas required to accommodate various programs. Parking spaces are grouped in twos to coincide with the width of the band paving. Folds in the surface bands are accentuated by a formal game within the palette of materials. There are three types of paving and materials for retaining walls, with steel sheeting for projections below 80 centimeters and higher retaining walls of reinforced concrete covered by steel, colored concrete paving in pedestrian areas, and cement mortar slabs on the project's perimeter, blending with the existing surface definition. The parking-lot surface itself is treated with float-finished reinforced concrete, which is surface-tinted with iron sulfate. A level pedestrian path traverses the park's topography in the north-south direction and the area is ringed by a one-way access road. Surface vegetation of ivy is contained in the geometry of the bands and the easy-to-maintain green is complemented by two types of trees: acacias and jacarandas.

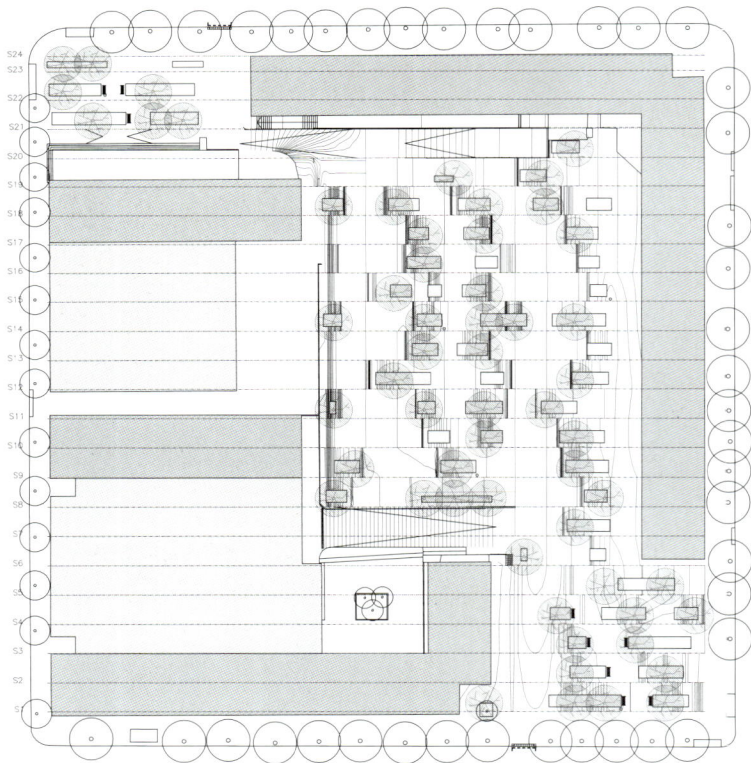

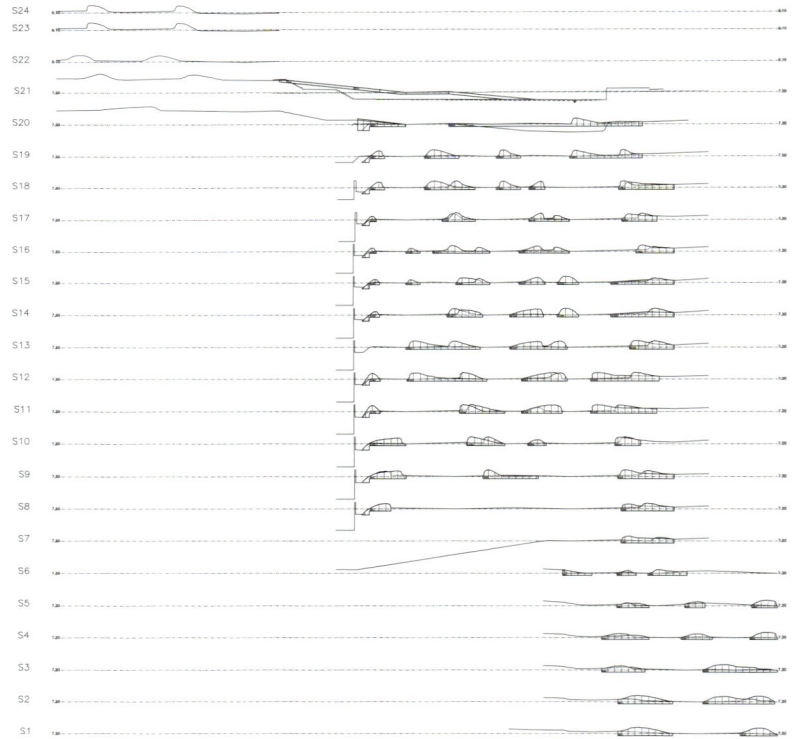

Choreographed Ascent

Toledo, Spain

Architect: Martínez Lapeña-Torres Arquitectes

Date: 1997–1998 (design), 1998–2000 (construction)

TOLEDO ESCALATORS AND CAR PARK

The steep slope of the hill upon which Spain's historic city of Toledo sits became an opportunity to merge topography and pedestrian movement. Martínez Lapeña and Torres elegantly embedded a mechanical stairs into the steep hillside of Rodadero — the inclined terrain between the medieval walls and the historic city center. They provided for an exceptional solution: a crack in the hill that simultaneously offers shelter and shade, outlooks and vistas, motion and public space.

The banishment of vehicles from Europe's historic city centers is becoming commonplace and Toledo, too, sought to limit car accessibility. A parking garage for 400 cars was therefore built on the Paseo de Reca- redo, and adjoining escalators take passengers to the upper part of the city. The 36-meter difference in height between the parking area and the summit is bridged by six sections of escalators that are embedded in the slope of the steep mountainside. The experience from car to historic city is boldly choreographed as a journey of initiation. Visitors first enter a tunnel under the city's lower, fortified medieval wall before being propelled upwards by the zigzag form of the escalators, inscribed in the topography. The construction appears as an incision or series of clefts in the mountainside, with retaining walls of folded concrete climbing toward the summit. The inclined roof, which pro-

tects the stairs and gives continuity to the terraced garden slope, does not follow the natural contour of the land but rises slightly to make a long and continuous opening, affording views of the Tajo and new Toledo. The signature of the project is the crack of the succession of clefts, illuminated at night. The otherwise bold project is softened by the monolithic ochre concrete, matching the colors of the ancient city's architecture. The project fuses pedestrian movement and topography while solving the difficult challenge of reconciling the pressures on a heritage site and controlling the flow of tourists. The modern incision in the town's foundations is emblematic of fusion into a new composite.

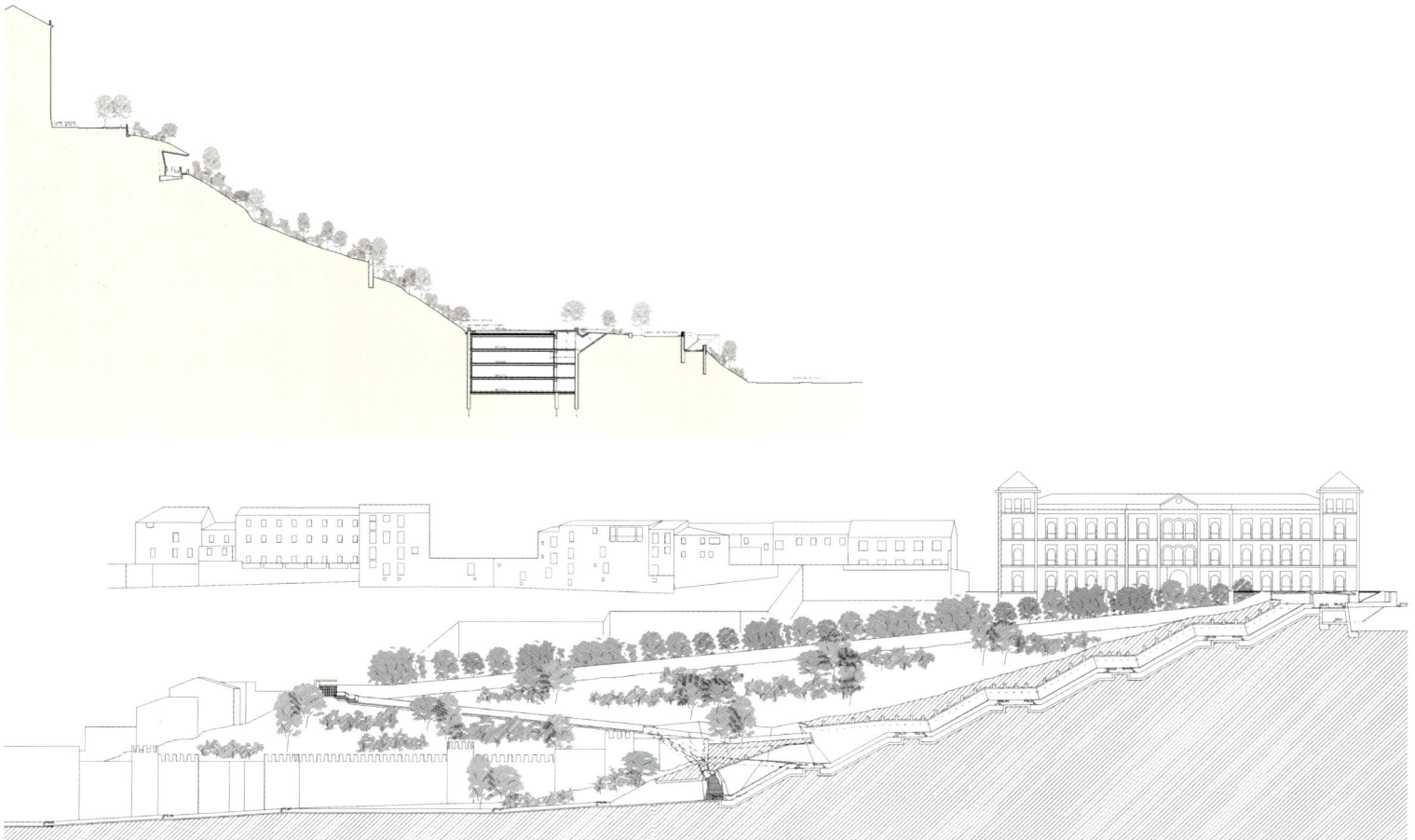

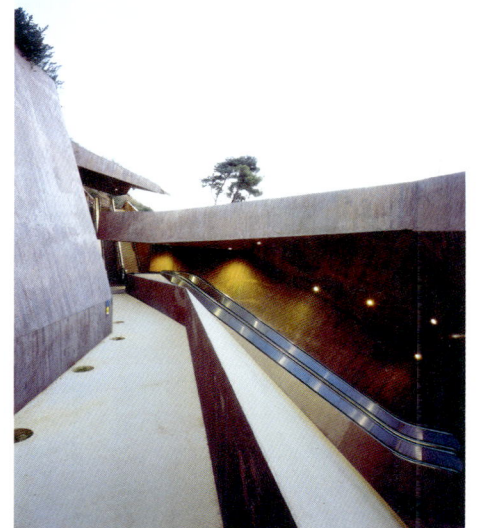

INCORPORATION INTO A PIECE OF MEGASTRUCTURE

The term megastructure, coined by Japanese architect Fumihiko Maki in 1964, was originally defined as a large frame in which many functions of a city could be housed. Its implementation was made possible by technology and turned into a "human-made feature of the landscape."[1] Reyner Banham, who popularized the term in 1976, claimed the megastructure to be "generally understood as a structural framework of great size into which smaller structural units can be 'plugged-in.'"[2] Over time, the notion of the megastructure evolved. Nowadays, it is generally intended to be constituted by several independent systems that can expand or contract with no disturbance to the others. No hierarchy is involved. Each system that contributes to the (trans)formation of the whole maintains the latter's identity and longevity. Without being affected by the other constituents, they remain in dynamic contact with them. In this sense, megastructures are repetitive systems that allow for a high level of variation precipitated by programmatic and contextual conditions.

The examples deployed under the category "Fusion Into a New Composite" (page 80), whereby the infrastructure is blended into a comprehensive new setting, reveal a strategy of an encompassing landscape design in which natural elements such as taluses and vegetation are complemented by a diversity of mineral textures and surface applications. A similar effect of inclusiveness can also be obtained by means of mere urban or architectural design. The infrastructure is then viewed as a large and complex structure or building with a very particular form that serves a highly unusual function. This megastructure can perfectly change in section and plan along its course. It can adapt to local circumstances but will generally be conceived as a single operation, by one designer. Even when it appears absolutely integrated into a specific context, it is basically formed by a hugely molded object in which all requirements of a complex brief have been met.

The replacement of outdated infrastructure and facilities through the manipulation of existing megastructures has spurred numerous projects in Europe, which have resulted in the qualitative morphological rearrangement of entire urban districts. The restructuring of the former military Chassé barracks in Breda, the Netherlands, led to the layout of a campus-like urban archipelago. OMA (urban design) and West 8 (landscape architecture) created a car-free environment by placing a large parking garage in the basement of the main square of the development. The infrastructural conversion of the 1960s-designed Gran Via de les Corts Catalanes by Arriola & Fiol in Barcelona has reshaped its eastern section – not only rationalizing traffic and providing new tram transport and parking places, but also reconnecting severed neighborhoods, setting up noise barriers, and creating a linear park along its route.

1 HIGHWAY PLAZA

Spanish urbanist Joan Busquets' Grotiusplaats in The Hague is literally a component of the megastructure of the Utrechtsebaan expressway. In a large area between the Court of Justice and the Royal Library, the rupture of the large traffic artery is tamed by covering part of the highway and thus creating not only a new public space but also extensive new plots for urban development. Busquets roofs over half of the Utrechtsebaan with translucent "alabaster wings" in longitudinal direction, allowing natural light to enter the traffic below.

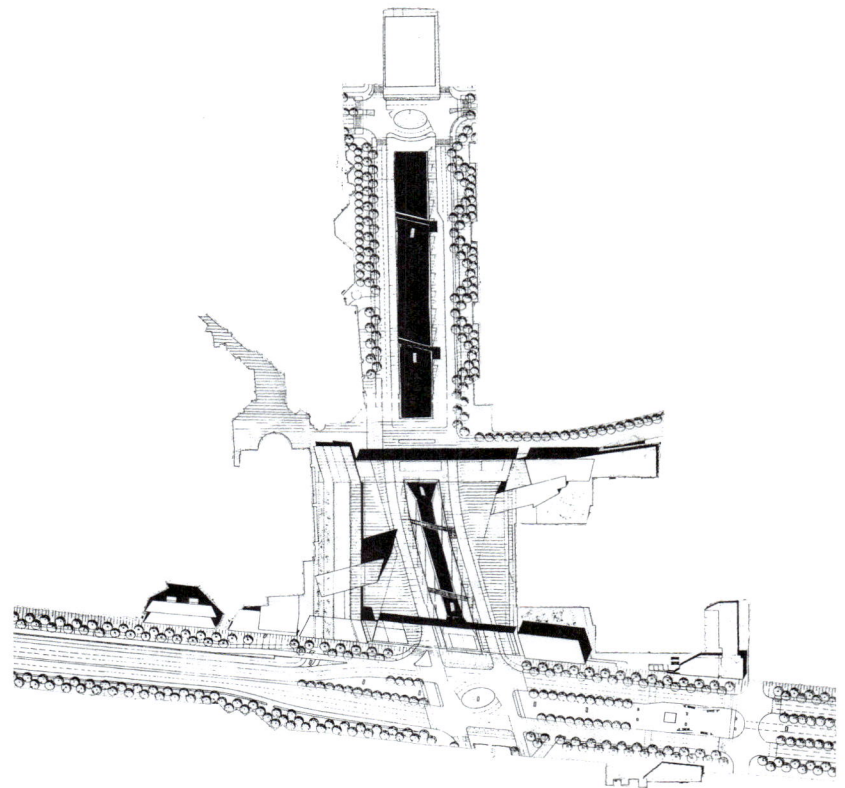

2 AIRPORT PLUG-IN

The sleek tubular spaceship-form of the ICE train station by BRT Architekten literally extends Germany's largest airport in Frankfurt. The 700-meter-long body of the station floats on pairs of splayed telescopic aluminum-clad columns over partially sunken tracks below. The 38,000-square-meter space within the flattened ribcage of steel clad in aluminum hovers next to the autobahn and is plugged into the arrival and departure terminals via a covered footbridge that cuts through a congress center block. Escalators connect an impressive section that also features randomly placed perforations for natural light above and 60-meter-clear spans of the tracks below. Tectonic expression and fluid morphology represent the landscape of 21st-century megastructure.

3 INTEGRATED VIADUCT EXTENSION

Odile Decq & Benoît Cornette incorporated a service structure into a highway viaduct, animating the otherwise dead space into a futuristic machine in the park that passes underneath. The sleek highway control volume suspended from the underside of the Nanterre A4 is situated where the road emerges from a tunnel that runs under La Défense. Workshops and the facility's parking garage are buried underground to allow the public park to pass unobstructed underneath the viaduct. The dynamism and symbolism of highway speed and movement melds a usually isolated object into a compelling structure nestled under a highway that appears to float over the landscape.

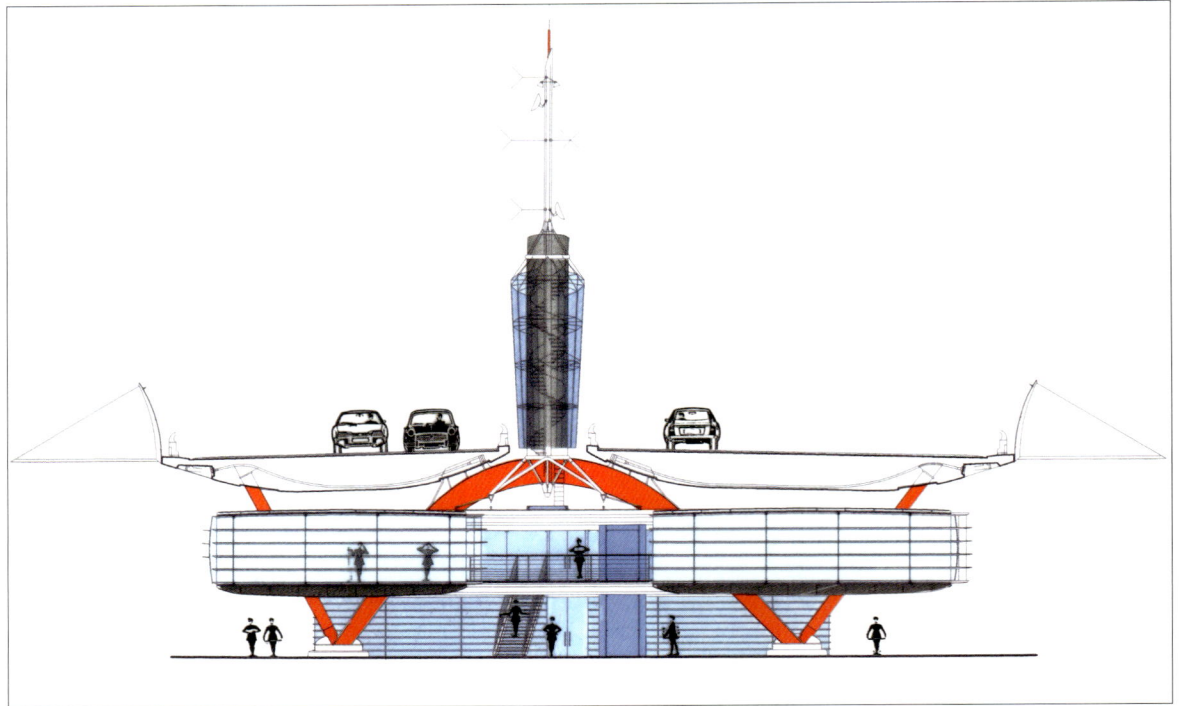

In Turin and The Hague, the new infrastructure has required even more radical restructuring of existing and the visible insertion of new megastructures. In Turin, the process of deindustrialization – coupled with the technical requirements of the high-speed train – resulted in the decision to completely bury 12 kilometers of railroad and to create a new station. At the core of the strategy was the notion of revitalizing derelict space and transforming the once peripheral zone into a central location. The sophisticated section of the resultant boulevard links a disparate collection of idiosyncratic, postindustrial fragments into new development areas. In The Hague, Joan Busquets conceived the zenithal slice that creates daylight in the tunneled highway underneath as outset for a new type of urban space [1]. In all these examples, traffic solutions are seen as comprehensive urban projects, as elements of urban centrality in their respective contexts. Traffic reconfiguration is considered as an instrument of order and congruent urban landscape where the integration of engineering and architecture is manifested with noticeable force and finesse.

The futuristic insertion of both the ICE train terminal at Frankfurt Airport and the highway control volume under the Nanterre A4 viaduct reveal another, more architectural manner of turning infrastructure into megastructure [2–3]. The new additions in this case are quite apparent and take visual clues from the notions of flux, speed, and movement. In another stylistic vain, the highly articulated traffic interchange-cum-pedestrian scenic promenade on Lake Maggiore confirms the transformation of a mere highway interchange into a sophisticated megastructural gateway.

1 Fumihiko Maki, *Investigations in Collective Form* (Washington University, School of Architecture, St. Louis, Missouri, 1964).
2 Reyner Banham, *Megastructure: Urban Futures of the Recent Past* (London: Thames and Hudson, 1976).

Parking Square

CHASSÉ SITE

Breda, the Netherlands

Architect: Office for Metropolitan Architecture (OMA)

Landscape Architect: West 8

Date: 1996–2000

The Chassé site is a former military barracks located in the city center of Breda, a mid-sized Dutch city with a low-density urban nucleus. OMA designed the master plan to transform the brownfield site into a high-density program of 1117 houses and large underground parking garage for 670 cars. The development is structured as a series of campus-like clusters that combine urban scale with open space. Different architects were commissioned for housing clusters that were set on the site with the aim of multiple perspectives. There are two prominent structuring pedestrian open spaces: the park and the square. The park's lawns, with planted oaks and informal pedestrian and cycle paths, contrast strongly with the hard surfaces of the square.

An overall development aim of Chassé site was to create a green enclave within the city and to keep it free of vehicular traffic. The large parking garage was therefore buried and its tilted roof became the "square." At ground level, the square is articulated by a series of black and white triangular granite plates. Wide strips of asphalt accentuate the edges and fold lines of the square and are cut through with thin sections of granite to create a visual play of lines. Below ground, the parking garage is revealed as a vast, light-filled space. Thirteen light wells or patios and a skylight over the main entrance connect the underbelly of the development to the public space above. The glass facade between the tilted square and the parking garage thus gives way to an important hybridity – not only for daylight purposes but also for fusion between square and garage. At the same time, the parking garage is an interesting atmosphere unto itself. The constantly sloping ground plane is finished with seven tones of blue polyurethane and the walls are clad with galvanized corrugated sheet steel.

Multilayered Roadside

Barcelona, Spain

Architect: Arriola & Fiol arquitectes

Date: 2002–2006

GRAN VIA DE LES CORTS CATALANES

In Barcelona, as in other European cities, the 1960s was an era in which large road infrastructure was built within the urban structure. In Barcelona, as in other European cities, amending such interventions has been a community-driven concern since the 1990s. The Gran Via de les Corts Catalanes was part of the city's Metropolitan Plan of 1976 to structure growth in the previously under-urbanized area. The sunken central axis, bordered by green slopes and flanking street-level access, was set within the Cerdà gridiron Ensanche. Bridges every three blocks (400 meters) connect the seaside and the mountain sides of the axis.

Today, the eastern section of the Gran Via, from the Plaça de les Glòries to the Besòs River – better known as the A19 highway – is one of the main entrances to the city. The noisy and polluting megastructural cut in the territory has been completely reconfigured by Arriola & Fiol to reduce the dominance of vehicular circulation, connect the urban tissue on the two sides of the axis, and create new public space. The transport artery has been remodeled into a multilevel boulevard with the section changing along its long route. The base spatial move was the 3.5-meter cantilevered projection of the service roads over the central carriageway, thus reducing noise (custom-designed acoustic barriers along the edge of the cantilevered sections) and pollution for the adjacent neighborhoods. At ground level, road installations are embedded in a linear park whose inclined sections manage the differences in levels between various routes and the existing urban tissue as well as ensure visual continuity for Gran Via. The cut is partially covered and pedestrian passageways extend the perpendicular streets.

A tramway is installed under the southern, seaside service road and its four stations are integrated into the topography of a new park. On the northern, mountain side, two parking levels 400 meters in length are constructed. Traffic is thus organized on three levels: a central trunk road that channels fast traffic; lateral roads over the elevated sections including a parking strip with service access to the central carriageway, parking garage entrances, loading bays, and bus stops; and service roads with a cycle lane. The boulevard quality is further expressed through the planting regime of six varieties of a single tree-species that form a grove-like promenade. A raised channel of water connects four ponds, each with a fountain, to one another, and the entire park is fitted out with a series of specially designed benches that furnish the squares as outdoor rooms.

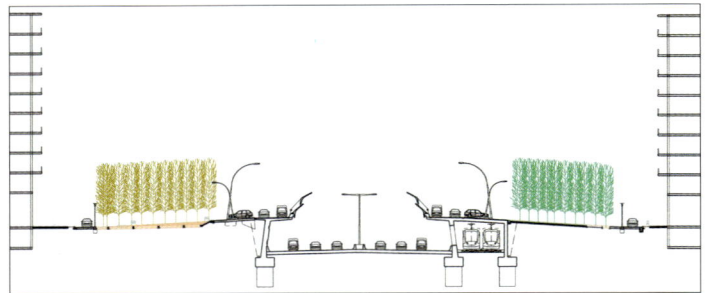

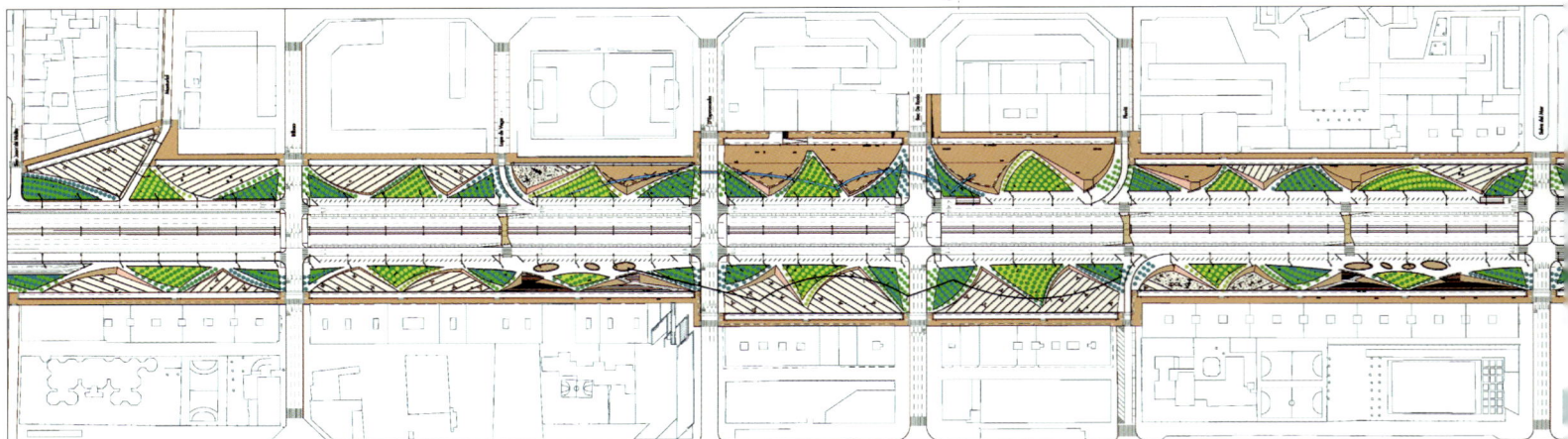

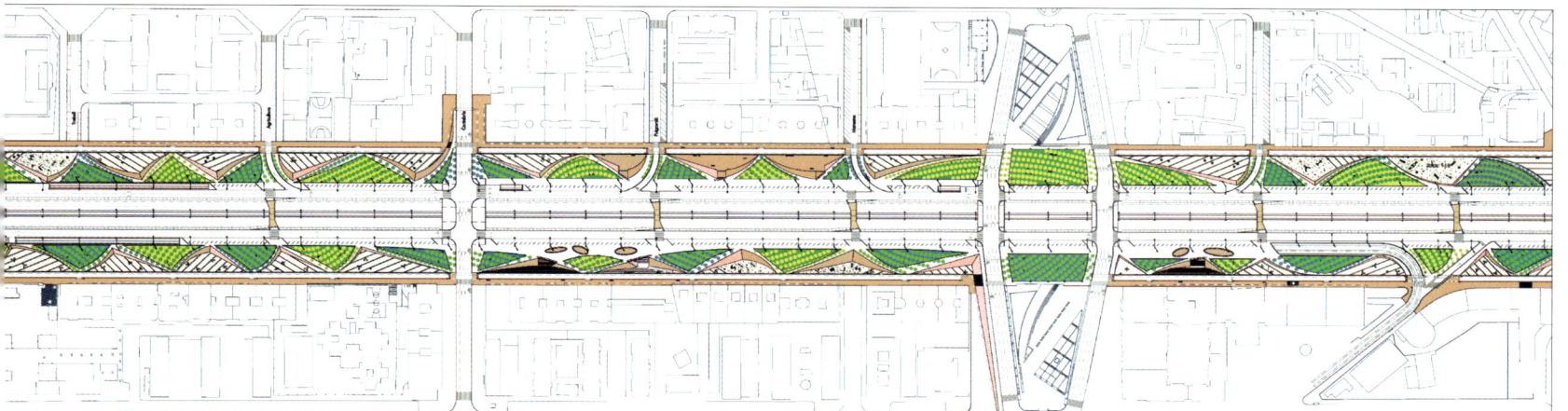

Multilayered Spine

PORTA SUSA TGV STATION

Turin, Italy

Architect: Architect: AREP Group (Jean-Marie Duthilleul and Etienne Tricaud), with Silvio D'Ascia and Agostino Magnaghi

Date: 2003–2008

The insertion of the Paris-Rome TGV line was the starting point for a comprehensive overhaul of Turin's city-center structure. It took the 2006 Winter Olympics to push the ambitious project into development, even though it has yet to be completed. When constructed, it will be a key element in the city's vast urban redevelopment program, part of which involves putting all train tracks underground and increasing the number of tracks. Interring the tracks allows for the creation of a north-south *Spina Centrale* (backbone), a 12-kilometer-long, 6-lane, oak-tree-lined boulevard that will reunite two sides of the town and structure four new redevelopment zones. The overall project adds close to three million square meters of space to the city through renewal of redundant industrial brownfield sites

alongside the tracks. The massive undertaking also includes the demolition of a steel railroad flyover and the creation of an interchange loop with Metropolitan Line 1.

Seven new stations are planned as part of the revamping and modernizing of the rail transportation system. A new Porta Susa, presently the provincial-looking 19th-century northern head station at the town's historic center (to be moved 500 meters further south), is to replace Porta Nuova as Turin's main terminal and intermodal hub. The station will be a centerpiece of the *Spina Centrale*. It will feature a 380-meter-long, 40-meter-wide glass roof linking the city and the old station to the new intermodal shopping concourse. From the gently inclined concourse, the street divides into

two parts, one ramping down 10 meters to platform level and the other a horizontal street. Together they form an intersection for the flow of train, underground, tram, car, and taxi passengers. The two sections join at the end of the axis, which culminates in a 100-meter-tall tower, to accommodate two hotels and offices. The complex sections create a variety of links with the different levels of the city and maintain and enhance thoroughfares on the site. The station area accentuates the north-south axiality, while at the same it is permeable thanks to transversal passageways. The architecture focuses on mobility flows and transparency; lighting is utilized to unite the series of spaces along the Spina's total length.

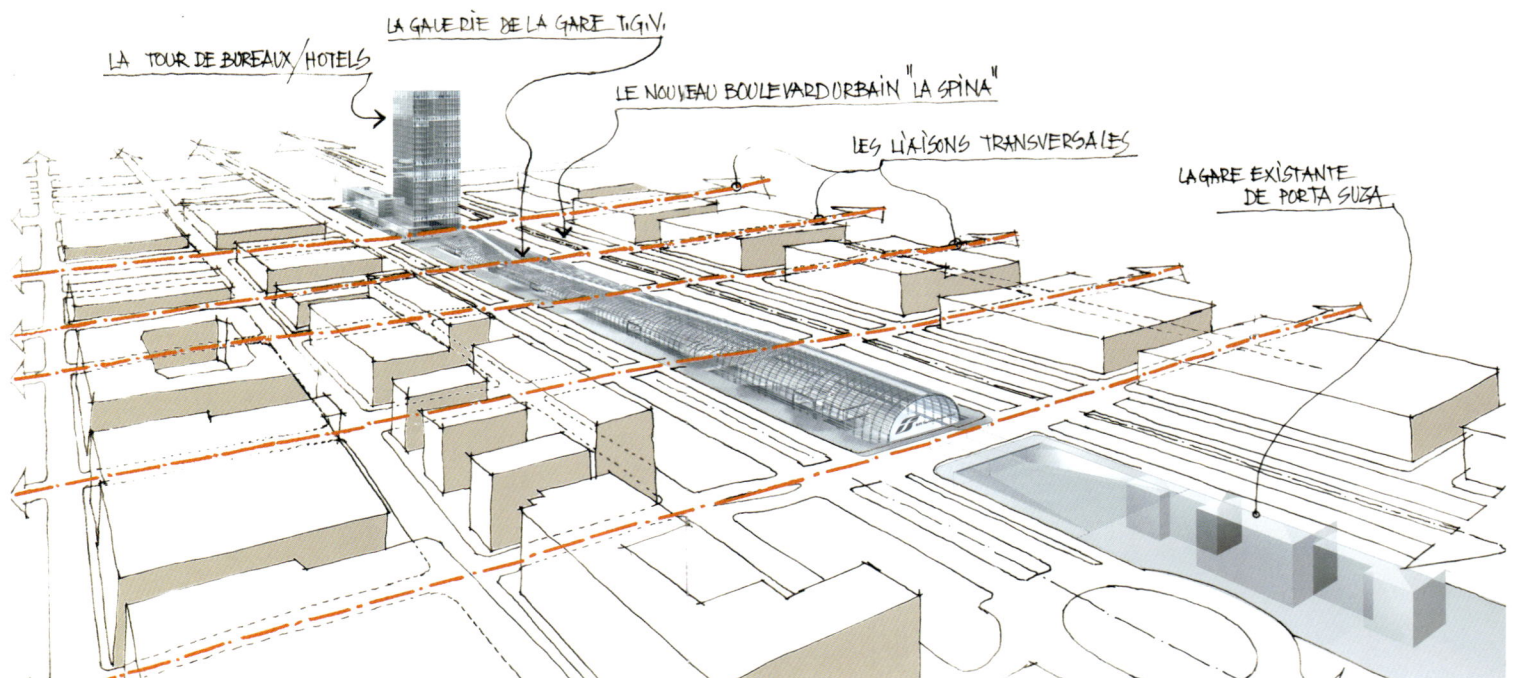

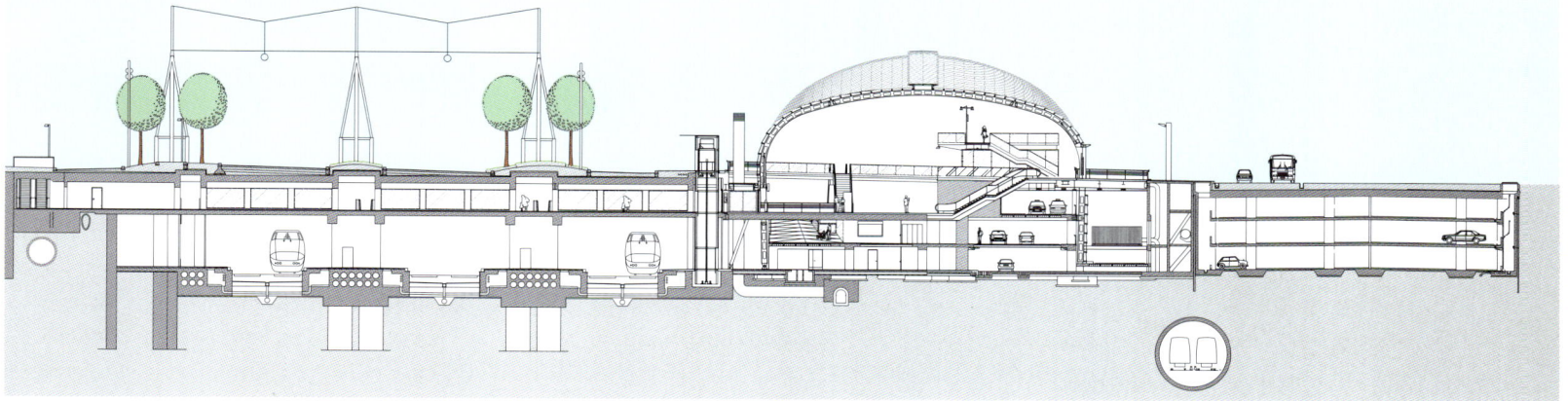

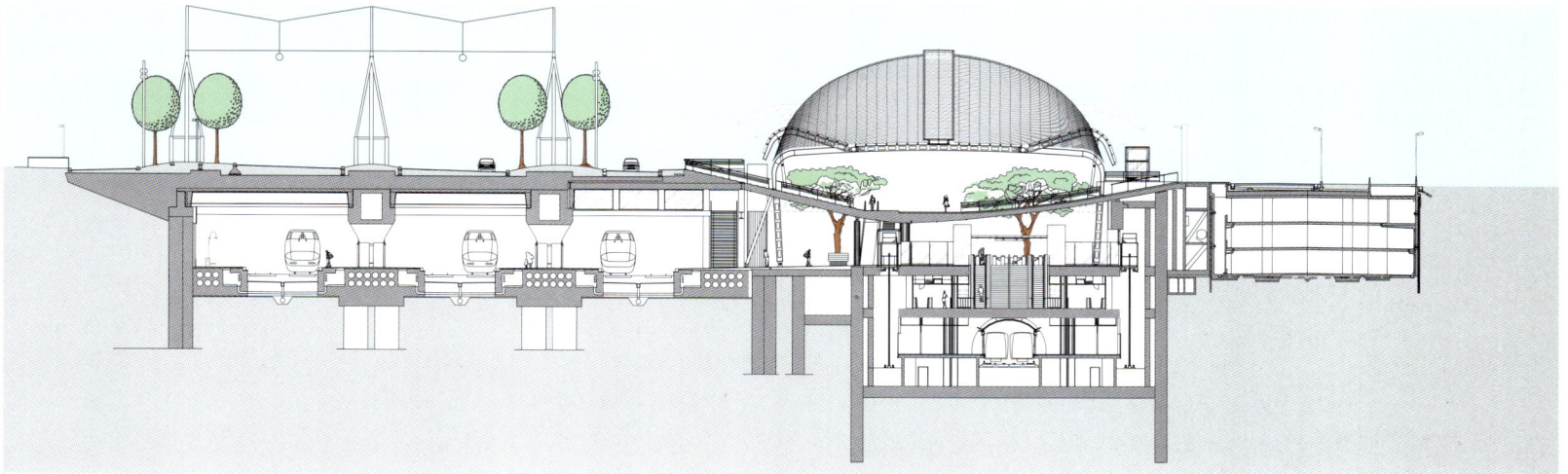

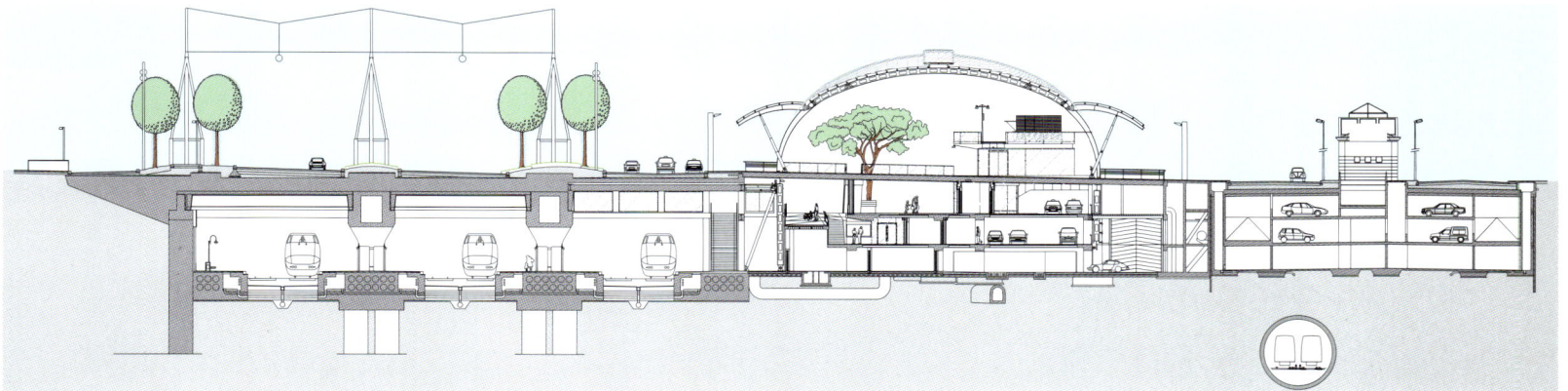

Iconic Passage

BAVENO BRIDGE

Baveno, Italy

Architect: Aldo Enrico Ponis

Date: 1992–1995

In the magnificent setting of Lake Maggiore's Ticino landscape, Aldo Enrico Ponis cleverly expanded the new interchange that links the Milan-Simplon highway exit to the Simplon trunk road to create a fantastic pedestrian passage along the lake, completely separated from vehicles. In this way, the interchange is treated as a gigantic piece of architecture. It becomes an immense, perhaps overly formal icon of a passage building. The entire ensemble – local traffic, highway traffic, cycle and pedestrian movement – is environmentally sensitive. New access ramps blend the terrain and vegetation of the land while the trunk road passes through the tunnel under the Milan-Domedossola railroad and joins the highway link road. Traffic leaving the highway to head north or south along the lake passes through the tunnel in the other direction, takes the road across the central deck of the new bridge, and joins the ramps to the viaduct.

The architectural expression is influenced locally by the distinctive Ticino school. The pillars and towers that support the crossbeams of the five-span viaduct (the main central span crosses over the trunk road) and the central deck carrying the link roads are clad in bands of alternating pink and gray Baveno stone. Their form resembles that of flat tuning forks, with two flat parallel uprights joining to form a single section at the base where they meet the ground or the lake's surface and bed. Completing the lakeside pedestrian and cycle route, a footbridge suspended on steel cables runs between the "prongs" of the towers and opens onto two small panoramic terraces. Its metal structure and wooden deck are an unmistakable reference to the landing stage on Lake Maggiore.

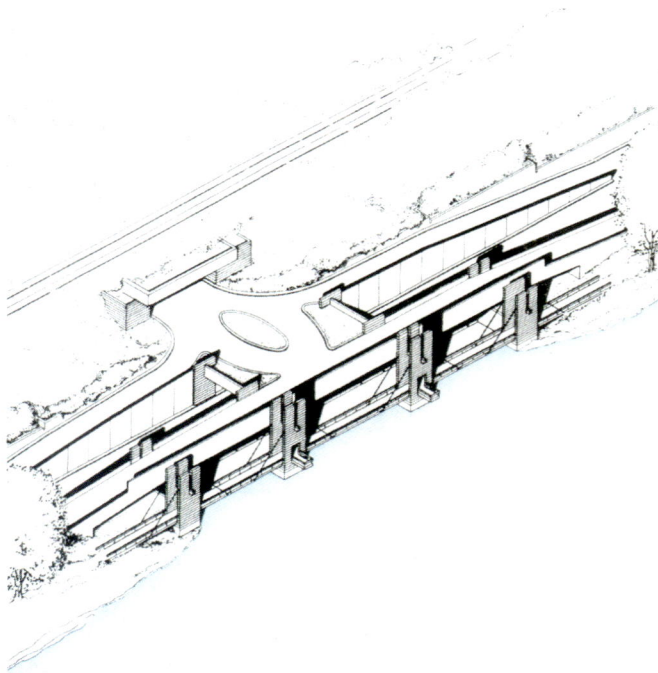

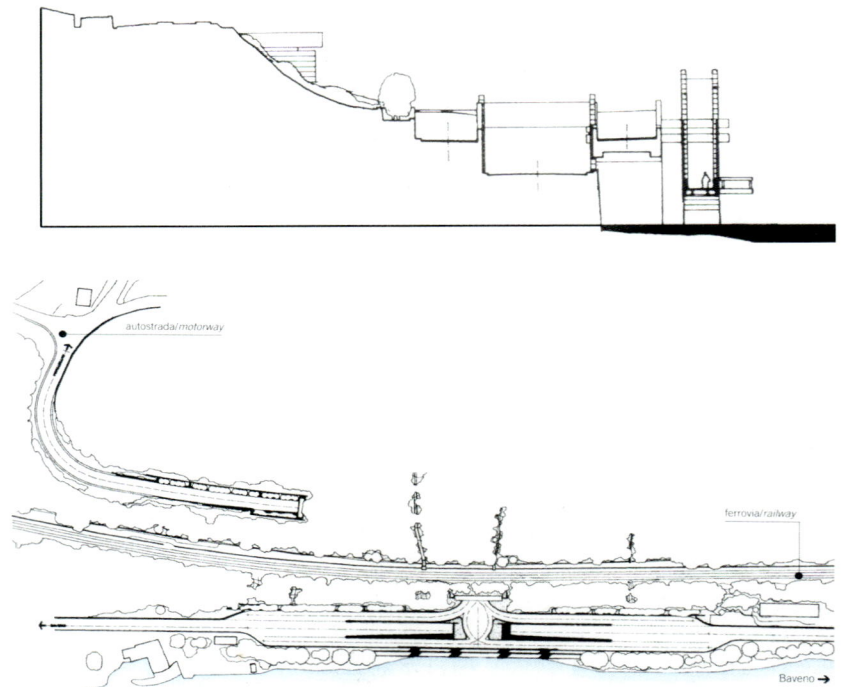

DETACHMENT THROUGH SELF-RELIANCE

As has been said by many people, the original sin of architecture lies in its very essence as an artificial construct. Man's mark of civilization is a defensive act that challenges nature. His interventions are defiant marks of difference, otherness, and an artifice of human culture – a celebration of all that is not nature. With the advent of urbanism, land ceases to be mere place. It becomes territory – with order, accessibility, and layered narratives. Infrastructure, by its very nature, is a colonization of land and there is a plethora of examples monumentalizing man's ability to tame and conquer nature though technology and innovation, engineering, and infrastructural feats. The self-reliance of objects through their detachment from their environs often results in astonishing spatial expressions – whereby technology is frequently paraded.

At the same time, infrastructure often appears to float over the landscape, seemingly leaving the latter untouched. In this sense, it maintains a relation of harmony with the environs, while simultaneously matching up to its own form-determining principles. The attitude thus permits the combination of self-adornment of the beautiful object with the appeal of an untouched natural landscape as backdrop. The attitude repeatedly leads to the creation of self-referential objects, attracting all attention and, in fact, to the absolute disregard of context. If cleverly designed, the splendor of settings can even be emphasized; by sheer dimension, infrastructure can indeed serve as a magnificent reference, underlining the presence of imposing landscape features. The architecture of bridge building is certainly an opportunity for elegant engineering feats, and in the early 20th century radical new forms began to blur the boundaries between civil engineering and architecture. The elegant, reinforced concrete structures of Swiss bridge designer Robert Maillart resulted from rigorous mathematical calculations, an astute perception of cost, an intuitive understanding of concrete's structural possibilities, and a marked sense of aesthetics [1]. Without a doubt the Swiss tradition continues, as exemplified by contemporary bridge engineer Andrea Deplazes and Christian Menn's curved cable-stayed Sunniberg Bridge [2]. Architects, too, are increasingly involved in bridge design, as is the case with Norman Foster's spectacular viaduct at Millau, France, and the railroad bridge over the Hollandsch Diep waterway in the Netherlands by Benthem Crouwel [3]. In all these cases, the astonishing beauty of the natural landscape is accentuated by the bridges. The measure and degree of the expanse or topographical change is underlined as valleys are spanned by a horizontal datum.

Detachment is also evident in works that reveal an indifference to or remoteness from their immediate surroundings. There are numerous examples of infrastructural projects that convey aloofness through reliance on the notion of construction and beauty for their own sake. The monu-

1 **INNOVATION IN CONCRETE**
Swiss civil engineer Robert Maillart (1872-1940) is regarded as a pioneer in innovative bridge building. His 1930 Salginatobel Bridge is a World Engineering Monument, applauded for both its structural efficiency and aesthetics. The 133-meter-long reinforced concrete three-hinged arch and hollow-box girder elegantly spans the Salgina gorge. Maillart revolutionized bridge building with simple designs that allowed for maximum use of materials and incorporated the engineered beauty of the structure against its harsh environment.

2 ENGINEERED ELEGANCE

The five-bay, curved cable-stayed Sunniberg Bridge (designed by Swiss architect Andrea Deplazes and well-known engineer Christian Menn), with a length of 526 meters and a height of 50-60 meters, ranks as one of the largest bridges in the Swiss Alps. In the largely rural Prättigau valley, the Sunniberg Bridge is the only major engineering structure of the Klosters bypass. This bridge over the Landquart River is supported by unusually low pylons on top of piers and a continuous slender slab with slightly thickened edges. The curvature in plan is an inseparable interplay of landmark aesthetics, structural efficiency, and economy. The pylons are flared in the direction (longitudinally) of the roadway and are tilted outward (laterally) to create a surprising visual character while solving crucial structural problems.

3 DETACHMENT THROUGH DIFFERENCE

The Dutch high-speed train (HST) line's longest bridge and most conspicuous structural work – at Hollandsch Diep south of Dordrecht – distinguishes itself from typical railroad bridges by its gently arching box structure. Designed by Benthem Crouwel with Ove Arup & Partners, the nearly two-kilometer-long bridge is supported by eleven Y-shaped pylons, the open triangles of which are illuminated at night. The bridge, situated between two existing bridges (the old railway bridge and the more recent road bridge on the A16 trunk road) is designed to provide a worthy entrance to Holland's impressive, richly watered landscape. Travelers will be able to enjoy the view for the 24-second sprint across the water before the train dives into a tunnel, and from this point onwards the Dutch landscape will be largely hidden from view by a camouflage of shrubs, acoustic screens, and embankments.

4 SELF-REFERENTIAL TECTONICS

Calatrava's signature is evident in Bilbao's new Sondica terminal by the structural expression of the project's components. The large glazed hall leading to the eight embarkation gates is a steel structure whose aerodynamic roof rises up toward the airfield to span the administrative areas and restaurants as well as the waiting areas behind the canted glazed facades that overlook the apron and runways. The triangular plan of the hall echoes the natural flow of passengers toward the transverse linear walkway leading to the gates, while the generously curved, glazed entrance on the northern side allows full use of the 36-meter-wide traffic drop-off area. In non-glazed areas, the concrete structure of the east and west wings is clad in a unifying skin of aluminum. The terminal is connected by a 100-meter-long subterranean passageway to a four-story (1400 car) parking garage that is partially recessed into the landscape.

5 THE BIG WHEEL

The Shanghai South Railway Station conceived by AREP, the architectural agency of the French Railways, is the world's first round station (270 meters in diameter). It is configured to promote operating efficiencies and traffic fluidity, and offers the 80,000-100,000 daily passengers the shortest possible walking distance to waiting rooms or directly to platforms. The huge spaceship-like object, powerfully illuminated at night, hovers over the landscape and has vertically stacked modes of transport. By coiling a typical Shanghai highway viaduct around the station concourse and its waiting areas, the designers were able to create what the Chinese call a "zero connection" station. The expansive amphitheater-shaped public area beneath a translucent roof has been transformed into a full-blown lifestyle center, further exemplifying the autonomy of the station.

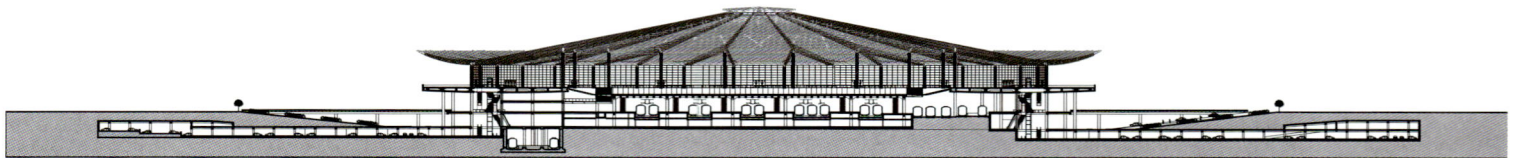

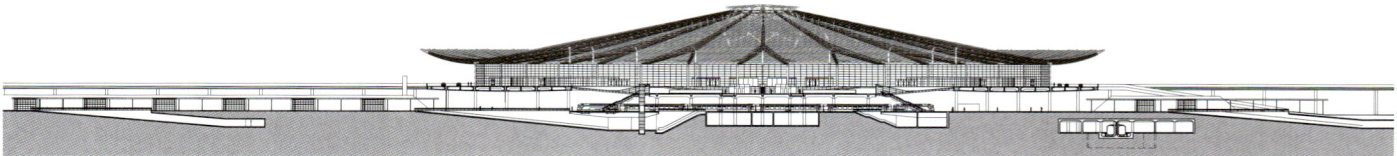

mental fascination with the relationships between function, technology, and aesthetics in a graceful structural form has long occupied architects. The work of engineer-architect Santiago Calatrava exemplifies such an approach where the monumentalization of construction makes objects estrange themselves from the natural surroundings. The self-referential tectonics of his work are further stressed by the fact that it is often painted a stark white, emphasizing its independence and artificiality. The Sondica Airport in Bilbao and the Oriente Station in Lisbon are evidence of this attitude of adornment of the beautified object [4]. The elevation of structure into sculpture, again in bright white concrete, is also evident in the impressive curving structure of the Casar de Cáceras Subregional Bus Station. The playfulness of these Spanish examples is contrasted by starkness in China, where the new Shanghai South Railway Station combines archetypal form and sheer scale to create a UFO-like object that hovers over a thriving transfer hub and entertainment center [5]. Although achieved in very different manners, both structures reveal a powerful autonomy and absolute distinction from their surrounding urban tissues. The trend of monumentalizing transportation infrastructure is a centuries-old heritage. The glorification of gateways automatically sets them apart from their surroundings and creates detachment though scale and meaning. In contemporary times, their emblematic expression ranges from the nostalgic, as evidenced by the high-tech, neogothic Washington National Airport to the whimsical, clearly expressed in the Fietsappel, a self-referential bubble organized as bicycle rack in the town of Alphen aan den Rijn in the Netherlands.

Floating Above the Landscape

MILLAU VIADUCT

Millau, France

Architect: Foster + Partners

Bridge Engineer: Michel Virlogeux

Landscape Architect: Agence Ter

Date: 1993–2005

The elegant 2.4-kilometer-long bridge over the Tarn Valley, connecting Clermont-Ferrand and Montpellier in southern France, appears to float over the landscape. Its slightly curving deck is 270 meters above the Aveyron River, making it the tallest vehicular bridge in the world (one mast's summit, at 343 meters, is taller than the Eiffel Tower). The bridge connects the highway networks of France and Spain (A75), opening up a direct route from Paris to Barcelona. The cable-stayed masted structure spans between two massive limestone ridges in the Massif Central mountain range (Causse Rouge to the north and Causse du Larzac to the south), making the crossing itself an event and the bridge a dramatic silhouette in the spectacular landscape. This sequence of perception, ideally placing the bridge within the field of view of the driver approaching transversally, along the valley, and then turning onto to the bridge, was carefully studied as part of the landscape design.

The awe-inspiring structure simultaneously overpowers the historic town of Millau and is tempered by the green valley floor of the gorge. The points of contact the bridge makes with the valley floor were explicitly minimized, and the concrete piers and cable masts were developed as graceful sculptural forms. The engineering has been fashioned so that the structure appears delicate and transparent; there is an optimum 350-meter span between columns. The columns range in height from 75 to 235 meters and, to accommodate the expansion and contraction of the concrete deck, split into two thinner, more flexible columns below the roadway and form an A-frame above the deck. The tapered form of the columns both expresses their structural loads and minimizes their profile in elevation. Eleven pairs of cables support each of the eight spans. The iconic landmark literally detaches itself from its landscape and creates an experience for the driver of floating above the dramatic landscape of the valley.

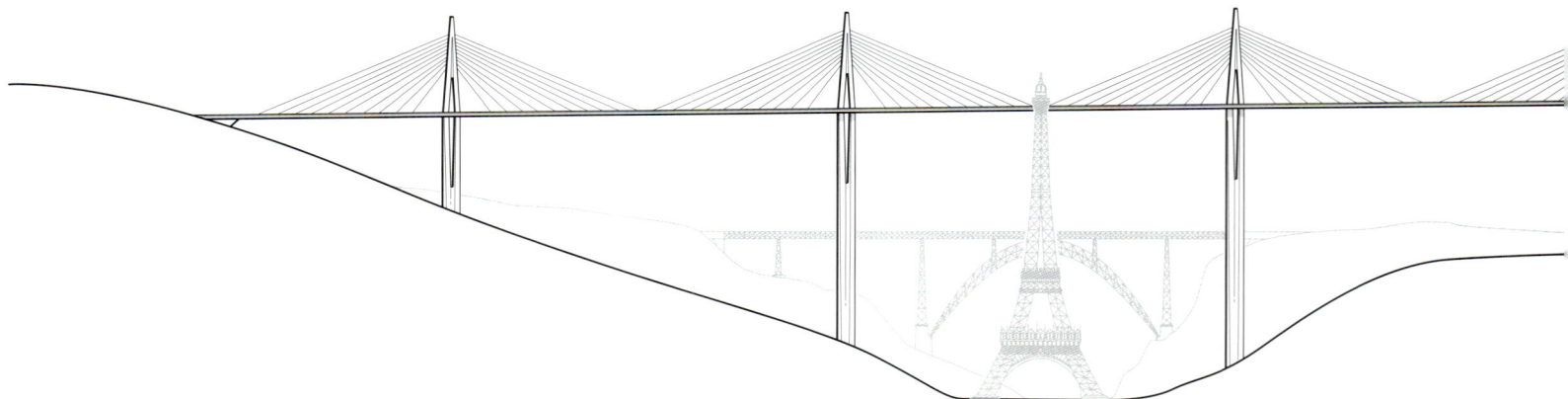

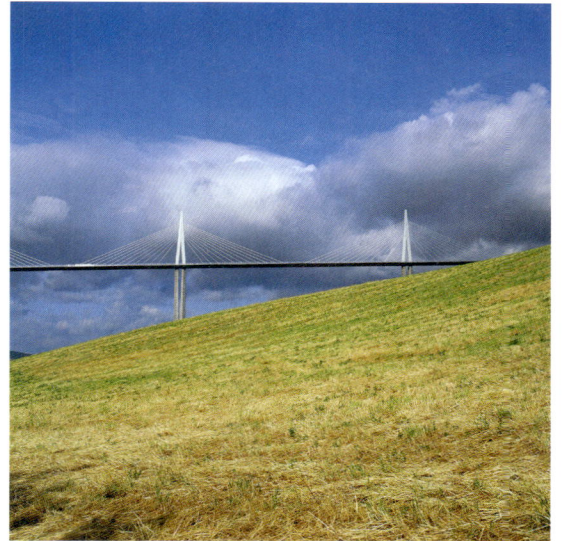

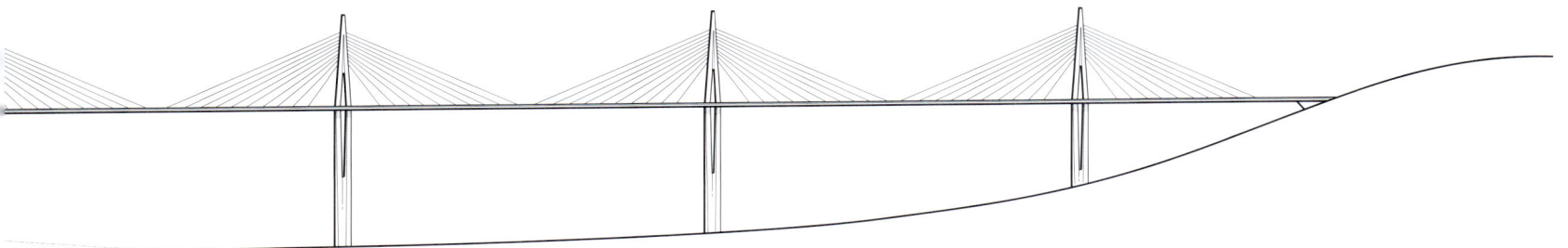

Monumentalized Engineering

Lisbon, Portugal

Architect: Santiago Calatrava

Date: 1993–1998

ORIENTE STATION

Monumentalization of construction and accentuation of structure – engineering as art – mark most of Spanish architect Santiago Calatrava's work as singular objects detached from their immediate environment. The Oriente Station, originally built as a gateway to Lisbon's 1998 Expo, is an important interchange between different types of transport – high-speed and standard trains, regional bus lines, metro, tram, and park-and-ride facilities for cars. The station became the main component and symbol of the revitalization and transformation of the formerly decaying industrial area of the eastern part of Lisbon called Doca des Olivais. By 2010, 25,000 people should be living in the new residential area along the Tagus River (once occupied by military barracks, oil refinery tanks, and industrial facilities). In this context, the Oriente Station works as the unmistakable gateway to the newly developed quarter.

However, unlike much of Calatrava's other work, the project is both a striking object and structuring component of the urban area. Calatrava pierced the Tagus River embankment to establish a visual and pragmatic link between the two separated (working-class residential and light industrial) areas of the district. The existing Avenida Berlin, perpendicular to the embankment, was extended to the river's edge. The Reciproca Avenida, a matching but slightly oblique avenue, was built on the northern edge to establish an important east-west axis penetrating the Expo site. This axis serves as the ordering principle and point of symmetry and reference for the entire proposal. The structuring avenues were complemented by elevating the station and relocating it to the north of the designated site.

The station is a huge, multilevel transport interchange with train, bus, park-and-ride facility, and metro link. It consists of two dramatic and visible parts: an elevated train station of eight tracks and four platforms (11 meters off the ground, 78 meters wide, and 260 meters long), and the sweeping wave-like glazed canopies positioned as in-situ concrete ribs along the main axis of the bus terminal located immediately to the west. The station's striking glass roof is supported by slender 25-meter-high steel supports resembling trees, creating an ostentatious gothic-inspired space. The structure is glaringly white. Structural expressiveness is explored throughout the various levels, though the actual mode of expression changes from two-legged columns to leaning columns, columns brazenly illustrating static forces, and canopies stretching their vertical supports.

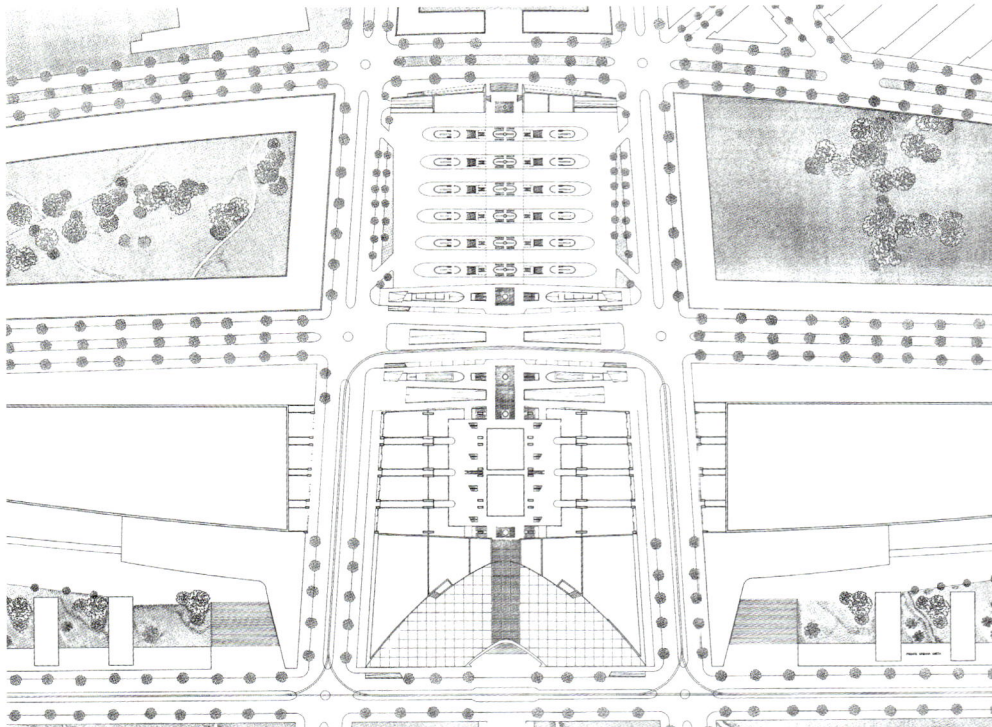

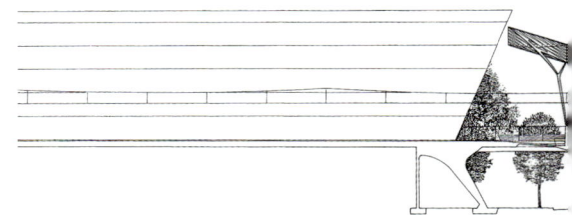

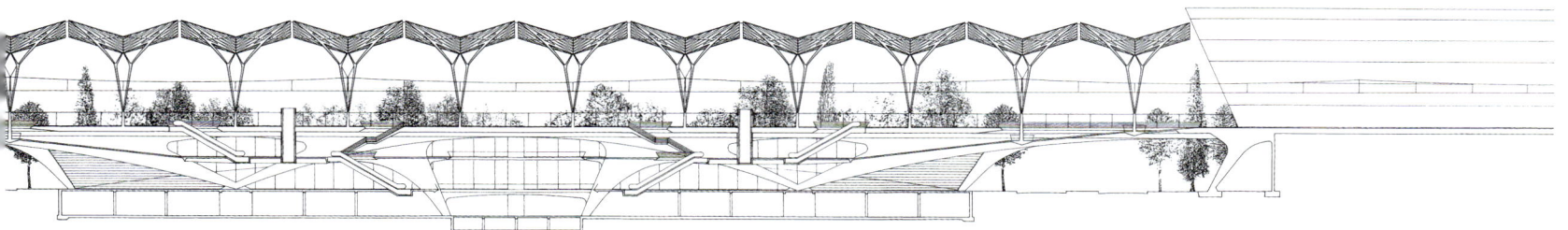

Dreamworld Canopies

CASAR DE CÁCERES BUS STATION

Casar de Cáceres, Spain

Architect: Justo Garciá Rubio

Engineer: Jaíme Cervera Bravo

Date: 1998–2003

The dreamlike quality of the curving canopies of the Casar de Cáceres Subregional Bus Station is understandable in the context of the town's vault-technique heritage and, at the same time, is an obviously foreign yet playful object in one of its residential neighborhoods. The station, set between a nursery and a school, with children passing in front of the building at all hours of the day, is made of a single material: white concrete. The thin and graceful curving band rises to become a sheet, a structure with a stability that originates from its form and that folds over on itself to fulfill all the program requirements. Buses go into and come out of the folds, intentionally enhanc-ing the traveler's sense of departing on or arriving from a journey.

Passengers generally arrive at the station from the town center, having passed under vaults that support houses that cover its crosswise streets. The station simultane-ously produces a similar condition of under-pass, yet its presence as a gigantic sculpture creates an undeniable attitude of detach-ment. Access to the station under the first, welcoming small sheet reveals the logic of the whole as intrinsic to itself and as a dominant yet playful object in the neighbor-hood context. A larger sheet arches over the small sheet and covers and protects the bus park. The formal solution at the corner frames the park at the rear elevation and relates to the low-rise housing neighbor-hood. Service functions including toilets, a store, and a bar are in the basement, freeing the ground plane of additional mass. The floor is of gray concrete, heightening the contrast between the white structure and the sculpture, or structure and architecture. The form designed for the main sheet of the project's two sheets is a simple hyperbola (34 meters long, 14 meters wide, and 12 centimeters thick). Detachment through self-reliance is achieved poetically.

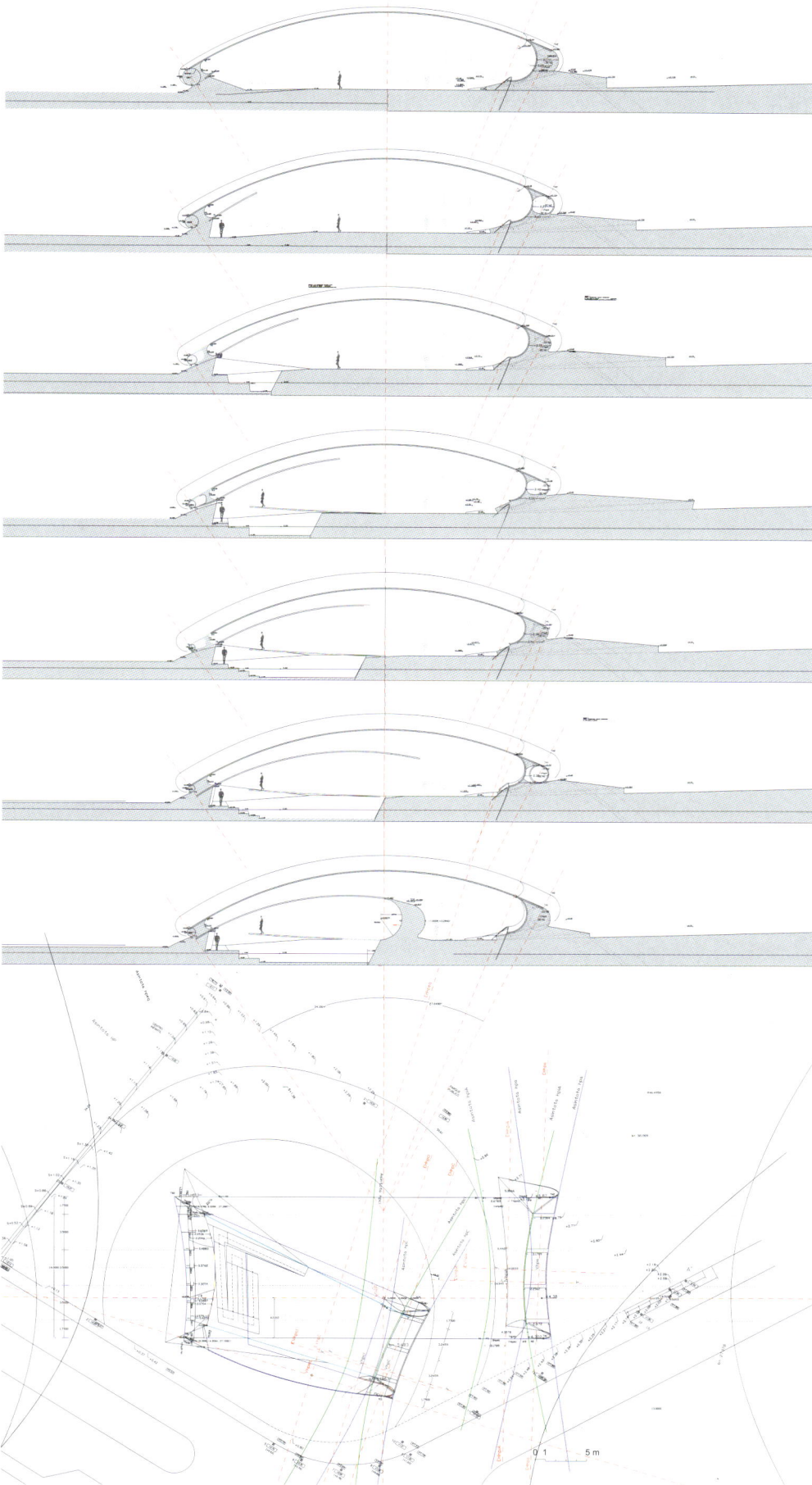

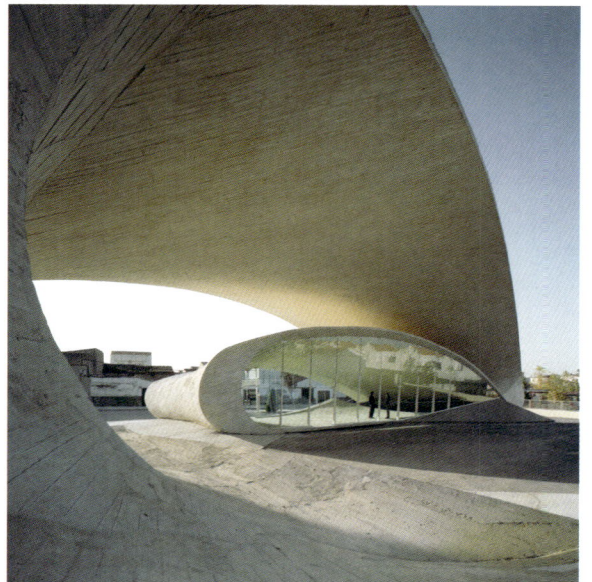

0 1   5 m

Neogothic Meets High-Tech

Washington, DC, USA

Architect: Pelli Clarke Pelli Architects

Date: 1990–1997

NORTH TERMINAL, WASHINGTON NATIONAL AIRPORT

Washington National Airport was planned as a gateway to a capital. The challenge to create an appropriate image while, at the same time, work with the logistics of one of the nation's busiest airports led Pelli Clarke Pelli Architects to design an elongated cathedral-like terminal that accommodates approximately 16 million passengers a year. The three-level, 35-gate structure of the new North Terminal is located between the existing 1941 South Terminal and the hangars at the north end of the landfill site, southwest of the Potomac River and in direct view of Washington's Federal Core and the Mall. Its detached categorization stems from the clear choice for a large vaulted insular space, for the demonstration of an impressive indoor volume that does not follow from its basic airport function of distributing people. In this sense, the triple-height concourse (500 meters long) becomes a grand space unto itself.

The technical complexity of the state-of-the-art airport is matched by an equally strong symbolic force of monumental civic architecture. The 45-×-45-foot (13.7-×-13.7 meter) square-module two-tiered cross section steel structure with vaulted roof dome trusses dictates the terminal's scale, flexibility, and architectural proportions. Outside, the static nature of the massive rhythmic structure (cladding with clear, patterned, and spandrel glass with a painted aluminum mullion system) is counterbalanced by the undulating arches of the roof. Inside, the orientation and quality of light entering the wide windows are reminiscent of gateway qualities of neogothic train stations. The naked simplicity of the 19th-century-style construction conjures up an archetypal image of glass and steel works of a bygone era. The reminiscence of the past is brought into the contemporary, fitting for an interface between the city and plane journey. The main concourse level, which is also the commercial street of the building, boosts a direct connection to the metro, parking garages, the South Terminal connector, and three perpendicular piers that serve 35 gates.

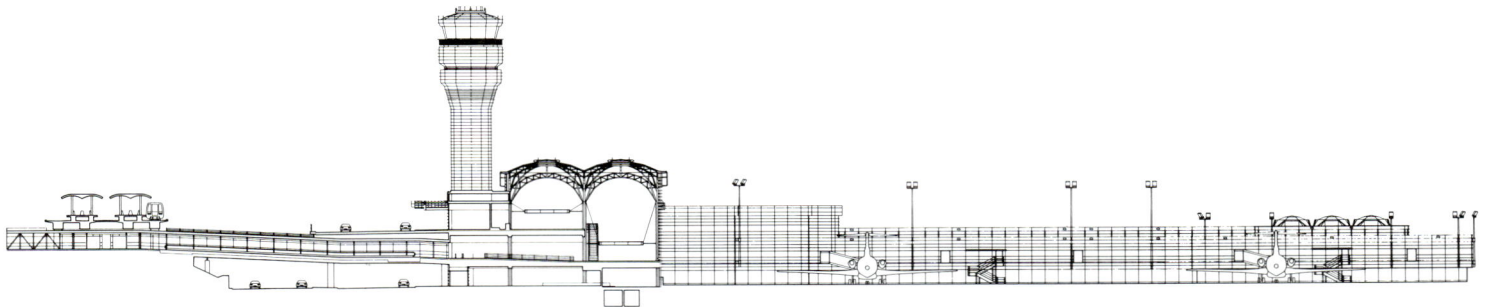

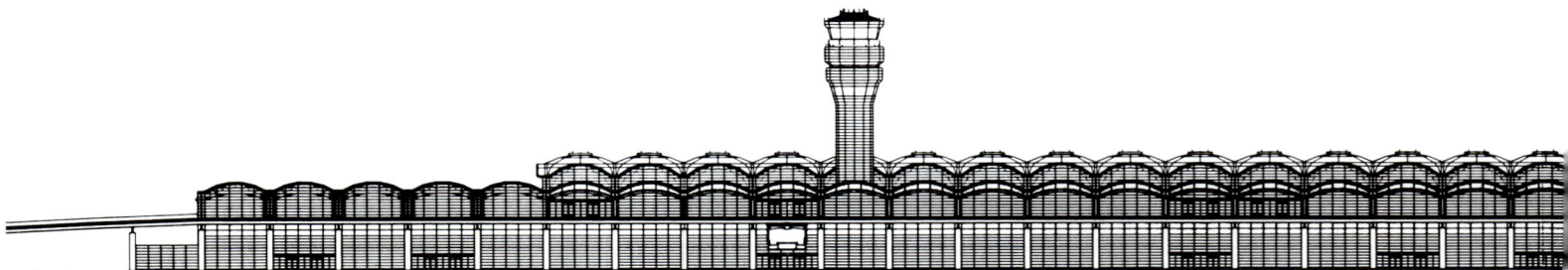

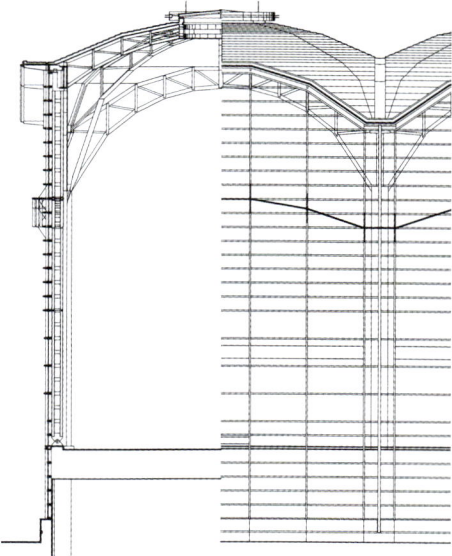

Super-Size Apple

FIETSAPPEL BIKE STORAGE

Alphen aan den Rijn, the Netherlands

Architect: KuiperCompagnons (Wytze Patijn, Silvian van Tuyl)

Date: 2005–2010 (projected)

This awkward translucent bubble — a parking place for 1000 bicycles in front of the Alphen aan den Rijn station — is a powerful illustration of an infrastructure of detachment. The Fietsappel (Dutch for bicycle apple) has the shape of its namesake; it is a large apple, the skin of which forms a ramped circulation spiral. The apple peel shapes the contours of the bicycle storage. The Fietsappel is the "jewel in the square" of a new urban area centered on the station of Alphen aan den Rijn in the Netherlands. The development includes 100,000 square meters of office space, 400 housing units, a hotel extension, and a new bus station. The

master plan proposes a scheme for the interconnection of different transport modes, and for the reconnection of the station with the center and with the Kerk and Zanen district.

The strangeness of the Fietsappel, its otherness, is intended to be both an efficient storage element (providing ample parking spaces that offer social control and security) and a lively object in the new city square. The unguarded bicycle storage is half sunken. From ground level there is a downward movement directly toward the platforms and an upward movement to the

bicycle storage. The bikes are cycled and eventually parked on the "peels" of the spiraling ramps. In the "core" of the apple, 12 columns form the main structure; they are linked through a web of cables to the outer skin. While the ramp loops around these columns, the stairs are situated inside. The two circulation routes cross each other at different moments along their trajectories. To improve social control and security, the outer skin is as transparent as possible. It is made of gauze of different sizes of wire mesh. At night it is designed to turn into the magic lantern illuminating the square.

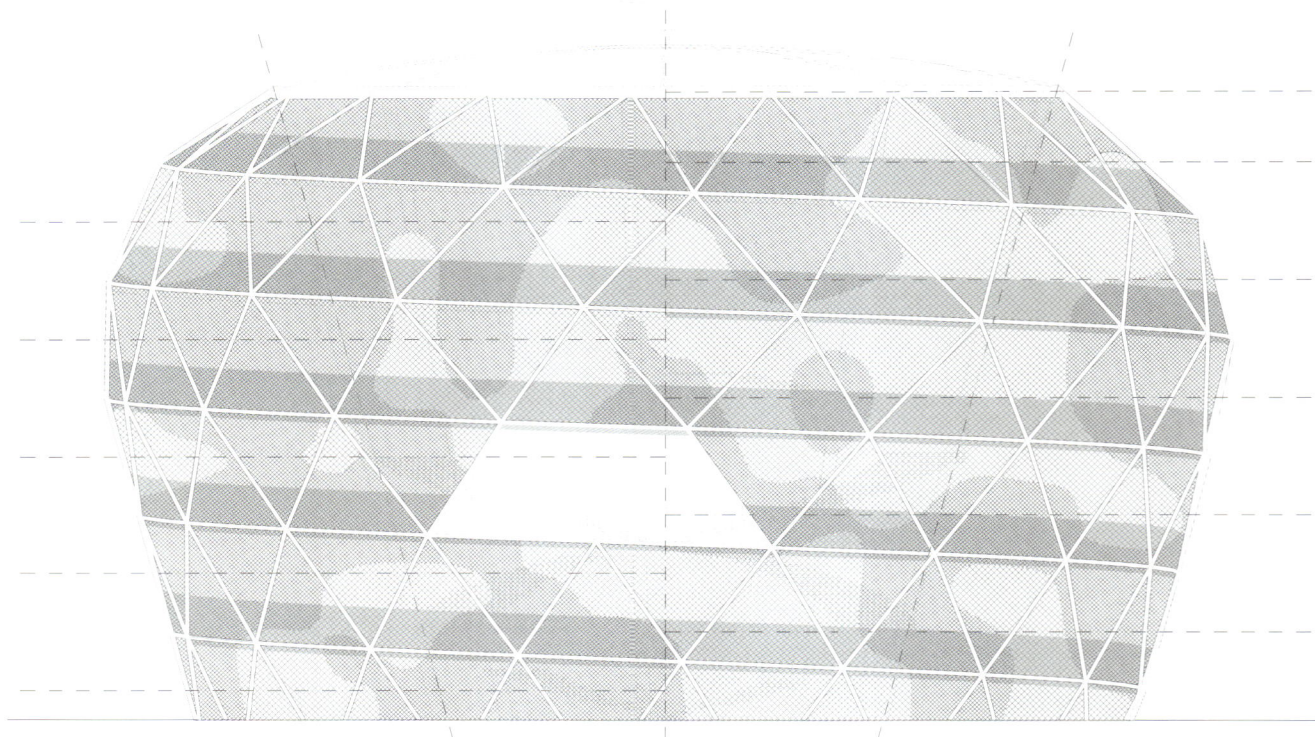

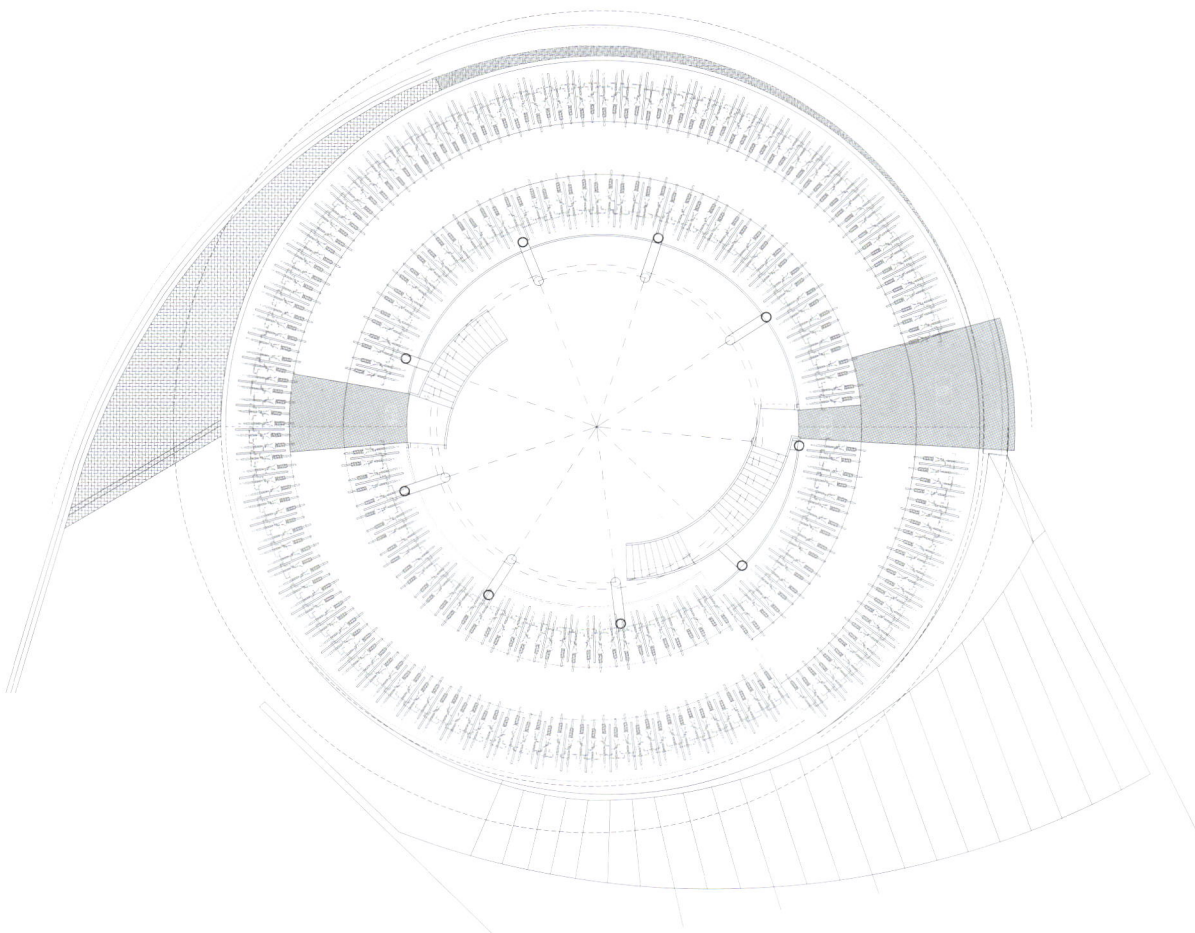

3

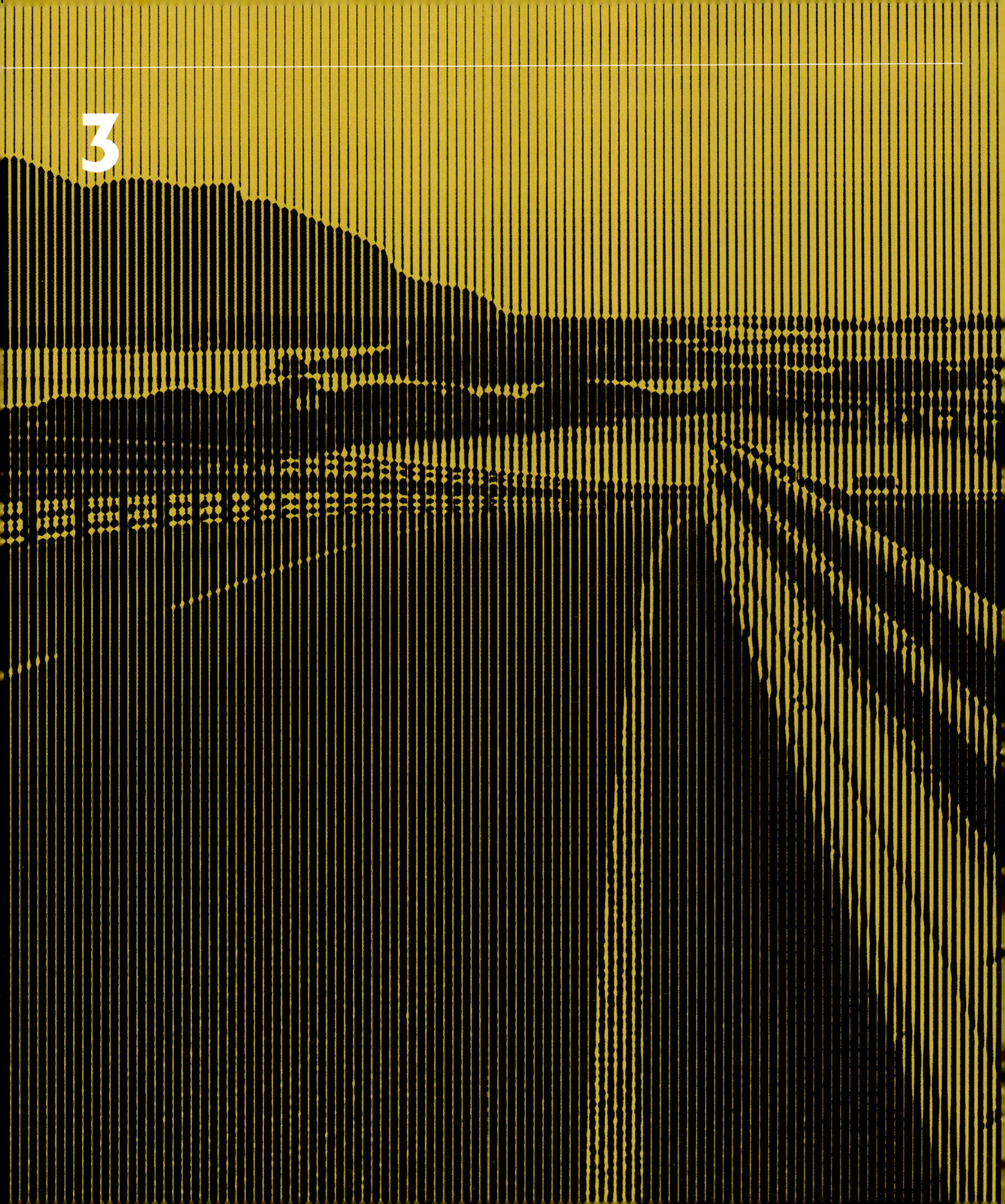

THE PERCEPTION OF LANDSCAPE THROUGH MOVEMENT

INTRODUCTION
CHANGING MODES OF PERCEPTION

Over the last two centuries, the perception of the landscape has changed in accordance with the altering modes and modifying forms of transport. Originally, the view of the surrounding environment was based upon pedestrian observation. Eventually, it gave way to choreographing the perspective gaze (with axes, privileged viewpoints, and elevated overviews) and organizing the picturesque view (with enclosures, composed visual entities, and vistas toward distant settings). Later, the various modes of mechanical locomotion instigated a full-fledged panoramic perception. The view of the landscape became inseparable from the speed and position of the observer in continual motion. Today's modes of transport allow mankind to experience ever larger territories, at ever greater speeds. Transportation technologies have thus fundamentally altered perception and, with it, the appreciation of the built environment. Furthermore, the sense of speed induced by technological advances has significantly affected the relation of man to his surroundings. It has radically reduced the range of senses with which he engages the territory through movement. Indeed, vehicles have reoriented the perception of the environment. Vision – rather than sound, smell, or touch – has become the primary sense through which the landscape is experienced. A form of kaleidoscopic vision arose with the side views afforded by boats, trams, and trains. From these forms of transportation, the world appeared as a blur on the foreground, while the background was reduced to an outline. Later, the car windshield restricted, focused, framed, limited, and directed forward a kinetic yet flattened view of the landscape. Mobility became associated with perceptual immersion amid social distance, personal detachment, the provision of comfort, and steady, mobile sight lines. Finally, the controlling view of air travel renders the landscape as a colorful mosaic of immeasurable abstract geometries.[1]

At the same time, there has been a paradigmatic shift with regard to the *sense* of movement, as experienced from foot to horse-drawn carriages, from trains to cars. The romantic 19th and early-20th-century exposés by Charles Baudelaire and Walter Benjamin about Parisian pedestrian wanderings come to an end in Lewis Mumford's reactive assault on the relation of *The Highway and the City* (1963), and in the deploring of highways as hideous scars in Peter Blake's *God's Own Junkyard* (1964). From that point on, the revo-

1 **EXPERIENCING THE CITY FROM THE ROAD**

In their groundbreaking book *The View from the Road*, Donald Appleyard, Kevin Lynch, and John R. Myer propose an alternative route for the planned ringroad around Boston. In their proposal, the driver's views of major landmarks are optimized, vistas to natural scenery are created, and sequences building up climaxes are constructed.

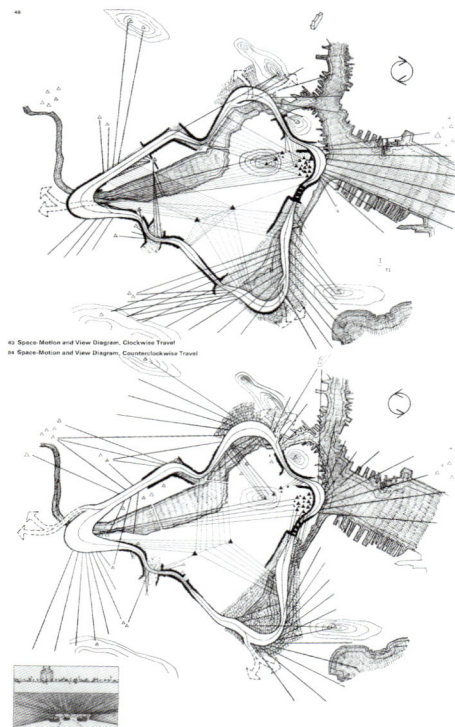

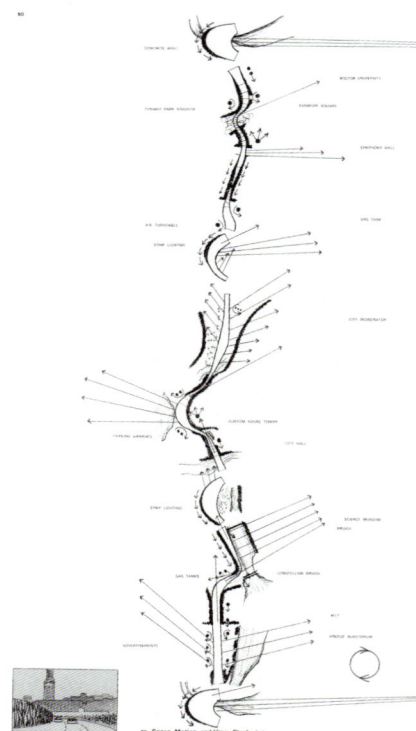

lutionary impact of *The View From the Road* (1964) by Donald Appleyard, Kevin Lynch, and John R. Myer instigated a new aesthetic in planning and design. This visionary study gave way to a focus on the perception of roadside detail. It stressed the need for a sense of motion and space, an awareness of orientation and position in the larger urban context, a clear understanding of the successive landscapes one passes [1]. It also claimed that "the roadside should be a fascinating book to read on the run."² More recently, Paul Virilio and Jean Baudrillard both have written extensively on modes of mediation, technology, and speed. In *Speed & Politics: An Essay on Dromology*, Virilio notes that the speed at which something happens may change its essential nature. In his view, that which moves with speed quickly comes to dominate that which is slower. "Whoever controls the territory possesses it. Possession of territory is not primarily about laws and contracts, but first and foremost a matter of movement and circulation."³ For Virilio, the visual aesthetics of the car driver are about penetration, not observation. They are not panoramic, but immersive. In a similar vein, Baudrillard, in his book *America,* states that "freeways don't denature the city or the landscape, they simply pass through and unravel it."⁴ Movement today is made more complex by new communication technologies, leading geographer Nigel Thrift to label the postmodern phenomenon of "feeling mobility." He writes that the shift from the physical to the immaterial, as exemplified by the Internet, has spawned developments in speed, light, and power that fuse with people to produce something like a cyborg.

It was, however, the train that began man's fascination with the perception of movement. The Swiss idea of leisure walks in the mountains was surpassed in the American Northeast with the invention in 1869 of the first mountain-climbing cog railroad up Mount Washington in New Hampshire's White Mountain National Forest [2]. Across the globe, a wave of tourist destinations was made accessible by rail and half of the experience was the ride itself, complete with moving scenery. The railroad required a fundamental rethinking of space, as distances shrunk and it was possible to travel farther in a shorter time. Rail voyages also enhanced an understanding of geography through units of time, eventually leading to the worldwide adoption of standardized time zones to meet the demands of rail schedules. The train, and later the car, recast the relationship between town and countryside. The "mobilized gaze," as Mitchell Schwarzer calls it, produced a new sense of distance and time. Space was ultimately compressed in time, leading Karl Marx to write of the annihilation of space by time. Due to the success of the rail network, places were, for all practical purposes, a lot closer. New modes of mobility also made places of work and home functionally separate spaces, and movement significantly reduced the distinctiveness of places. Travel became a necessity for everyday life and was no longer signified by "the grand tour" as an extended voyage around the sites of Europe taken by well-to-do gentlemen. Mobility became central to what it is to be modern and it represented freedom, and the railroad was instrumental in ordering modern life through the production of

2 SCENIC RAILROAD
The invention of the cog railway – an engineering marvel with the technology of toothed cog gears, rack rails, and tilted boilers – allowed for extremely steep grades to be accessed for tourism. In 1869 the first such railroad operated from a base elevation of 820 meters to the 1917-meter summit of Mount Washington in New Hampshire.

abstract time and abstract space. For many, the railroad was a symbol of 19th-century progress that facilitated economic wealth, social betterment, democracy, freedom, and much more. However, for others, metaphors of trains as mechanical monsters, iron horses, and beasts of burden underscored the downsides of pollution, danger, and despoliation of rural beauty.

Quite literally, the wheels of progress developed further and, in 1885, Karl Benz invented the automobile. By the early 20th century, the development of parkways in the United States and Europe led to a landscape *of* the road and from the viewpoint of the driver. Parkways were intended for pleasure driving and rooted in the picturesque, romantic landscape tradition of Frederick Law Olmsted. A number of parkways even had the stated purpose of *adding* beauty to the landscape. The car became the privileged means of discovering scenic routes, giving rise to automobile and tourist associations that were connected with tour guides and hotel evaluations like the Michelin Guides [3]. Parkways and associated service areas made people aware of their surroundings, while transportation infrastructure was utilized to form the basis of a new perception of the landscape. Roads were designed through parks, with sinuous curves adjusted to the existing topography to break the monotony of driving [4].

Such a bucolic infrastructure/landscape relation was soon superseded as the countryside became an obstacle to be overcome by highways. By the end of World War II, the cultural shift from cities, hotels, and railroads to suburbs, motels, and highways was well-established in North America and soon after evident across the world. The landscape became a place of transience and transit, and the predominant visual order became one of horizontality. The sense of pleasure driving, of delight and discovery, was soon replaced by a modernist ambition to cover distance, an aspiration of effectiveness and dominance over the environment. According to Sigfried Giedion, "The space-time feeling of our period can seldom be felt so keenly as when driving, the wheel under one's hands, up and down hills, beneath overpasses, up ramps and over giant bridges."[5] "Serial vision" was the term that Gordon Cullen coined in *Townscape* (1960) to identify the phenomenon that generated a new symbolic order determined by movement, isolation, and consumerism – as pointedly revealed in *Learning from Las Vegas* (1972) by Robert Venturi, Denise Scott Brown, and Steven Izenour. The aesthetics of the automobile view were modern, dynamic, and often infinite sights, all shaped by the brief encounter and a stream of forms that somehow elude conscious form. Automobiles encourage an understanding of architecture as landscape instead of landmark; and although they greatly facilitate access to individual landmarks, "cars are impatient with stasis and singularity."[6]

The road in the landscape dramatically changes not only the perception of the environment but also, quite literally, the landscape

3 **PRECASTING THE VIEW**
By their detailed and well-sketched tours and information, Michelin's green guides have been predetermining the view of motorized tourism through France and Europe ever since they were first published in 1926.

itself. For John Brinckerhoff Jackson, chronicler of landscapes, a national highway system has always been what he calls a "political landscape."[7] For the most part, it follows three canons: first, a vastness of scale; second, a disregard for local features, topographical as well as man-made; and last, a persistent emphasis on military and commercial (economic) functions. For Jackson, the road obviously changed perception of man's travel through the landscape, but even so important it was the physical manifestation of infrastructure and enacted on the landscape the visible expression of order and power. The landscape created by the physical presence of infrastructure is therefore, obviously, inseparable from the perception of landscape through movement.

Yet, today, the psychology of perception seems to be largely sidelined not only in the design of infrastructure as engineering logics, but also in the pressures of sustainability, compatibility, and environmental impact that have risen to the fore. In fact, in most cases, visual perception of the landscape along infrastructure routes is dominated by advertising – a disturbance and obstacle to the continuity of perception. Nowadays, it is exceptional if projects explicitly organize vision into an aesthetic experience, and indeed, most of these are choreographed as scenic routes serving as tourist attractions. These aim to emphasize dramatic effects and the sequential organization and exploitation of privileged viewpoints, and to simulate naturalness or authenticity. At the same time, slow routes are counterbalanced by a whole new array of high-speed routes, particularly high-speed train (HST) networks. The national footprints of France and Japan, at the forefront of HST investment, have significantly shrunk, and in the process these HST lines have once more changed the perception of travel and of the landscape through which they move. Ultimately, it is the tension between the systematic approach with the latest technology, on the one hand, and the site-specific attitude attuned to environmental characteristics, on the other hand, that determines the contemporary perception of the landscape through movement. In today's era of a shrinking world and ever more time-space compression, the control of outside interferences indeed needs to be balanced with a visual orientation that highlights the navigability of the system and the specificity of the landscape.

1 A more thorough discussion of these topics can be read in Mitchell Schwarzer, *Zoomscape: Architecture in Motion and Media* (New York: Princeton Architectural Press, 2004) and Tim Cresswell, *On the Move: Mobility in the Modern Western World* (London: Routledge, 2006).

2 Donald Appleyard, Kevin Lynch, and John Myer, *The View From the Road*. (Cambridge, MA: MIT Press, 1964), 18.

3 Paul Virilio, *Speed and Politics: An Essay on Dromology* (New York: Semiotext(e), 1977), 11-12.

4 Jean Baudrillard, *America* (London and New York: Verso, 1998), 53

5 Sigfried Giedion, *Space, Time and Architecture: The Growth of a New Tradition*, fifth edition (Cambridge: Harvard University Press, 1967), 831.

6 Mitchell Schwarzer, *Zoomscape: Architecture in Motion and Media* (New York: Princeton Architectural Press, 2004), 72.

7 John Brinckerhoff Jackson, "A Pair of Ideal Landscapes," in *Discovering the Vernacular Landscape* (New Haven and London: Yale University Press, 1984), 9-56.

4 **AUTOBAHN PICNIC**
A 1936 cover of the journal *Die Strasse* ("The Road") romanticizes the modernity of the autobahn with the pastoral imagery of a weekend picnic -- a curious mixture of obtrusive Nazi propaganda linking the military roads to tourism.

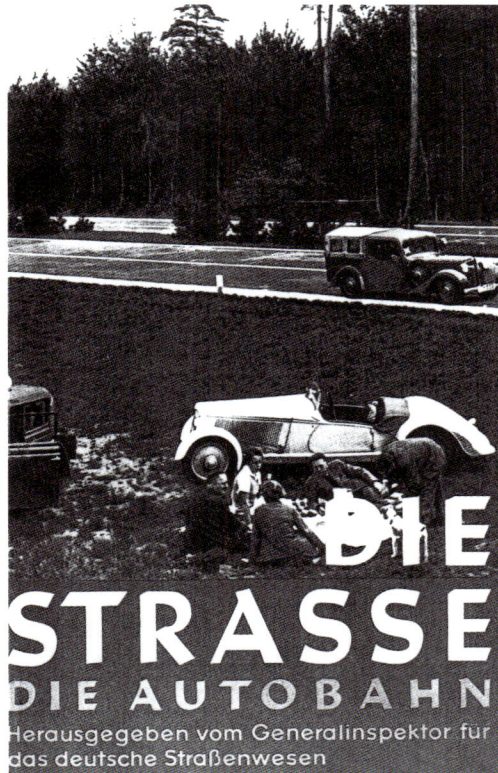

STAGING THE SCENERY

The creation of infrastructure places the designer in the position of directing the gaze. The trajectory of the journey and the view of the voyager are determined by the course and the implantation of the road, rail, air, or sea line. A contemporary sense of the picturesque is instigated by aligning the infrastructure in a way that underlines the striking features of the landscape it crosses. Architect Alwin Seifert, the original inventor of this theory for the German autobahn in the 1930s, saw such staging of the existing landscape as a means of highlighting regional identity. In 1933, with the intention of rivaling the Mount Vernon Memorial Highway, Fritz Todt, general inspector of the German autobahn system, laid out the highway from Munich to the border across the Irschenberg. It created a most prestigious piece of scenery by affording a three-kilometer-long view of the Alps. Generally, the intention of Seifert was to meld the highway with the Bavarian landscape, and have the spatial order of farming land continue throughout the authentic landscaping of middle and side stretches on the autobahn. Rhythm and variation for the auto-tourist was guaranteed by designing oscillating trajectories, and alternating open (farmland) and closed (wood) sections, climbing and descent, and panoramas unto mountain ranges, sea, or lakes [1]. In the United States, in the northeastern states around New York, parkways choreographed the vehicular route as a landscaped road through ribbon-like parks. Robert Moses, a gifted opportunist and pragmatic administrator, created a vast network of parkways in the environs of New York City, the most iconic of which was the Henry Hudson Parkway (1934-38), which connected five major parks and was structured as a scenic waterfront highway [2].

Today, the tradition of scenic routes continues, though perhaps not so much as choreographing the entire route as creating stops along the way. The landscape as scenery, as a contemplative object for the eye, has led to the deliberate choice of particular points of observation for the attainment of visual effects and accommodating what British sociologist John Urry has coined the "tourist gaze." According to Urry, such an expression is the result of the desire of tourists for rapid movement, the search for panoramic views, and spatial and temporal removal from their normal routine.[1] This aspiration to stage experience is evident in the National Tourist Routes program in Norway. Travel through the Norwegian countryside is enhanced by this encompassing project that offers the country's best architecture and design though a series of pullouts, rest areas, lookout points, parking lots, and emergency shelters. The new amenities and interventions have a narrative function. Their ambition is to interpret well-known places and endow lesser-known ones with names and identities. As such, nature is tamed and organized and the experience for the viewer composed. A striking example is the Mannheller Ferry Terminal, which optimizes transport logistics and enhances the site's distinctiveness as a small spit on Norway's largest fjord [3]. In

1 **MEANDERING MOTORWAY**
Taken from the famous survey on the great works of Adolf Hitler published by Georg Fritz in 1939, this symbolic drawing entitled "The autobahn approaching Dresden," exemplifies the ideal of inserting new highways into the specific geography of the landscape they cross.

2 **RIVERFRONT PARKWAY**
Following the Great Depression, Robert Moses – the most polarizing figure in American urbanism – set about making "cities for traffic" to stimulate the economy. The 17.8-kilometer-long Henry Hudson Parkway provided an uninterrupted, limited-access route from Lower Manhattan to the wealthy northern suburbs of Westchester County. The new parkway, which had six lanes separated by a center median, was constructed on top of landfill directly along the Hudson River. This afforded motorists on the parkway a direct view of the Hudson shoreline, but limited access to the shoreline for park visitors.

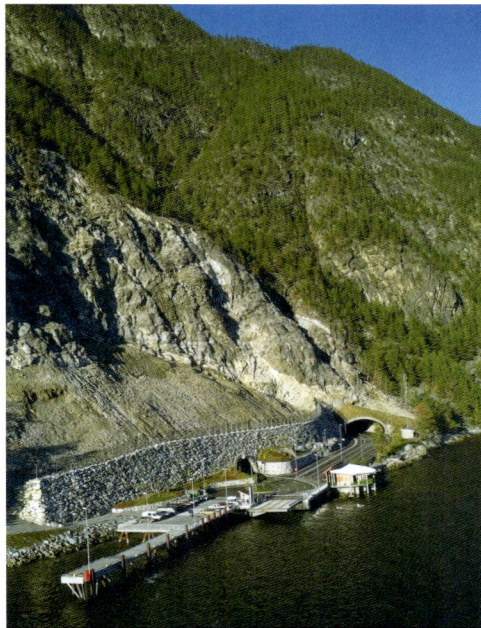

3 **FJORD FERRY MODESTY**
Landscape architects Bjørbekk & Lindheim worked with road engineers on the tunnel boring through mountains to frame a magnificent view of Norway's longest and deepest fjord, the Sognefjord. At the same time, the terminal serving the ferry from Mannheller to Fodnes has been melded into the landscape, and material left over from the tunnel's stone retaining wall was used to create two tree-planted terraces – a reference to the agricultural traditions of the region. The line of coast available has been equipped with wooden benches that, with an 80-person amphitheater of brick and stone, constitute areas for resting, waiting, and contemplating the powerful landscape.

4 **WALKING ON WATER**

The longest wooden bridge in Switzerland is in Rapperswil-Hurden and spans the narrowest part of Lake Zurich. The bridge (841 meters long, 2.4 meters wide) is part of the historic Route of St. James (also known as Jacob's Path) traveled for centuries by pilgrims on their way to Santiago de Compostela. A rickety bridge (the first of which was erected in 1360) was rebuilt in a contemporary style in 2000–2001 and the new L-shaped oak bridge elevated on timber piles not only provides a route but also allows the spectator to take in the surrounding landscape in a serene and meditative environment.

5 **PLANTED VIADUCT PROMENADE**

A mid-19th-century train line through the 12th arrondissement in Paris included a 1.5-kilometer-long limestone and brick viaduct with 67 linear vaults. When the line from Bastille to Bois de Vincennes was discontinued in 1969, the viaduct became an overgrown and unkempt relic of a bygone era. The conversion of the structure into a pedestrian walkway in the air was made by architect Patrick Berger (the interior of the viaduct) and landscape architects Philippe Mathieux and Jacques Vergely (the planted roof). The vaults contain shops, arts/crafts spaces, and exhibits, while the roof of Le Viaduc des Arts serves as an elevated park that affords changes in perspective and opens unexpected views of the urban tissue.

6 **QUARRIED REST STOPS**
The 1997 rest stop of the
Crazannes Quarries on the
A837 highway between Saintes
and Rochefort-sur-Mer in
the southwest of France is
representative of the general
approach of Bernard Lassus,
whereby the interactive
nature of landscape is underlined. Lassus – unconvention-
ally designing on site and in
close cooperation with the
engineers, the workers, and
local people – sculpted and
transformed an abandoned
quarry field into a landscape
to be experienced at high
speed. A system of rest areas,
wooden footbridges, paths,
and belvederes strategically
engages the traveler, out of
the car, in an enriching visual
and tactile experience of the
fragile and secretive site.

Garabit, France, the entire rest stop on the A75 highway is conceived as a gigantic stage, exhibiting the historic viaduct by Eiffel and Boyer that spans the gorge of the nearby Truyère River. A huge landform integrates the service station into the site and arranges service facilities in a linear sequence that begins as motorists step out of the car and overlook the landscape, their view directed toward the railroad bridge by a constructed vista. The viewing platform makes a playful reference to the panorama tables of Michelin and the Touring Club of France, the leading cartographers for motorists from the 1930s to the 1960s.

However, the attention for the moving gaze did not start with the era of the automobile. Panoramas, vistas, and perspectives have been framed as scenery by landscape designers since the Renaissance. Promenades and walks have only gained in popularity ever since.[2] Varying views of the landscape have been opened and made accessible by choreographed routes through the landscape. Signaled paths – from treks in the Alps to walkways along military fortifications such as China's Great Wall – draw more and more visitors as time passes. In this way, great pilgrimage routes have led to spectacular interventions that highlight the beauty of the landscape. Part of the legendary Route of St. James to Santiago de Compostela crosses Lake Zurich with careful attention paid to the view, approach, path, horizon, and mountains [4]. Even more dramatic a setting and approach is the magical aura of Mont Saint-Michel. Today, the UNESCO world cultural heritage site draws approximately 3.6 million tourists every year and the beautiful new jetty was designed to carry such a load while simultaneously restoring the site's maritime character, preserving its symbolism and notion of pilgrimage.

In fact, the desire to stage the scenery for passers-by is inherent in many types of present-day projects. In some cases, whereby the transformation of neglected industrial ruins allows for adaptive reuse of abandoned viaducts, it has engendered a new rhythm of public spaces and an unexpected perception of the urban landscape. The Paris walkway created atop Le Viaduc des Arts has become extremely popular [5]. It inspired the urban regeneration of the popular quarter around it and formed an evident precedent for the High Line in Lower Manhattan. Industrial heritage has also given rise to the interesting French landscape and highway intervention by Bernard Lassus at Crazannes along the A837 [6]. Both sides of the highway were sculpted and transformed into a striking landscape by the construction of a visual itinerary at high speed that involved excavating and clearing an abandoned quarry. A similar stage-like quality of mobility through the landscape was also staged in the underground Bibliothèque François-Mitterrand Station of Paris's Météor-Line 14, where Antoine Grumbach and Pierre Schall literally put the movement created by the users of the metro on show. In this case, the landscape they highlight is the animation of urban mobility itself, which is made a focus for observation from a large amphitheater at a critical and busy pedestrian crossway.

1 John Urry, *The Tourist Gaze: Leisure and Travel in Contemporary Societies* (London: Sage Publications, 1990).
2 The changing meaning of promenades is analyzed in Marcel Smets, "Promenade – einst und jetzt / Promenade, past and present," *Topos 41,* December 2002, 6-17.

Tourist Itineraries

NATIONAL ROUTES PROJECT

Norway

Architect: 3RW (Jakob Røssvik) (Askvågen, Atlanterhavsvegen); Manthey Kula (Myrbærholmen, Atlanterhavsvegen); 3RW (Sixten Rahlff) (Ørnesvingen, Geiranger-Trollstigen); Knut Hjeltnes (Rjupa, Valdresflya)

Landscape Architect: Smedsvig (Askvågen, Atlanterhavsvegen and Ørnesvingen, Geiranger-Trollstigen)

Date: 2005–2006

The national tourist routes project of the Norwegian Public Roads Administration aims to showcase the country's magnificent landscape scenery in a harmonious and non-exploitive way. With several routes already realized, the project is slated to continue until 2015. In total, 18 sections of thoroughfares (1850 kilometers in length) are to be designated tourist routes through quintessential Norwegian countryside. Overlooking fjords, coasts, mountains, and waterfalls, stopping points are designed for taking breaks, parking for hikes, and taking photographs. The majority of the tourist routes will be open all year, enabling motorists to experience the Norwegian outdoors under changing weather and light conditions. A number of practical needs are met in the interventions – parking places, rest areas, information points, public toilets, small cafés and so on. Several of the interventions feature viewing points where visitors can enjoy the spectacular landscape while at the same time not intruding on it. They therefore work as a way to manage the landscape as a limited resource. The interventions are designed to intensify the experience of the scenery as tourists pass through.

Among the various routes is the northwest Atlantic Ocean Route, with a road that hugs the coastline and where bridges cross waterways as sinuous arcs melding with the rocky terrain. In Myrbærholmen, Beate Hølmebakk of design firm Manthey Kula created an 80-meter-long pedestrian bridge and parking space alongside the national route for use by recreational fishermen. In Askvågen, architect Jakob Røssvik of 3RW and landscape architect Smedsvig projected a new notion of a rest area that combines weathering steel steps leading to a pier/belvedere on a rock with a simple glass balustrade. Sixten Rahlff of 3RW and Smedsvig also collaborated on a dramatic lookout point in Ørnesvingen, on the Geiranger-Trollstigen Route. A curve on the winding road along precipitous mountains was exploited and extended to create a spectacular viewing point of the blue-green Geiranger Fjord 600 meters below. The river running through the site was manipulated to form a waterfall on a glass plate. Pedestrians occupy three concrete slabs positioned askew to one another, and simple concrete benches provide safety between cars and people. At Rjupa on the Valdresflya Route, architect Knut Hjeltnes created a simple yet elegant parking and small rest area amidst the setting of lakes and mountains. There are numerous other wonderful examples of the National Routes Project, all of which stage the scenery with modest means and beautiful detailing, and stress the Norwegian craft of highlighting the magnificent landscape.

Rjupa

Ørnesvingen

Myrbærholmen

Askvågen

21st-Century Panorama Table

GARABIT HIGHWAY REST AREA

Garabit, France

Landscape Architect: Latitude Nord (Gilles Vexlard, Laurence Vacherot)

Architect: Bruno Mader

Date: 1994–2002

Located on the new A75 highway, this rest area in the French Massif Central was created as a panoramic viewpoint overlooking the spectacular 1884 railroad viaduct by Gustave Eiffel and Léon Boyer. The station, situated halfway between Clermont-Ferrand and the Millau Viaduct, radically manipulates the landscape to underscore its inherent beauty and to frame the Garabit iron bridge, a monumental testament to exceptional engineering. More than 300,000 cubic meters of landfill were employed to remold the terrain, creating a tour through the landscape along a purposefully inflated ellipsoidal traffic circle and forming a terrace from which to enjoy the historic viaduct. An exaggeratedly dimensioned exit/entry cloverleaf takes motorists along a sloping and scripted series of views of the unfolding landscape – a safe distance away owing to the logistical functions and noise of the highway. When travelers arrive at the level of the station they are also at the same elevation as the Eiffel Bridge, made possible by placing the earthwork terrace 11 meters above the existing topography. Parking is developed with a lawn, isolated trees for shade, and pedestrian passageways that evoke the characteristic subdivision of agricultural allotments in the region. The parking lot directs the view toward the river and connects to the Maison du Cantal, an exhibition pavilion about the region by a three-meter-wide boardwalk.

The pavilion itself, designed by architect Bruno Mader, is positioned parallel to the elevated terrace and forms part of an elongated landscaped strip defining the edge of the plateau and marking the river valley. Conceived as a slightly elevated glass-box structure, it affords magnificent views of the landscape and viaduct. Its nondescript tones of concrete and gray wood cladding unambiguously offset Eiffel's bright red bridge as a contrast and focal point. Most spectacular, however, is the modest terrace at the edge of the undulating plateau, with its unusual geology. It demarcates the Truyère River limestone gorge by a 200-meter-long elongated granite panorama table. The massive horizontal surface is superimposed on the valley, as a tangent to the road.

Elegant Maritime Jetty

MONT SAINT-MICHEL JETTY

Mont Saint-Michel, France
Architect: Dietmar Feichtinger Architects (jetty)
Engineer: Schlaich, Bergermann & Partner (jetty)
Landscape Architect: Agence HYL (parking areas)
Date: 2002–present

The causeway bridge, connecting the continent to the insular territory of the monumental Mont Saint-Michel, was conceived as a jetty, a light crossing on piles. The new minimalist structure, which replaces a 120-year-old, 2-kilometer-long dike, restores the fragile coastal ecology and reinforces a horizontal datum, thereby heightening the majestic aura of the monument. From afar, the jetty reads as a sliver of a line standing on a row of thin piers. The structure's dimensions are reduced to an absolute minimum to merge the intervention with the horizon. The route is the result of the overlay of conceptual and complex hydraulic considerations. The sinuous, flowing curve of the causeway allows pedestrians to experience the Mont and the landscape from different perspectives, without ever having the head-on view. The geometry accentuates and prolongs the tangential approach to the monument, which is discovered gradually. As pedestrians complete their approach, with Tombelaine and the inner bay steadily coming into view, they discern the Mont surrounded by nothing but sand and ramparts. The jetty itself is divided into three primary sections with 4-meter (eastern) and 1.50-meter-wide (western) oak flooring pedestrian passages flanking the central 7-meter-wide shuttle-bus roadway, which is sunk 10 centimeters and stops 200 meters short of the end of the jetty).

The jetty is conceived not only as scenic promenade but also as a major landscape restoration project. The project is designed to free the Mont of the stranglehold of the surrounding salt marshes, which through the combined forces of the sea and the Couesnon River have accumulated 15 meters of sediment. The new dam under construction in conjunction with the jetty will allow the excess sediment to be flushed away by tidal and river currents and the bay's landscape to recover its marine character and the river to rediscover its natural meander. Tidal wetlands will also be recreated. The parking lot, too, is a major consideration in such a project, not left to an ad hoc solution but integrated into the entire landscape scheme. All vehicles remain on the mainland, where the wooded lots for 4000 cars and buses will not be seen from the access roads. To the south, the parking lot will be concealed by a gentle slope and slightly raised fields that form a screen without blocking the open view over the horizon of the bay on which the Mont Saint-Michel appears to float. To the north, the parking area is enclosed behind a dike or promenade overlooking the polder landscape. The entire Mont Saint-Michel project is about staging the scenery. Not only is the approach to the Mont carefully framed, but also the entire scenery of the coast is reconfigured to its more natural state.

Before

After

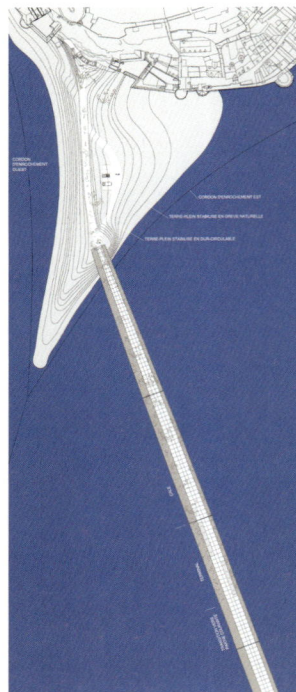

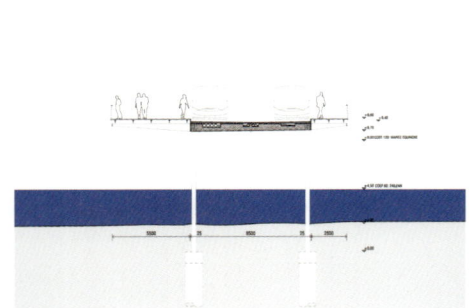

Before

After

Modern-Day Hanging Garden

HIGH LINE PARK

New York City, New York, USA

Architect: Diller Scofidio + Renfro

Landscape Architect: James Corner Field Operations

Date: 2005–2010 (projected)

Built in 1930, the 2.3-kilometer-long elevated freight railroad – the High Line – along 20 blocks of Manhattan's industrial western edge has been a scene in and of itself since its abandonment in 1980. The massive cast-iron structure of the viaduct and the melancholic, unruly beauty of the wild succession of overgrowth atop the rails was slated for demolition but saved by a high-profile nonprofit citizen group called Friends of the High Line, which was formed in 1999. An international competition drawing 720 entrants was staged to convert the industrial relic into a linear public park in the air. The Agri-Tecture team, led by Field Operations in collaboration with Diller Scofidio + Renfro, has since been developing the site's found beauty by changing the rules of engagement between plant life and pedestrians. The strategy involves the juxtaposition of simple, wild, quiet, and slow landscapes of woodland, grassland and wetland above, and the bustling urban life

below. The two are connected to each other by prolonged transitional spaces consisting of gentle flights of steps, ramps, and elevators.

The park itself combines organic (soft) and building materials (hard) of diverse proportions to accommodate "the wild, the cultivated, the intimate, and the hyper-social." The park is designed as a continuous ground surface built from precast concrete units that can fold down to permit pedestrians to travel through the thick structural section of the High Line or fold up so pedestrians can pass over it without destroying natural preserves. The kit of precast concrete components forms the linear planking and planting system that echoes the vanished train tracks and articulate furniture, planting beds, and large platforms. Along its route, the pathless landscape park includes floating ponds, sundecks, and lookout spots over the Hudson River, the Empire State Building,

and the Statue of Liberty. And whereas the railroad formerly linked adjacent industrial buildings at multiple levels, it will now link communities, providing residents and visitors with a public space to promenade, exercise, and relax. Programs are not explicitly designed, but the amount of paving is calibrated to accommodate a variety of uses. Flanked by 22 blocks of dense urban fabric, the transformed High Line is a high-profile public space that will endow the lower West Side with a new driver of development. The High Line exemplifies a new form of staging the scenery in which a picturesque linear pastoral landscape is enjoyed from above and premised upon the way in which nature has reclaimed a once vital piece of urban infrastructure. The neglected industrial ruin has been converted into an expanded public realm, a postindustrial instrument of leisure through both historic preservation and modernization.

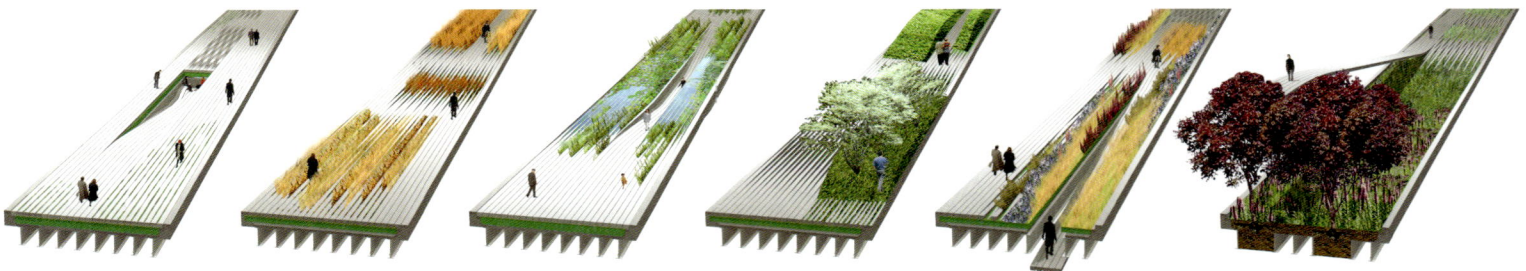

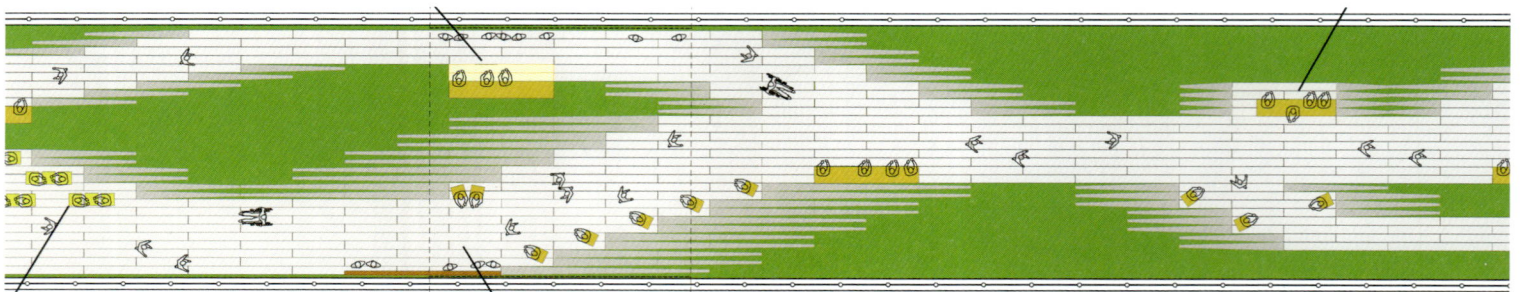

Before

Métro Stage-Set

BIBLIOTHÈQUE FRANÇOIS MITTERRAND STATION

Paris, France

Architect: Antoine Grumbach and Pierre Schall

Architect Météor Line 14: AR thème (Bernard Kohn, Jean-Pierre Vaysse)

Artist: Jean-Christophe Bailly

Date: 1990–1998

The new Météor (Métro Est Ouest Rapide) Line of Paris runs from Place de la Madeleine to Bibliothèque Nationale de France in under 15 minutes. It exemplifies a literal staging of the subterranean urban scenery. The Bibliothèque François Mitterrand Station, the interchange between Line 14 and the RER (the lines used by trains arriving from Austerlitz Station for Avenue de France and the shopping and office buildings that will make up the future Left Bank quarter), is simultaneously a component of the high-tech line and set apart from it through its subterranean monumental expression. The classical vocabulary of the 15-meter-high vaulted-roof amphitheater setting of the station designed by Antoine Grumbach and Pierre Schall is complemented by a complete range of features made in case aluminum, including walkways over the platforms and skylights at the top of the green pylons.

The architectural vocabulary was derived from the affinity between form and structural necessity, thus giving rise to the 120-meter-diameter semicircle placed below the platforms, where the rails make way for the RER platforms. The 19-step amphitheater, a place where all travelers converge, was conceived as a subterranean site that could be appropriated by users as a public lounge and meeting place. According to Grumbach, "We have tried to create a place that will be remembered, with a large public, slightly archaic square, which is not 'datable' or perverted by effects of fashion, because the underground is a place appropriated by people in a special way. Nowadays it is hard to find one's way about the city without these interconnecting points, and its spatial geography is organized around these transport junctions." The specificity of the place is also contrasted with more universal references through the art of writer Jean-Christophe Bailly. A "shower of quotations," a hybridization of art and literature, adorns the walls and floors, while the steps of the amphitheater are engraved with symbolic signs of nineteen existing or vanished civilizations. The amphitheater, 25 meters below street level, has been appropriated by various events and stages the everyday life and movement of the Paris underworld.

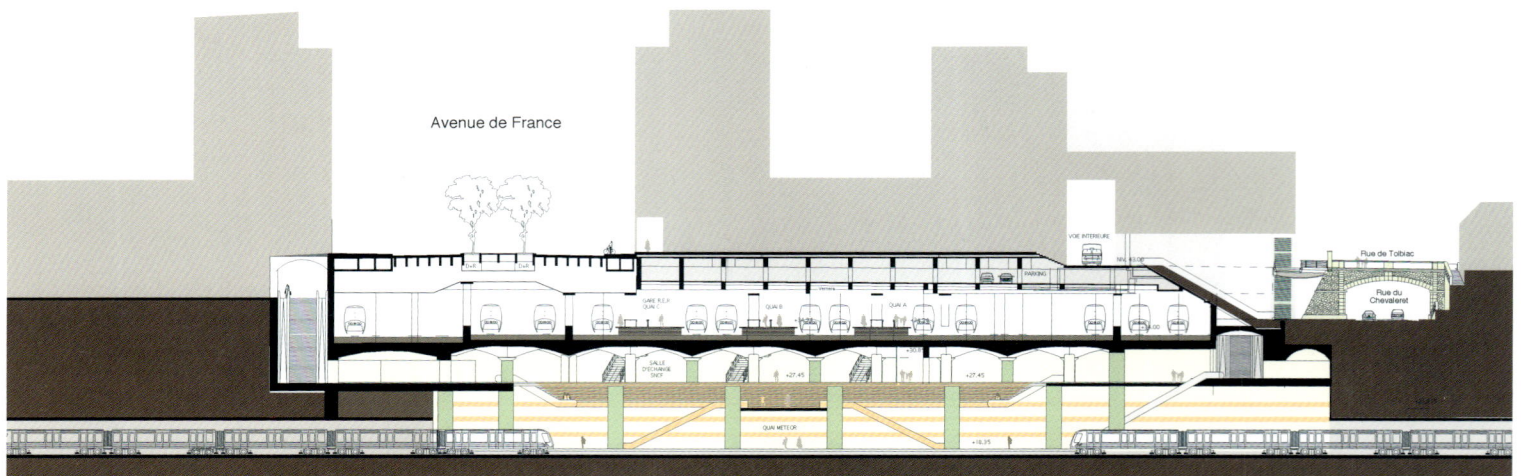

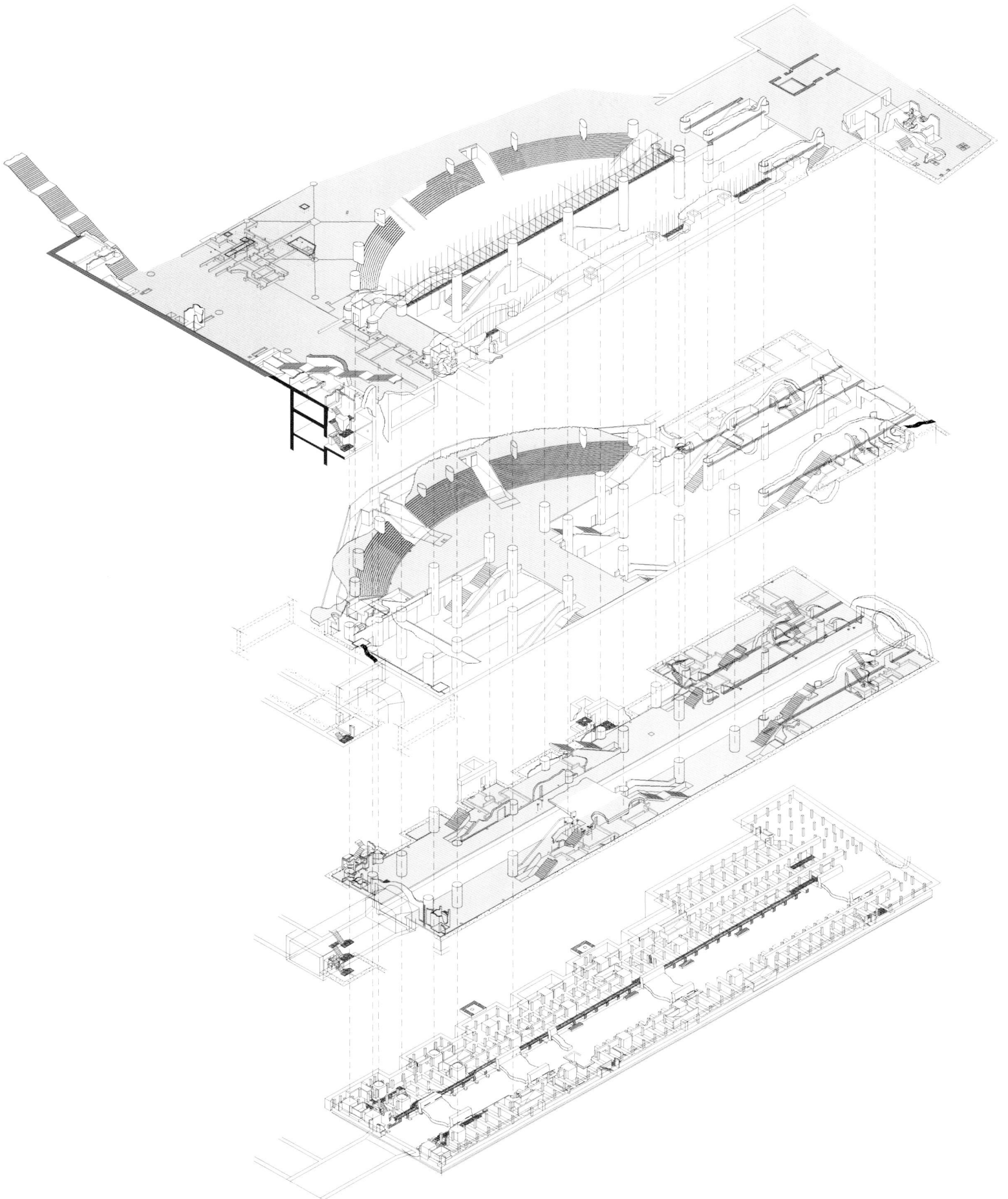

MARKING TRANSITIONS BY A THRESHOLD

Along a journey, infrastructure crosses a changing landscape. Territorial differentiation is recognizable through identifiable sections of natural settings or manmade environments that, in turn, create points of reference as to the distance covered and progression of the journey along the route. The passage from one environment to another is often celebrated by designers as a compressed transition, a threshold that provides the key to the connection between divergent landscapes and, at the same time, as a place in its own right. Thresholds are in-between spaces that provide an opportunity for accommodation between adjoining worlds. They are the points of transgression that create the spatial condition for the meeting and dialogue between different orders. In many instances, the clarification and concretization of the threshold as an in-between is intended as a setting for welcomes and farewells, arrivals and departures – thresholds expressed as gateways. Prominent landmarks or focal points address the identity of the local environment and symbolize destinations.

The idea of passage from one place to another is inherent in the very nature of many types of infrastructure. Bridges are privileged structures in this respect, since they mark a connection and also highlight the transition between two sides. Numerous examples could prove this point and the one employed here, a bridge traversing a gorge in the mountains of Switzerland, is a surprising threshold expression in a natural setting [1]. Its curving momentum is simple, light, and graceful – celebrating the crossing of rushing water below in an otherwise wild and remote landscape. In another pedestrian bridge, the symbolism of crossing was pushed even further. The Memorial Bridge in Rijeka, Croatia, links the historical city to its post-industrial port area and marks the spot where soldiers were sent to the front during the recent civil war. The functionally elegant bridge commemorates the passage it marks.

Not just the open-air crossing of territories but also highway tunnels – as routes literally bored through the landscape – powerfully mark transitions. The moment the dark confines of the tube conduit meet the open-air environment, light conditions, views, and broadened horizons are revealed. In Pittsburgh, Pennsylvania, the most magnificent entrance to the city is through the Fort Pitt Tunnel onto a bridge that spans a mighty river below. The city's skyline is framed by the tunnel opening and more intimately exposed as the journey to downtown continues [2]. Just as dramatic, but through a more naturalized landscape, are the series of tunnel (and road interchange) interventions on the completed 23-kilometer-long stretch of mountainous A16 highway between Delémont and Porrentruy in Switzerland. The twinning of tunnel gates creates stages of rhythm and measurement, while the striking architecture of the tunnel mouths and maintenance buildings underscores the idea of passage.

1 TIGHTENING PASSAGE
In the heavily wooded site of Boudry in western Switzerland, Geninasca Delefortrie connected the two banks of Areuse River – one formed by a low, open field and the other by steep rocks – with a graceful 27.5-meter-long arching footbridge. In plan, the sinuous S-shaped span narrows in width from 3.5 to 1.2 meters and constricts in section as it approaches the steeper bank. The passage through the steel-framed structure is mediated by slatted blades of dark-stained fir on the sides and top, filtering the sun, screening views, and accentuating the effects of perspective.

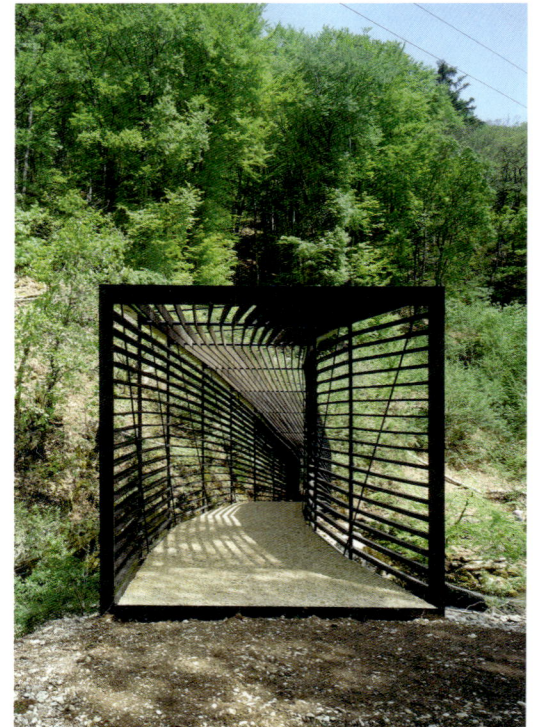

2 FRAMED VIEW

Before entering the I-279 Fort Pitt Tunnel at its southwest end, motorists observe the commonplace view of Western Pennsylvania's rolling green hills, but upon exiting at the northeast end, they are struck by the spectacular view of Pittsburgh's Golden Triangle skyline. The tunnel extends beneath Mount Washington before the power of the city is revealed from the Fort Pitt Bridge that crosses the Monongahela River.

3 BEACON OF LIGHT

The asymmetrical, parabola-shaped, 50-meter-high metal-frame lighting tower was specifically designed to function as a city beacon and to provide adequate illumination at a crossroads between the A86 highway, the railroad line, and the new bridge of La Courneuve, France. The tower, by Marc Mimram (architect-engineer) and Alexandre Chemetoff (landscape architect), solves the problem of "patchy linear lighting" by creating a central system of smooth circular lighting of the ground from a single source.

4 ESCALATOR-ELEVATOR-BRIDGE

The Catalan town of Lérida, high in the Pyrenees and on the bank of the Segre River, is composed of urban terraces, culminating on a rocky plateau with its citadel, gothic cathedral, and upper historical district. In line with Joan Busquets' urban plan to revitalize the town, Lluís Domènech and Roser Amadó designed an outdoor escalator (built by the municipality), a 47-meter-high triangular elevator, a steel bridge, and a 20-meter-high retaining wall that hugs the topography and forms the new Palace of Justice that connects the upper and lower cities through a new system of public spaces.

5 AERIAL UPLIFT

The city council of Medellín, Colombia's second largest city, is actively trying to overcome the city's association with danger and insecurity related to the vast criminal organization called the Medellín Cartel. Liberalized development policies have gone hand in hand with investment in education, security, and accessibility. In line with this policy, the metro system has been expanded with a number of Metrocable lines – hydraulically powered aerial tramways designed to reach a number of the poorest and least-accessible barrios (informal housing neighborhoods) that are built on the steep terrain of the Aburrá hillsides.

6 WEIGHTLESS TRANSITION

The Naoshima Ferry Terminal in the Shikoku region by SANAA (Kazuyo Sejima + Ryue Nishizawa) links this tourist and art-centered island to the larger islands of Japan's archipelago. The minimalist, super-lightweight, and transparent structure modestly accommodates ferry functions and provides a large flexible space for various public events under a massive and light roof (70 meters long, 52 meters wide, 15 centimeters thick) that rests on slender tubular columns (85 centimeters in diameter). The dematerialization of this structure underlines the inherent beauty of the Inland Sea landscape.

The notion of thresholds along vehicular transport routes is, to a certain degree, commonplace. Entrance and exit ramps, tollbooths, and crossings of other hierarchies in the mobility system all mark alterations of the rhythm along the line. However, there are occasions when the notion of gateway is unambiguously developed – as is the case with the lighting tower on La Courneuve, France, where the object is something between an instrument and monument, functional and yet symbolic [3]. Similarly, on the outskirts of Melbourne, Australia, the Craigieburn Bypass is configured as a functional and scenographic noise wall and an expressive northern framing of the city. The design explores how otherwise static objects begin to reveal a dynamic movement activated by the motorist.

In some instances, the challenges of topography require other types of transition. In the medieval Spanish hilltown of Lérida, a promenade of exterior escalator, public elevator, and bridge links the lower commercial town to the historic citadel city [4]. In Medellín, Colombia, the necessity of public transport, difficulty posed by steep topography, and limited surface available at the ground floor sparked the development of Metrocable lines that create a transition from the city core to housing areas in the air [5]. In Portland, Oregon, an aerial tramway connects a hillside health facility to an expansion area on a riverfront site with a simple yet powerfully expressed series of support towers and landing stations.

In addition, there are the ferry terminals, perhaps the sharpest representation of thresholds because they literally constitute the doorstep to another shore. Japan's Naoshima Ferry Terminal elegantly announces its presence with a lightness that emphasizes the surrounding landscape more than the functional space of the terminal itself [6]. In Cape Town, South Africa, the terminal serves as a highly charged departure point to Robben Island, the infamous site where political prisoners were detained during the apartheid era. The threshold is designed with modesty and respect and avoids the commercial gluttony that typically dominates tourist civic spaces of this kind. And, finally, there is a quite particular threshold between land and water: that of a lock and dike system in Enkhuizen, the Netherlands, where architects Zwarts & Jansma with landscape architect Lodewijk Baljon projected a "water bridge" that cleverly allowed naval and road traffic to be celebrated as important gateways.

Folded Memorial

RIJEKA MEMORIAL BRIDGE

Rijeka, Croatia

Architect: 3LHD

Date: 1997–2001

The Memorial Pedestrian Bridge plays the dual role of Croatian war memorial and link. It is an unostentatious memorial to the most recent era of death and destruction during the Balkan conflict and also serves as a footbridge connecting the city's historic center with its former port in the east – an area now separated from the old city by a canal, but slated to become a public park. The architects wanted the bridge to be a monument and to balance the utilitarian and symbolic functions, construction and form. The structure consists of two archetypal elements: a super-thin, box-steel plank (47 meters long with a 35.7-meter clear span, 5.4 meters wide, and only 65 centimeters thick) laid over the canal as the bridge and a 9-meter-high concrete slab driven into the

earth as the monument. These two elements form an L-shape in which the horizontal of the bridge meets the vertical of the monument. Symbolic emphasis is accomplished by a cleft in the vertical element and a red memorial slab embedded in the walkway as a shadow of the void.

This strikingly abstract yet contemplative bridge and memorial is simultaneously inviting to cross and works as a barrier that requires conscious perception of the object. The cleft in the vertical is just wide enough for the passage of one person. Reminiscent of a tombstone, the tall, geometrically pure wall is confronting, forcing groups to walk single-file through the aluminum-magnesium-clad monoliths. At night, a thin LED

beam located in the teak handrail on the glass railing magically illuminates the plank and defines the edges of the monoliths and the red path between them. A small plaza at the bridge's east end continues the utilitarian and commemorative balance. Cantilevered, L-shaped benches of steel and teak echo the bridge, while the scar of crushed red brick and epoxy remind us, again, of the bloodshed. It is the place where Croatian soldiers were sent off to war. The 150-ton steel structure of the bridge was constructed in a local shipyard and floated into position on a specially adapted barge. It was able to pass under other bridges at low tides, and was positioned by turning the barge round at high water and reducing its height in the water.

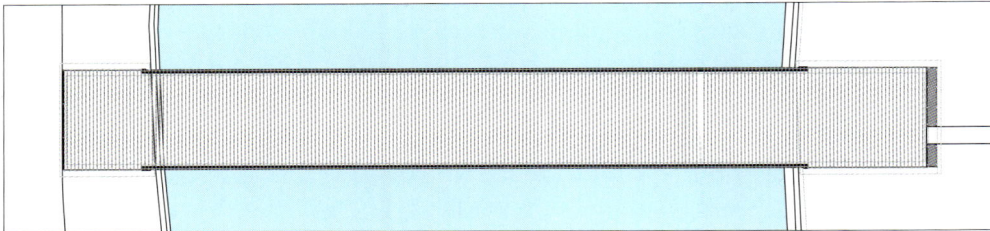

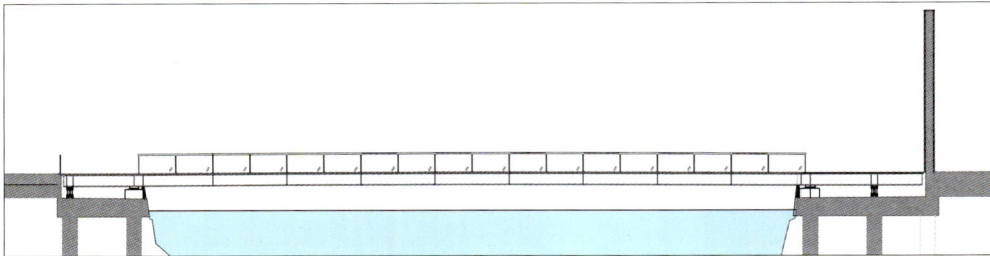

Tunnel Artifices

A16 HIGHWAY

Bienne (Switzerland) to Belfort (France)

Architect: Renato Salvi and Flora Ruchat-Roncati (section 4, 5, 6), Renato Salvi (section 3, 7/8)

Date: 1988–1998 (section 4, 5, 6), 1998–2008 (section 3, 7/8)

The architectural language of the A16 Transjurane highway, which follows a route across the Jura mountain range between Bienne in Switzerland and Belfort in France, explicitly celebrates the notion of thresholds. An entire repertoire of components was developed as a family of recognizable parts – from the tunnel entrances with the necessary ventilation towers to the formal cut-and-cover tunnel, abutments, pylons, and balusters of bridges, viaducts, and power stations. The appearance is one of clear-cut forms and powerful geometries, all rendered in rough concrete. Each solution is singular, but the common vocabulary assembles them into a succession of memorable events. This marriage between the pragmatics of engineering and the poetics of passage is successfully conveyed in a number of tunnel entrances and egresses that are convincingly suited to the scale of the landscape as portals to the mountainside.

Renato Salvi, who has been working for twenty years on the project, constructed an artificial landscape that not only emphasizes the uniqueness of the natural scenery but also distinguishes the route that one follows. His thresholds mark sections of the landscape and set up a rhythm. They initiate an entry and exit point with a majestic gesture and repeat the same vocabulary and design solution at both ends of the valley one encounters in between. By replicating the succession of access portals in both directions, the architect is able to architecturally mark the transition from each segment of the A16 to the next. Examples of this design device are the four ventilation intakes, which are installed at the tunnel entries to Mount Terri and Mount Russelin. By their dimension and form, they take on a symbolic value against the background of the rugged landscape. At the northern side of Mount Terri and the southern side of Mount Russelin, the entries to the tunnels read as impressive doorways, each articulated as three elementary volumes of strong angles and determined forms, strange objects in a romantic landscape. The

ventilation shafts on the southern side of Mount Terri and the northern side of Mount Russelin appear as slotted masks against the face of the mountains. Two sizeable structures facing each other at both ends of the Grippons interchange are defined by concrete fans cut by the louvers that admit fresh air. They appear as two giant tombstones or totems, marking the direction of the highway in the flank of the mountain. Finally, the spent-air-extraction conduit of the Russelin Tunnel appears as a crack in the mountain, protected by high concrete walls and able to receive service vehicles. It hides a base on which the cylindrical volume (more than 35 meters high) of the extraction stack sits, inclined by 28 degrees from the natural slope of the site. A service elevator drops down the more than 300-meter-deep shaft that descends into the depths of the mountain to reach the highway tunnels to permit maintenance work. Elements apparently extraneous to the landscape have become design tools for enhancing it and creating imposing thresholds.

Porrentruy (section 3) portal Banné Est – viaduct Rasse – portal Perche Ouest

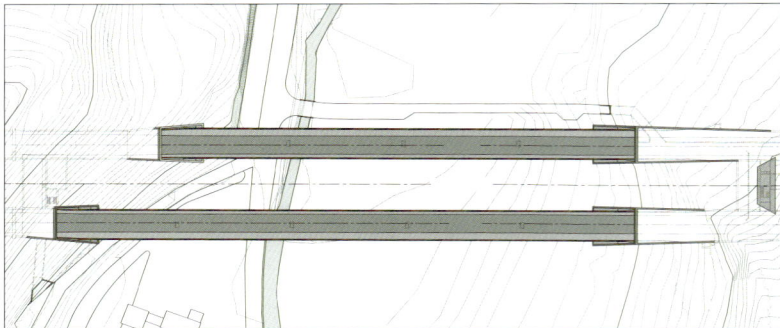

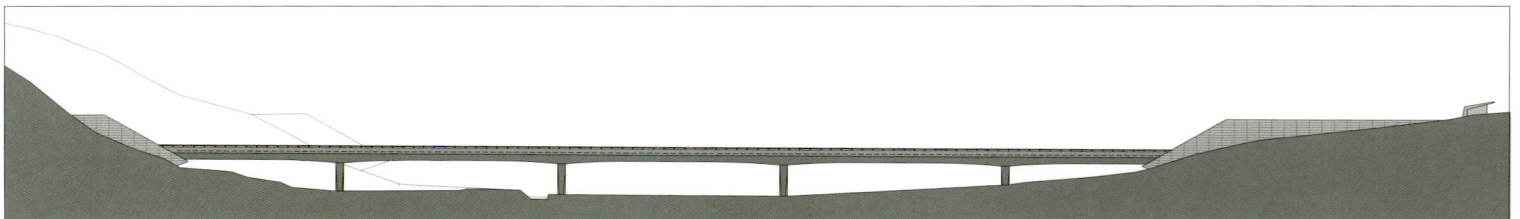

St.-Ursanne (section 5) portal Russelin Nord

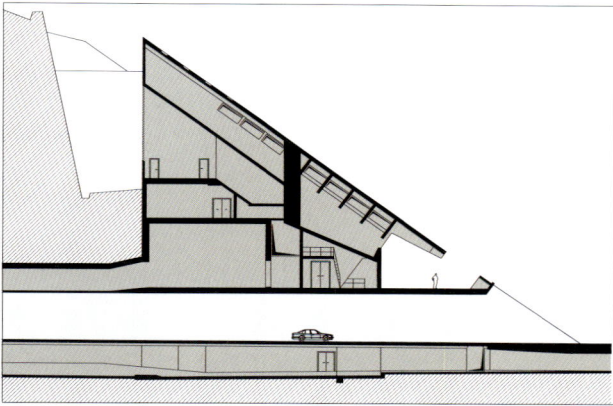

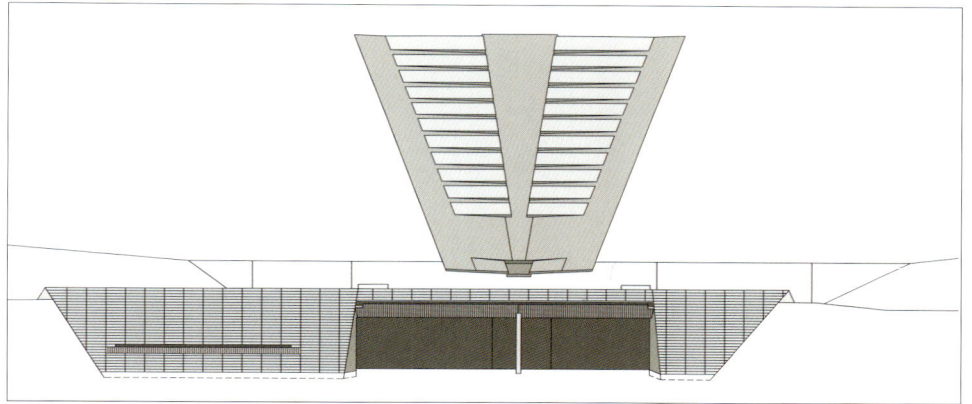

St.-Ursanne (section 5) portal Terri Nord

Sinuous Steel & Blue Blades Gateway

CRAIGIEBURN BYPASS

Melbourne, Australia

Architect: Tonkin Zulaikha Greer

Landscape Architect: Taylor Cullity Lethlean

Artist: Robert Owen

Date: 2003–2005

The northern gate to Melbourne on the 17-kilometer-long Craigieburn Bypass (alleviating congestion on the Hume Highway, the conduit connecting the city to Sydney) is simultaneously a noise attenuation wall, a dynamic sculptural element, and a pedestrian passageway. The Craigieburn Bypass was conceived as a sequential gateway experience at a speed of 110 kilometers per hour. Two types of noise wall were developed, each reflecting very different contextual surroundings. Coming from the north, the motorist is first confronted by the scrim wall that protects one of Melbourne's dormitory suburbs. It transfers the image of the domestic vernacular that characterizes this environment to the grand scale. This first sound wall resembles a giant window, with sandblasted, patterned acrylic panels (with a filigree reminiscent of lace curtains) and a

rhythm of 10-meter-high, striking blue vertical louvers (reminiscent of Venetian blinds) in front of the acrylic panels. The louvers, although compositionally static at a singular view, are rotated five degrees on axis in relation to each successive post. This creates a spinning effect at speed, an impression of constantly opening and enclosing as the motorist travels past. At night, the acrylic panels of the scrim wall are illuminated by *Northern Lights*, an artwork produced by electrical impulses that reflect the intensity of traffic stimuli by changing LED sequences.

As the scrim wall ends, a dramatic gateway frames the Melbourne skyline. It crosses the highway and primarily serves as a pedestrian bridge from the eastern residential area and linear park to the western authentic land-

scape – the ancient basalt plains, Craigieburn grasslands, and Merri Creek catchment area. But this majestic gesture does not stand alone. For the driver entering Melbourne, it constitutes the apotheosis of the scrim wall and is clearly part of a more wide-ranging signal. The bridge, a complex curve in plan and elevation, is a tubular steel truss covered with facetted weathering steel sheets modeled in simple concave and convex folds. Its material and tectonic language is continued in a second sound wall type – the curtain wall – a gently undulating, fluid ribbon of weathering steel waving in the wind and floating on a recessed base of dark concrete. The dark-gray roughly textured concrete base provides continuity between the two wall types.

High-Flying Urban Link

PORTLAND AERIAL TRAM

Portland, Oregon, USA

Architect: agps architecture (M. Angelíl, S. Graham, R. Pfenninger, M. Scholl)

Engineer: Ove Arup & Partners (structural/mechanical); Dewhurst Macfarlane and Partners (facade engineering);
GeoDesign (geotechnical); W&H Pacific (civil)

Date: 2003–2007

Portland, Oregon, lies in a valley at the confluence of the Willamette and Columbia Rivers in the Pacific Northwest. It has a spectacular landscape with Mount Tabor rising on the city's east side and with Mount Saint Helens and Mount Hood visible from many places in the city. Its aerial tramline connects the hillside Oregon Health and Sciences University with an expansion campus area under construction on a defunct shipbuilding site on the Willamette River. An aim of the city's well-known planning measures was to improve the quality of Portland's urban core and metropolitan area by introducing territorial growth limits, densification strategies, and networks of public transportation. The tramline is approximately one kilometer long, spans a ravine, and runs high above the city's old

historic district, urban parks, and an eight-lane highway. By its very nature, it constitutes an urban link where the boarding of the sky tram, and the experience of the amazing panorama the aerial ride provides, mark a prominent and potentially much cherished threshold.

The tramline is designed as a minimal intervention in the urban fabric. Its light and open forms make the transportation infrastructure almost invisible. The whole enterprise includes an upper station, an intermediate support tower, a lower station, and two tram cars, which operate in a jig-back configuration. The upper station is an open-air covered platform supported by asymmetrically skewed braced steel legs balancing on a steep site and wedged between

hospital buildings, one of which is connected to the ninth floor of the station by a bridge. The intermediate tower is built of steel plate. Shaped in response to statics, it leans at a 90-degree angle to the tram cables; it is wider at the base, tapering as it moves up to provide clearance for the tram cars and then flares outward to support the saddles. The lower station, a covered open platform at street level, is the public center of its new neighborhood. Like the upper station, its steel frame is internally and externally clad with expanded-aluminum mesh panels that are animated by shimmering moiré patterns. The tram car, curvilinear with reflective aluminum and glass, is designed to dematerialize against the sky as it passes over the urban neighborhood below.

Gateway of Dignity

ROBBEN ISLAND FERRY TERMINAL

Cape Town, South Africa

Architect: Lucien le Grange Architects & Urban Planners

Date: 1999–2001

For nearly 400 years, Robben Island, 12 kilometers from Cape Town in Table Bay, was a place of banishment, exile, isolation, and imprisonment. It was a place for political troublemakers, social outcasts, and the unwanted of society. The island served as a leper colony from 1836 to 1931 and as a maximum security prison for political prisoners until 1991. South Africa's former President and Nobel Peace Prize winner Nelson Mandela spent 18 years of his 27-year sentence in a tiny cell on Robben Island. Today, the island is a place of pilgrimage, a tourist haven with grand-scale political mythology of the somber days of its apartheid past. Unsurprisingly, the new ferry terminal has been named the Nelson Mandela Gateway and its construction initiated renewal of the Victoria and Alfred Waterfront. The terminal doubles as a landside museum, a preamble to the heritage of the island. Its overall architectural composition reinterprets the classical language of plinth and porch to designate its civic nature while simultaneously operating as a gigantic window to Table Mountain.

The ferry ride itself symbolizes a major transition from freedom to imprisonment and the terminal works as a powerful threshold. Located between the Clock Tower Square and the edge of the waterfront, the building serves as a point of embarkation. The structure was conceived as a quiet and modest transitional space and informed by a number of themes and metaphors, including the building as a giant portal, a prospect between different conditions, and a vessel that conveys the island's message to the mainland via a permanent exhibition of images, archival material, and audiovisual devices. The building, extremely transparent and making use of explicit public components like square and forecourt, is one of reserved dignity and strong urban presence. Its slate facade makes direct reference to the slate-clad prison on Robben Island. The terminal is neither a destination in itself nor a monument, but an opening and gateway between different conditions.

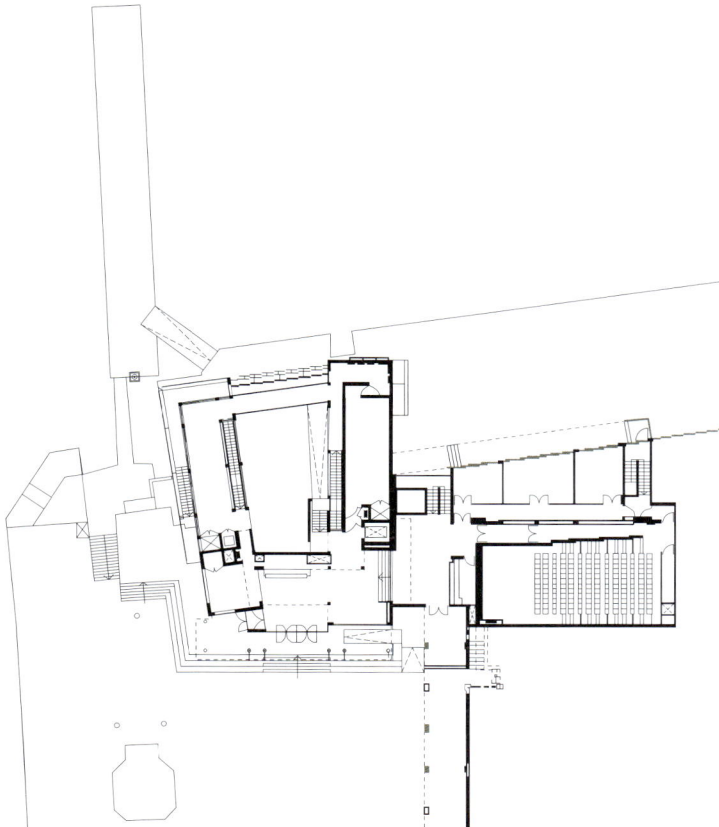

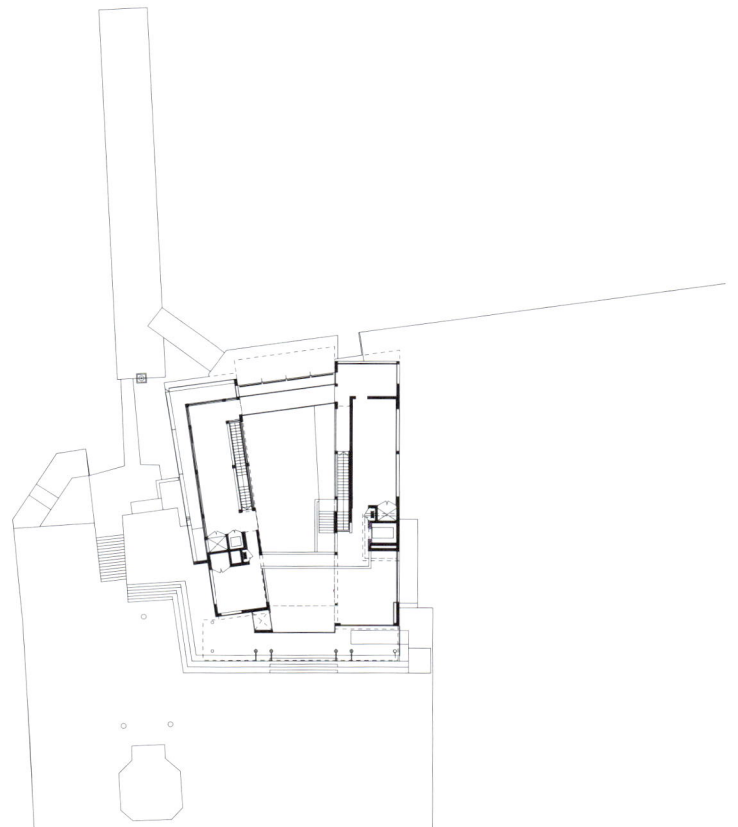

Landscaped Lock

ENKHUIZEN NAVIDUCT AND DIKE

Enkhuizen, the Netherlands

Architect: Zwarts & Jansma Architects

Landscape Architect: Lodewijk Baljon

Date: 1998–2003

Due to its limited capacity, the Krabbegat Lock in the Netherlands resulted long waiting times, not only for the boats that used it for entering the primarily recreational port of Enkhuizen from the IJsselmeer but also for the traffic on the Houtrib Dike between Enkhuizen and Lelystad, which had to pass over this lock by a drawbridge. The new lock complex, east of the existing one and commissioned by the Dutch Directorate-General for Public Works and Water Management, avoids the conflict between naval and road traffic by lowering the road below the lock. At the same time, it tremendously enlarges the lock capacity by installing two separate lock chambers, each 120 meters long and 12 meters wide. As such, the new infrastructure simultaneously works as a lock and an aqueduct – hence its designation as a "Naviduct."

The Naviduct clearly operates as an immense threshold for the vessels entering the local port of Enkhuizen. By its configuration, the lock is positioned in the dike and acts as a passageway between two large bodies of water. Because the roadway passes under it, the lock is disconnected from the earth rather than buried in it, as is usually the case. It appears as a "water bridge," a passage of water over a void, a sensation that certainly accentuates the character of threshold. Finally, the dike raised on the IJsselmeer side to protect the new lock from high waves and floating ice gives way to an artificial lagoon, an enlarged channel acting as a doorway through which vessels have to pass before approaching the Naviduct and the port.

This new dike, conceived as an integral part of the overall intervention by Dutch landscape architect Lodewijk Baljon, is an intelligent way to use the mass of silt and earth generated by the digging of the lock and the road underneath. The outer side of the dike was configured as a tight curve with a riprap revetment. The leeward side was planned as a lagoon area featuring elongated creeks, with the intention of nurturing a biotope with natural vegetation into a habitat for undisturbed wildlife. The contrast between the clear geometry and the bright concrete appearance of the lock, on the one hand, and the meandering naturalness of the protection dike, on the other hand, only heightens the functional character of both elements.

THE MONTAGE OF DISTINCTIVE SEQUENCES

The succession of identifiable sections on a journey constitutes a sequential chain of events. Rather than the episodic value of the transition points, it is the nature, rhythm, and progression of consecutive components that mark the identity of the route. In the contemporary era of transport and mobility, the image of towns and landscapes perceived by the moving spectator is increasingly emblematic for promoting their uniqueness. In the design of contemporary infrastructure, this notion of sequential diversity marking the distinctiveness of the place one crosses routinely underlies many a design approach. It comes to the fore in various new road schemes of successive and differentiated section profiles, but somehow appears more attributable to the existing surroundings, or the coincidental succession of tunnels, gallerias, panoramas, river crossings, canopies, and filtered prospects. Points of reference, variation in radii of curvature, texture of surface, distance and location of visual markers can simultaneously elaborate a sense of continuity, create variants that avoid too much monotony, and establish perceptible rhythm. The most illustrative cases are those in which the intervention intensifies the geographic constituents of the existing landscape, thereby reinforcing the meaning of the urban or landscape section at hand.

The designers of the new E4 highway in Sweden wanted to mark the districts along the route by embellishing each highway exit and the surrounding landscape in a different way [1]. The aesthetics of the highway are conceived as the basis of visual sequences for the observer in motion; the various sequences reflect the meaningful landscape found by the roadside. The qualities and differences of the existing landscape are recognized and enhanced along the route with subtle yet powerful landscape moves. In Sundsvall, the route becomes a point of orientation, the access roads designed intelligibly and with variety to punctuate and mark travel. Similarly, for Helsingborg, the narrowest point of the Øresund, the six differently designed sections choreograph the approach to the city center. At Norrköping on Bråviken, a bay on the Baltic Sea, an even more differentiated set of seven sequences with four differently designed sections marks the route along different landscapes, with columnar poplars employed for orientation.

A similar and even more radical expression of creating sequential singularity is employed in the design of tramways that a number of midsize French cities (including Nantes, Grenoble, Montpellier, and Bordeaux) have convincingly used as motors for restructuring open space within their city. In Strasbourg, the tramway system has successfully restructured entire neighborhoods along its route. From the Hoenheim terminus station – the powerful and effective interface between car and tram by Zaha Hadid (see page 88) – the tramway operates as a moving walkway in the city, endowing edges with unprecedented vitality and dynamism. The landscape treatment along the tramline itself – from a grassy green in the north, to the mineral sur-

1 DISTINCTION BY SECTION

In the north of Sweden, the new E4 highway formed the impetus to rethink the entrance to a number of cities. In Sundsvall, the drive from the highway interchange to the city center was conceptualized as a "voyage in six acts," and interventions underline broad vistas of the sea that alternate with wooded hills.

2 INTERCHANGE COMPOSITE

The rail and bus terminal in Santo André, Brazil, creates a series of different sequences for road and pedestrian traffic through and over a highway in a peripheral postindustrial area. Architects Marcelo Ferraz and Francisco Fanucci designed a bus terminal that operates as an armature linking residents to potential new programmatic areas. The building is a passerelle, a bridge that crosses the train tracks and transforms into a mezzanine overlooking the bus terminal. It is intended as a spark for urban renewal. The circulation structure becomes a new topography that also functions as an outlook beacon over the industrial landscape.

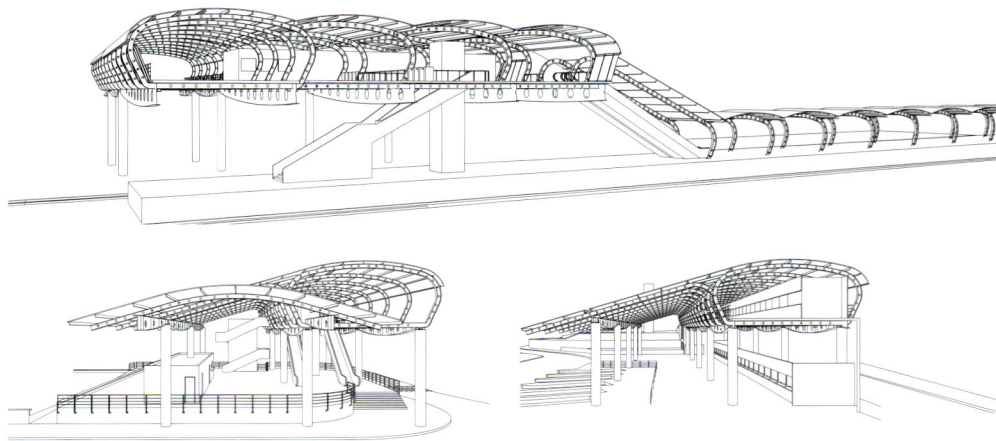

3 BRIDGED SEQUENCES

The Normandy Bridge (by Michel Virlogeux, François Doyelle, Charles Lavigne), an elegant cable-stayed concrete and steel structure that spans 856 meters over the Seine River and connects Honfleur to Le Havre, is part of a larger sequence that extends over the entire width of the estuary. Crossing the sparsely populated area of industrial estates along the Grand Canal, parallel to the river and at a high altitude to allow the passage of large vessels, a curved bowstring viaduct acts as a prelude for the grand finale of the bridge, whose elegant A-shaped pillars support a majestic bundle of cables that demarcate a translucent enclosure with breathtaking views of the river.

faces of the city center to the gravel bed through the southern industrial area – becomes an identity of distinction amidst the continuity of the movement corridor. One could say that the tramway is configured like a chameleon: it takes on the colors of the background it traverses. From the tram window, images of the landscape and buildings multiply, simplify, and compress into montage-like sequences.

The slower speed of pedestrian movement was the basis of the altering settings along the river and coastal promenade of Porto and its sister city of Matosinhos. The distinctiveness of the urban and landscape geography led to a wonderful collection of interventions by a number of renowned urban designers, each of them taking up in the transversal section the quintessential character of the historical relationship between settlement and river/sea. In its total length, the promenade thus engenders a perception of the territory through the establishment of formal compositions, intervals, accents, and priorities in the interesting topography, and coexistence of simultaneous landscapes. It is explicitly choreographed and highlights the beauty of the natural and constructed landscape. The pedestrian route is also a chief component of the train and bus interchange station and terminal in Santo André, Brazil [2]. The montage effect is realized twofold: by transformation of the postindustrial context itself; and by movement through the structure, which is essentially a bridge and covered walkway. Visual sequences are staged for pedestrians as they pass though the subsequent sections of the elongated building and discover the new topography of this urban trail.

Finally, there are bridges themselves, where the distinctive sequences are usually a product of the physical constraints imposed by the obstacle to be crossed and the static options of overcoming the barrier. This proves especially evident in super-long bridges, whereby the engineering itself creates a succession of spatial experiences linked to horizontal and vertical movement. In Normandy, the A29 highway dramatically descends from the terraces along the cliffs before bottoming out at the vast expanse of the Seine valley, where the two imposing bridges – a curved bowstring supported by concrete columns at regular intervals and a cable-stayed construction supported by two enormous pillars at both ends of the wide river – highlight the differing conditions of the landscape they cross [3]. Perhaps even more dramatic is the Øresund Link that connects Denmark and Sweden by a journey through a grand-scale landscape by way of a clear sequence of experiences with an understandable narration of portals, gateways, spaces, traces, transitions, and monuments. Perhaps less broken up in landscape sequences, but just as powerful due to its sheer scale is the Hangzhou Bridge in the Yangtze River Delta in China. Owing to its magnitude, it joins a number of more or less independent constructions into a succession of distinctive parts.

Tramline Chameleon

STRASBOURG TRAM (LINE A)

Strasbourg, France

Architect: Norman Foster, Jean-Michel Wilmotte (tram stops); Guy Clapot (Place Kléber, Place de l'Homme de Fer); Gaston Valente, Richard Normand, Bernard Aghina, Bernard Barto (Place de la Gare, underground station)

Landscape Architect: Alfred Peter

Date: 1990–1994 (Line A)

Alfred Peter, the landscape architect of the tramway network in Strasbourg, unabashedly declares to "see the tram as a vehicle for designing public places." Since its creation in the early 1990s, the network has been the impetus to recreate the city's urban landscape. The 10-kilometer-long stretch of the first line (Line A) linking the northwest to southwest through the city center reprofiled existing roads by transforming three-lane car-oriented streets into single lanes and recuperating one lane each in each direction for tram and pedestrian circulation. The basic route was conceived as three distinct sequences, each taking clues from and enhancing the existing character of the adjacent urban tissues. The most northwesterly section — extending from the highrise neighborhood of Hautepierre to the edge of the city center, past the large hospital complex and the district of Cronembourg — was developed as a tramway through a grassy green and

dramatically reduced the overscaled street section to a new type of parkway with a separate tramway subdivision. Public space is thus introduced into an area that historically had none. Downtown, the material of the tracks — pink granite and pale concrete slabs — is similar to the facades along the narrow streets. In the south, the tramway was developed as a ribbon of tamped sand running along the middle lane of the former state highway to Colmar. Linden trees edge the track.

The tramway is a powerful spine that restructures the city and is able to endow the contexts it passes with a new vitality and dynamism. A new system of loops and highway ramps frees traffic in the city center and allows for an enlargement of the pedestrian zone. The tram — a moving walkway in the city — provides continuity while highlighting differences in the perception of the territory. It adapts to the territory it traverses

and establishes a vocabulary for the chain of public squares along its route for whose refurbishment it provides the opportunity. As a first gesture, Place Kléber was transformed from a traffic throughway into a pedestrian square. A ring-shaped pergola marks Place de l'Homme de Fer as the junction for the trams, buses, cars, and pedestrians. The city's station square, by Normand-Valente-Aghina-Barto, is a huge glass roof covering the underground tram station that is married to an intermodal connection (railroad and parking lot). Particularly striking, though, is the attention that the landscape design pays to the quality of street furniture and the refurbishment of tram stops in the poorer outer areas. Here, the tram is deployed as an instrument to enhance solidarity between different sections of the population by the careful treatment of public spaces in areas that are typically neglected.

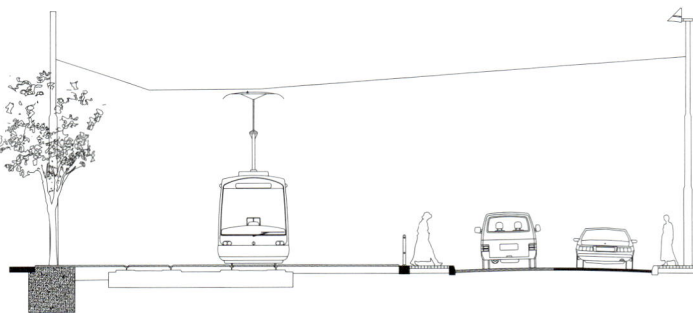

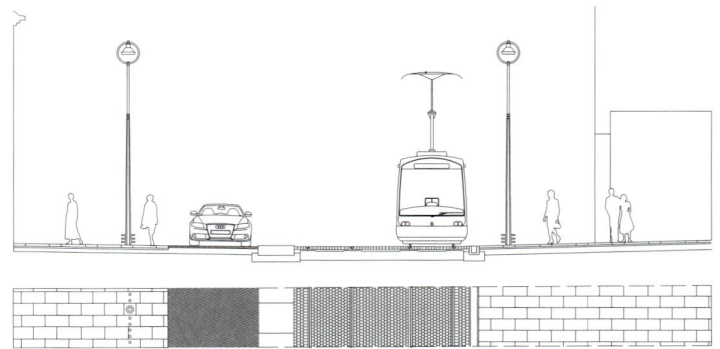

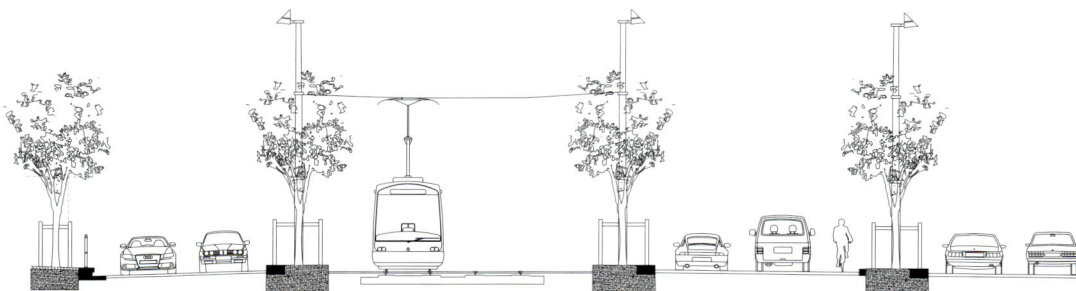

Shifting Waterfront Promenade

DOURO PROMENADE

Porto to Matosinhos, Portugal

Architect: Eduardo Souto de Moura (Atlantic promenade, northern Matosinhos), Manuel de Solà-Morales (Atlantic promenade, southern Matosinhos / northern Porto & city park), Manuel Fernandes de Sá (Douro Promenade & Marginal road bridge), Menos é Mais (restaurant pavilions); Landscape Architect: Beth Figueras and Isabel Diniz (southern promenade)

Date: 2000–2003

The transversal section of the Marginal, the coastal roadway that connects Porto to the Atlantic Ocean and the neighboring city of Matosinhos, has been restructured through a series of exemplary interventions by a number of renowned Mediterranean architects, urban designers, and landscape architects. This revitalization project was boosted by Porto's status as European Cultural Capital 2001 and the EU-funded Polis Programme. The most acknowledged part of this pleasant promenade is certainly the three-kilometer-long boardwalk in Matosinhos that has been realized along the seafront by Eduardo Souto de Moura (northern section) and Manuel de Solà-Morales (southern section). The layout of the Atlantic promenade by Souto de Moura is remarkable for its simplicity: a granite boardwalk (740 meters long, 19 meters wide), framed by a seating wall, which allows an unobstructed view of port activities and the sea. The promenade is to serve as the backbone of a number of future buildings along the waterfront. The section further south by de Solà-Morales is part of a larger effort to renaturalize the valley, and the

path was literally set into the coastal edge, with its irregular points and rocky valleys integrated and accentuated by the sensitive inclusion of a series of small retreats, viewpoints, terraces, support walls, and kiosks. The road embankment was demolished and replaced by a viaduct, which in turn created a natural system of beach and park as a new landscape with a palette of materials including wood, asphalt, concrete, and weathering steel. Concrete-framed flower beds, lowered into the ground, protect plants as well as visitors on windy days. By raising the local section of the Marginal on a viaduct, de Solà-Morales was also able to link the 60-hectare city park to the ocean. An open, four-story building acts as meeting point of the "green and blue" and frames panoramic views of the ocean and the inland landscape.

It should be noted that the exemplary public waterfront is only a segment of a wide-ranging project that embraces the successive neighborhoods along river mouth and sea. In each case, the particular response of individual designers has resulted in a sequence of layouts that respond to specific

local conditions. Along the Douro River, in the historic part of the city, it led to the refurbishment of the embankment, and to the sinuous curving bridge over the river by Manuel Fernandes de Sá, which routes traffic away from the quayside to preserve the 18th-century quay wall and hide the city's new sewer system. Further downstream, a series of transparent steel-and-glass box restaurants have been constructed by Menos é Mais in a large boardwalk park. Besides the reconfiguration of the public realm, the promenade joins together many noteworthy actions of revitalization, such as the renovation of the Serralves Museum (Álvaro Siza, 1997) and the Crystal Palace (José Manuel Soares, 1998) and the plan for the new housing district on the site of the former canneries in southern Matosinhos (Álvaro Siza, 1996). The entire project is remarkable for its driving force and constant reiteration of the coast's natural qualities, highlighted by that which can be newly constructed. The continuity of the promenade – contemplative rest and beauty of the changing scene – is distinguished by differences in architectural expression.

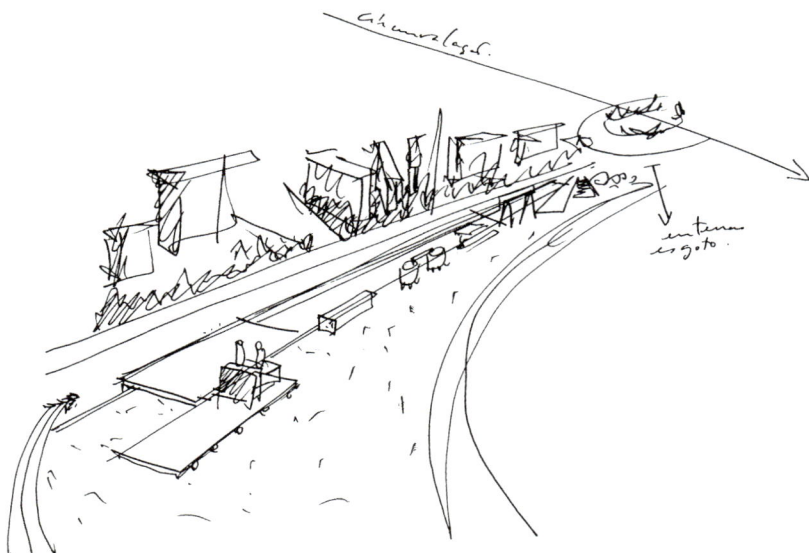

Atlantic promenade, northern Matosinhos

Atlantic promenade, southern Matosinhos / northern Porto & city park

Civil Engineering in Four Acts

ØRESUND BRIDGE AND TUNNEL

Copenhagen (Denmark) to Malmö (Sweden)

Architect: Georg K. S. Rotne

Engineer: ASO Group, Øresund Link Consultants

Date: 1992–2000

The Øresund Link, joining Denmark's capital (Copenhagen) and Sweden's third city (Malmö), is a part of the ambitious Trans-European Network connecting the countries in northern and eastern Europe to the Mediterranean. It comprises four vast civil-engineering enterprises joined to form a spatial sequence that makes the passage one of transience.

First, there is an artificial peninsula at Kastrup on the Danish side, which is characterized by technical complexes, logistical installations, and the route of the road and rail infrastructure, which is underscored by an earth berm between them. Slopes and retaining walls conceal the logistical installations and open up a series of differentiated views of the marine landscape. Second, there is the aluminum-clad and exposed-concrete sink tunnel (3.5 kilometers long) under Drogden. A screen of horizontal panels on the entrance and exit ramps eases the transition between daylight and artificial

light. Third in the sequence is the artificial island of Peberholm, the location and form of which was determined by the conditions of the strait, the distance to the seal and bird reserve of Saltholm, and constraints of depositing dredged material from channels and water traffic routes. The four-kilometer-long island marks the transition from the tunnel to the bridge. Finally, there is the curving bridge itself, an elegant two-level structure of steel trusses and diagonals. Trains travel within the truss itself, with four lanes of cars on the deck above. The truss has a constant 20-meter bay length along the full length of the bridge and a single span of 490 meters over the international navigation channel, which has a maximum headroom of 57 meters. The cable-stayed bridge and the viaduct together have a total length of 7845 meters.

This wide-ranging project is more than an impressive feat of engineering. Beyond the new connection it creates, it serves as an

international gateway and exemplifies the sensitive insertion of a large project into the fragile ecosystem of the Baltic Sea. Once an inland lake, this sea is one of the world's largest bodies of brackish water with unique marine life. Consequently, the construction of this project had to be undertaken in such a way that it obstructed the exchange movement of water as little as possible. The trajectory of the intervention – with the gentle swell of the great curves and the lack of dramatic abutments – relates to the wide sea and the rolling landscape on either side. The bridge is a series of episodes that extends from an open landscape in Denmark to a submerged tunnel with diminishing vanishing points, to a passage over a new island as a relaxed pause before the curved course of the bridge, to the vertical monument in the space defined by pylons in the center of the bridge, and finally to the landing on a protruding limestone deposit on the coast in Sweden.

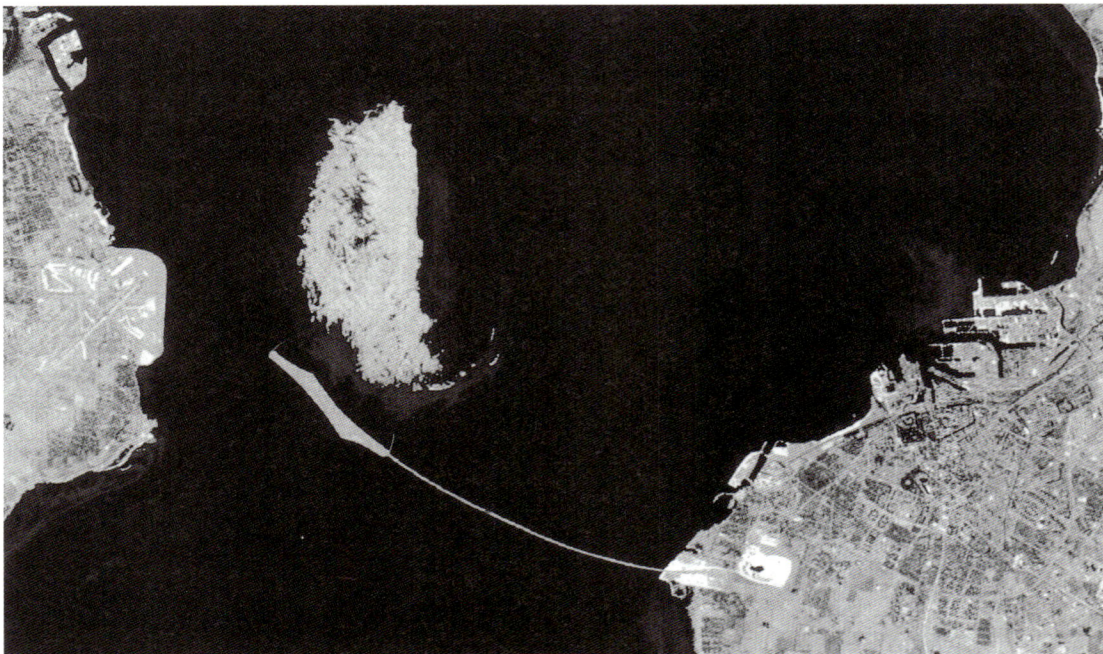

Impressive Concrete Reptile

HANGZHOU BAY BRIDGE

Hangzhou, China

Engineer: CCCC Highway Consultants

Date: 1994–2008

The Hangzhou Bay Bridge in the East China Sea connects the municipalities of Shanghai and Ningbo in the Zhejiang province. The bridge crosses the bay and spans the Qiantang River. This cable-stayed bridge is the longest transoceanic crossing in the world. It is located in China's so-called Golden Industrial Triangle between Shanghai, Hangzhou, and Ningbo (presently China's second largest cargo port) in the Yangtze River Delta. The delta presently accounts for 21% of the national gross domestic product and is home to 8% of China's total population. The vital bridge connection is expected to boost the already prosperous region to become the sixth largest urban agglomeration in the world after Paris, London, New York, Tokyo, and Chicago. The Hangzhou Bay New Zone (for investment in industrial areas), at the starting point of the bridge in Ningbo, is expected to boost industrial

output significantly. The bridge will be an important connection along China's East Coast Superhighway and will shorten the ground transportation distance from Ningbo to Shanghai by 120 kilometers and travel time from four to two hours.

The distinct sequences of the bridge are, to a certain degree, determined by its very construction. The S-shaped bridge is 35,673 kilometers long, 33 meters wide, and counts 6 expressway lanes (3 in each direction). The northern approach rests on low piers with posttension concrete box-girder spans and leads to the 448-meter-long cable-stayed span, with twin diamond-shaped towers. The middle bridge approach rests on low piers with 70-meter, posttension, concrete box-girder spans with a total length of 9.4 kilometers. The southern bridge, with an A-shaped single tower, has a span of 318 meters and is navigable thanks to

a clear height of 62 meters that enables fourth and fifth-generation container ships to pass through. Technically, the bridge structure had to overcome the strong waves and the fast waters of the Qiantang River, and withstand the frequent typhoons and earthquakes of up to 7.0 on the Richter scale. The southern landing area has three components: a section over the water (6 kilometers long), a mud-flat component (10 kilometers long), and a land section (3.2 kilometers long). Between the two spans is a 10,000-square-meter service island, which simultaneously serves as a sightseeing location for motorists (with hotels, restaurants, service stations, and a viewing tower) and supports rescue services. It is also expected that the island will become a tourist destination in and of itself for watching the Qiantang River. The service island will be built entirely on piers to avoid disrupting the tide.

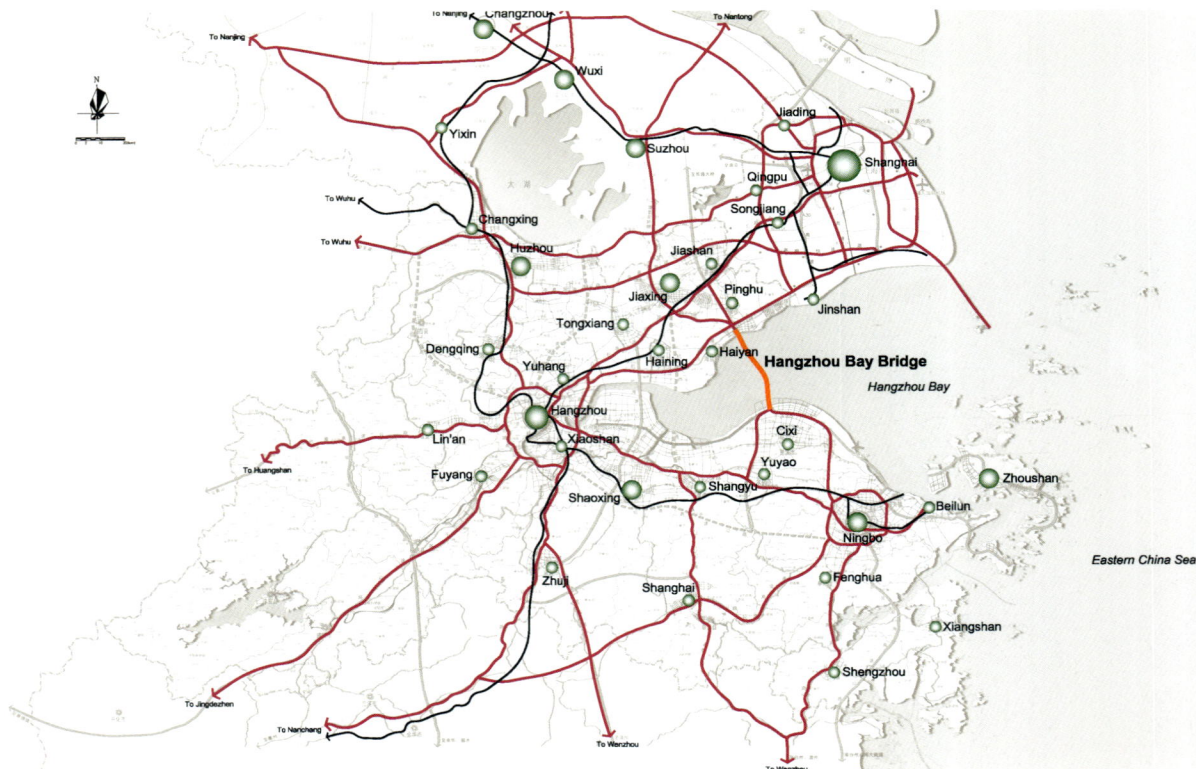

CONSTRUCTING A CINEMATOGRAPHIC ITINERARY

Ultimately, the moving view is very similar to a motion picture. It is constructed from a multitude of slightly varying images whose internal variation gives evidence of the movement. In that sense, most infrastructural projects influence the moving gaze in one way or another. However, there are differences. One could conclude, for instance, that emphasizing a limited number of distinctive sequences (see page 156) comes down to compressing a movie into a slide show. Even if none of the sequences can really be considered as stills, the distinction into separate scenes solidifies movement. Such an attitude reminds us of the picturesque approach. In the 19th century, though, the gaze changed as the observer moved about. The tram and train turned the built environment into something of a moving picture show, presenting the changing view of the passing landscape along a smooth horizontal trajectory. The view in motion is mediated by continuity versus fragmentation, speed versus slowness, and shifting versus empty spaces.

The cinematographic view becomes all the more evident with the advent of the automobile. The sensation of driving a car is primarily one of motion and space, felt in a continuous sequence. In 1966, Lawrence Halprin pointed to the "kinesthetic calligraphy" that the "crisscrossing geometries" of freeways offered to the driver.[1] In his opinion, the laws of motion created a sensation of art, of being positioned in the midst of a gigantic sculpture. Even today, this appeal of the fascinating beauty of the freeway intersection still exists among highway designers as a primary metaphor. It emblematizes an ultimate engineering proficiency by producing an autonomous piece of art, a sovereign experience. The intention of this design attitude is clearly not to relate to the landscape, but to *create* a landscape. Vision is the principal sense called upon (more than sound or smell) to induce an uninterrupted sense of spatial sequences. In the meantime, the creation of kinesthetic sensations and dynamic impressions for travelers extends far beyond roadway infrastructure.

Much of the work of the American artist Vito Acconci is emblematic of such an approach. He has stated that he strives to "design freedom" and create interactive links with users and onlookers alike. His preferred site is not the institutionalized museum, but highly visible and used public spaces. Both his bicycle parking structure in the Netherlands and the Mur Island bridge/ampitheater/playground/café in Graz, Austria, are introvert objects in their respective environments that force the public to engage with both the site and the world of the created object [1]. Their curved forms, changing volumes, and sweeping gestures engage the spectator in a continuous discovery of unremitting spatial and sensual evolution. Juxtapositions of nature and technology are thus synthesized into radical expressions of motion and movement.

1 SPIRALING AMONGST TREES

The never-ending loop of steel and polycarbonate that forms a free-standing bicycle storage facility around a group of three trees inside a park in The Hague creates a fluid and continuous movement. It is an animated object in the landscape in which the dramatis personae (the cyclists and the people moving away on foot) become part of the movie they watch while passing through. Acconci Studio combines function with fantasy in this project in which ramps are circulation and parking places and the central node of the structure is a floating, transparent dome that doubles as a guardhouse. Visitors park bicycles after entering the transparent tube and walking through the trees, finally emerging by the guardhouse to collect tickets before exiting down a ramp. The structure's support stanchions may be fitted with accessories and used as a playground at ground level.

2 JUMP CUTS AND PANS

The 200-meter-long Jan Schaefer Bridge by Ton Venhoeven, spanning the IJ River and connecting Java Island and Oostelijke Handelskade in Amsterdam, traverses abrupt changes of scenery that appear as jump cuts and pans framed by the trajectory and relative speed of three types of traffic: pedestrians, cyclists, and cars. An urban screenplay unfolds as a series of shots from diverse perspectives.

3 KINETIC FOOTBRIDGE

The reconstructed foot-bridge (62 meters long, 3 meters wide) in Évry, France, by DVVD Architects connects the rundown housing district of the Pyramids to Place des Miroirs. The helix-like steel footbridge creates a continuously changing tube that encloses the pedestrians and lets light pierce through. The structure of the bridge is a set of diaphragms connected by four tubular, helicoidally formed beams that rest on three bays of 24.4, 26.3, and 11.3 meters, all preserved from the former bridge. The light and playful bridge expresses the notion of flow, with the curve of the wooden deck and the four-meter rhythm of the diaphragms working as a kinetic whole and providing the neighborhood with an urban landmark.

4 INTERTWINED SPANS

Between Pont Royal and Pont de la Concorde in Paris, Marc Mimram's Solférino footbridge elegantly links the upper and lower embankments of the right and left banks of the Seine. The shallow deck of the single span between the upper embankments and the lower arch produces structural lightness and a high degree of transparency. Slung underneath and tied to the upper deck at its highest point, the arch links the lower quays and allows pedestrians to move from one level to another, allowing for two very different experiences of crossing the river. The cinematographic effect is created, on the one hand, by the framing — particularly on the lower crossing where the pedestrian is at the heart of the structure — and, on the other hand, by the very diverse perspectives of the surroundings.

In this regard, bridges, more generally, are typologies where a great deal of innovative design work is occurring. The Jan Schaefer Bridge spanning the IJ River in the Netherlands creates an urban screenplay, a new panorama composed of a series of successive impressions [2]. The area in which it is located, the eastern docks area of Amsterdam, is a motley assemblage of buildings and situations and the bridge cuts across the landscape and frames the abrupt changes of scenery as a well-directed cinematic experience. In Évry, France, the very shape and construction of a new footbridge by DVVD Architects creates a moving sequence of framed views through a series of twisted structural diaphragms [3]. In Paris, the 1999 pedestrian Solférino Bridge between Museé d'Orsay and Tuileries by Marc Mimram can be regarded as a predecessor to the Simone de Beauvoir Footbridge by Dietmar Feichtinger [4]. Both bridges generate a multiplicity of experiences and, in fact, are many bridges in one. They connect different urban levels and walkways, create artificial topographies, and reconcile technical logics with spatial experiences. They join technical and formal originality to indisputable urban usefulness. The Paris bridges majestically combine the crossing of the Seine with the interlinking of the higher and lower embankments that characterize the river section.

The cinematic effect is also powerfully displayed in terminals. In Salerno, Italy, the new maritime terminal by Zaha Hadid displays her signature dynamism and radical geometry. It emits a surreal abstract beauty that is highly cinematographic. Her forms seamlessly change shape, endowing the space with a fluid spatiality and making it morph as one passes. The multiplicity of perspectives rendered possible though flowing geometries is also the driving force of the Arnhem Central multimodal hub in the Netherlands by Ben van Berkel and Caroline Bos of UN Studio. Instead of a single heroic gesture, the asymmetrical interweaving of concavities creates an unexpected progression of dynamic and hollowed-out spaces, all abiding by the logistics of complicated infrastructural requirements. Finally, the Ground Transportation Center of the Incheon International Airport in South Korea by Terry Farrell and Partners applies a plasticity of form that is evocative of flight to an intermediary transport interchange of massive proportions. Farrell's projects, like many others that construct a cinematographic-like itinerary, feature spaces that work in succession, revealing a force of motion and forward momentum while creating different rhythmic intervals in a binding continuity.

1 Lawrence Halprin, *Freeways* (New York: Reinhold, 1966), 23.

Floating Fluidity

MUR ISLAND

Graz, Austria

Architect: Acconci Studio

Date: 2001–2003

This playful crossing over the Mur River in Graz was designed on the occasion of Graz European Capital of Culture in 2003. The island, made of glass and reticular steel, is 47 meters long and 18 meters wide. It is simultaneously a bridge, theater, café, and playground. By this intervention, the highly polluted (by sewage water and industrial effluent) Mur River – the previously neglected, back facade of the city – was strikingly turned into a provocative event space. The curved piers of the bridge turn into an island in the middle of the river, half-covered by a glass vault and half open in the shape of an amphitheater. The circulation route itself is a mischievous filmic event. The itinerary passes through the tube of the piers, which then becomes a dome that morphs into a bowl, then morphs into a dome and a tube again. Lucite and perforated-metal panels provide enclosure

and views out. Under the glass roof dome cooled by water, a café in blue and white offers the opportunity to enjoy being close to the river. The bowl functions as a theater, lined inside with transparent bleachers made of grating or perforated metal that steps down to a stage at the bottom of the bowl. When there is no show on, the bowl is used as a public space. The structure between dome and bowl serves as monkey-bars for children. The playground stretches into the dome and is usable both inside, behind the surface of the dome, and outside, on top of the water running down to the inside of the bowl.

Acconci's scheme conquered the fluvial space as a part of the urban fabric. Mur Island, literally and metaphorically, brought the Mur River back to the inhabitants of Graz. The hinged piers are anchored to the

gradually sloping shore while the island floats on large pontoons, allowing it to rise and fall with the water level in the river. The bridge connects the historic town center to newer neighborhoods on the other side of the river. The island also acts as a catalyst for further contemporary art and architecture initiatives in the city. Its inventive melding of form and function works as an inspiration for local artists and promoted the idea of "the city as theater." Originally intended as a temporary structure, Mur Island became so popular that it was maintained as a permanent fixture. The flowing structure is now a landmark in the city – even at night, when the access piers are illuminated from underneath, while the island is illuminated blue from within for navigation purposes.

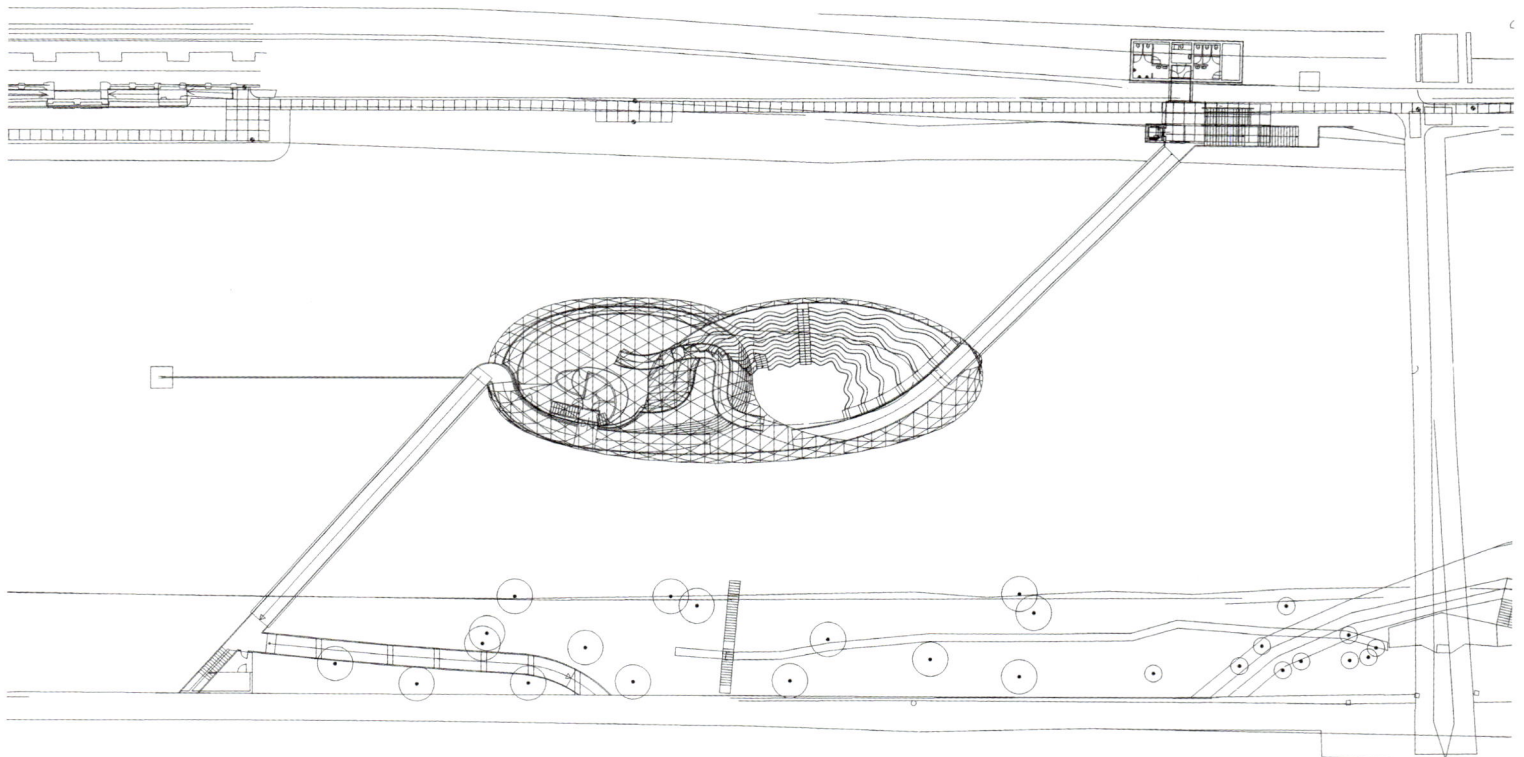

Arc & Catenary Crisscrossing

SIMONE DE BEAUVOIR FOOTBRIDGE

Paris, France

Architect: Dietmar Feichtinger Architects

Engineer: Rice Francis Ritchie

Date: 1999–2006

The light and elegant 270-meter-span Simone de Beauvoir Footbridge simultaneously links the postindustrial redevelopment site of the south bank of the Seine around the public plaza of the new François Mitterrand National Library with Bercy Park on the north bank and the two areas to the quayside promenades along the river. A slender arc in tension between the quays is balanced by a pretensioned, suspended catenary curve in compression in the opposite direction. The latter crosses the two busy roads parallel to the river and links the urban districts that were formerly separated by the Seine. The gentle incline of the structures permits easy access and a fluid crisscrossing of paths at the intersection of the two geometries. This option allows for a diversity of choice in routes to experience the river and urban landscape. The intersection of the arc and the catenary itself creates a symmetrical "lens," which serves as a two-story, 65-x-12-meter public space suspended above the water. It is the stabilizing element in the new landscape and was intentionally designed without furnishings. The upper area serves as a magnificent viewing platform that can be transformed into a grandstand seating area for entertainment events on the water. The lower terrace is conceived as a place for temporary installations or events – kiosks, fairs, used-books stalls and so on – and is sheltered by the platform above.

The footbridge has been efficiently constructed using the two levels to support each other. The decks are covered with oak slats, preventing slipping, and the aluminum handrail, with integral illumination, silhouettes the bridge at night. The woven-steel mesh of the balustrades conveys a sense of lightness and contrast to the steel structure, and the transparent net between the bridge and river provides security but does not hinder views. Pedestrians walk both on and in the structure, and the interweaving of the pathways responds to the force lines of the hybrid structure, enabling visitors to move down closer to or up away from the water. The bridge can be described as three paths running alongside one another while interweaving (in the sense of creating a ribbon), and opening up the landscape of the city and the river. From the arc of the bridge pedestrians can see Notre Dame Cathedral and the historic city center, while the path that links to the bridge's lower level directs the gaze to the water below. The bridge does not simply provide a way to reach a destination; it grants an opportunity to observe and experience the continuously changing landscape of the river crossing.

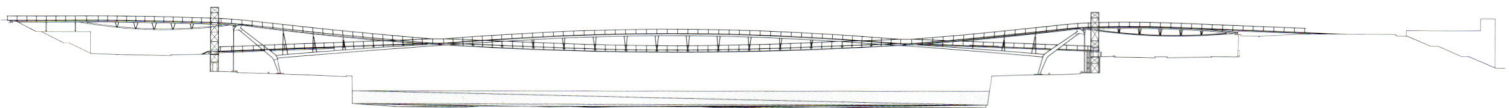

Dynamic Threshold

SALERNO MARITIME TERMINAL

Salerno, Italy

Architect: Zaha Hadid Architects

Date: 1999–2009

Salerno, located on Italy's renowned Amalfi Coast, is the geographical center of the so-called Tourist Triangle of the 3Ps (Pompeii, Paestum, and Positano). It is a tourist destination in itself and a great deal of ferry and cruise-ship traffic passes through its harbor. Zaha Hadid's new maritime terminal signifies a novel, intimate relationship between the city and water. Metaphorically, the terminal is likened to an oyster, with a hard protective shell and a soft fluid interior. While the large ribbed roof acts as the supporting structure and protection against the powerful Mediterranean sun, the interior of the terminal reads as a consistently fluid and softer landform that merges land and water. The terminal is composed of three main interlocking levels: administrative facilities, terminals for ferries, and a terminal for cruise ships. The entry floor provides a view of the structural set-up and the various amenities are evident and highly differentiated as spatial experiences in the dynamically sculpted form. The ground floor functions as the area where passengers purchase tickets and wait for departure; it is shaped and illuminated as a topography to guide passengers along the length of the terminal. As passengers ascend to the upper levels, they reach the boarding entrances to the ships. The route of daily commuters is the most efficiently organized and facilitates speed of movement.

The interconnected swathe of dynamic spaces is characteristic of Hadid's vocabulary and the sculpted lines and forms are strong in the visual and performative senses. The structure provides a smooth transition between land and sea, starting at ground level as an artificial landform and reaching the top as it melts away and presents the scene of an aquatic landscape. The bold form is both a transitional and a monumental space. Its lighting effect echoes the symbolic lighthouses of the city's Norman and Saracen past.

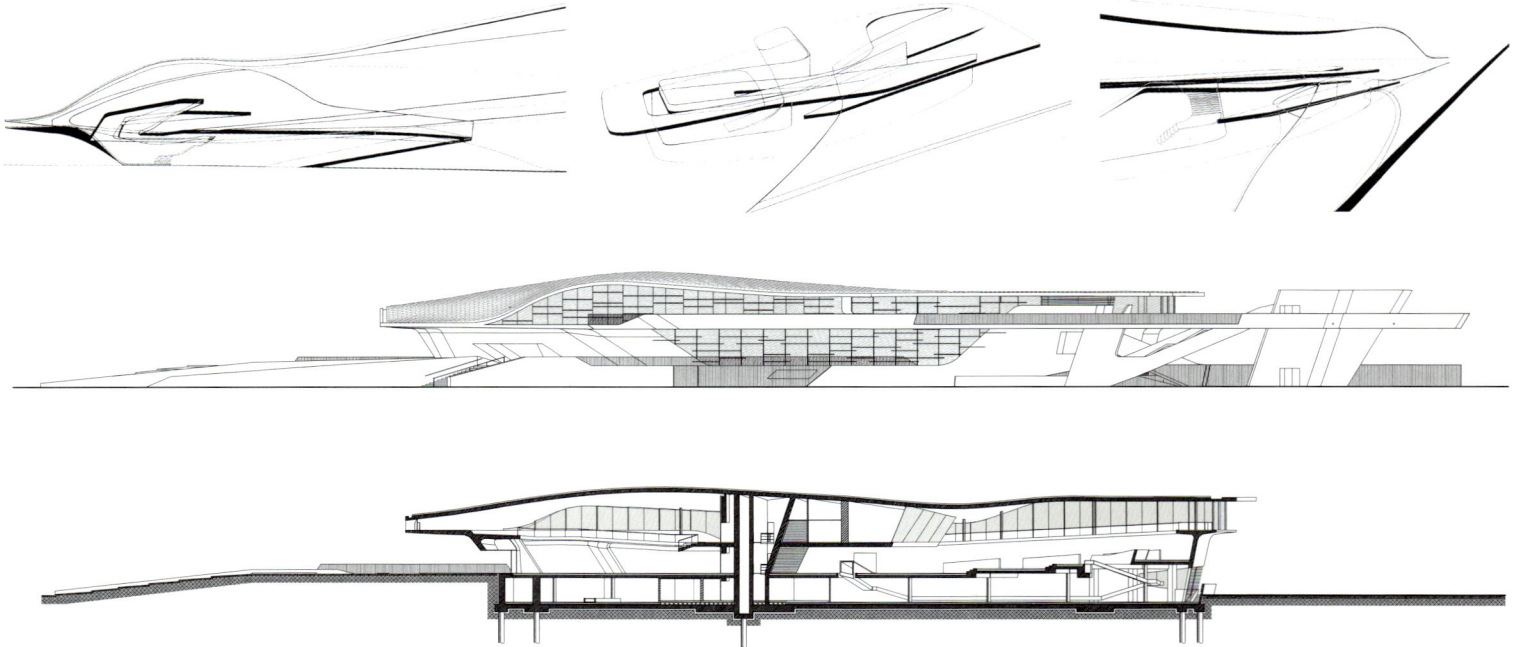

Fluid Transfer Zone

ARNHEM CENTRAL STATION

Arnhem, the Netherlands

Architect: UN Studio

Engineer: Ove Arup & Partners

Date: 1996–2020 (projected)

In Arnhem, the Netherlands, the area of the city's former railyards has been reconceived and rescaled to create a new multimodal transportation hub (including a new station hall, fourth station platform, bus terminal, railroad underpass, car tunnel, storage for 5000 bicycles, and parking garage for 1000 cars). A massive area of new development – 80,000 square meters of office space (in two 15-story towers) and 11,000 square meters of shops and 150 housing units – is also planned. The redevelopment area is organized as a roofed, climate-controlled plaza that connects with and gives access to trains, taxis, buses, bikes, parking, office spaces, and the route to the town center.

Movement studies were the cornerstone of the project and the city's natural topographical differences are exploited to create overlaps in circulation routes. Conceptually, the ground plane – traditionally at one level – has been multiplied and works in section to create a public realm that weaves vertically through the structure. The key to the project is the development of a series of dynamic blob-like fluid sections that encourage vertical pedestrian movement through the building's extra-large mega-form.

Logistically, the circuit routes of buses and cars were configured to be clear of pedestrian routes. The overlapping areas of shared interests, where one layer of urban landscape falls into another one, determined the placement of various program components. The massing allows natural light to penetrate the lower entrances to the station, garage, and offices, and creates clear and lengthy vision lines, aiding pedestrian orientation and giving an acceptable degree of safety and liveliness. The pedestrian flows, transport systems, lighting, construction, and distribution of entries and amenities fuse to form one continuous landscape. This flow chart and circulation pattern through the complex work as the kinetic spine that animates the whole megastructure development that is grafted on it.

level 24.5 + NAP

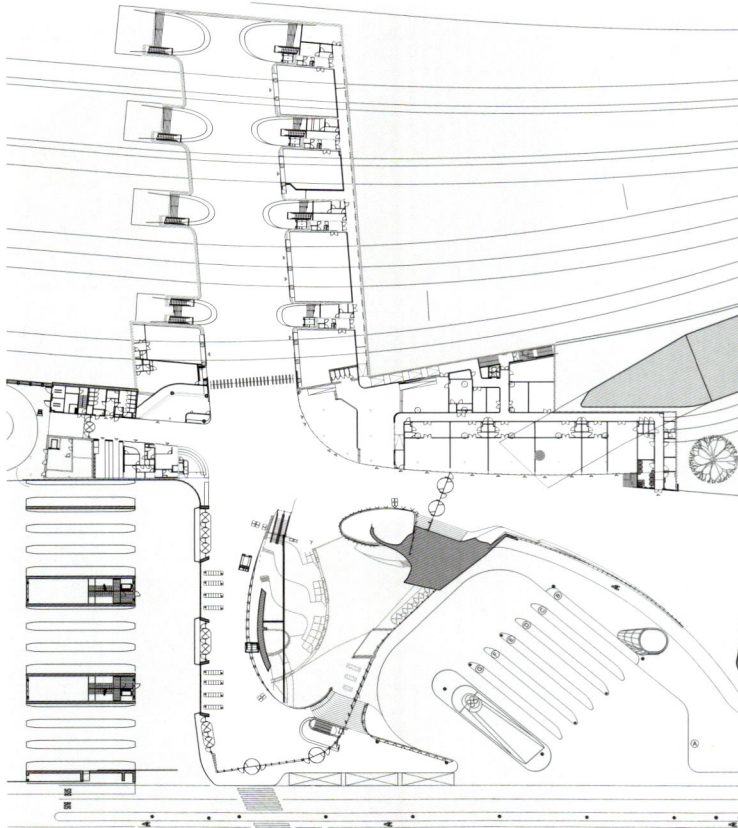

level 32.5 + NAP

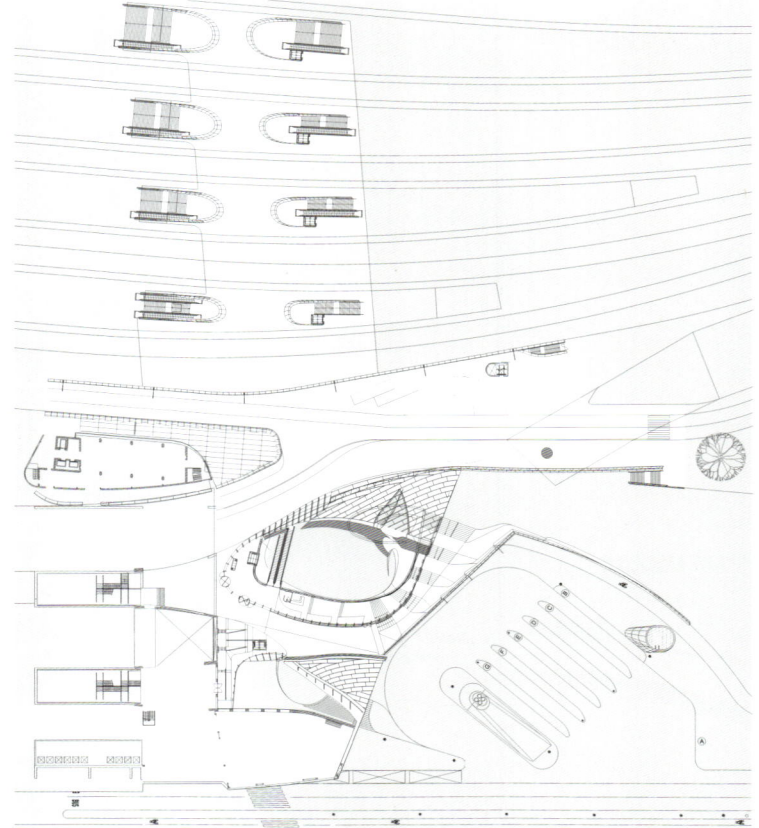

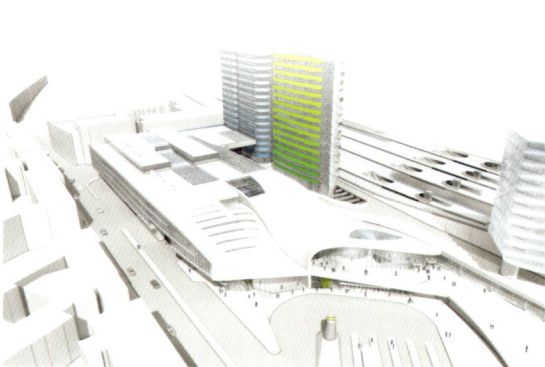

Terminal Transport Itineraries

Seoul, South Korea

Architect: Terry Farrell and Partners, with Samoo Architects and DMJM

Date: 1996–2002

INCHEON INTERNATIONAL AIRPORT

Incheon International Airport, 50 kilometers from Seoul, prides itself as the premier gateway to northeast Asia and expects to achieve an ultimate capacity of 100 million passengers per year. The global presence, regional ambition, and national inspiration of the airport itself are mirrored in the enigmatic and immense (250,000 square meters) Ground Transportation Center (GTC). Both accommodations are situated on an artificial island in the Yellow Sea. A freestanding structure between two existing terminals, the six-story GTC is conceptualized as a seamless transition from one mode of transport to another. It houses three rail systems (metro, standard train, and high-speed train); a bus and coach station; taxi, car rental, hotel, tour-bus pick-up points; and vast parking lots for 9000 cars. Terry Farrell

has combined the organizational intricacies of such a program with strong forms that allude to local myths and international aviation icons like Eero Saarinen's TWA Terminal at JFK Airport in New York.

The GTC complex nestles into the arc of one of the existing terminals. The many forms of ground transportation and the passengers they carry converge in a central 190-meter-span Great Hall, a truss-roofed, day-lit space that recalls the grand rail terminals of the Victorian Age and forms a dramatic tribute to arriving and departing aircraft at the airport. Its geometry and determined spatial expression lead passengers toward the adjoining terminals. A 200-meter-long glazed pedestrian gallery links the underground parking garage with the Great Hall,

while exterior parking areas are linked to the same space by long, low spreading wings. Sunken gardens between the Grand Hall and parking access gallery are landscaped in the traditional Korean style. They contrast with the sleek materiality and space-age flows of the interior, replete with a complex interplay of curves, tubes, and rich three-dimensional pierce-throughs. Atop the Great Hall is a dolmen-like steel-frame structure that evokes a bird in flight and functions as a wind accelerator to allow the GTC to be partially ventilated naturally. The scale of the complex, clad with stainless-steel panels and glass, makes it a grand civic gesture in the landscape. And yet, the intricacies of the interior and overlapping circulation routes create an array of interesting cinematographic spaces and itineraries.

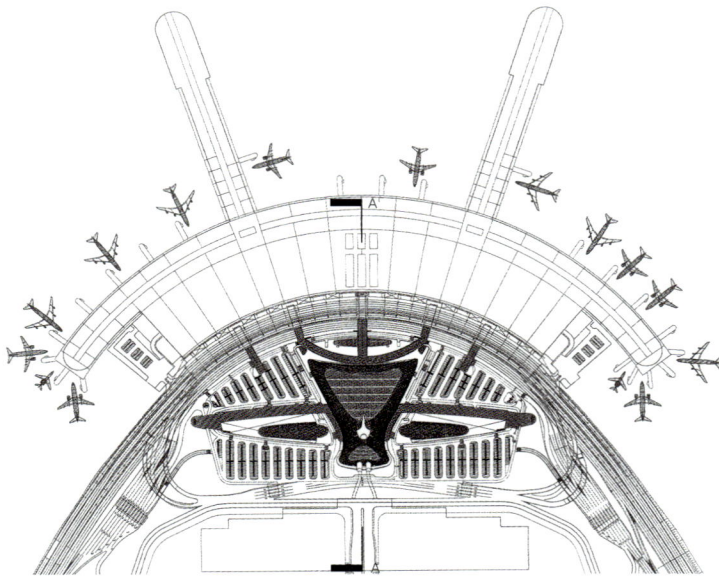

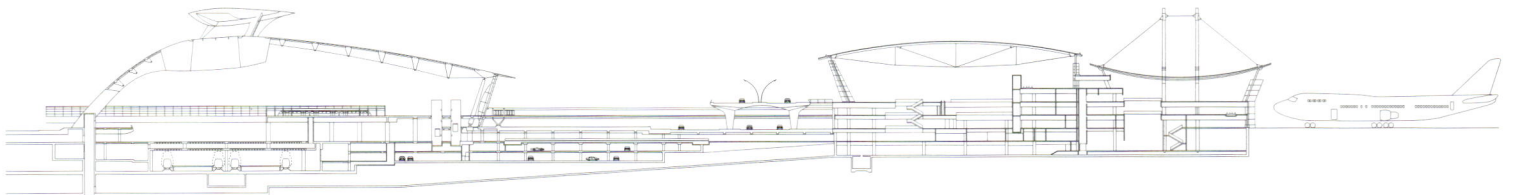

4

INFRASTRUCTURE AS
PUBLIC SPACE

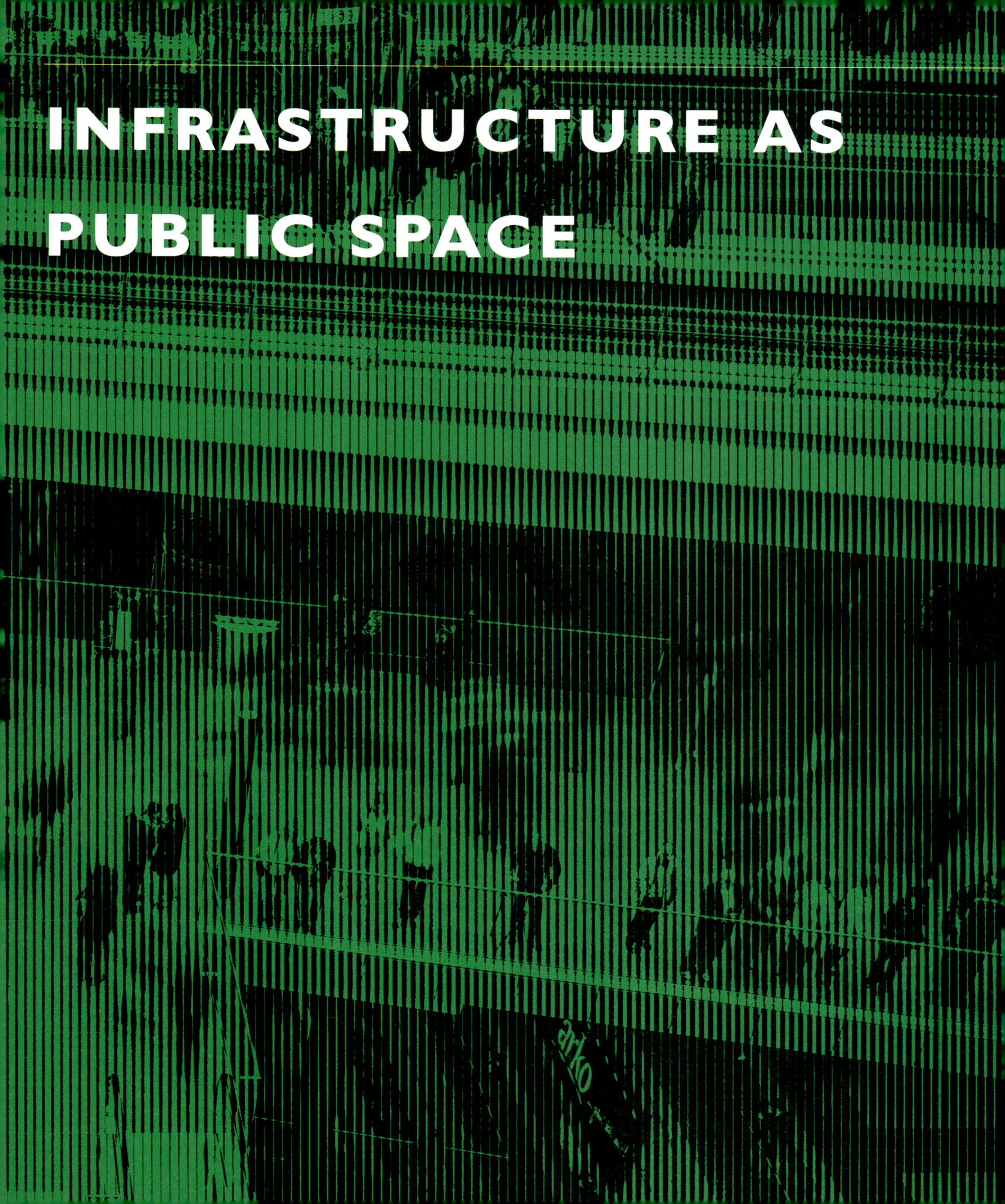

INTRODUCTION
CHANGING PERCEPTIONS OF THE PUBLIC REALM

Infrastructure may be seen as the ultimate public space: it is generally paid for by public authorities, it is accessible to almost everyone, and it marks a common itinerary or a collective place. Infrastructure, by its very nature, expands the public realm beyond the boundaries of a single space. It articulates the aspirations and dignity of contemporary society. Infrastructural investments thus allow for a form of public management or partnership in a more complex urban transformation. Judiciously planned infrastructure may indeed be one of the most effective means of both achieving quality control over private development and realizing strategic urban improvements. For that reason, the creation of infrastructure always potentially involves a more inclusive landscape or urban project.

Throughout history many projects have built upon the civic realm afforded by transportation. The general democratization of space – evident in places of transportation – has inspired a paradigm shift in the articulation of the public realm. From the mid-19th century on, public buildings have emblematized a bourgeois conception of the public sphere. Contrary to the palaces, parks, ball-

rooms, and other collectively used private spaces of the aristocracy, a series of new collective spaces – opera, theatre, station hall, school – were, in principle, open to all citizens and edified them by encouraging behavior that was in accordance with the norms of civil society [1]. Through their monumental form, their vast stairs and hallways, and the extent of their common spaces and interiors, they were designed to impress and inspire respect, and ultimately to pay tribute to and show consideration for the user. The public nature of such spaces relied heavily upon the fact that access was open to all. The mixture of residents, visitors, strollers, and travelers is nearly indiscernible and fluxes produced by the town and the transfer constantly intermingle. The resultant, fascinating bustle and enthralling congestion has kept transportation nodes central to present-day public space, despite the contemporary predilection to privatize public space in the name of security and economic logic.

A brief history of transport reveals the shift in the perception and spatial articulation of the public realm. Beginning with steamships – which dominated the early 19th-century transatlantic mar-

1 **SUMPTUOUS WAITING ROOM**
At the turn of the twentieth century, Le Train Bleu was a lavish and luxurious restaurant in the Gare de Lyon train station in Paris. It not only catered to first class passengers before they boarded trains to the Mediterranean coast but also functioned as place of encounter for the Parisian bourgeoisie.

ket of passenger transport – the quality of the voyage had everything to do with class distinctions. Business travelers and tourists were accommodated in cabins and had extravagant dining and entertainment halls, while the steerage in the hold of the ship offered a more primitive passage for immigrants. Terminals were also conceived with distinction in mind and built on quays with carriage ramps that carried rich customers to the *piano nobile* and from there across horizontal walkways to the upper decks of the ships moored to the quayside. Poorer passengers, along with goods, entered directly from the quays to the lower decks of the ships. By the early 20th century the concept of the superliner was developed and shipping companies competed to launch exquisite, massive, and ornate floating hotels. The luxury and the romance of the voyage was heavily marketed while the design of the ships steadily increased speed. The first nonstop transatlantic flight in 1927 by Charles Lindbergh (from New York City to Paris) signaled the start of the end of business for ocean liners. Yet in the 1960s the industry was revived by the "fun ship" cruise industry, where the role of ships for transporting passengers to a particular destination was replaced by an emphasis on the voyage itself. Terminals became common large halls, with class distinction only occasionally made in executive or business class lounges, like in airports. The commercial exploitation of terminals took advantage of the profits made in duty-free trade. Over time, the distribution and addition of programmatic components over a larger area led to even greater public use of the terminal.

The 19th-century popularization of train travel accommodated the values of the new bourgeois society, and transport space took on an urban image. While assigned train carriages mirrored class distinctions, the station hall and platforms were common spaces through which everyone passed. In this way, train stations became the true initiators of transport infrastructure as public space. Once railroad networks were established, their stations replaced market halls and civic buildings as the most democratic places, simply on account of the sheer number of daily users. Stations were points of urban assembly where the spectacle of society, the culture of congestion, could be witnessed, and where a token of modernity and the worship of movement were clearly evident. Stations were iconic structures, with an importance similar to churches and opera houses in terms of their position within the urban fabric, such as at the termination of monumental axes. They articulated prominent civic spaces with material extravagance. They were nodes of interchange and exchange, links between local, national, and international travel, and places of transfer between various modes of transport (initially horse-drawn carriages, and later trams, metros, and taxis). Great vaulted roofs above the platforms celebrated technological advancement and enhanced civility by their awe-inspiring impressiveness. Conversely, the station hall was a grandiose civic space replete with dining spaces and waiting halls, a gateway to the city [2-3]. Most often, the two worlds, of shelter and voyage, were connected by a grand staircase, since the platforms and tracks were usually on elevated viaducts.

2 GRAND PUBLIC HALLWAY

Early train stations in important cities, like Penn Station in New York over a century ago, were gathering places for passengers of different social class and status. Station halls constituted important public spaces and formed the transition between the city and the train voyage.

3 STANDARDIZED ELEGANCE

With the rise of the middle class, train travel became more standardized and specifically geared to ensure passenger comfort. Sophisticated facilities like this elegant diner in the Cincinnati Union Terminal (1929-33) were introduced.

Until recently, stations remained fully public in terms of accessibility. They were even seen as places of refuge for the homeless and played host to many informal economic activities. This highly public nature was obviously related to the fact that stations were owned and operated by the state. In the past decades, however, increased concerns over security and privatization are starting to radically challenge this premise.

The longer waiting times at train stations fundamentally distinguish them from the more incidental use of metro, tram, or bus stations. With regard to the great number of stops and the diversity of accommodation involved, the design of stations is obviously more directed toward practical purposes. Yet, in many instances, their architectural expression also fosters an air of civic pride and an ambition for modernity. Due to their utilitarian nature, though, explicit public space is often scarce. To a large degree, their public character is typically dependent on their use by all sectors of society. This is most clearly evident in the case of metros, where casual encounters between the rich and poor are an everyday occurrence [5]. Once the wealthier members of society are not part of the clientele, the civic nature of this form of transport infrastructure changes. Such an observation is particularly evident in bus stations. The introduction of Greyhound services in the United States was originally aimed at the middle classes, for whom long-haul air travel was too expensive. Accordingly, the Greyhound bus stations were well-furbished, replete with restaurants, showers, and

waiting and recreation rooms. They were representative icons of modernity [4]. Today, with perhaps the exception of the highly innovative bus networks in Latin America, long-haul bus networks and their stations cater more to low-budget clientele and their facilities often merely reuse the side-spaces of existing facilities. For example, Eurobus makes use of existing parking lots and occupies side entrances to train stations in larger towns, which are often unguarded and sometimes unsafe. Alternatively, parking lots can also temporarily turn into public plazas when the gathering involves a company of people that are already acquainted or share a common goal. Such appropriation generally takes place when parking lots next to local road networks and regional-scaled highways are utilized as assembly points for tour-guided trips.

It may seem paradoxical to mention car travel in relation to public space. However, road infrastructure is a paramount constituent of the public realm. In some car-oriented cultures, driving acts as a replacement for walking and generates comparable experiences of gathering, encounter, and discovery at the scale of the extensive town that city-strolling does at the scale of the concentrated town. Moreover, the private, capsular, cocoon-like car is used for trips that become a collective experience because of their reoccurring nature – the daily journey of the commuters, the weekend recreation at the seaside, the yearly holiday migration, and so on. Such collective journeys undertaken in individual cars are compressed into road conduits of a relatively small stretch of territory. Initially,

4 **WELL-DESIGNED AMENITY**
Well-organized Greyhound bus stations played a major role in boosting the popularity of long-haul bus travel among the American middle class. In terms of publicity, they were icons of modernity that combined comfort, speed, and service. Pictured here is Pittsburg station in 1943.

travelers stopped as they pleased, went to the lavatory in the bushes, and consumed home-prepared picnics [6]. In the past decades, regulations have been enforced to establish a middle ground between ensuring safety (not just stopping and starting on a fast highway) and imposing consumption (buying your food, paying for the toilet). Travelers are treated as customers at the public spaces of service stations, roadside restaurants and motels, and their habits of consumption determine the appearance and organization of such collectively experienced service areas. Rest stops have become increasingly complex. They have developed into miniature cities, acquiring an assortment of generally accessible public amenities. Toilets are not only free and well-maintained, and picnic areas well-provided, but one can just as well find shopping markets, a range of restaurants and hotels, showers and washing places, theme-parks, exhibition halls, and cinemas.

Finally, there is air travel. Almost the opposite of train stations, airport terminals have secured access only. They are essentially screened off from the wider public. This seclusion from the public realm did not always exist. Initially, airports were articulated as places to visit and gather, and watching flight take-offs and landings was considered a recreational activity [7]. Airports were a part of the town. It was safety and noise regulations that led to the eventual distancing of airports from city centers. And, as air traffic grew, so too did the ancillary programs of hotels and business centers. Today, the largest part of an airport is usually inaccessible to those without tickets. Yet for the traveler, a whole new form of public realm has come into being to create distractions that take up the waiting time associated with flying. Airports are measured by the number and diversity of side-programs – ranging from food courts to shopping arcades to casinos to spas to museums. The most recent development in airport design has been the integration of urban activities into the airport realm – a secure zone for air passengers with adjacent areas for the non-flying public who take advantage of the node in the air-traffic network. Shopping facilities and meeting spaces are now included in airports for people who do not have anything to do with flying. The public nature of transportation is forever in a process of evolution and transformation.

5 **SPACE OF MAXIMUM UTILITY**

Public space is scarce in most buildings that accommodate high-frequency transport services. Passenger platforms with functionally determined dimensions are usually the only provision. By minimizing spatial excess, such buildings minimize comfort too, as is evident on this metro platform in São Paulo, Brazil.

6 **INFORMAL ROADSIDES**

Before security and consumption restrictions were imposed, roadsides functioned as spaces for informal, recreational use. Road shoulders often provided sites for spontaneous picnics and camping grounds, as seen in the 1960s in the Netherlands.

7 **WATCHING THE PLANES**

In the days before security, efficiency, and noise regulations transformed airports into self-contained capsules, the concourses and terraces of early airfields served as tourist attractions, providing spaces for visitors to view the planes. Pictured here is Schiphol airport in Amsterdam, the Netherlands.

BEAUTIFIED LEFTOVER

By the 19th century, it was formally recognized that providing infrastructure as a technical amenity created leftover space along its fringes – neglected taluses, derelict bits and pieces, and abandoned in-betweens. In 1890, Josef Stübben, the City Engineer of Cologne, Germany, classified such "traffic places" in his systematic and structured manual of city design, *Der Städtebau*.[1] Combining the efficient city with the city beautiful, he sought to develop "practical aesthetics" both to improve traffic planning and mobility and to make the appearance of streets, and particularly intersections, more agreeable for passers-by [1]. Today, the tenets of Stübben have been embraced by the New Urbanism movement in their pursuit of "Traditional Neighbourhood Development." In the United States, the Institute of Transportation Engineers and the Congress for the New Urbanism published a Recommended Practice, which advances the successful use of context-sensitive solutions in the planning and design of major urban thoroughfares for walkable communities.[2]

Embellishment of infrastructure often takes the form of an amenity serving neighboring housing districts, or improvements to the surroundings through some form of adornment such as planted taluses, wastelands, or vacant strips and stretches. These operations commonly follow existing patterns of planting and set up stereotypical buffer landscapes. Often they try to highlight regional character by incorporating emblematic features (symbolic displays on traffic circles) or experimenting with local species or planting arrangements (taluses with native shrub bundling, or plant patterns and earth configurations intended to blend with the surroundings). In many cases, these projects suffer from awkward interpretations of local character and/or poor accessibility. Successful operations require the alteration of movement patterns through the reconfigured sites.

The beautification of forgotten territories, of the non-places of cities, of urban fallows, has been the task of urban design since time immemorial. The most interesting examples, however, are those that transcend mere aesthetics and reprogram sites. In Nantes, France, Agence Tetrarc transformed a street verge into an urban landmark at the southern entrance to the city and close to the confluence of the Erdre and Loire Rivers, endowing the vast site with a tram station and market place [2]. The Brinkpark in Apeldoorn, the Netherlands, was more asphalt than grass until landscape architects OKRA reconfigured the parking lot and created a decisively artificial landscape that turned cars into the guests on the site and parking into the underground component of the new topography [3]. A similar spatial tactic was employed by José María Torres Nadal in Murcia, Spain, where the underground parking garage and the ground-level public space are visually connected and the animated section has fundamentally upgraded an elongated site between the urban fabric and the Segura River. Long and narrow left-

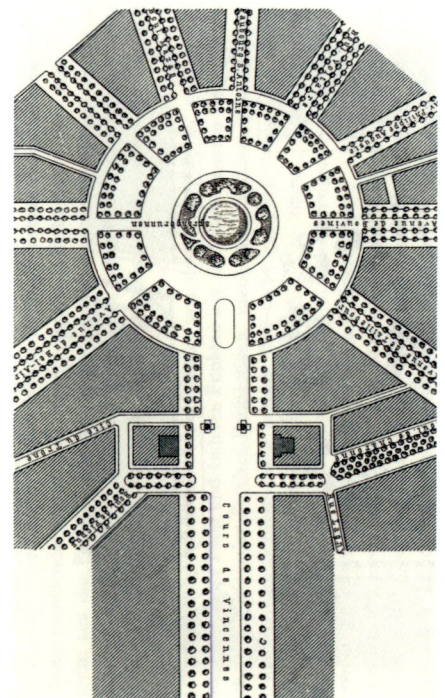

2 ROOFED PLATFORMS

Place Pirmil in Nantes, France, was transformed by Agence Tetrarc from a forgotten place into a vibrant transport node with a tram station (in the west) and market place (in the east). Two large roofs (70 meters long and 7 meters high) composed of three folded sails of corrugated aluminum and supported by 12-meter-high pennants reprogram the no-man's land. The northern part of the site, stretching towards the rivers, is buffered from the busy road beyond by a small garden and car park on banks of raised earth with rocks and trees and defined by fin-shaped granite bollards.

3 GREEN INFILL

The triangular Brinkpark in the Veluwe area of Apeldoorn, the Netherlands, was transformed from a spatially complicated convergence of infrastructure (cars, buses, and parking lot) into a green entrance to the city. Its shape is determined by the triangular leftover space between two street directions. Landscape architects OKRA combined underground parking and a park with an artificial topography where traffic is treated as a "guest." A patio in the car park forms a vertical link between the worlds above and below ground.

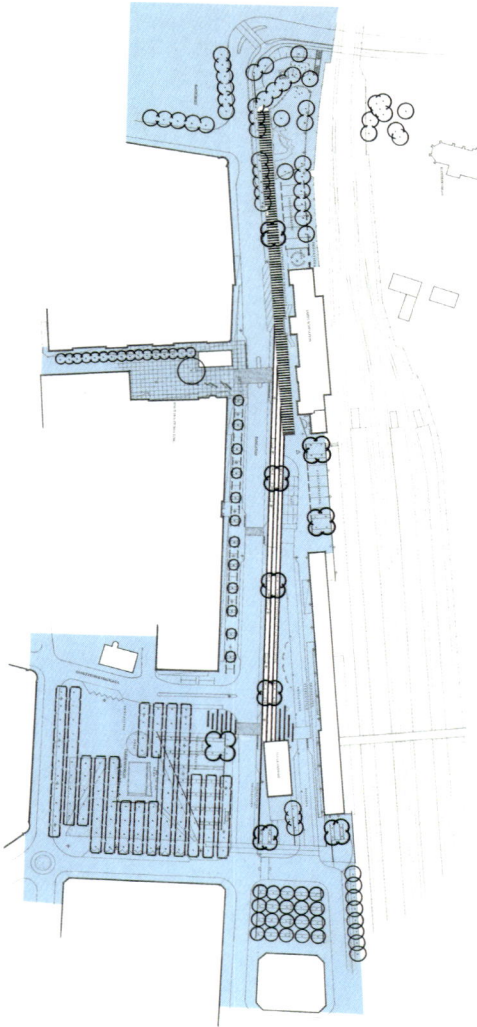

4 RAG RUGS, GRANITE WALLS, AND LINDENS

Landscape architect Sven-Ingvar Andersson transformed a ribbon-like space along the railroad in Lund, Sweden, into a unified and dignified large pedestrian mall. Two long "rag rugs" (each 400 meters long and 7 meters wide) were created with cobble stone paving, one bonded as horizontal strips and the other as vertical strips, and accented with paving curbstones. Adjacent to the rugs, lindens were planted in clusters of four trees. Low Swedish granite walls separate bicycle parking from pedestrian areas and provide seating.

over sites are common on railroad yards, and their convincing rearrangement and programming is not a particularly easy task. In the university town of Lund, Sweden, the 500-meter-long railroad right-of-way along the western border of the medieval city was beautifully restructured by Sven-Ingvar Andersson into a dignified entry plaza from the train and bus station [4].

The abandonment of infrastructure, too, offers opportunities for reprogramming. The decommissioning of railroads often results in the conversion of lines into bicycle and pedestrian paths, as has been the case with many of the more beautiful bicycle tracks in the Flemish countryside or the more extensive landscape recovery project by Jones & Jones for the Cedar Lake Park in Minneapolis-St. Paul in Minnesota [5]. Railroads to bicycle paths is perhaps an easier conversion than the challenge faced by the Roma Design Group with the demolition of the Embarcadero raised freeway in San Francisco, California. The width of the former road made the reconnection of the city to its waterfront difficult to reconcile with the urban fabric, the reconfigured surface transport network, and the open spaces. Nonetheless, the repaired urban landscape has resulted in a polite, recreation-oriented, slightly romanticized urbanism with a predictable amalgam of street furniture, paving, and planting. Finally, a more radical or perhaps merely more fashionable urban and architectural approach to beautification is displayed by Subarquitectura in Alicante, Spain. This team of young architects turned a large traffic circle into a new park with tram platforms, the coverings of which are huge pock-marked steel boxes seemingly suspended in the air. The combination of such pragmatism combined with the aesthetics of adornment, one could argue, continues the line of thinking developed by Stübben over a century ago.

1 Joseph Stübben, *Der Stadtebau*, facsimile reprint of 1st edition, 1890, (Braunschweig/Wiesbaden: Vieweg & Sohn, 1980), 562.
2 "CNU and ITE Unveil New Street Design Manual – Proposed Recommended Practice Paves Way for True Urban Thoroughfares," www.cnu.org/node/617 (posted 21 July 2006, accessed 24 August 2009).

5 FROM TRAIN TO CYCLE TRACKS

Since train engines cannot master steep grades, train tracks have always been more or less horizontal. Such a straight and flat trajectory is exactly what recreational cyclists prefer in order to cover reasonable distances without too much effort. For this reason, disused railroad lines are often put to use as cycle paths. In Belgium, the country with the densest railroad network in the world, many cycle paths of this type are becoming part of tourist routes and cross nature areas without requiring substantial investment. An example is the former line 74 between Diksmuide and Nieuwpoort.

Much More Than a Lot

Murcia, Spain

Architect: José María Torres Nadal

Date: 2002–2004

MURCIA PARKING GARAGE AND PLAZA

On an underutilized urban edge, which was formerly the site of an army barracks, in the southern Spanish city of Murcia, José María Torres Nadal created an underground parking garage. The ground surface above forms a stage to host the public realm. The revitalization of the elongated site adjacent to the Segura River establishes a new relationship between the city and the river, park and parking, ground and underground. The project is all about an intelligent configuration of the section. An elevated pedestrian promenade offers views of the river and extends to become a large and colorful multipurpose public space — an artificial public green that will eventually make a transition to a planned park to the west. Large openings

in the roof of the garage below not only allow for ample natural light and ventilation but also underscore the notion of parallel flows of water, cars, and pedestrians. This multilayered upgrading project has certainly beautified a leftover. In addition to refurbishing the vacant lot, the architect redefined Murcia's critical city edge and intervened in a strategically located area of the town.

With the river and countryside beyond as a serene backdrop, the area above ground can host street markets, an outdoor cinema, and exhibitions. The ground plane is colorfully painted with spots of green and bull's-eye symbols in brightly saturated colors,

while the parking spaces below are painted a vibrant blue). Metal-mesh and shading canopies screen the strong sunlight. They are supported by columns whose bases form colorful seats. Lighting fixtures spring from the underground parking garage and arc over the public space, creating vertical markers on the predominately horizontal plane. At night the plaza is illuminated indirectly from the openings in the parking garage. The long striations of the plan and spaces reveal an overall lightness and playfulness in the detailing of the street furniture, the surface colors, and the shading canopies that seem to float overhead.

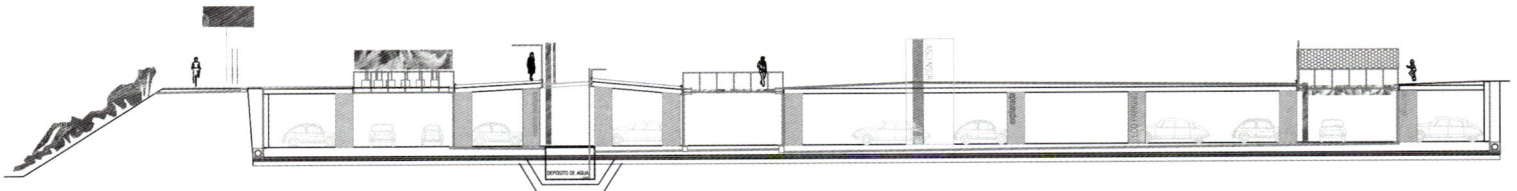

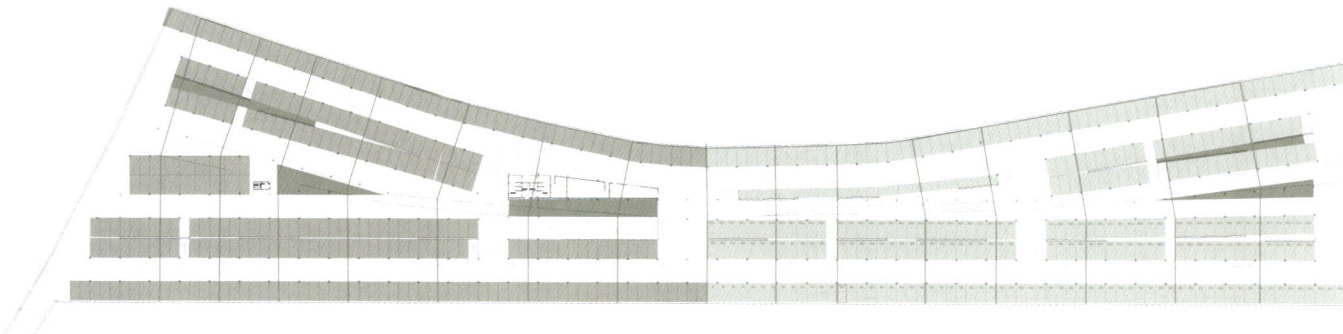

Ecology-Designed Cycle Path

CEDAR LAKE PARK AND TRAIL

Minneapolis, Minnesota, USA

Landscape Architect: Jones & Jones

Architect: Richard Haag Associates

Date: 1992–1996

The twin cities of Minneapolis-St. Paul in Minnesota developed in a landscape of deep forests and lakes on the Mississippi River and, as early as 1883, a park system linked lakes, streams, and rivers to the cities. In the 19th century, Minneapolis-St. Paul thrived as a lumber and grain milling center and was connected to the rest of the United States by an extensive railroad network. The area north and east of Cedar Lake played an important role in the early history of the railroad as the site was a major switching yard. Despite the presence of the railroad, land was purchased around the perimeter of Cedar Lake between 1908 and 1975 and the lake was eventually connected to the other nearby lakes to create the well-known

"Chain of Lakes." During the 20th century the economy underwent drastic change, and this was accompanied by a decline in the rail industry. Although the Burlington Northern Railroad still continues to operate daily trains north of Cedar Lake, most of the major railroad facilities had closed by the mid-1980s. Tracks were removed, buildings razed, and the area was slowly reclaimed by nature.

In 1992, landscape architects Jones & Jones teamed up with Richard Haag Associates to convert an abandoned railroad right-of-way on Cedar Lake into a seven-kilometer-long pedestrian and bicycle commuter corridor, linking residential neighborhoods with the

heart of downtown Minneapolis-St. Paul and the Mississippi River waterfront. It was proposed as a new kind of park: a wild, yet urban, nature preserve linked by trails to the Mississippi River and other parts of Chain of Lakes Regional Park. The natural process of succession on the postindustrial site was enhanced by site changes in micro-relief that in turn affected the site's moisture regime — wet, semi-wet, semi-dry, dry — supporting the growth of different native prairie grasses and wildflowers. The landscape architects considered ecology an active design agent, weaving together and differentiating atmospheres between the various pedestrian and cycle paths.

Before

After

From Port to Leisure City

San Francisco, California, USA

Architect: Roma Design Group

Date: 1991–2004

THE EMBARCADERO

San Francisco's history is closely tied to its waterfront, which provided access to ocean trading routes. The relationship between city and port changed significantly after World War II as truck and rail systems started to dominate freight transport. The proliferation of the automobile led to the construction of an elevated freeway, the Embarcadero, originally designed to connect the Bay Bridge and the Golden Gate Bridge. Skirting the waterfront, the road effectively separated the city and the water. The water became the city's backside, formed by a raised freeway and a string of pier head-houses. To make matters worse, due to a citizens' protest in 1958, the road itself remained incomplete, rendering it a useless

nuisance, a "freeway to nowhere." Controversy beset the road ever since it appeared. In 1989 the Loma Prieta Earthquake struck the city, and in 1991 the Embarcadero was finally dismantled owing to concerns about public safety. The in-between space has since been transformed into an urban boulevard, spatially reconnecting the city to San Francisco Bay.

The new bayside promenade along the city's seawall now celebrates the transition from a maritime area to a place of recreational opportunities. The project by Roma Design Group includes a redesigned Embarcadero roadway (two banks of thoroughfare traffic, three lanes going in each direction), the

reintroduction of historic streetcars (running down the center of the traffic lanes), a series of new waterfront parks, a pedestrian promenade marked by a continuous ribbon of light, and the renovation of Pier 1 and the historic Ferry Building with a large forecourt. The redevelopment has spurred improvements to other areas, including the old industrial South Market area. Pedestrian and waterborne traffic has expanded. The area has a festive, resort-like quality to it, with palm trees creating a grandness of scale and formality. At the same time, the excessive width of the Embarcadero remains a challenge for a lively urban realm.

Before

After

Floating Boxes

ALICANTE TRAM STOP

Alicante, Spain

Architect: Subarquitectura

Date: 2005–2006

In the south of Spain, a new tram line was created by reusing the tracks of the old local railroad. The new line connects a string of towns along the Mediterranean coast. In Alicante, the tram links the city to the beach. Subarquitectura designed the main tram stop, and in the process turned a traffic circle into an eye-catching public space that enlivened tram travel with a fresh image. Two large open boxes of steel (36 meters long, 3 meters wide, 2.5 meters high) mark the center of the circle and appear to float above passengers' heads as they wait for trams on the platforms. The structure and envelope is one and the same, and each box contains 25 tons of steel and

cantilevers 22 meters. The floating boxes seem to defy gravity as they each rest on two slender columns located asymmetrically along their length with merely a pair of tension cables near one end to counterbalance the cantilevers. A number of crossbraces strut diagonally through the interior of each box, working in a composition with 13 angled fluorescent lighting tubes The boxes are perforated by 800 holes in 5 different diameters ranging from 10 to 50 centimeters. The holes reduce the weight of the boxes and are irregularly distributed to take account of critical points in the structure. They also animate the boxes and allow light and cooling breezes to pass through. The

position of the boxes is calculated to cast a permanent shadow – necessary under the hot Mediterranean sun. At night, the boxes glow like gigantic lanterns.

Access to the platforms is by way of 32 possible pathways, which together with remolded topography of bermed grass redefine the traffic circle as a public space. The fractal-like path system is deformed on either side to accommodate existing trees. Combined seating and lighting units adorn the pathways and invite lingering. The leftover is not just beautified but is integrated into an encompassing urban project.

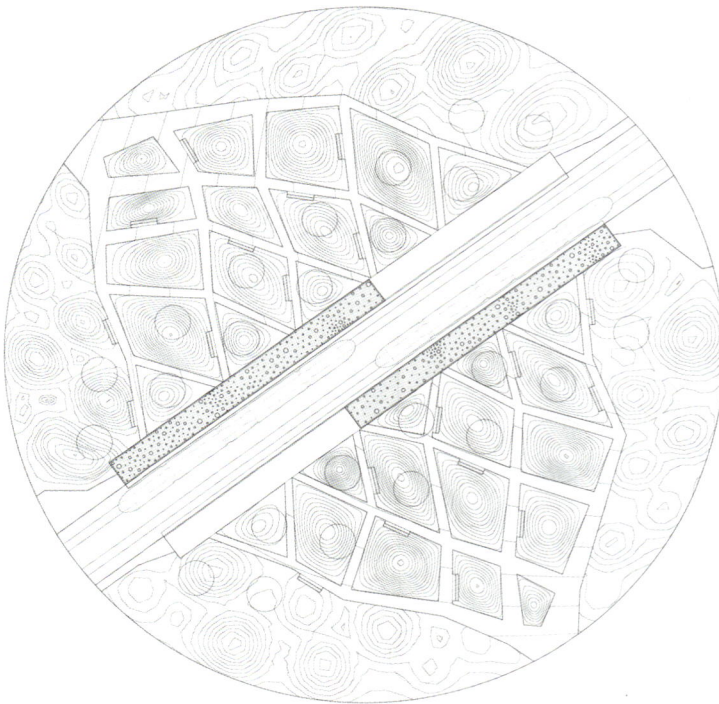

MONEY-MAKING COMMODITY

Multimodal transfer facilities generate a lot of activity. They are points of accessibility, visited by nontravelers who make use of the many amenities but not the transport services. Airports, ferry terminals, and train stations are prime locations for retail and entertainment facilities, and many of them are complex shopping malls whose clientele is not confined to passengers. The mall, a descendent of the 19th-century arcade and 20th-century department store, has evolved into a large, windowless space of self-contained experiences that creates imagineered and artificially differentiated worlds. In reality, these new sites of global capitalism are much the same everywhere. Typically, the commercial facility is conceived as a capsule that simulates a lifestyle centered on consumerism. The spatial arrangement is embedded in a politics of branding and constructing a make-believe public realm inside an extensive privatized arena. "Junkspace," as Rem Koolhaas calls it, "is the result of the conjunction of escalator and air conditioning, conceived in an incubator made of plasterboard (…) Junk space is (…) designed to carry brand names (…) it consists of orphaned particles searching for a plan or a model."[1]

The 1970s construction of the Forum des Halles in Paris, France, is emblematic of the trend to bring the large mall, until then located in peripheral housing districts, to the urban core [1]. The subterranean connection to the suburban commuter rail line (RER) and metro created access to and from the whole agglomeration, while claims for public space (the park on the site of the former covered market halls) and the demand for other social amenities (swimming pool, mediathèque, cinema complex) resulted in a new combination of programs that has since been replicated in projects worldwide. Initially, train stations served not only as the meeting place for passengers, but also as an unrestricted place for all. This unreserved and truly public character, which initially also supported the concept of the Forum des Halles, has gradually disappeared.

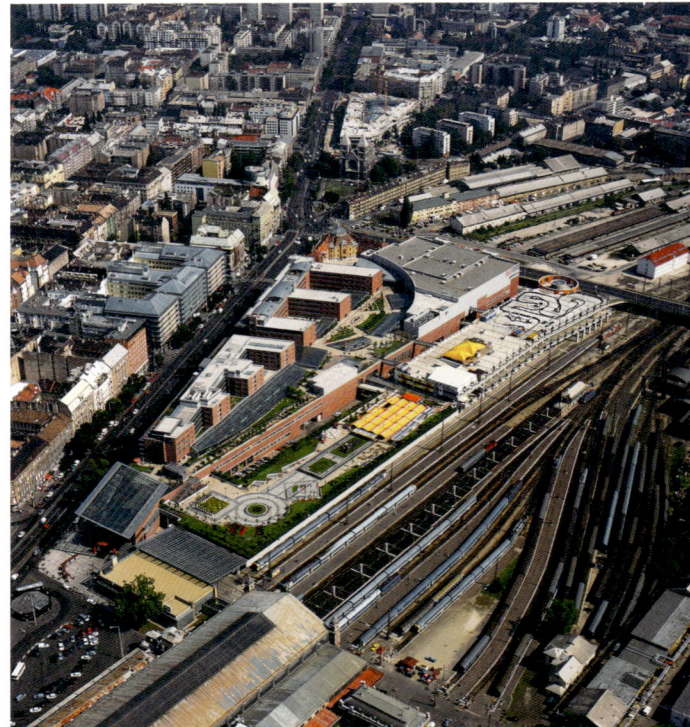

The modern-day closed passage or the protected mall has progressively replaced the 19th-century open hall. Covered passages and corridors have increasingly been treated as separated galleries, and independent shopping levels were inserted into single-vaulted hallways. In Eastern Europe, shopping and entertainment centers next to train stations have been used as an economic stimulus. The Westend City Center in Budapest, Hungary, is the prototype of a new-style shopping arena, developed by the American architect Jon Jerde [2]. Like the Sony Center in Berlin, Germany, it stands contextually free, is self-referential and emblematic of the artificial notion of "place making." In Leipzig, Germany, a new shopping arcade by Hentrich-Petschnigg & Partner has been completely integrated into the station; hallway, platform accesses, and the different levels of the mall form one single space. Shopping is used here to enliven the train voyage and, at the same

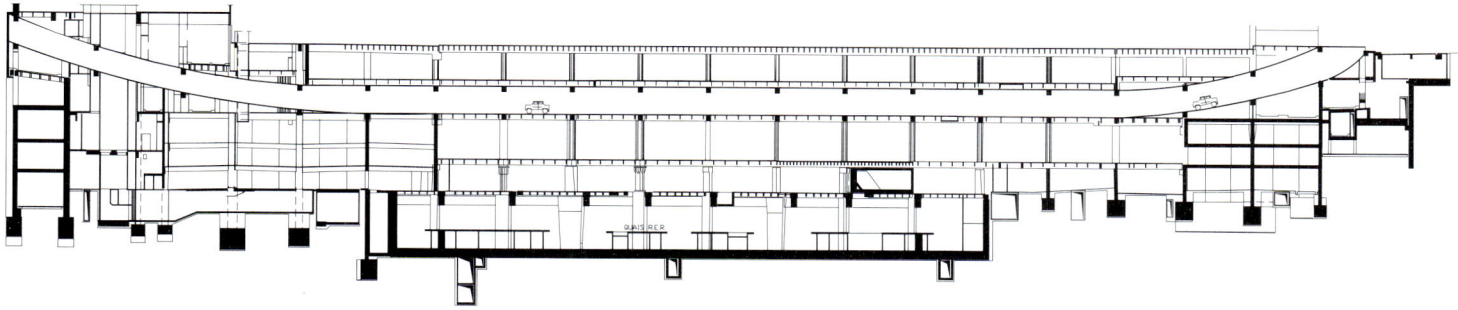

1 BELLY OF PARIS

The Forum des Halles was built in 1979 as an underground mall that connected to the Châtelet-Les-Halles RER suburban rail line. The 15-hectare site, once the central market of the city, was transformed into a multilevel shopping center that essentially imported the commercial model (and the customers) from the periphery to the center of Paris. A large proportion of the 45,000-square-meter shopping facility was buried underground, and many social and cultural functions were added, among them a swimming-pool, a library, a médiatheque, exhibition halls, and cinemas. They created a world and a microculture of their own. The complex has become an aging eyesore, and was the object of a competition in 2007 to remodel the whole site.

2 TERMINAL MALL

Westend City Center, built adjacent to the Western (Nyugati) Train Station in Budapest, Hungary, is one of Central Europe's largest mixed-use retail and entertainment projects. Designed by the highly experienced architect of shopping facilities Jon Jerde in association with local architects Finta Studios, the 186,000-square-meter complex physically connects to the transit station to attract the 400,000 people who pass through the site daily.

3 ECONOMIC REVIVAL

Transbay Transit Center, the intermodal bus and rail transit (intercity, commuter, light rail) station by Pelli Clarke Pelli Architects, for the San Francisco Bay region is to become the anchor of a major mixed-use redevelopment (220,000 square meters) that includes adjacent underutilized parking lots and irregular parcels of state-owned land left over from the Loma Prieta earthquake. In addition to the high-density retail, office, and hotel precinct, there are 3000 housing units in the development. The rooftop park is designed to compensate for the busy commercial activity below, and together they offer two atmospheres as an attraction for residential settlement.

4 AIR-RIGHTS DEVELOPMENT

The redevelopment of Charing Cross Station (London's most densely utilized terminus station) included the use of air rights over the tracks to create 41,800 square meters of mixed use development (hotels, offices, retail). Terry Farrell and Partners' creation of Embankment Place was possible by 18 columns, which rise through the station platforms to support the arch from which the seven to nine office floors are suspended and isolated from the railroad vibration. The Charing Cross development is an iconic London landmark, particularly at night with the illuminated building sitting alongside the other "palaces on the Thames."

5 HOVERING UFO

Bothe Richter Teherani Architects created a UFO-like object to hover over the rail tracks of the train station in Dortmund, Germany. The 240-meter-diameter sleek disk houses just over 250,000 square meters of space, a large part of which is relegated to an "urban entertainment center" spread over five levels that is complemented by a ring parking system for 3800 cars. In the otherwise introvert building, a broad raked pedestrian bridge penetrates the multilevel panoramic window over the city center. The structure's clear and memorable form of technological machinery gives a fresh image and identity for a city and region facing economic difficulties.

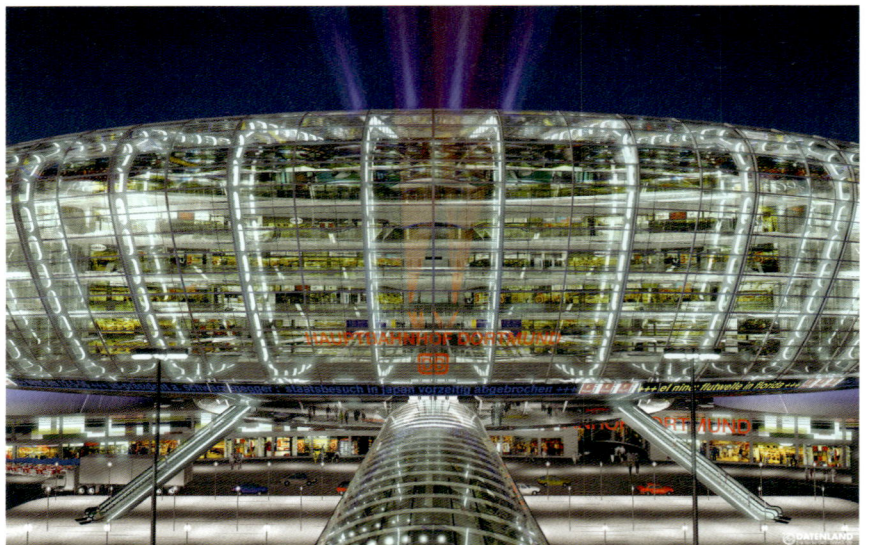

time, to generate the income needed for restoring this important and majestic historical building.

Shopping as an impetus for urban renewal and economic stimulus was also a driver for the Transbay Transit Center in San Francisco, California. Pelli Clarke Pelli Architects designed an intermodal bus and rail transit as the anchor of a major mixed-use redevelopment project. Unusually, housing is also combined into the more typical mix of retail and office space [3]. Similarly, housing is included in the Nordseepassage by Von Gerkan, Marg und Partner with Volkmar Sievers in Wilhelmshaven, Germany. In contrast to the exuberance of expression in San Francisco, the modesty and understated nature of the German multipurpose complex does not immediately reveal it as a money-making commodity. Yet its exploitation of the peripheral areas of the railroad yard, combined with its composite programming (parking, retail, offices, housing) cleverly disguises the commercial aspect. By contrast, without any modesty at all, Hiroshi Hara designed a colossal new train station in Kyoto, Japan, that forms a gateway and an investment anchor for the ancient city. The full and complex program of activities turns the huge compound into an internalized mini-city. In other contexts, the profit potential of railroad areas has been exploited by taking advantage of the air rights – the area over the tracks themselves. Embankment Place, by Terry Farrell and Partners, was developed over the Charing Cross Station and is representative of a new breed of multifunctional train stations that became common in London after the deregulation introduced in Thatcher era [4]. A similar tactic, yet more spectacular, is the rejuvenation project of the main train station in Dortmund, Germany. The hovering UFO by Bothe Richter Teherani Architects over the unused vacuum above the tracks is a symbolic gesture, seeking to create iconic identity for this city-region facing economic difficulties [5].

Finally, airports must be mentioned since they increasingly integrate shopping and entertainment facilities. Moreover, airports are often likened to global cities and work as obvious boosters for local economies. Their inherent typology, however, leads to a particular situation since security issues prohibit contact between passengers and the outside world once they have passed the security checkpoint. Two separate but clearly complementary spheres come into being: the capsular airport and the urban dependence, which benefits from the transport lines that serve the multimodal transfer point. The modification of the circulation system in the design of a new terminal at Schiphol Airport in the Netherlands by Benthem Crouwel led to a configuration that deviates from the standard separation of flying passengers and nonflying visitors. Schiphol Plaza combines modes of transport and transfer in a threshold building that is animated by shopping and eating and that is truly open to the public [6]. Conversely, the airport as a shopping destination in itself is evident in Dubai, United Arab Emirates, where the price of a plane ticket is often offset by the duty-free deals on offer in the expansive and luxurious concourse of the new terminal recently realized by the French-based architect Paul Andreu.

6 HUB CONVERGENCE
Schiphol Plaza is a 22,000-square-meter interchange building between a new shopping center and an integrated train station. It serves as a forecourt to the security measures befitting Amsterdam's international airport. Benthem Crouwel redesigned the circulation and integrated arrival, departures, trains, and shopping into a spatially clear system that creates new relationships between airport travel, train travel, and shopping, and also attracts new non-flying customers to the specialized and easily accessible shopping amenities.

1   Rem Koolhaas, "Junk-Space," in *Archplus* 149, April 2000.

Shopping Hall

LEIPZIG CENTRAL STATION

Leipzig, Germany

Architect: HPP (Hentrich-Petschnigg & Partner)

Developer: ECE Projektmanagement

Date: 1994–1997

The refurbishment of Leipzig Central Station into the Promenaden shopping arcades is the highlight of a nationwide commercial investment program intended to renovate German train stations and their surroundings. In the 19th century, the railroads had been the backbone of Germany's industrial and urban development, and almost all important stations were centrally located. With the purpose of recovering commercial profit from these well-positioned and superbly connected sites, the German railroad company and ECE (a real estate and retail company set up for this objective) launched a number of implementation competitions for the adaptation and transformation of the central train stations in Cologne, Düsseldorf, Bremen, Stuttgart, Nuremberg,

Mannheim, Munich, and many other cities. As in Leipzig, the problem of commercial exploitation had to be keenly combined with the heritage value of the civic buildings many of these stations represented.

In Leipzig, the original central station dated from 1915. It was built after a competition won in 1906 by the Dresden architects William Lossow and Hans Max Kühne, and was the largest rail terminus in Europe. Particularly impressive was the concourse hall (267 meters long, 24 meters wide and 17.7 meters high), that gave direct access to 26 tracks. Located 3.84 meters above street level, it was easily reached from the vast east and west entrance halls by imposing flights of stairs. To connect the concourse

with the 140 shops, cafés, and restaurants covering approximately 30,000 square meters, competition-winners HPP Architects proposed a lens-shaped opening in the original concourse floor. This alteration to the original structure allowed natural light to be brought in and created views into the two floors under the access level to the trains. The arcades on three levels around the lens-shaped opening holding lifts and stairs thus become a multilayered shopping hall that acts as central hub for the renovated station complex. The intervention drastically changes the original civic connotation of the station hall, and reduces the entrance to the tracks to a glazed doorway occupying half the top arcade of a shopping center hollowed out in a historical hall.

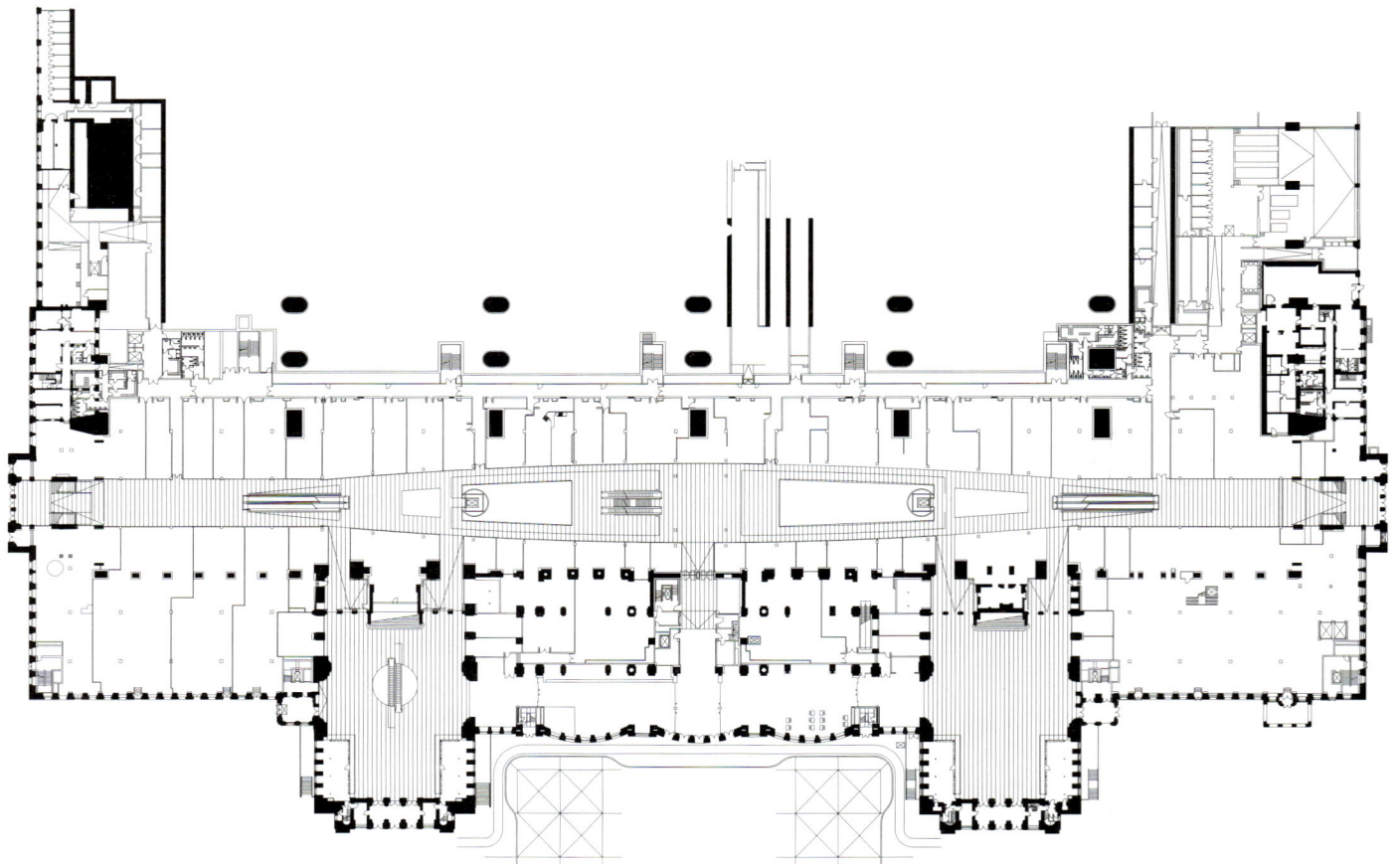

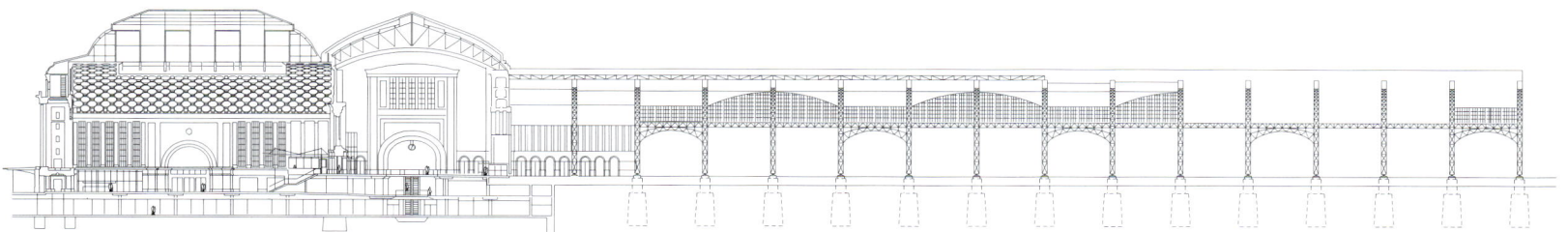

Integrated Urban Hybrid

NORDSEEPASSAGE

The Nordseepassage in Wilhelmhaven, Germany, not only combines the predictable programs of a new shopping mall, bus terminal, parking garage and offices with the city's rail terminus, but also includes housing. Two multistory parking garages, positioned parallel to both sides of the tracks and with expressive open-air parking ramps at one end, culminate in a larger building block that directly connects the city and tracks. The new bus station is integral to the complex and the four-story end building features shops at ground level and offices and apartments on the floors above. The light-red brickwork, characteristic of the area, is used both externally and internally and its material density contrasts with the large expanses of glass.

The huge renovation project covers a 4.3-hectare site, most of which was a railroad yard, and consists of 22,300 square meters of retail space, 3400 square meters of office space, and 2100 square meters of residential space. With such a comprehensive program, including its own parking space, the development constitutes a city-in-miniature in what is already a small city on the North Sea. But the investment benefits a wider area, since the extensive covered passage (250 meters long and 19,400 square meters in area) through the megastructure completes the long-awaited pedestrian connection between the inner city and the seaside. Moreover, a new 9000-square-meter pedestrian square designed by WES & Partner in front of the new station extends the historic Marktstrasse. The new bus terminal extends the Virchowstrasse with a forecourt and forms the start of the Nordseepassage through the building. The careful readjustment of the rail terminus led to a rare case of balanced programming and created a structure that genuinely embodies various aspects of urban life. No doubt the limited catchment area contributes to the avoidance of excessive shopping and office development.

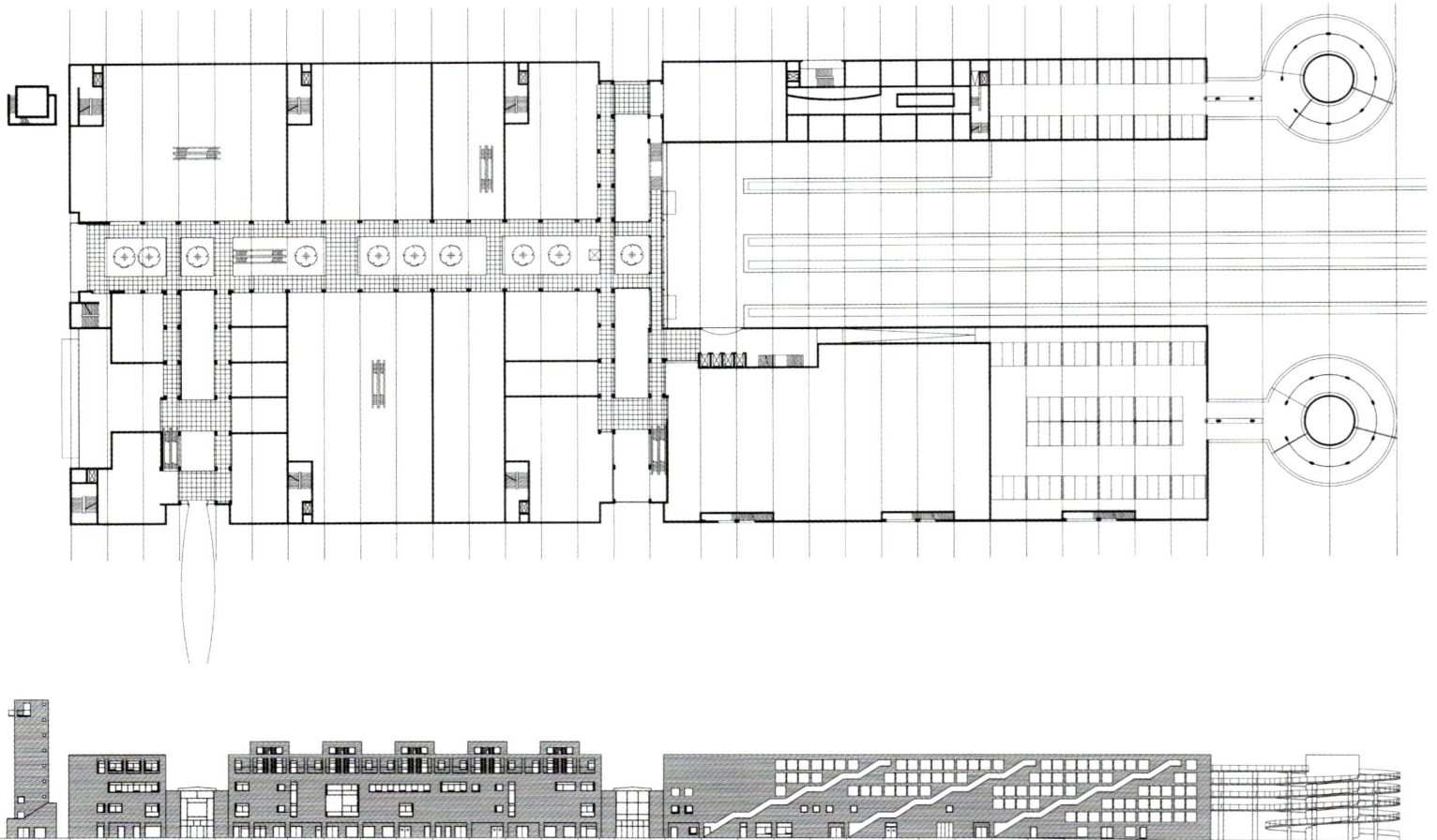

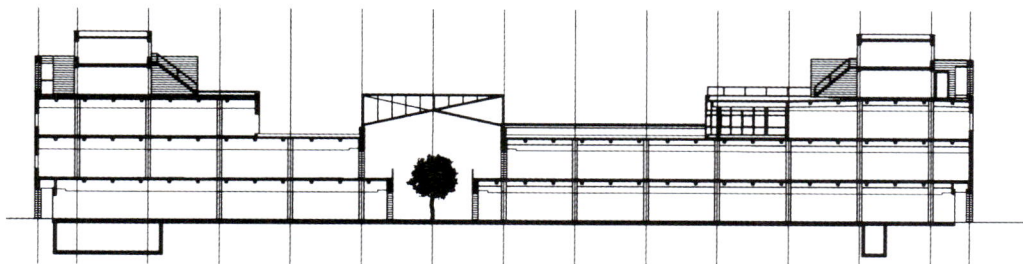

Futuristic Megalith

Kyoto, Japan

Architect: Hiroshi Hara + Atelier Phi

Date: 1991–1997

KYOTO STATION

In 1987, Japan privatized its national railroad company. The main station of the medieval, 1200-year-old former capital city of Kyoto became part of JR West. A new, modern station was to be built and an international competition was launched in 1991. Hiroshi Hara won the commission and created a hybrid building that, despite the fact that the station only accounts for 10% of the area, has the feel of a train station throughout. The 38,000-square-meter site features 238,000 square meters of program, including a department store, amusement facilities, a small theater, a parking area, and a hotel. A building height restriction of 60 meters, in keeping with the city's skyline, placed another limitation on the complex. The building acts as both a gateway to and center of the city. It is a major point of entry

for the 40 million tourists Kyoto annually hosts and also represents its largest commercial development.

Hara created a 470-meter-long rectangular building organized around a "geographical concourse," a v-shaped atrium that is wide at the top and narrower at the lower levels. The concourse has a spatial grandeur that is framed by wide escalators that step back on both sides of the space. Access to the concourse from the exterior is on the ground level. On one side (the west) of the large hallway, a grand staircase leads to a sky garden. An observatory passageway, termed a "skyway," is hung from the roof at a height of 45 meters above ground to allow pedestrians to experience the view of the atrium from above the multilevel public space. The

atrium is roofed by a glass, barrel-vaulted structure and complements the open-air plaza in front of the station. The whole complex is endowed with a lobby-like quality: its diverse, publicly accessible domains are clearly given particular attention and are architecturally differentiated. Artificial landscapes are created by 70 different kinds of stone and a variety of plants, lighting towers, and bridges. Due to its sheer size, the building is very much part of the cityscape of Kyoto. Glass was extensively used, especially in the upper parts of the building, to perceptually diminish the volume. The architectural expression of the slightly irregular cubic facade of plate glass over a steel frame is unabashedly contemporary, even futuristic, and yet components like the barrel roof recall the train stations of a previous era.

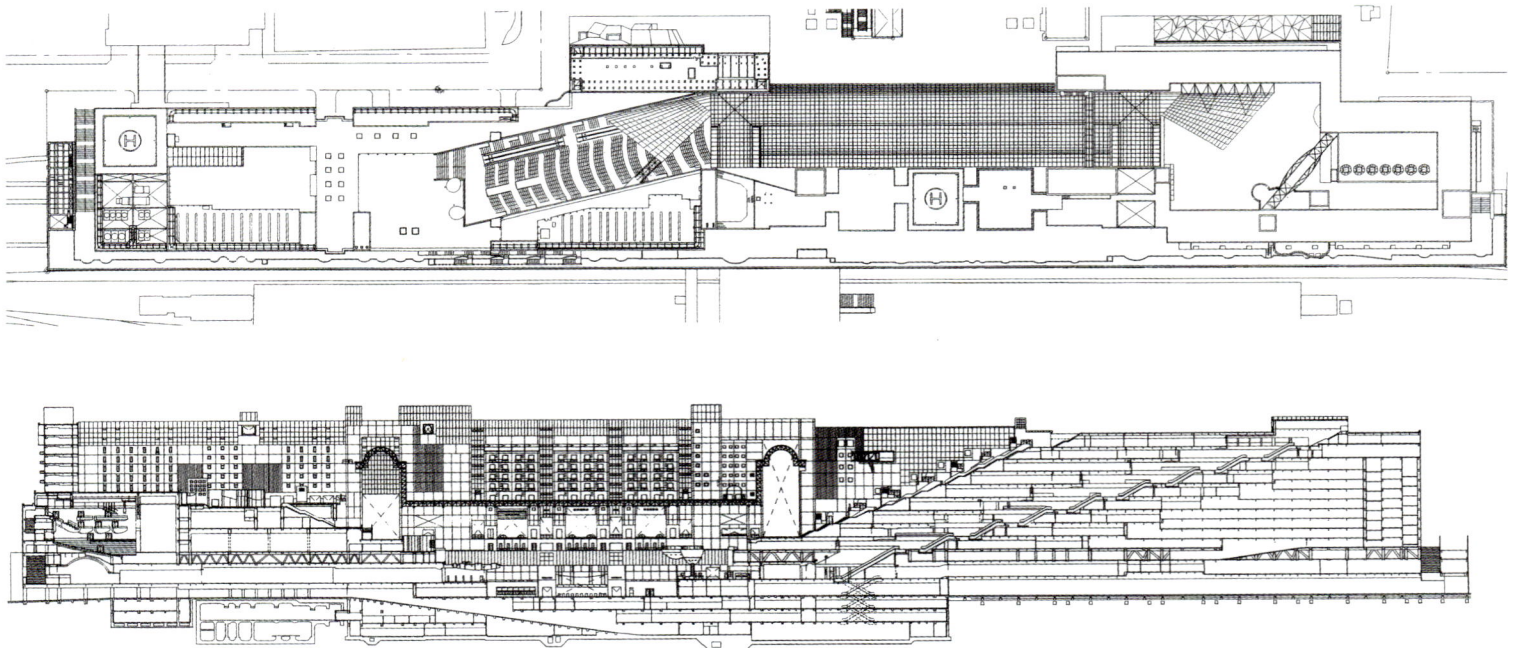

Duty Free H(e)aven

DUBAI INTERNATIONAL AIRPORT

Dubai, United Arab Emirates

Architect: Paul Andreu (Terminal 3)

Date: 2000–2005

Dubai International Airport boasts the largest duty free shopping mall in the world, and was the first airport in the Persian Gulf to have a duty free shop. The airport first opened in 1960 and immediately sought to extend the city's laissez-faire commercial tradition – it had been a commercial entrepôt since the 1880s – into an "open skies" policy. Oil revenues, which now account for just 6% of the city's income, initially spurred infrastructure development and Dubai – as the most populous of the United Arab Emirates (UAE) along the southern coast of the Persian Gulf on the Arabian Peninsula – soon became a major international point of assembly between Asia, Africa, and Europe. In 2008, it was the sixth busiest international airport in the world and the flight hub for the Emirates airline. By the 1990s, the airport itself became a major shopping center, offering luxury goods with low duty fees and no sales tax.

The airport prides itself on being ultra-luxurious and indeed it is a colossal facility with a particular lifestyle branding, perhaps rivaling Las Vegas in terms of opulence. The golden metal palm trees of the earlier concourses are complemented in the newer terminal with lush green Zen gardens and fountains, all set among food courts and world-famous shops selling designer labels. In addition to the shopping mall, the airport complex also counts a Dubai Airport Free Zone, which operates as a regional base for manufacturing, distribution, and services. Situated within the vicinity of the airport, it benefits from the availability of low-wage, nonunionized workers. Activities permitted in this free zone are limited to the fabrication and assemblage of high-value, low-volume products that require rapid access to markets (including high-tech and IT products, luxury items, jewelry, light operations, and airplane components). As such, Dubai airport has typically acquired a wealthy clientele that flies in from the many poorer destinations of the three surrounding continents where these luxury or convenience goods are not easily available.

فنـــدق دبـــي العـالمي

CENOTAPH FOR TECHNOLOGICAL ABILITY

Throughout the history of architecture, there have been grandiose expressions of construction that pushed statics to its limits. Seemingly defying the laws of nature, these audacious structures gave the impression of being related to the divine or the supernatural and therefore inspired awe and respect. They were places of reverence, as exemplified by the pantheon and the gothic church, or works of infrastructure that appeared impressive owing to their combination of size, ingenuity, and elegance. Examples include aqueducts, arched passages, and canal bridges. In the 19th century, challenging the laws of gravity stood for progress. By their tantalizing display of structure and use of steel, the breathtaking spans of stations, bridges, and market halls bore evidence of the building capacity of the industrial era. This glorification of technology gained momentum in the early 20th century. Technologically inspired visionaries such as the Futurists – Sant'Elia wrote his *Città Nuova* in 1914 – and generations of later architects (including Buckminster Fuller, Pier Luigi Nervi, Jean Prouvé, Frei Otto, and Konrad Wachsmann) created heroic expressions that embodied the novelty of modern times in the technological appearance of its architecture [1]. The notion that the *zeitgeist* of modernity resides in advanced technology often inspired a machine-like appearance in which technical aspects were exploited for their representative aesthetics. This attitude came to the fore in many projects for visionary housing or pioneering urban plans built up around the centralizing capacity of the road as circulation spine: Le Corbusier's famous scheme for Algiers (Plan Obus, 1933), his concept for a linear industrial city (ASCORAL, 1942), and Leonidov's project for Magnitogorsk (1930) [2]. This celebratory stance towards technology finds expression today in a number of recent infrastructure projects. More often than not, a fetishized technological aesthetic prevails over the cultural history of the location. Projects of this category aim to create public space representative of advanced engineering.

Airports remain the most emblematic infrastructure hubs for this attitude. Ever since Eero Saarinen's expressive TWA Terminal at JFK Airport in New York – and perhaps, according to historian William Curtis, as part of a mood of dissatisfaction with the restrictive minimalism of the International Style – there has been a long line of experimentation with form in airport typology [3].[1] Conceptual elegance and formal power have pushed airport design expression to new limits. In addition, the metaphorical associations with flight have led to structures that reveal a lightness and airiness, despite the physical massiveness. French engineer-architect Paul Andreu has spent more than three decades developing airports across the globe. Since 1967, he has been working on the successive terminals of Charles de Gaulle Airport in Paris, which are representative of the changes taking place both in architecture and engineering. Terminal 2E is a majestic expression of grandeur with seemingly endless curving spaces and delicately filtered daylight [4]. The same aspiration is cultivated more intensively in the modernizing

1 FUTURIST IMAGINATION
In his manifesto *Futurist Architecture*, published in 1914, the Italian visionary Antonio Sant'Elia describes the industrialized and mechanized city of the future, not as a mass of individual buildings, but as a vast, multilevel, interconnected, and integrated urban conurbation designed around the spine of urbanity and infrastructure. His unbuilt projects embodied bold forms inspired by modern technology. Included in his famous series of drawings for *La Città Nuova* ("The New City"), the central train station and airport are conceived as one monumental structure.

2 LINEAR INDUSTRIAL CITY

During World War II, the French-Swiss architect and founder of the modern movement Le Corbusier assembled a group of French modernist thinkers and designers to prepare the reconstruction of the country in terms of architectural renovation. With this *ASCORAL* group he prepared a number of models that closely linked the organization of the planned settlement (in this case the linear industrial city) to the configuration of the transportation networks.

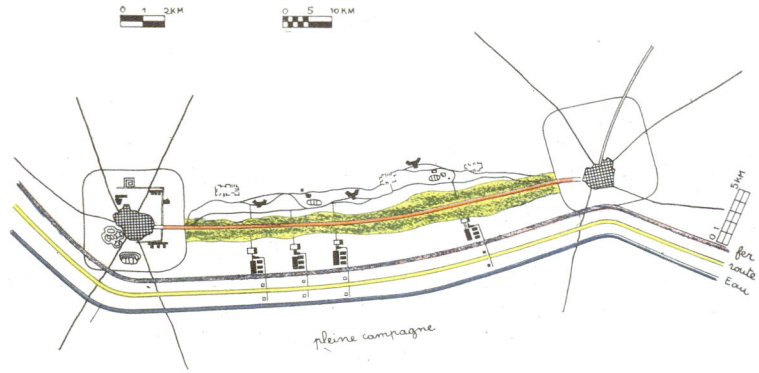

3 SCULPTURAL CONCRETE

The iconic TWA Terminal at New York's JFK Airport, completed in 1962 by Eero Saarinen, remains a symbol in airport design. The curving contours of concrete, soaring roof, and expressive interior spaces evoke a bird in flight, and the sculptural gracefulness celebrates the modern drama of airborne travel. Saarinen pushed the relation of architecture and engineering to new limits, combining an expression of dynamic form with the possibilities of concrete.

4 TUNNEL TECHNOLOGY

Terminal 2E (104,000 square meters) of Charles de Gaulle Airport in Roissy, north of Paris, France, by Paul Andreu applies the flow and flux of air-travel passengers as the primary driver of form. Pragmatism and functionality give way to innovation and restraint. Tunnel-building technology, combined with circular lenses spared out of the shuttering and cofferdam, allows for vast spans of the elliptical reinforced concrete shell (covered with African timber in the check-in area) and diffuse daylight of an almost magical quality.

5 BALANCED SUSPENSION

The 320-meter-long stainless steel Millennium Bridge, hovering lightly over the Thames, by Foster + Partners links the area of St. Paul's Cathedral to the north with the Globe Theatre and Tate Modern on Bankside. The shallow suspension bridge is formed by two Y-shaped armatures that support eight cables that run along the sides of the four-meter-wide deck, while steel transverse arms clamp onto the cables at eight-meter intervals to support the deck itself. This structural configuration means that the cables never rise more than 2.3 meters above the deck, allowing pedestrians uninterrupted panoramic views of the surrounding buildings.

6 CANTILEVERED AWNING

Designed by the French architect-engineer Marc Mimram, the supporting structure of the huge awning covering the Éprunes toll station at Melun on the A5 highway between Troyes and Dijon in France consists of a hinged half-arc portico in steel box beams of variable inertia. It shapes a long asymmetrical and cantilevered vault formed by long palm-shaped leaves that not only shelters motorists but marks a memorable sign of passage at the scale of the highway and the extended landscape around it.

7 **CONTAINER TECH**

Completed in 2003, Union Pacific Railroad's Global III Intermodal Facility in Rochelle, Illinois, is an interchange hub and container loading/unloading terminal for rail and truck shipments. It is a logistical platform that has a capacity of 25 trains and 3000 containers daily. It is equipped with an automated gate system, software to maximize terminal efficiency, on-site refrigeration capabilities, and lead tracks to allow trains to access the switchyard at higher speeds. The facility is a state-of-the-art transfer terminal for standardized cargo and for trailers to and from railroads and interstate highways.

region of Asia where new, large airports are conceived to display the ideal of progress through technological expression. The Suvarnabhumi Airport in Bangkok by Murphy/Jahn Architects convincingly combines size and structural bravura with innovative climate engineering to resourcefully address the tropical climate of Thailand.

Bridges are also structures where engineering is often tied to aesthetics. Arup engineers have been working with architects – and artists – over the past decades to create spectacular pedestrian bridges. Both London's Millennium Bridge and Melbourne's Webb Bridge spring from a collaboration between architecture, art, and engineering [5]. Norman Foster's team created a bridge with a uniquely thin profile, forming a slender arc across the Thames and spanning the greatest possible distance with minimum means. A thin ribbon of steel by day, it forms a glowing blade of light at night. In Melbourne architects Denton Corker Marshall worked with artist Robert Owen to create a cocoon-like structure that would not have been possible before the era of computer-aided three-dimensional modeling. Both the Millennium and Webb bridges not only allow users to appreciate the surrounding views and activities, but also have become destinations in their own right.

The fascination for technology is also expressed in many service buildings along highways. Clearly, such a high-tech approach is a form of branding. It emblematizes the modernity of the amenity and, by extension, of the gas, catering, or toll-highway company that is providing it. Because these technical facilities have to be grasped at a glance, their form is often more geared to presenting an iconic image than to achieving tactile refinement. Marc Mimram's toll-booth canopy on the A5 highway at Melun, France, works as an impressive gate [6]. By designing a long arch over the highway that counterbalances the palm structures holding up the awning, he avoids the habitual roof-supporting columns that visually divide the space between the ticket booths. Similarly, on the E19, near Nivelles in Belgium, Philippe Samyn constructed a service station that appears like an elegant single-span bridge building, avoiding any support structure in the service area and offering a formidable translucency to the long, vaulted restaurant that makes the slim overpass light up at night as a shimmering gateway. The final examples of this attitude are of a wholly different nature. Their mark of technological ability resides not so much in their expression of sophistication and stylishness, but in the raw force of technological advancement required to master the demanding objectives they were set to resolve. The first is the new railroad connecting the northwestern Chinese city of Qinghai to Tibet. Working on "the roof of the world" in extreme climatic conditions led engineers to develop a number of innovative techniques to allow such a remote area to be conquered. The second example, the Global III Intermodal Terminal in Rochelle, Illinois, is representative of a new generation of transfer terminals between modes of transport [7]. It is designed as a vast and highly efficient machine, with little regard for the landscape. No doubt, its enormous size is awe-inspiring and for that reason supernatural. Because of its magnitude, it prompts a fundamental rethinking of the dimensions of freight transport.

1 William Curtis, *Modern Architecture Since 1900*. (Englewood Cliffs: Prentice Hall, 1982), 309.

Moment Diagrams + High-Tech Membrane

SUVARNABHUMI AIRPORT

Bangkok, Thailand

Architect: Murphy/Jahn Architects

Structural Engineer: Werner Sobek, Martin/Martin

Environmental Engineer: Transsolar Energietechnik

Date: 1995–2005

The new passenger terminal at Suvarnabhumi Airport (*suvarnabhumi* means "land of gold") in Bangkok is a modern gateway to Thailand, at once revealing an affinity for global technology and local cultural tradition. The highly engineered roof of the terminal and the technologically mediated spaces are counterbalanced by shaded gardens flanking the terminal, a jungle garden between the terminal and the concourse, and traditional Thai patterns and colors on glazed surfaces and floors. It is the extraordinary roof, however, that leaves the most awe-inspiring and lasting impression on the visitor. A 570-x-200-meter structure spans the completely glazed central terminal hall and covers the two large gardens. The great cantilevered canopy that appears to float over the hall rests on eight pairs of columns, each supporting a primary truss. The three-chord trusses of welded steel are essentially the built geometry of moment

diagrams and thereby change in section depending on which chord is in compression. The megatrusses liberate the massive column-free space. Tubular concourses appended to the central hall consist of typical bays. The concourses are roofed by a total of 104 identical three-chord, five-point trusses of varying depth that resemble linked wishbones. The membrane stretches 27 meters between the trusses and alternates with areas of glazing.

Bangkok's intense tropical heat, humidity, and sunlight, in addition to structural and acoustic demands, led to the development of a now-patented translucent fabric membrane made up of four layers: an outer structural and weatherproofing surface composed of Teflon-coated, high-performance glass fiber; a middle airtight layer of polycarbonate panels that block out aircraft noise, absorb interior sounds, and stiffen

the membrane against wind; an inner skin of open-weave fiberglass, transparent to sound; and an interior aluminum coating that reflects outside heat back toward the exterior. The continual cooling and dehumidification of the spaces places high demands on the building envelope to minimize the effects of solar loads. The facades in the central hall used fritted glass (95% opacity) on the north side and solid panels limiting the solar gain to 1% of the radiation striking through the south side. A cantilevered, louvered roof shades the 40-meter-high vertical glazing. The configuration and materials eliminated the need for artificial illumination during daylight hours, and even with a graduated frit the glazing appears entirely clear from the interior. After dark, the metallic inner surface becomes an effective reflector for indirect lighting.

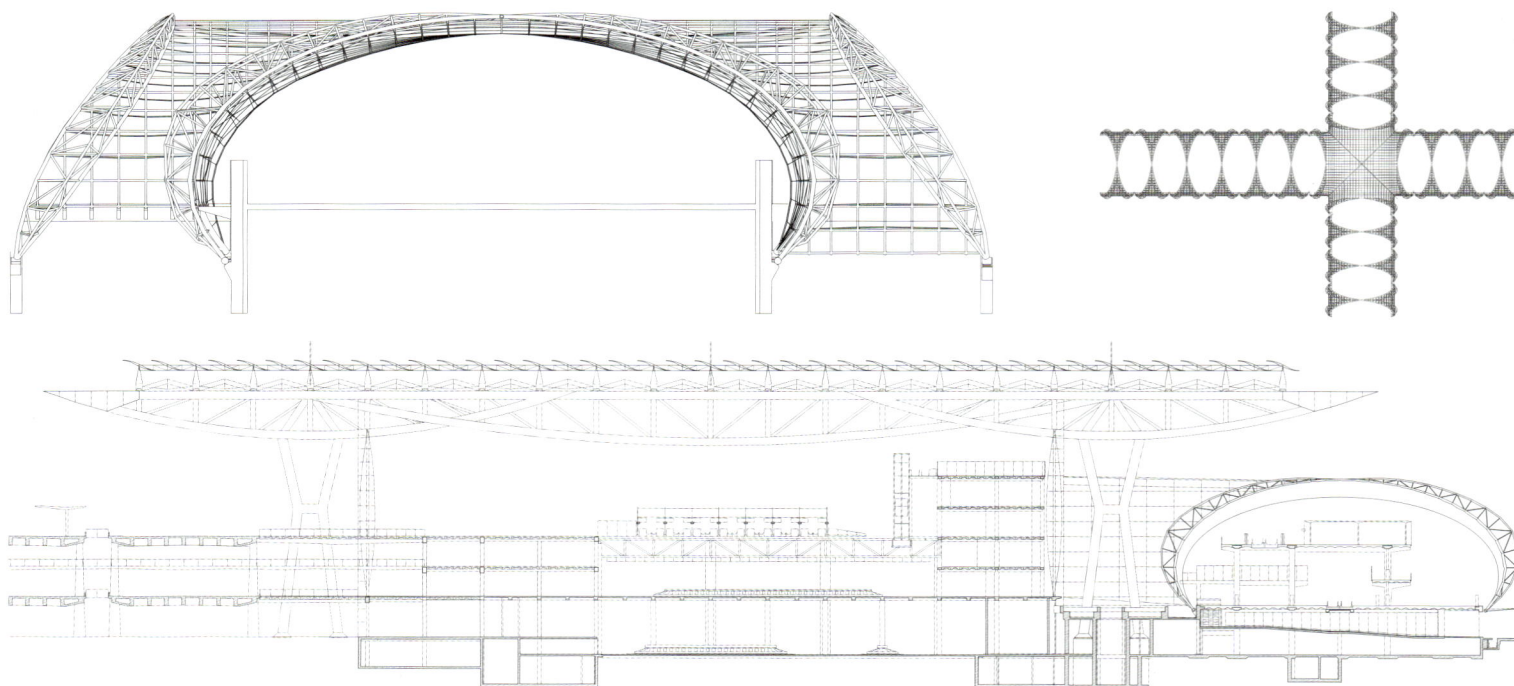

Steel-Lattice Cocoon

WEBB BRIDGE

Melbourne, Australia

Architect: Denton Corker Marshall

Engineer: Ove Arup & Partners

Artist: Robert Owen

Date: 2000–2003

The new sculptural pedestrian and cycle bridge, which includes a wheelchair ramp, over the Yarra River was part of a public art project (1% of the budget of new development) in Melbourne's Docklands area. The 80-meter-long snake-like form of the hairpin curve section of the bridge is seamlessly joined to 145 meters of an existing remnant of the Webb Dock Rail Bridge. The new, ramping and sinuous connection accommodates level changes and links the Docklands on the north side to the new residential developments on the south side. Architects Denton Corker Marshall teamed up with local Australian artist Robert Owen, who is known for mixed-media installations, and

Arup engineers to create the simple and yet complex structure – postrationalized for its resemblance to the woven-stick eel traps that Koorie aborigines used two centuries years ago in local rivers.

The structure consists of a steel box topped by a pigmented concrete screed deck contained within ribs of ovoid-shaped hoops that vary in diameter from 5 to 8.7 meters and from 4 to 8.9 meters in height. They are constructed from hot-dip galvanized steel sections measuring 15 by 150 millimeters, with their flats facing outwards, placed at varying centers along the bridge. They are connected to one another by a series of

hot-dip galvanized mild steel straps 150 millimeters wide. At the northern bank, the structure begins as a series of plain hoops that grow further apart towards the middle of the span. As one approaches the south bank, the hoops increase in density again to form a filigree cocoon. The entire bridge was assembled on barges in Victoria Harbor and floated into position at high tide. By night, the bridge floor is backlit with white cold-cathode lamps mounted under the side edges and metal-halide lamps at the handrail that bounce light up against the inner surface of the arches.

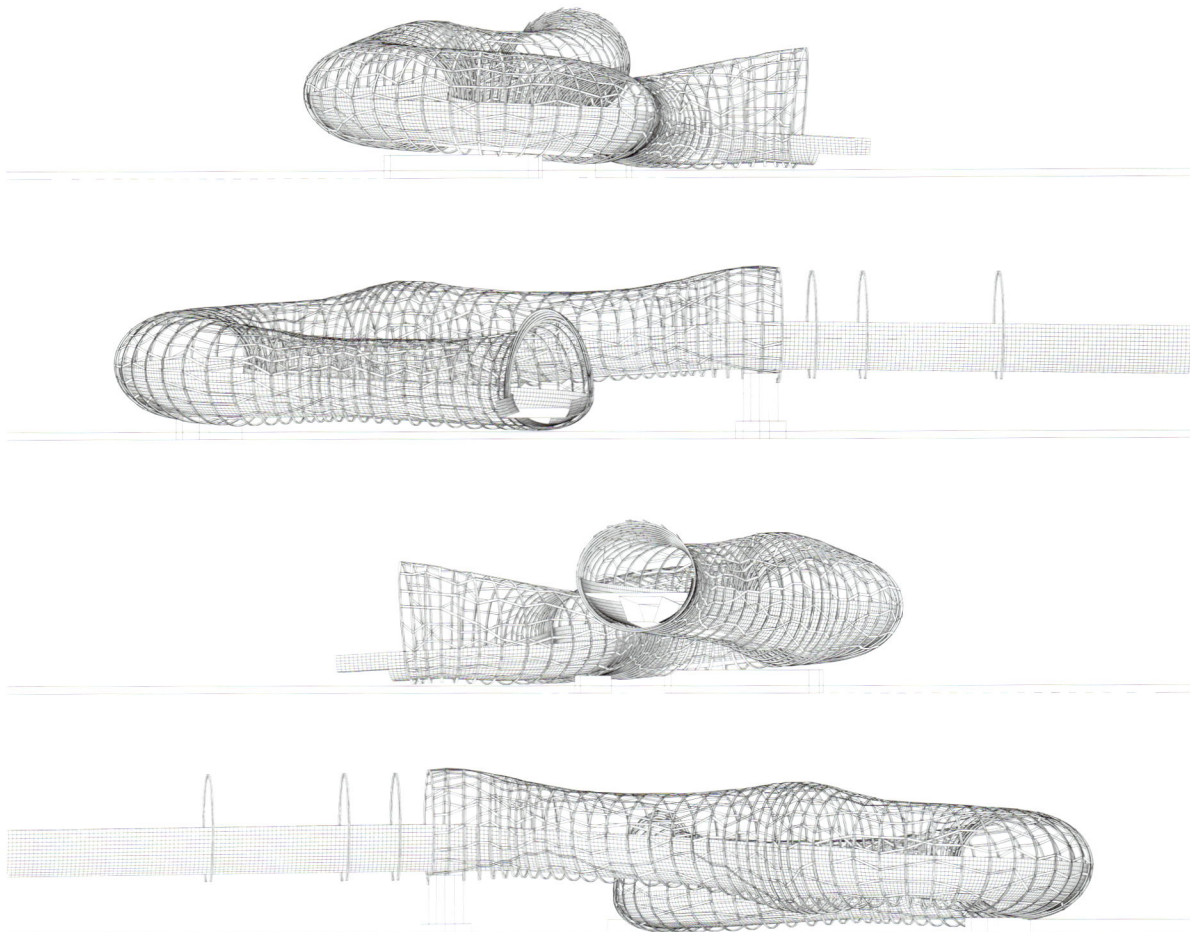

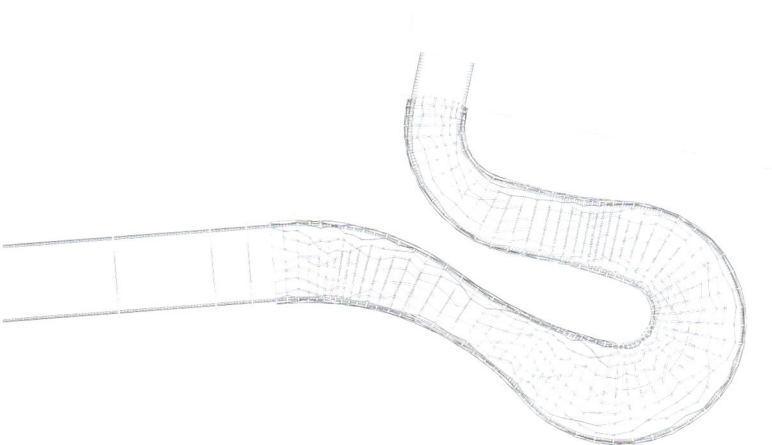

Perched Over the Highway

ORIVAL SERVICE STATION AND RESTAURANTS

Nivelles, Belgium

Architect: Samyn and Partners

Engineer: Setesco

Date: 1998–2001

Samyn and Partners' elegant design won the competition launched in 1998 by the Belgian Walloon Region for a rest area with two service stations, two self-service restaurants, 200 parking spaces, playgrounds, and picnic areas. By melding the two restaurants together in a building perched over the busy E19 highway between Brussels and Paris, the architects produced a compact footprint, inserting all roofed constructions into a single intervention, and thus left the rest of the site open for a landscape treatment with speed-reducing curved parking zones and ample grass surfaces, complementing the undulating Brabant countryside.

The elongated building as a thin circular slice refers to the characteristic form of the local landscape. Instead of two arches bowing over each direction of the highway as was called for in the competition brief, the solution was a rectilinear opening that marks a stylish gateway and avoids the potential collision danger of a central pier. The two 210-meter-long tapered Warren Truss girders rest on two supports placed 70 meters apart from each other. The position of these piers not only allows for an unbuilt area of 10 meters on each side of the motorway, but also leaves the entire service area free of columns. To cover the service stations, the catering building spanning the highway is extended on each side with two cantilevered awnings. Four secondary awnings are suspended under the cantilevers of the principal lattice girders and complete the protection. Access to the bridge building is through glazed circulation shafts extending from the supporting piers that protect the service area from the noise of the highway.

The interior of the catering building gracefully reflects the structural concept. The elongated vault relates to the overall form of the roof and the ample provision of diffuse daylight reflects the trussed girders on both sides. The highly insulated covering and metal screens against direct sunlight penetration were made in aluminum to minimize weight and keep the structure as slender as possible.

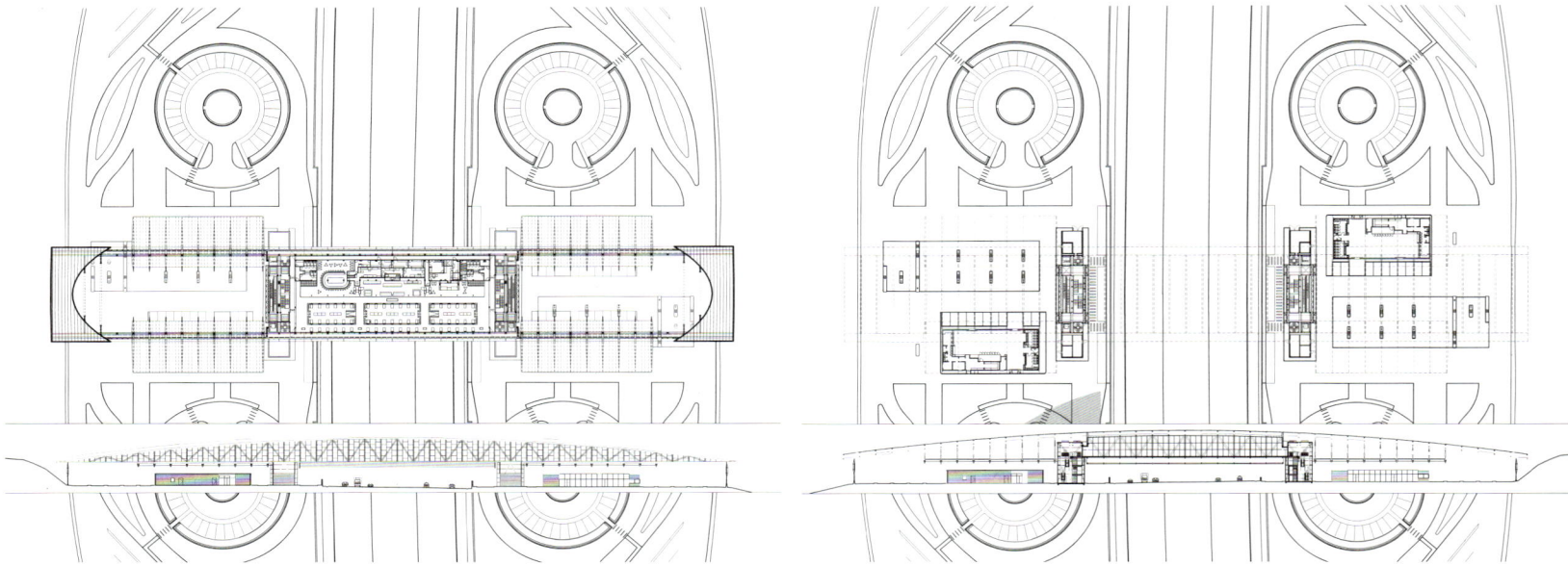

Colonizing the Roof of the World

Xining (China) to Lhasa (Tibet)

Engineer: Li Jin Cheng

Date: 2001–2006 (last section)

QINGHAI-TIBET RAILROAD

Opened in 2006, this 1956-kilometer-long railroad connects Xining in Qinghai Province to Lhasa in Tibet. Chinese dreams of a rail connection to Tibet were already included in Dr. Sun Yat-sen's 1912 plan to build 100,000 kilometers of tracks across the entire country. Concrete plans for the mountainous railroad were drawn up as early as 1955 and a first section, from Lanzhou to Xining, was completed in 1959. However, the project was suspended at the start of the Cultural Revolution in 1966. Since then, it has had a number of technical setbacks due to frozen soil and very high altitudes. The plan was finally pushed through by the Chinese government – and predictably with a good deal of controversy. For the government, the railroad represents not only an enormous economic corridor for the exploitation of animal resources, tourism, and the transport of minerals, but also national unity and a means of stabilizing borderland control. For critics, the project has and will continue to have numerous detrimental effects on the environment – foremost of which is the dramatic opening of the Tibetan Plateau to more tourism – and it is seen as a forceful means for China to strengthen its political and military control over Tibet.

The Qinghai-Tibet railroad runs through some of the most difficult terrain on earth, rising at one point (Tanggula Pass) to 5072 meters above sea level. Extreme temperatures and unstable permafrost proved a challenge to its construction. The 1338-meter-long Fenghuoshan tunnel is the highest rail tunnel in the world at 4905 meters above sea level. The line crosses 675 bridges, totaling a length of 160 kilometers. Some 550 kilometers of the railroad connection are laid on permafrost. This necessitated construction on elevated tracks with foundations sunk deep into the ground. Metal sunshades and hollow concrete pipes beneath the tracks keep the rail bed frozen. Similar to the Trans-Alaska Pipeline System, portions of the track are passively cooled with ammonia-based heat exchangers. Since the air in Tibet contains 35 to 40% less oxygen than at sea level, special passenger carriages with enriched oxygen had to be developed, as were oxygen factories along the railroad, ultraviolet protection systems, and methods to heat water in the toilets to prevent freezing. Today the railroad is glorified as one of China's major technical accomplishments of the 21st century.

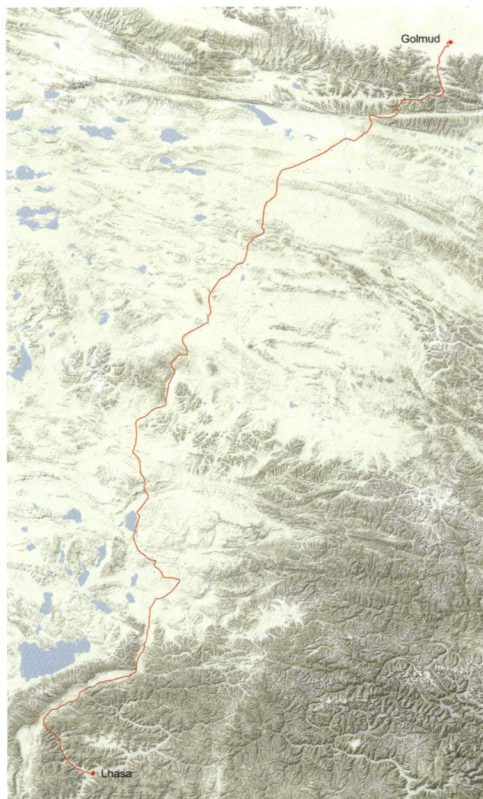

BACKDROP FOR FLUX ANIMATION

Massive flows of movement are often a backdrop for a number of contemporary infrastructure projects. Entry and exit points of transportation networks usually present themselves as intermodal transfer hubs, particularly where collective transport systems connect or meet with individual means of travel. In fact, some central transfer hubs go so far as to make an aesthetic of flows, where the voyeurism of travel meets the dynamism of city. Flow planning, the spatial sequencing of program components and the organizing principle of projects, enhances and celebrates the ebb and flow of travelers. Indeterminate, in-between, transit, mingling spaces are often included in the projects and are able to accommodate various unplanned events and encounters. Spaces of hybridization result and the pragmatic demands of motion have become a contemporary choreography, an aesthetic of movement. The projects that utilize such an approach are most often located at strategic places in the city and both reply upon and intensify the notion of infrastructure as an urban generator. Such transport-network nodes have become places of urban hyperactivity – fields of chance and movement.

The work of Bernard Tschumi is emblematic of such notion. His "event cities" are made by the movement of bodies in space and portray an infrastructure, or architecture in general, that acts as a backdrop for flux animation.[1] For Tschumi, architecture is indeed not static, but has its origins in the concept of mobility. Completed in 2001, his Flon Interchange bus and train station formed a component of his theoretical Bridge-City project for Lausanne, Switzerland, begun in 1988 [1]. The idea of topological displacements and cross-programming literally enabled the connecting of levels between the historical city and the Flon Valley via "inhabited bridges" where transit spaces melt with urban programs. Each bridge accommodates two categories of use: a core element for public or commercial functions; and a deck level for pedestrian traffic and spaces for appropriation by unpredictable urban events. The potential of producing urban activity with places of transport exchange was also fully exploited in the new Berlin Central Station development in Berlin, Germany. Von Gerkan, Marg und Partner modeled the massive structure on the different vectors of the train tracks, their interrelation, and the idea of hyper accessibility. As a requirement of the client, and working with economics and the desire to make the station key to the urban regeneration of the area, the architects inserted a substantial shopping center into enlarged transit spaces. As such, flows of different nature systematically interact with the clear intention of generating animation and unanticipated public gathering.

A rich mixture of activities to stimulate a qualitative confrontation with movement was also behind the winning competition entry for the Tromsø Ferry Terminal in Norway by Space Group [2]. The organization of a

1 URBAN GENERATOR

Bernard Tschumi Architects exploited the naturally steep topography of Lausanne, Switzerland, to create a bus and train station that adds to the city's network of bridges, elevators, and escalators. Located in the heart of the Flon Valley at the Place de l'Europe, the Flon Interchange links four different lines of commuter services by the convergence of "inhabited bridges" – rectilinear steel-framed structures, sheathed in red-printed glass – and links the industrial valley to the historic city above. The north-south connections generate densities of people and hybrid programs: bridges are walkways and departure areas, the station platforms serve as streets, and the public plaza provides an urban garden.

2 CHARGED SCENOGRAPHY

Won in an international competition by Space Group, the Tromsø Ferry Terminal in northern Norway rethinks the city's threshold between land and water through the organization of flows of busses, ferries, and speedboats, as well as guests of the hotel, congress center, and spa. A new landfill wraps the existing coastline and creates an artificial topography where streets penetrate the structure and ships sail straight to the raised "urban floor." Each program is spatially distinguished. The waiting rooms and mingling areas have a varied scenography (inner garden versus terrace to the sea), while the terminal itself forms part of the city's public promenade.

3 SLOPED PLANES

The continuous ramping floors (100 meters long, 17.5 meters wide, 3% grade) of the temporary bicycle storage building near Amsterdam Central Station in the Netherlands by VMX Architects form an animated series of artificial ground planes and an open stage for the comings and goings of cyclists. The extremely efficient stacking and routing system for 2500 bikes consists of a single surface folded onto itself and suspended over the quay wall of a canal. The same red asphalt of the city's cycle routes covers the metal slopes, and the steel structure has been detailed to appear light.

sequence of events and "symphony of objects" is developed as a continuous interface between the citizen and traveler. The raised urban floor, an artificial topography that allows for panoramic views of the spectacular natural landscape, was pursued even more radically by Foreign Office Architects in the Yokohama Port Terminal in Japan. Designed on the dynamics of movement, the terminal appears as a terrain in motion and its materiality recalls the world of boats. The structure blurs the distinction between architecture, engineering, and landscape, and the transportation node and civic gathering space meld into one. The elegant origami-like surface of the ground that folds onto itself shares a formal and metaphorical likeness to the Olympic Sculpture Park in Seattle, Washington, by Weiss/Manfredi Architects. In Seattle, the design integrates architecture, landscape design, and urban infrastructure (railroad, vehicular approach, waterfront promenade) to unify three separate parcels of land previously separated by train tracks and roads, and unites art, city, and coast into one unremitting landscape.

The fascination and instrumentality of the folded plane where wall, roof, and structure merge is a feature of a wide range of infrastructure projects and is evidently a logical tactic for parking garages, where sloping planes are part of the vocabulary. The temporary bicycle storage in Amsterdam, the Netherlands, by VMX Architects is simply made of ramped plates screened by a protective mesh balustrade system – literally creating a stage for urban movement of the cyclists and viewing platform over the flows of trains in the station and tourist boats in the canal it is suspended over [3]. And, finally, a similar fascination for flows leads to the underground artificial topography by OMA and LAB-DA for the Souterrain Tunnel Complex in The Hague, the Netherlands. An amazing underworld is constructed here by a series of interconnecting parking garages, ramps, galleries, and tram stops that meld together to form the enlivened spaces of the richly developed section of this narrow tunnel of the Souterrain project.

1 Bernard Tschumi, *Event Cities* (Cambridge: MIT Press, 1994).

Animated Crossing

BERLIN CENTRAL STATION

Berlin, Germany

Architect: Von Gerkan, Marg und Partner

Engineers: Schlaich, Bergermann und Partner; ivz / Emch + Berger

Date: 1994–2006

The new impressive train station for 30 million passengers per year was planned after the reunification of Germany and the decision to make Berlin once again the nation's capital. However, the idea was not new. In Nazi Germany, the site of the 19th-century station in the bend of the Spree River was destined to become the grandiose termination of the north-south axis of the city – and for this it became a target of allied bombing. Today, Berlin Central Station is Europe's largest train station. In addition to the new north-south u-Bahn and the east-west s-Bahn, the station accommodates two high-speed ICE tracks: a north-south line that forms part of the Scandinavia-Sicily route; and an east-west line that forms part

of the London-Moscow route. In addition to the complicated rail line geometries and engineering, the commission explicitly requested "a shopping center with rail link"; it was deemed an important, even symbolic, component of the larger area's redevelopment.

The station is straightforward in its section: pedestrian, tram, taxi, bus, and car access are situated at street level, east-west tracks at 10 meters above ground and north-south tracks at 15 meters below ground. The east-west tracks are covered by a 430-meter-long barrel-vaulted glass roof whose tensile cable structure lends it a modern look while also echoing the skeletal structure of older

train sheds. The concourse hall (170 by 50 meters and 50 meters high) cuts across two building slabs that contain retail, office, service facilities, and a hotel. The glass-and-steel constructed, column-free hall serves as an open, transparent, and inviting passageway, a salient beacon on the route from the Moabit neighborhood in the north, to the parliament and government buildings in the south. Large openings in the floor of the concourse carry daylight to the deepest spaces of the station and allow people to observe the bustle on the many levels of the building. The entire complex is spatially bound by a 4.4-meter-high plinth that acts as a huge public space for pedestrians.

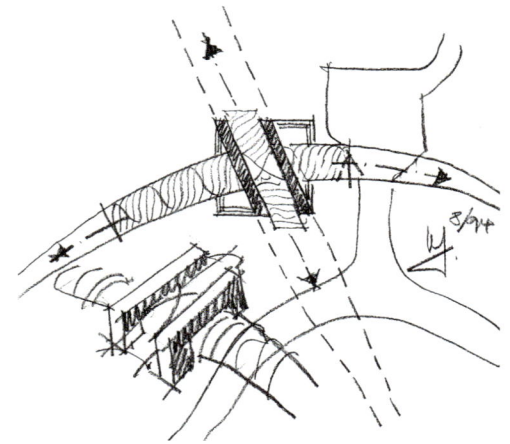

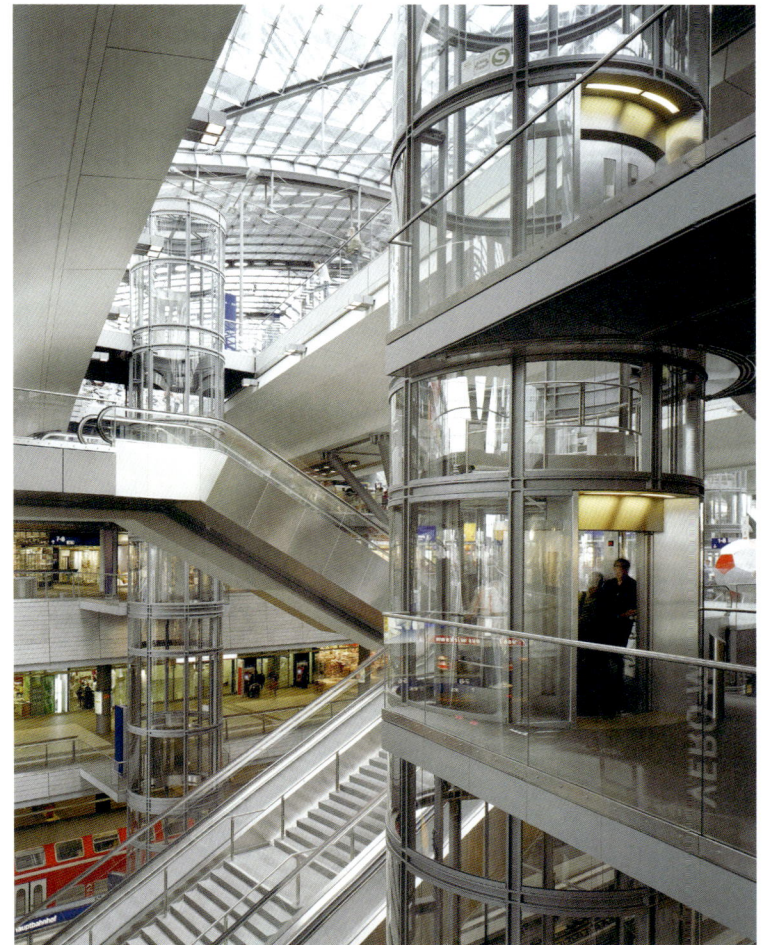

Mediated Harbor Garden

Yokohama, Japan

Architect: Foreign Office Architects

Engineer: Structure Design Group (1998-2002) / Ove Arup & Partners (1995-96)

Date: 1995–2002

YOKOHAMA PORT TERMINAL

Yokohama Port Terminal is an icon of its time. It was touted as a paradigmatic example of an artificial topography and computer-generated form, where multiple modes of infrastructure, public space, and ferry terminal programs are indistinguishably blurred into a continuous passage. Its uniqueness is unchallenged, yet it is importantly part of a larger restructuring of the city's port and part of the urban-leisure chain of programs on the Japanese coast from Tokyo to Yokohama. The client's request for the project was the concept of *ni-wa-minato* ("mediation") between garden and harbor and also between the citizens of Yokohama and those from the outside world.

The new ground surface is created as a 430-meter-long, 45-meter-wide pier protruding into Yokohama Bay as well as a seamless extension of Yamashita Park. The boarding level of the terminal is conceived as an extension of the city itself and the paths intensify the experience of passing through the structure by duplicating the number of events that are encountered. The building's circulation system is organized as a series of loops in which the borders between the dynamic and the static have been removed. Travelers and locals can inhabit the main passenger hall with its faceted dark-steel ceiling as well as its visceral passages and chambers, stroll along the sweeping flows of the warm-colored ironwood (Brazilian Ipe) flooring, occupy

the terraced steps that form a 500-seat amphitheater, or retreat to any number of grassy knolls. Mobile or collapsible physical barriers and surveillance points enable the reconfiguration of the borders between territories, allowing the terminal to be occupied by locals or overtaken by foreigners. The folding topography of warping planes melds inside and outside as the multi-level interior envelops the outdoors within. The artificial earthwork affords sweeping waterfront views from the rooftop park. The entirely steel structure (to resist earthquake forces) of different sections (27 trusses at 16-meter intervals) allows interior and exterior to morph into each other.

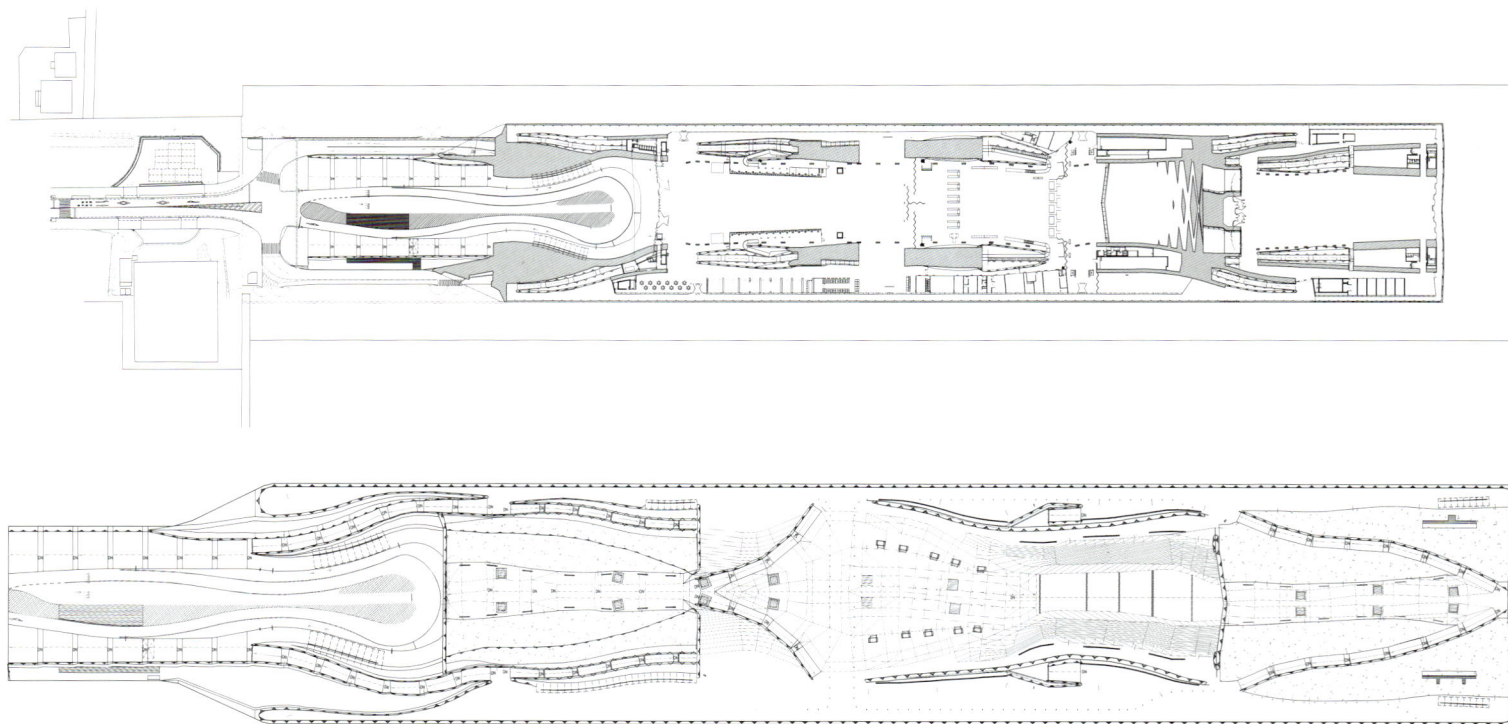

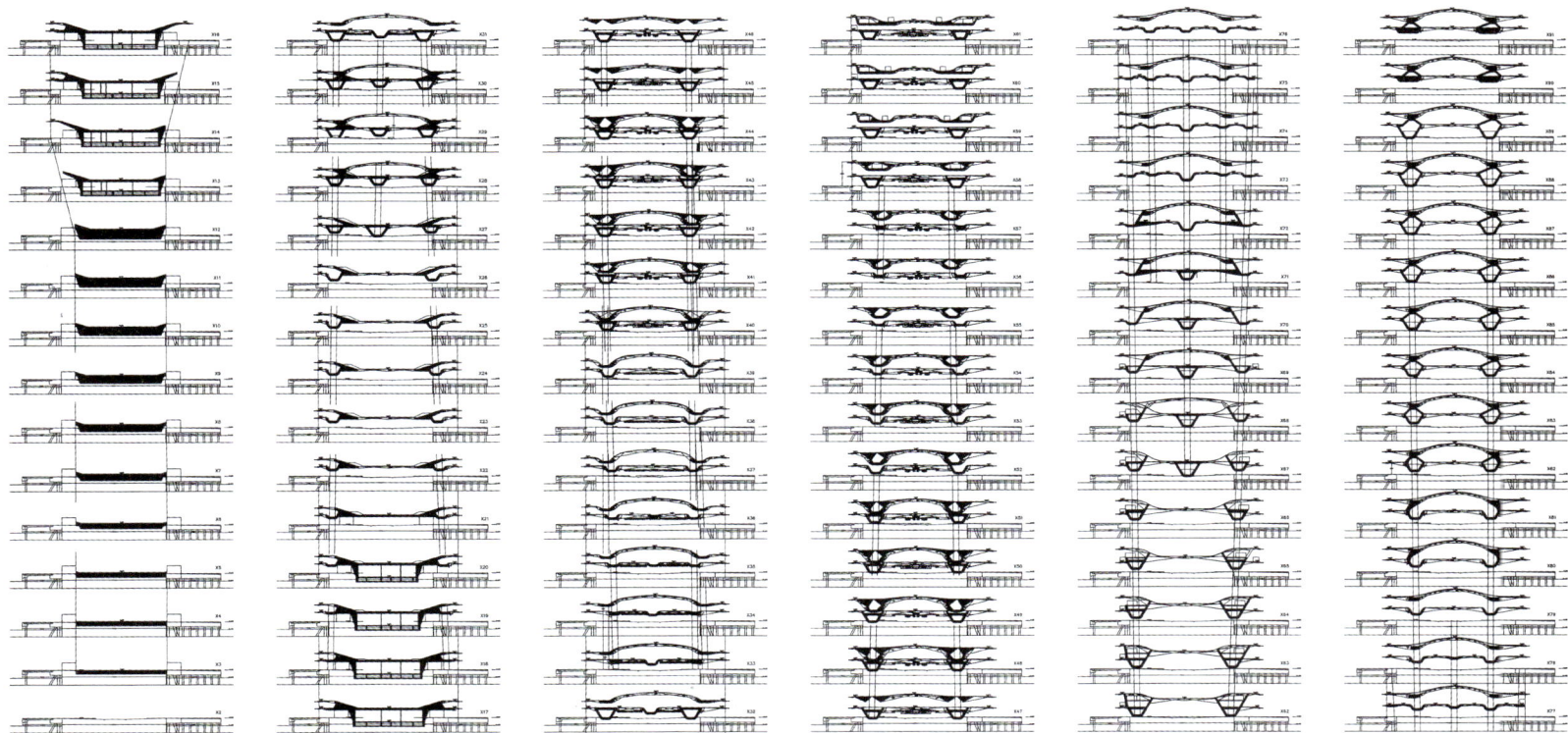

Vector Works

SEATTLE OLYMPIC SCULPTURE PARK

Seattle, Washington, USA

Architect: Weiss/Manfredi Architects

Landscape Architect: Charles Anderson Landscape Architecture

Date: 2001–2007

After winning an international competition, Weiss/Manfredi Architects transformed a difficult city edge into a vibrant civic area. The site is emblematic of many North American coastal locations: obsolete brownfield areas cut off from the urban fabric by large works of infrastructure. In the case of Seattle, the location of Unocal (Union Oil of California), an oil transfer facility, was on a leveled hill and landfill in Elliott Bay on Puget Sound. It was severed from the city by the Burlington Northern Railroad line and four-lane thoroughfare of Elliot Avenue. The area was slated to become a hotel and condominium complex, but due to the entrepreneurship of the Seattle Art Museum and the Trust for Public Land, the city instead received an urban sculpture

park and revitalized public waterfront. The 3.6-hectare site is structured by a 760-meter-long Z-shaped platform that bridges but does not hide the infrastructure lines. It also ensures topographical continuity over a 12-meter height difference of the newly constructed landscape with sloping panels of precast concrete, gravel paths, and carpets of grass. The pedestrian route (including smaller paths and detours) begins in the southeast corner of the site with a 3200-square-meter glass and metal exhibition pavilion (which becomes a luminous beacon at night) and descends to the waterfront via three segments, each imbued with a contemporary reinterpretation of archetypal landscapes of the Northwest. The geometric clarity, with strong converging and

diverging edges, frames different views of the city, water, and mountains. The middle segment is directly on axis with Mount Rainier (monument of the Olympic Mountain Range, from which the park takes its name). At the waterfront, the new park is seamlessly connected to Myrtle Edwards Park, which runs along bay shore to the north. The folds and turns of the constructed topography create series of outdoor rooms for a range of modern sculpture, including pieces by Richard Serra, Teresita Fernández, and Mark Dion. The site is more than a sculpture park with a strong identity; it is a passageway from the high ground to the water, an open park of domesticated infrastructure in the middle of the city.

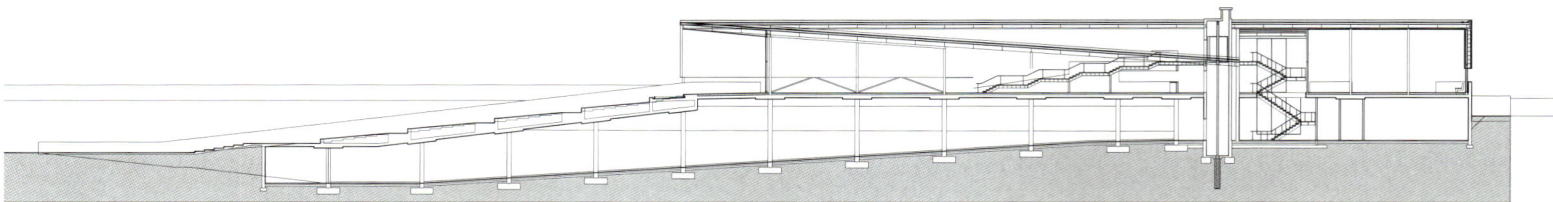

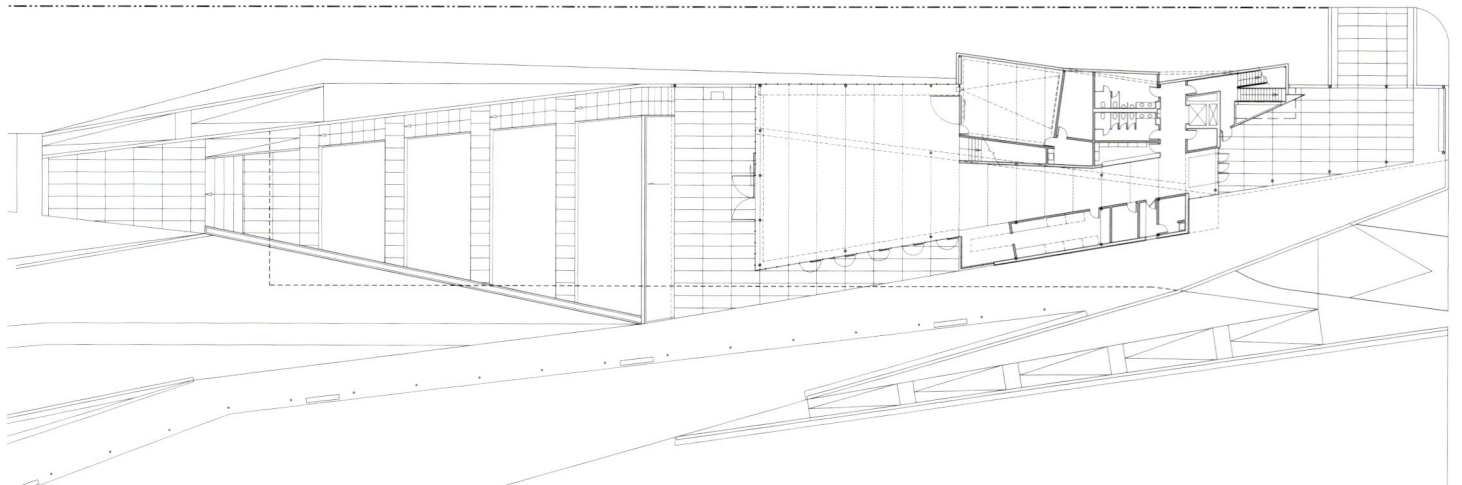

Before

After

Vibrant Underground

SOUTERRAIN TUNNEL COMPLEX

The Hague, the Netherlands

Architect: OMA and LAB-DA

Date: 1994–2004

This multistory tunnel complex runs beneath The Hague's main shopping street, the Grote Marktstraat. The development includes two underground tram stations at its ends, a two-level parking garage for 375 cars immediately below ground level, and a permanent archeological exhibit and poster museum. The tunnel is flanked by department stores on both sides and connects, by way of other parking garages, to the so-called parking ring-road that encircles the one million square-meter island of CBD development. The Souterrain complex liberates the street above for the exclusive use of city strollers. Its longitudinal section (1250 meters long and 15 meters wide) is determined by the route of the tramway, with gentle slopes descending to level -2 at both ends and ample space (the lowest point is 12 meters below ground level) for

a variety of uses, such as parking spaces in the hollows above the tram tracks.

The challenge of such an extensive underground complex was met by varying the width and height of the cavern to create a sequence of different spaces, to connect physically or visually to other parts of the tunnel program, to provide views of the city or sky outside, and to link the tunnel to the surrounding shops. The structural integrity and economical efficiency of tunnel design were fully exploited. In terms of ventilation, the tunnel functions as a duct; in terms of structure, the walls, floor, and ceiling act together to support the whole complex. The parking garage is organized in response to the linearity of the structure, and transparent walls to the tram stations animate the garage. The longitudinally inclined con-

crete slabs of the garage form part of the platform's ceiling and the glazed galleries and ramps that give access to the garage levels suggest uninterrupted passage. The many entry points and walkways, as well as the direction of the movement they generate (along the tunnel axis, or orthogonal or oblique to it) create a dynamic sensation of multiple users. All these interpenetrations produce an unmistakable sense of people on the move. Together with the daylight penetration, they create a reassuring sense of security in an underground space perceived as urban hallway, even though the interior finishing – poured concrete walls molded and enlivened by daylight and artificial lighting and contrasting wooden floors – is almost nonexistent.

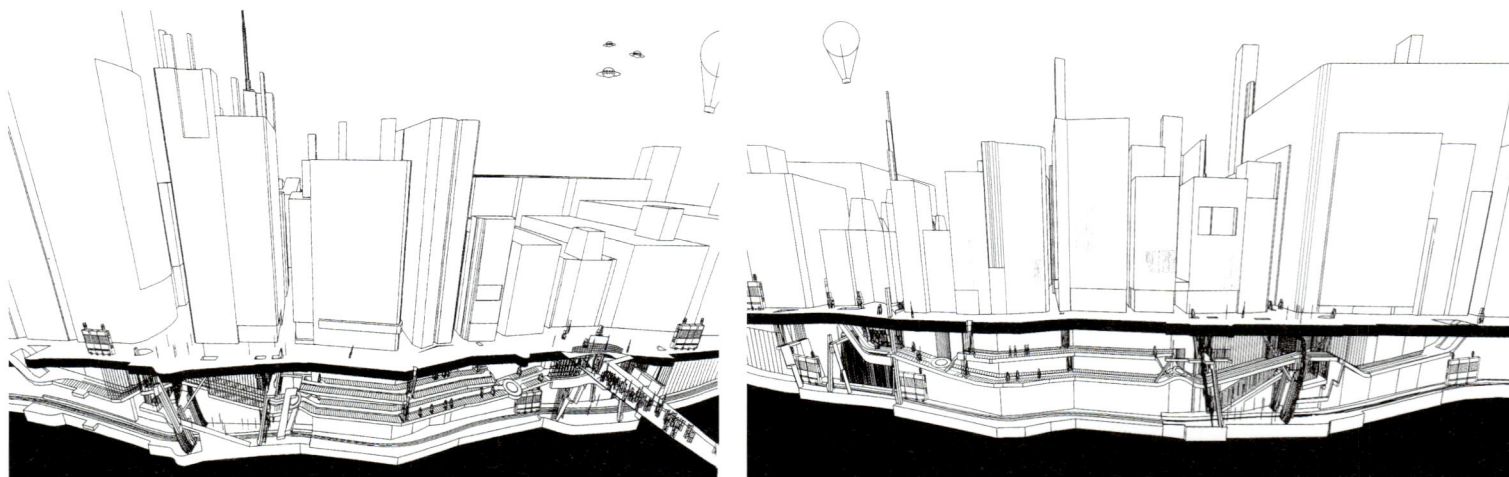

GALLERY OF CIVIC UNDERSTANDING

Today, governments invest heavily in infrastructure projects. At the same time, public engagement in sectors like urban renovation, civic improvement, and the provision of public amenities has been shrinking over recent decades. Along with this withdrawal of the public hand in urban development projects, the meaning of the collective realm has altered and infrastructure has gained renewed recognition as public space. Such perception indicates that the conventional idea of the public sphere has been maintained in most forms of contemporary public transport. More often than not, the ticketing price is low enough to make systems accessible for all types of public, and even when slight price discrimination occurs – in the case of air travel, for instance – there remain opportunities for unforeseen encounters. Transport hubs often work as the prolongation of conventional streets. They are centers of urbanity where the consciousness of the other, awakened by the sharing of a single space, refers to the common understanding of the public realm. People experience this sense of rubbing shoulders in the hustle and bustle while changing modes of transportation. As transport infrastructure guides people's travels and movements, metro, bus, tram, and train stations become real places of gathering. They attract bigger crowds than those usually attracted to other public activities.

The history of public transportation is replete with splendid examples of vast, imposing concourses, vaults and waiting halls that express exuberance and civility. In Moscow, the lavishly designed underground stations, known as "People's Palaces," were part and parcel of Soviet propaganda [1]. Throughout the world, train sheds of the 19th and early 20th centuries were great engineering feats and important symbols that displayed the prestige of cities. The Helsinki Railway Station in Finland by Eliel Saarinen is emblematic of this era of grand station halls that not only embodied a sense of civic dignity but also echoed nationalist sympathies in the materials and detailing [2]. In terms of transportation, the public realm has two faces. Besides the sense of public gathering that spaces of transport engender, there is the collective consciousness that individually made journeys over common itineraries provoke. In this second kind of public sphere it is the spatial memory of the route that is meaningful. As landscape architect Chris Reed commented, "Infrastructure has the capacity to be appropriated and transformed toward social, cultural, ecological and artistic ends. Architectural accretions, layerings of program and use, existing infrastructures made useful – herein lies the basis for a new civic realm, one created by appendage and insertion."[1] Evocative infrastructure makes the traveler aware of the passage, either by setting up sequential spatial events or by drawing attention to the landscapes and places crossed. To go beyond the fugitive impression and address a civic quality, the routes must construct a spatial sequence by stimulating an understanding of the landscape's construction or by engendering contemplation of its natural or architectural splendor.

1 **"PEOPLE'S PALACES"**
Moscow's underground system was planned as early as 1902, but was set back by the October Revolution and the Russian Civil War. When the first station opened in 1935, it was meant to symbolize Stalin's Soviet project to supposedly construct a radically new world of abundance, justice, and happiness for all. Stations were an architectural extravagance, with elegant designs and ample use of marble, chandeliers, and stucco ceilings. They were known as "people's palaces" and featured sculpture, mosaics, and murals in styles that ranged from classicism to art deco to social realism.

2 SIMPLE GRANDEUR

The Helsinki Railway Station (1919) designed by Eliel Saarinen is not only one of Finland's clearest examples of National Romanticist architecture, but also emblematic of the grand train stations of the early 20th century. Inspired by the Vienna Secession, the main hall is an impressive civic gesture rendered in a simplicity of lines and visual mass. The power of the Finnish granite front facade, with its great portal archway flanked by giant male statues holding globes and a 48.5-meter-high clock tower, is carried into the interior, with vaults of reinforced concrete and elements of traditional rural architecture.

3 AUSTERE ELEGANCE

Cruz y Ortiz Architects have created a freestanding city landmark for the Santa Justa Train Station in Seville, which serves the new high-speed rail line connection with Madrid. The long, low spacious station built of pale bricks has a modest monumentality reminiscent of early modernism. An off-center projecting canopy leads into the white-walled and floored concourse with huge floor-to-ceiling windows and flush detailing. Access to platforms is via gentle ramps and these transitional spaces boast roof heights that allow for a play of daylight. Six long tunnel-like hooped arches cover pairs of tracks and the detailing of all the roofs heightens the wonder and appreciation of such a public space.

4 POWER OF GEOMETRY

In Madrid, the station for Spain's high-speed train (known as Atocha) has been married to the 1892 steel-and-glass terminus, which has been transformed into a palm house. Rafael Moneo laid down a strong urban and architectural arrangement in which approach ramps bring cars over the tracks to the columned concourse that, in turn, supports a flat canopy in steel and a bold geometric pattern of I-beams. The civic ensemble is completed with the roofs over the tracks, a parking garage covered by a grid of segmental domes, and a large paved plaza that connects the different levels by pedestrian ramps.

6 DIGNIFIED PARK(ING)

The parking garage for Terminal 2 of Nice Airport in France by Cuno Brullmann Jean-Luc Crochon + Associates dignifies the pragmatic program with inventive massing, two landscaped linear east-west patios, and an elegant pedestrian circulation system. The 2700 parking places are relegated to three independent volumes of four levels that are separated from one another by large gardens of palms and bamboo. The circulation around the gardens takes pedestrians over footbridges and along promenades. A ramp with a 10% grade makes negotiation between the various levels easy.

5 CAVERNOUS PUBLIC REALM

Opened in 2002, the Copenhagen Metro designed by KHR arkitekter is easily navigable and uncomplicated, yet exquisitely detailed. The standardization of all the architectural elements is based on a 5.5-meter grid based on the size of the automated metro wagons. Glazed pyramidal rooflights with small prisms, which move according to the position of the sun, deflect daylight down to the platforms submerged 20 meters below. The single entrance to each station begins with a broad flight of stairs from the street to an intermediate level with escalators. Materials are restricted to pale granite, concrete, and stainless steel, and are accentuated by an aluminum clock.

In today's world, the legitimacy of the public realm is threatened by privatization and market opportunities, in which programs such as shopping prevail in transport interchanges. There are, however, a number of notable exceptions. In Spain, the high-speed rail network required the building of new stations. Both the Seville and Madrid stations, by Cruz y Ortiz and Rafael Moneo respectively, have a sober monumentality that escapes crass commercialism and restores an old-fashioned dignity to train travel [3, 4]. The noble spaces in the stations have a lot to do with the manipulation of daylight and the generous height of halls and passageways. The Copenhagen Metro network, by KHR arkitekter, should also be mentioned here as an intelligent kit of parts with a sobriety and elegance also premised upon the manipulation of daylight in its cavernous interiors [5]. Also located in Madrid is the terminal extension to Barajas International Airport by Rogers Stirk Harbour + Partners and Estudio Lamela. This building is conceived with a self-explanatory layout, an immense hallway covered by an undulating pattern of daylight-monitoring devices that enhance the sensation of movement in the arrival and departure lobby.

Piers are explicit travel transitions. They address a clear idea of departure connected to leaving the land and moving onto the water and, as such, they are places of shift and observation. The Wall Street Ferry Terminal in Manhattan is part of a concerted attempt to upgrade the public realm. Architects Smith-Miller + Hawkinson and landscape architect Judith Heintz have, in a modern industrial idiom appropriate to the waterfront, created an array of open and closed waiting areas where Wall Street office workers and local residents mix and linger while waiting for the ferries. Against the overpowering background of Manhattan, the fine-tuned modesty of the intervention makes travelers fully aware of the unique and vulnerable location of the pier.

Projects that identify the second kind of public realm focus on the connection between functional spaces or on the circulation within the connection space itself. Encouraging interaction with the surroundings is exemplified by Jun Aoki's Mamihara Bridge in rural Japan, and in Manuel de Solà-Morales's Louvain bus station and parking complex in urban Belgium. In the former, Aoki superseded the notion of the bridge as *connector* to bridge as a civic place. In Louvain, the intricate spatial finesse of premeditated relational flows infused the station square with a new vitality, an interplay between infrastructure, urbanism, and landscape premised on dignifying the public realm. Even the underground garage is generously transformed into an exciting passageway in its own right. Knowing that functional requirements and the drive for efficiency contribute to making parking garages unpleasant places, Cuno Brullmann Jean-Luc Crochon + Associates designed an exceptional new parking garage at the airport in Nice, France [6]. It enriches the passage of the pedestrian between parking garage and terminal with lightwells and broad walkways that focus on beautiful gardens.

1 Chris Reed, "Public Works Practice," in *The Landscape Urbanism Reader*, ed. Charles Waldheim (New York: Princeton Architectural Press, 2006), 282.

Wavy Roof and Colored Structural Trees

BARAJAS AIRPORT EXTENSION

Madrid, Spain

Architect: Richard Rogers (Rogers Stirk Harbour + Partners) and Estudio Lamela

Engineer: Anthony Hunt Associates, INITEC, and Tarmac Professional Services (TPS)

Date: 1997–2010

The Barajas Extension by Richard Rogers (Rogers Stirk Harbour + Partners) and Estudio Lamela adds more than a million square meters of functional floor area to Madrid Airport and increases capacity to 70 million passengers a year. The new, fourth terminal of the airport is flanked by two new runways and is intended to consolidate Madrid's position as a major intercontinental hub and the focal connection between Europe and Latin America. The building is developed with an 18-×-9-meter module structural grid that allows for infinite extensions of the repetitive structure.

The distinguishing feature of the new terminal is its roof — a repeating sequence of narrow waves formed by great wings of prefabricated steel supported by slender concrete branching tree-like columns. The roof is punctuated by rooflights providing carefully controlled natural light throughout the upper level of the terminal. Its form reflects the pattern of stress forces by providing a deeper section in the areas of high stress. The roof is kept clear of all services and is divided into three parallel bars. The first contains check-in, passport and security control; the second contains the departure lounges; and the third contains the boarding pier (1.2 kilometers long and large enough for 38 aircraft). The bars are separated by large, full-height courtyards filled with daylight and spanned by passenger bridges that establish a sequence that incorporates landscape into the interior space. Internally, the roof is clad in laminated bamboo strips and the structural trees are painted to create a vista of graduated color. The skillful use of natural light — daylight from the canyons reaches the lowest level of the automated transport system — and ample shading reduces the energy demands of the building. The building benefits from a north-south orientation with the primary facades facing east and west — the optimal layout for protecting a building against solar gain. The facades themselves are protected by a combination of deep roof overhangs and external shading.

Self-Effacing Urban Pier

WALL STREET FERRY TERMINAL

New York City, New York, USA

Architect: Smith-Miller + Hawkinson Architects

Landscape Architect: Judith Heintz Landscape Architect

Engineer: Ove Arup & Partners

Date: 1995–1999

The modest and elegant new Wall Street Ferry Terminal building that Smith-Miller + Hawkinson Architects designed on the former Pier 11 forms part of the long-term strategy of New York City to improve its alternative transportation infrastructure and to provide waterfront public access and open space in Lower Manhattan. Pier 11, whose original function had vanished when cargo ships abandoned New York for more affordable anchorage in New Jersey, is located on the East River under the girders of FDR Drive and has been reconceptualized as a vibrant public space giving New Yorkers access to the waterfront. The 260-square-meter terminal, the first built in decades in New York, serves small scale private ferries

to New Jersey, Brooklyn, Staten Island, and LaGuardia Airport.

The delicate, predominately horizontal building provides a flexible transition between interior and exterior, land and water. The large, south-facing glass-and-anodized-aluminum hanger door tilts up and stows overhead, transforming the main waiting area from a fully interior environment to an open porch, indistinct from the rest of the pier. A café is located at this inside-outside threshold and serves both commuter and visitor. Translucent fiberglass and steel canopies protruding from the east and west of the building extend the space of the open-air waiting area to the

ferries. The terminal, offices, support spaces, and seating occupy the northern edge of the jetty, liberating the majority of the pier for unprogrammed open space. The terminal provides both shelter and shade, a place not only for the traveler but only for the local community and Wall Street workers during lunch breaks. The building materials are low-tech, low-key, and functionally sympathetic to waterfront construction. The terminal is like an urban loft atop an open platform on the water. Landscape architect Judith Heintz designed benches made of timber that was salvaged from the old Pier 11, as well as catwalks with griled decks to walk over the water.

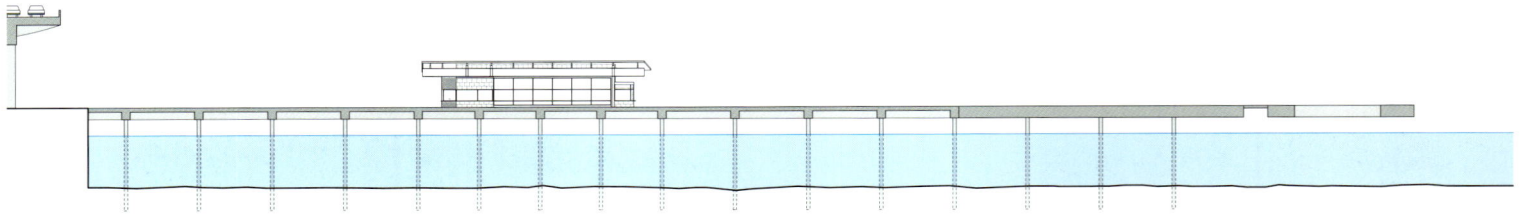

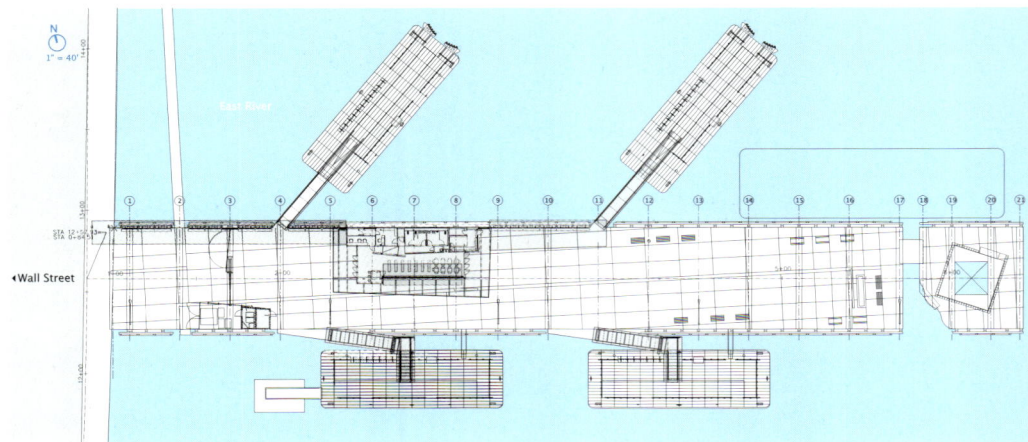

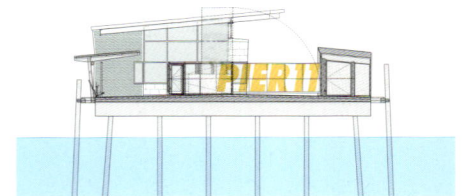

Bridge of Passage and Contemplation

MAMIHARA BRIDGE

Kumamoto, Japan

Architect: Jun Aoki & Associates

Engineer: Chuo Consultants

Date: 1994–1995

The Mamihara Bridge, in the center of Soyo in the Kumamoto Prefecture in Japan, is part of the Kumamoto Artpolis Project (KAP), a simple but innovative system of stimulating a new spatial and symbolic strategy to develop public buildings and structures in the provincial regions of Japan. KAP is a large-scale regional development plan to generate social infrastructure across the entire Kumamoto prefecture on the southern island of Kyushu. It is of importance in that public projects (including bridges, homes for the aged, museums, and cultural centers) have been targeted for the entire prefecture, village and city, island and mountains, in an attempt to redirect existing administrative policy to address the diversity of cultural conditions.

The Mamihara Bridge is conceived as a public station by architect Jun Aoki. The 38.25-meter-long, modified steel-frame Vierendeel bridge was designed to serve its purpose as a connector while, at the same time, inviting occupation of the structure for the enjoyment of the landscape. Soyo is located at a crossroads along a national road in the mountains and once flourished as a post town. The road crosses the river as a bridge, thus maintaining continuity of the street pattern and, hence, the urban fabric. Shaped like a pair of lips, the bridge inverts the traditional curve of Japanese arched bridges and was intentionally configured to invite people to linger. The span is divided into upper and lower chords with posts between them. The lower chord is the ten-

sion element and posts are compression elements. The resulting 5.8-meter-wide upper level for pedestrians and cars leads toward a pair of rocks joined by a sacred rope at the other end of the bridge. The 7.5-meter-wide lower level, solely for pedestrians, dips down toward the river. The inverted arch reaches its lowest point in the middle, 3 meters below the level of the street above. The lower deck is finished in planks of local cedar 45 millimeters thick. It has two round holes with diameters of 2.8 and 2.2 meters through which passers-by can contemplate the watercourse below. Apart from the railing on the lower bridge, standard specifications for public works are used for all details.

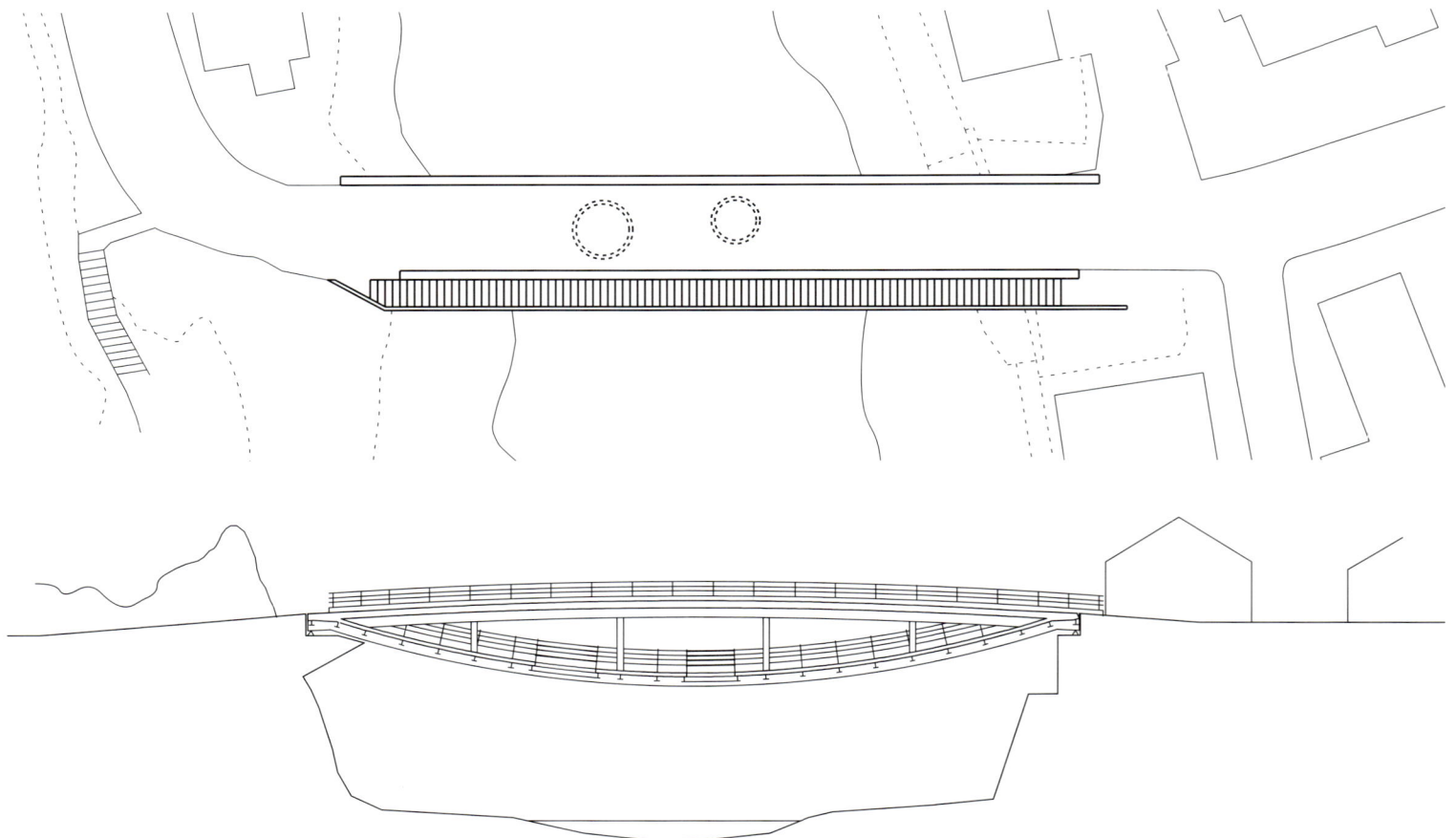

Sectional Manipulation

INTERMODAL STATION SQUARE

Louvain, Belgium

Architect: Manuel de Solà-Morales/A33

Urban Design: Projectteam Stadsontwerp, directed by Marcel Smets

Engineer: SWK

Date: 1996–2002 (1st phase)

Benefiting from the real estate opportunities created by the improved railroad access to Brussels and the international airport, the university city of Louvain in Belgium has seen a major transformation of its rail gateway and immediate surroundings. The elongated reserve areas of the station have been developed in line with the morphological concept put forward in the urban design by Projectteam Stadsontwerp. On its city side, the linear development is structured by major public buildings at both ends. On its suburban Kessel-Lo side, it provides an urban balcony with multipurpose center and elongated park, and a landscaped passage for pedestrians and cyclists to a major housing expansion on the former railroad site nearby. The eclectic train station itself is adorned with a sweeping new steel-and-glass canopy by Samyn and Partners, and the entire station square has been reconfigured. The previous clutter of bus stops has been

rationalized by Manuel de Solà Morales in a new bus terminal compressed into the large L-shaped office building belonging to the bus company that closes the station square at its northern end. The terminal is marked by its seven distinctive sky-lit shed structures, each corresponding to a bus lane, and red brickwork that allows the large structure to discreetly interact with the surroundings.

The bus terminal is set at a right angle to the train station and is connected to a large underground parking garage by a system of underpasses, pathways, and underground ramps leading out from center of the square. Car traffic along the beltway, which once cut the historic city off from the station area, has been relegated to an eye-catching tunnel that passes under and gives access to the parking garage, restoring the dignity and magnitude of the vast open space in front of the station. The existing war memorial has

been cleaned and accentuated with a light-well and staircase to the underground garage, creating sectional unity between interior and exterior, and between the spaces above and below ground. Passage from the city to the station occurs equally on both levels, while the square has been formalized with bluestone paving and perimeter light columns. The underground parking garage itself is one of unusual civility, with its landscape of flowing ramped floors, height differences, unexpected views, and elegant top-lit mushroom columns. The pedestrian underpass, connecting the city square to the train platforms and Kessel-Lo on the opposite side of the tracks, is a dynamic, ramped, and animated space that receives plenty of daylight. The power of the entire station area resides in the sectional manipulations whereby the different itineraries of congestion and movement gain a new interdependence.

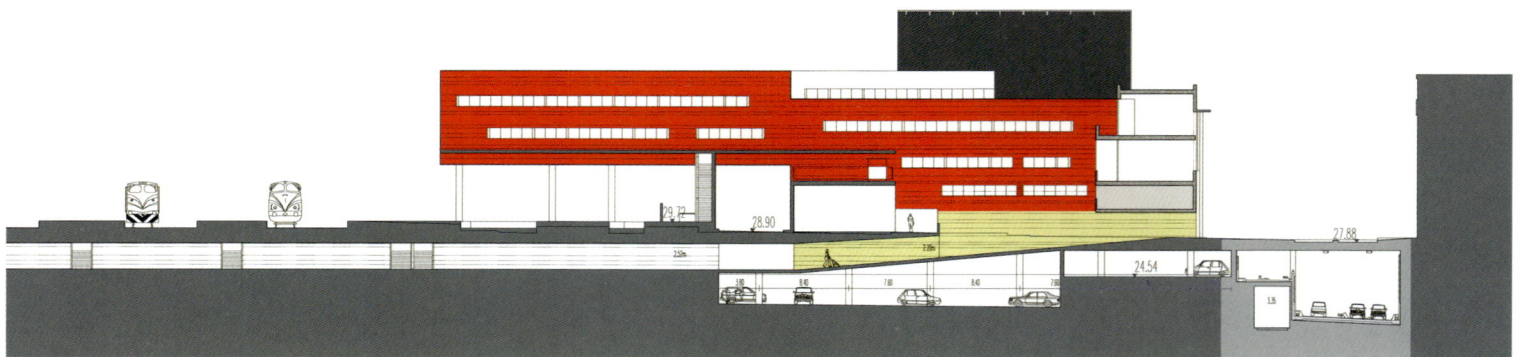

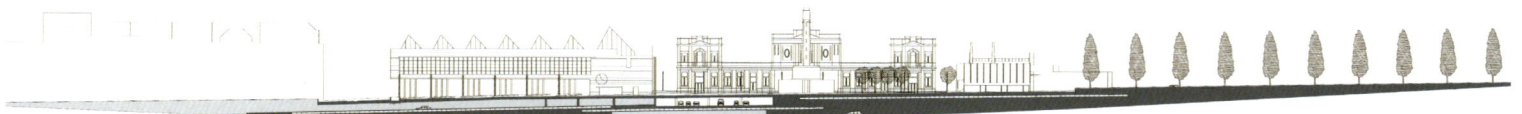

BIBLIOGRAPHY

GENERAL BIBLIOGRAPHY

Allemand, Sylvain, François Ascher, and Jacques Lévy. *Le sens du mouvement*. Paris: Belin, 2004.

Allen, Stan. *Points + Lines: Diagrams and Projects for the City*. New York and Princeton: Architectural Press, 1999.

Alonzo, Eric. *Du rond-point au giratoire*. Marseille and Paris: Parenthèses/Certu, 2005.

Appleyard, Donald, Kevin Lynch, and John R. Meyers. *The View from the Road*. Cambridge: MIT Press, 1964.

Ascher, François and Mireille Apel-Muller, eds. *The Street Belongs to All of Us*, Vauvert: Au diable, 2007.

Augé, Marc. *Non-places: Introduction to an Anthropology of Supermodernity*. Translated by John Howe. London: Verso, 1995.

Banham, Reyner. *Los Angeles: The Architecture of Four Ecologies*. New York: Harper & Row, 1971.

Barles, Sabine, and André Guillerme. "L'urbanisme souterrain." *Moniteur architecture AMC* no. 100 (1999): 46-53.

Binney, Marcus. *Architecture of Rail: The Way Ahead*. London: Academy Editions, 1995.

Castells, Manuel. *The Rise of Network Society*. Cambridge: Blackwell Publishers, 1996.

Clifford, James. *Routes: Travel and Translation in the Later Twentieth Century*, Cambridge: Harvard University Press, 1997.

Cresswell, Tim. *On the Move: Mobility in the Modern Western World*. New York and London: Routledge, 2006.

Cullen, Gordon. *Townscape*. London: The Architectural Press, 1961.

Easterling, Keller. *Organization Space: Landscapes, Highways, and Houses in America*. Cambridge and London: MIT Press, 1999.

Feldman, Leslie. *Freedom as Motion*. Lanham: University Press of America, 2001.

Flink, James. *The Automobile Age*. Cambridge: MIT Press, 1988.

Hall, Peter. "A Tale of Two City Railways." *Town & Country Planning* 68, no. 5 (1999): 146-49.

Halprin, Lawrence. *Freeways*. New York: Reinhold, 1966.

Henley, Simon. *The Architecture of Parking*. London: Thames & Hudson, 2007.

Il paesaggio delle freeway = The View from the Road. *Lotus Navigator* no. 7 (2003).

Infrascape. AREA no. 79 (2005).

Jackson, John B. *Landscape in Sight*. New Haven: Yale University Press, 1997.

Jones, Will. *New Transport Architecture*. London: Mitchell Beazley Publishers, 2006.

Julià Sort, Jordi. *Metropolitan Networks*. Barcelona: Editorial Gustavo Gili, 2006.

Kaplan, Caren. *Questions of Travel: Postmodern Discourses of Displacement*. Durham: Duke University Press, 1996.

Loyer, Béatrice. "Lieux de transport: design et environnement." *Techniques et Architecture* no. 440 (1998): 101-5.

Marx, Leo. *The Machine in the Garden*. Oxford: Oxford University Press, 1964.

Mazzoni, Cristiana. *Stazioni: architetture 1990–2010*. Milan: Federico Motta Editore, 2001.

McCluskey, Jim. *Road Form and Townscape*. London: Architectural Press, 1979.

Mialet, Frédéric. "Dossier. Transports: le siècle de l'intermodalité." *d'Architectures* no. 92 (1999): 30-31.

Mostafavi, Mohsen, ed. *Landscape Urbanism: A Manual for the Machinic Landscape*. London: AA Publications, 2004.

Mumford, Lewis. *The Highway and the City*. New York: Harcourt, Brace and World, 1963.

Parcerisa, Josep, and Maria Rubert de Ventos. *Metro*. Barcelona: Edicions UPC, 2002.

Pascoe, David. *Airspaces*. London: Reaction Books, 2001.

Périmètres d'intermodalité/Transport Territory = Techniques & Architecture no. 491 (2007).

Prelorenzo, Claude, and Dominique Rouillard, eds. *Le temps des infrastructures*. Paris: L'Harmattan, 2007.

Prelorenzo, Claude, and Dominique Rouillard, eds. *La métropole des infrastructures*, Paris: Picard, 2009.

Rambert, Francis, ed. *Architecture on the Move: Cities and Mobilities*. Paris: City on the Move Institute and Barcelona: Actar, 2003.

Richards, Jeffrey, and John M. MacKenzie. *The Railway Station: A Social History*. Oxford: Oxford University Press, 1986.

Russell, James S., ed. *The Mayor's Institute: Excellence in City Design*. New York: Princeton Architectural Press, 2002.

Sassen, Saskia. *The Global City: New York, London, Tokyo*, 2nd ed. Princeton: Princeton University Press, 2001.

Schwarzer, Mitchell. *Zoomscape: Architecture in Motion and Media*. New York: Princeton Architectural Press, 2004.

Sert, José Luis. *Can Our Cities Survive?* Cambridge: Harvard University Press, 1944.

Smets, Marcel. "The Contemporary Landscape of Europe's Infrastructures = Il nuovo paesaggio delle infrastrutture in Europa." *Lotus international* no. 110 (2001): 116-43.

Southworth, Michael, and Eran Ben-Joseph. *Streets and the Shaping of Towns and Cities*. Washington, Covelo and London: Island Press, 2003.

Stilgoe, John. *Metropolitan Corridor*. New Haven: Yale University, 1982.

Taxworthy, Julian, and Jessica Blood. *The Mesh Book: Landscape/Infrastructure*. Melbourne: RMIT University Press, 2004.

Thorne, Martha, ed. *Modern Trains and Splendid Stations: Architecture, Design, and Rail Travel for the Twenty-First Century*. London: Merrell, 2001.

Tiry, Corinne. *Les mégastructures du transport*. Lyon: Certu, 2008.

Tunnard, Boris, and Christopher Pushkarev. *Man-Made America: Chaos or Control?* New Haven: Yale University Press, 1963.

Tschumi, Bernard. *The Manhattan Transcripts*. New York: St. Martin's Press, 1994.

Urry, John. *Sociology beyond Societies: Mobilites for the Twenty-First Century*. London and New York: Routledge, 2000.

Venturi, Robert, Denise Scott Brown, and Steven Izenour. *Learning from Las Vegas*. Cambridge: MIT Press, 1972.

Virilio, Paul. *Speed and Politics: An Essay on Dromology*. New York: Columbia University Press, 1986.

Waldheim, Charles. *The Landscape Urbanism Reader*. New York: Princeton Architectural Press, 2006.

Webb, Bruce. "Engaging the Highway." *a+u: Architecture and Urbanism* no. 94 (1994).

Whyte, William H. *The Last Landscape*. New York: Doubleday & Co, 1968.

CHAPTER 1

Kowloon Rail Station, Hong Kong, China (p. 17)

Binney, Marcus. *Architecture of Rail: The Way Ahead*. London: Academy Editions, 1995, 52-57.

Blackburn, Andy. "Kowloon Station: The Integrated City." *Asian Architect and Contractor* 28, no. 9 (1999): 12-13, 15-16.

Cairns, Robert. "Kowloon, Hong Kong's Landmark Station." *Asian Architect and Contractor* 27, no. 6 (1998): 35-36, 38, 40, 42.

Farrell, Sir Terry. *Terry Farrel: Selected and Current Works*. Mulgrave: Images, 1994, 206-16.

"Kowloon Station, Hong Kong." *World Architecture* no. 48 (1996): 124-25.

"Masterplanning a City." *Asian Architect and Contractor* 28, no. 9 (1999): 18-19.

Mazzoni, Cristiana. *Stazioni: architetture 1990–2010*. Milan: Federico Motta Editore, 2001, 146-59.

Melvin, Jeremy. "Under one Roof." *Blueprint* no. 196 (2002): 38-42.

Pitman, Simon. "Contract 503C: Kowloon Station." *Asian Architect and Contractor* 27, no. 8 (1997): 41-42, 44, 46-48, 51.

Thomas, Ralph. "The Great Indoors." *Blueprint* no. 212 (2003): 62-66.

Thorne, Martha, ed. *Modern Trains and Splendid Stations: Architecture, Design, and Rail Travel for the Twenty-First Century*. London: Merrell, 2001, 66-69.

"Union Square." *Asian Architect and Contractor* 32, no. 1 (2003): 12-14, 17.

"A Very British Consulate." *Architects' Journal* 205, no. 4 (1997): 38-39.

Underground Pedestrian Passages, Montreal, Canada (p. 18)

Besner, Jacques, and Clément Demers. "La face cachée de Montréal = The Hidden Face of Montreal." *Architecture d'aujourd'hui* no. 340 (2002): 100-105.

Lachapelle, Jacques. "Unterirdisches Montreal." *Werk, Bauen & Wohnen* no. 7-8 (1994): 14-23.

Jubilee Line Underground Stations, London, UK (p. 19)

Aldersey-Williams, Hugh. "Down the Tube: An Extension to the Jubilee Line Will Reverse the Neglect of London Underground's Design Legacy." *Architectural Record* 181, no. 6 (1993): 120-25.

"Arqueología ferroviaria: Estación de Westminster, Línea Jubilee", "Una gruta abovedada: Estación de Canary Wharf, Línea Jubilee." *Arquitectura Viva* no. 71 (2000): 30-33, 36-39.

Baillieu, Amanda. "Jubilee Line, Londra." *Domus*, no. 748 (1993): 48-55.

Hall, Peter. "A Tale of Two City Railways." *Town & Country Planning* 68, no. 5 (1999): 146-49.

Hardingham, Samantha. "Norman Foster: stazione di Canary Wharf, Jubilee Line Extension, Londra = Canary Wharf Station, Jubilee Line Extension, London." *Domus* no. 825 (2000): 50-55.

Irace, Fulvio. "Canary Wharf." *Abitare* no. 396 (2000): 106-9.

"Jubilee Line Extension, Londres." *Techniques & Architecture* no. 455 (2001): 34-41.

"Larvas de cristal: stación de metro en Canary Wharf, Londres." *Arquitectura Viva* no. 65 (1999): 48-49.

McGuire, Penny. "Grand Canary: Underground Station, Canary Wharf, London." *Architectural Review* 207, no. 1240 (2000): 51-55.

"Norman Foster: Canary Wharf Station, Jubilee Line Extension, London, U.K." *GA document* no. 62 (2000): 120-27.

Pashini, Luca. "Architetti per la metropolitana di Londra = The Jubilee Line Extension Project, London." *Casabella* 64, no. 678 (2000): 64-83.

Pawley, Martin, and Romano Roland Paoletti. "Going Underground." *Architects' Journal* 211, no. 4 (2000): 26-37.

Powell, Kenneth. "Modern Movement: London's Jubilee Line extension." *Architecture Today* 105 (2000): 36-38, 41-42, 44-48, 51-52, 55.

Powell, Kenneth. *New London Architecture.* London: Merrell, 2001, 30-31.

Russell, James S. "Engineering Civility: Transit Stations", "Canary Wharf, Jubilee Line Extension, London." *Architectural Record* 188, no. 3 (2000): 129-33, 138-41.

Slessor, Catherine. "Underground Jubilation." *Architectural Review* 205, no. 1227 (1999): 54-55.

"U-Bahnstation Canary Wharf in London = Canary Wharf Underground Station in London." *Architektur + Wettbewerbe* no. 185 (2001): 34-37.

"U-Bahnstation Canary Wharf in London = Canary Wharf Underground Station, London = Stazione della metropolitana Canary Wharf a Londra = Station Canary Wharf à Londres = Estación de metro en Canary Wharf, London." *Detail* 41, no. 1 (2001): 88-91.

"U-Bahnstation Westminster in London = Westminster Underground Station in London." *Architektur + Wettbewerbe* no. 185 (2001): 32-33.

"Underneath the Politics: Underground Station, Westminster, London." *Architectural Review* 207, no. 1240 (2000): 60-63.

Wegerhoff, Erik. "Die Erweiterung der Jubilee Line." *Baumeister* 97, no. 6 (2000): 36-47.

Welter, Volker. "U-Bahnbau als Stadtpolitik: die Erweiterung der Londoner Jubilee Linie." *Bauwelt* 91, no. 23 (2000): 34-37.

Wessely, Heide. "Stationen der Jubilee Line, London = Jubilee Line Stations, London = Jubilee Line Extension: nuove stazioni metropolitane a Londra = Les stations de la ligne du Jubilé, Londres." *Detail* 40, no. 4 (2000): 620-24.

"Westminster." *Abitare* 396 (2000): 112-13.

Woodward, Christopher. "Simply the Best: Canary Wharf Metrostation van Foster and Partners in Londen." *Architect* 31, no. 6 (2000): 44-50.

Zunino, Maria Giulia. "Londra: Jubilee Line Extension." *Abitare* no. 396 (2000): 104-105.

Rail Station Renovation, Stuttgart, Germany (p. 20)

Bund Deutscher Architekten BDA et al. with Meinhard von Gerkan, eds. *Renaissance of Railway Stations: The City in the 21st Century.* Stuttgart: BDA, 1996, 156-63.

Davey, Peter. "In the Public Eye: Underground Station, Stuttgart, Germany."
Architectural Review 213, no. 1274 (2003): 66-69.

De Matteis, Federico. "La nuova stazione di Stoccarda." *Industria delle costruzioni* no. 337-338 (1999): 76-79.

"Hauptbahnhof in Stuttgart." *Architektur + Wettbewerbe* no. 178 (1999): 14-17.

"Hauptbahnhof Stuttgart." *Arch plus* no. 159-160 (2002): 74-79.

"La nuova stazione centrale di Stoccarda = Stuttgart Hauptbahnhof." *Spazio e società* 20, no. 83 (1998): 58-65.

Lynn, Greg. "Hauptbahnhof: Ingenhoven Overdiek, Kahlen & Partner." *Quaderns d'arquitectura i urbanisme* no. 220 (1998): 130-31.

Meyer, Ulf. "Ingenhoven Overdiek Architekten: Main Station Stuttgart, Stuttgart, Germany 1997–2013." *a+u: Architecture and Urbanism* no. 396 (2003): 78-87.

Pacey, Stephen. "The Natural Look." *RIBA Journal* 110, no. 2 (2003): 79-81.

Pavarini, Stefano. "La stazione di Stoccarda = A New Cathedral." *l'Arca* no. 128 (1998): 4-9.

Sayah, Amber. "Hauptbahnhof Stuttgart." *Bauwelt* 88, no. 30 (1997): 1658-59.

Thorne, Martha, ed. *Modern Trains and Splendid Stations: Architecture, Design, and Rail Travel for the Twenty-first Century.* London: Merrell, 2001, 91-92.

Tiry, Corinne. "Stuttgart ouvre la voie vers le ciel." *Architecture d'aujourd'hui* no. 321 (1999): 32-35.

"Visionär: Bau-, Licht- und Lufttechnik zum Projekt Bahnhof Stuttgart." *Intelligente Architektur* no. 12 (1998): 66-69.

Tramline and Terminal, Nice, France (p. 21)

"Au chausse-pied." *Techniques & Architecture* no. 455 (2001): 30-33.

Boudet, Dominique. "Le Ray: La nouvelle entrée nord", "La mise en valeur des grands espaces historiques: La place Massena", "La mise en valeur des grands espaces historiques: Place Garibaldi." *Moniteur architecture AMC*, no. 163 (2006): 164, 168-69, 170-71.

Boudet, Dominique, Jacques Peyrat, and Claire Reclus. "Nice: l'urbanisme catalyseur du développement." *Moniteur architecture AMC* no. 163 (2006): 151-59.

Dana, Karine. "Atelier Barani: centre de maintenance du tramway, Nice." *Moniteur architecture AMC* no. 180 (2008): 92-99.

Dana, Karine, and Marc Barani. "Atelier Barani: centre de maintenance du tramway, Nice." *Moniteur architecture AMC* no. 184 (2008): 88-99, 224.

"Le tramway: Un grand projet à l'échelle de la ville", "Deux nouveaux pôles de centralité", "De nouvelles entrées de ville." *Moniteur architecture AMC* no. 120 (2001): 158-63, 164-69, 170-75.

"Marc Barani: Tramway of Nice and its Greater Surroundings, Nice, France 1996–1997." *a+u: Architecture and Urbanism* no. 370 (2001): 62-65.

Redecke, Sebastian. "Die Linie 1 in Nizza: das Depot- und Werkstattgebäude der Strassenbahn in Nizza: Marc Barani." *Bauwelt* 99, no. 25 (2008): 14-35.

A29 Highway, Haute-Normandie, France (p. 23)

"Autostrada di Normandia." *Lotus Navigator* no. 7 (2003): 106-11.

Boyer, Charles-Arthur. "Architectuur als landschap = Architecture as Landscape: Atelier Badia-Berger: project in Normandië." *Archis* no. 8 (1997): 54-59.

"Équiments." *Techniques et Architecture* no. 429 (1996): 101-6.

Kerveno, Yann. "Une belle discrète." *Construction moderne* no. 89 (1996): 11-15.

Smets, Marcel. "The Contemporary Landscape of Europe's Infrastructures = Il nuovo paesaggio delle infrastrutture in Europa." *Lotus international* no. 110 (2001): 116-43.

A77 Tollstations, Dordives/Cosnes-sur-Loire, France (p. 23)

Arnaboldi, Mario Antonio. "La rivoluzione ha le tempie grigie: A Toll Station in France." *l'Arca* no. 162 (2001): 62-67.

Metro Line 14, Paris, France (p. 24)

Barles, Sabine, and André Guillerme. "L'urbanisme souterrain." *Moniteur architecture AMC* no. 100 (1999): 46-53.

"Design et transport: meteor, urbanité souterraine." *Techniques et Architecture* no. 427 (1996): 92-93.

Fitoussi, Brigitte. "Linea metropolitana 14, Parigi = The Métro Line 14, Paris." *Domus* no. 812 (1999): 48-49.

Fitoussi, Brigitte. "Roger Tallon: météor, la nuova metropolitana automatica di Parigi = Météor: The New Automatic Paris Metro." *Domus* no. 812 (1999): 54-58.

Houzelle, Beatrice. "Connexions: transports publics à Paris." *Techniques & Architecture* no. 412 (1994): 50-57.

Loyer, Béatrice. "Lieux de transport: design et environnement." *Techniques et Architecture* no. 440 (1998): 101-5.

Mialet, Frédéric. "Dossier: transports: le siècle de l'intermodalité." *d'Architectures* no. 92 (1999): 30-31.

"Réalisations 1998: Equipements." *Moniteur architecture AMC* no. 94 (1998): 152-53, 128.

Roulet, Sophie. "Renouveau du métro ou l'espace en question." *Architecture intérieure créé* no. 286 (1998): 70-73.

Rouyer, Rémi. "Météor, maîtrise d'ouvrage, génie civil, architectes: les conditions du débat." *Architecture intérieure créé* no. 286 (1998): 32-39, 42-47.

Tramline, Saint-Denis/Bobigny, France (p. 24)

"Alexandre Chemetoff." *Architecture d'aujourd'hui* no. 303 (1996): 65.

"La tranvia di Saint-Denis = The Tramway of Saint-Denis." *Casabella* 53, no. 553-54 (1989): 66-67, 123-24.

Lucan, Jacques. "Seine-Saint-Denis: tramway." *Moniteur architecture AMC* no. 41 (1993): 30-31.

"Paseo del Tranvía, Saint-Denis, La Courneuve, Drancy, Bobigny, Francia." *Escala* 40, no. 199 (2004): 71.

Rocca, Alessandro, and Jacques Lucan. "Saint-Denis-Bobigny." *Lotus international* no. 84 (1995): 86-101.

"Tranvía = Tramway." *Quaderns d'arquitectura i urbanisme* no. 225 (2000): 101.

Vanstiphout, Wouter. "De tuinman en de stad: het werk van Alexandre Chemetoff en het Bureau des Paysages." *de Architect* 25, no. 2 (1994): 68-69.

High Speed Bus Track, Amsterdam, the Netherlands (p. 25)

Costanzo, Michele. "N10 architecten: una nuova vita per gli 'spazi tecnici' = N10 architecten: New Life for 'Technical Spaces'." *Metamorfosi* no. 57 (2005): 44-53.

Guardigli, Decio. "La forma delle idee: Fluid Vehicle and Cyclopes." *l'Arca* no. 194 (2004): 12-17.

"High Speed Bus Track in Kerntraject Zuidtangent: Maurice Nio." *C3 Korea* no. 252 (2005): 130-41.

Jansen, Joks. "De flexibiliteit van een systeem: ontwerp Zuidtangent in regio Amsterdam van VHP en Dok." *de Architect* 32, no. 2 (2001): 34-39.

Kersten, Paul. "Die Südtangente in Holland = The 'Zuidtangent': The Southern Tangent in the Netherlands." *Topos: European Landscape Magazine* no. 42 (2003): 26-31.

Van Cleef, Connie. "Sheltering in Style: Bus Shelters, Haarlem, the Netherlands." *Architectural Review* 216, no. 1293 (2004): 40-41.

Lechwiesen Service Station, Munich-Lindau Highway, Germany (p. 26)

Dawson, Layla. "Autobahn prototype." *Architectural Review* 203, no. 1214 (1998): 56-58.

"Drive in: Tank- und Rastanlage Lechwiesen." *Deutsche Bauzeitung* 132, no. 4 (1998): 66-77.

Herzog, Thomas. "Prototyp: Tank- und Rastanlage Lechwiesen." *Deutsche Bauzeitschrift* 46, no. 8 (1998): 51-56.

Sowa, Axel. "Thomas Herzog et associés: prototype en bord de route, Allemagne." *Architecture d'aujourd'hui* no. 322 (1999): 40-45.

Bilbao Metro, Bilbao, Spain (p. 28)

"Bauen für den Aufschwung." *Werk, Bauen + Wohnen* no. 12 (1996): 38-42.

"Bilbao Metro, Spain." *Architecture + Design* 21, no. 1 (2004): 162-65.

"The Bilbao Metro." In *Two Projects by Foster and Partners: The Carré d'Art, Nîmes & The Bilbao Metro*, introd. P. G. Rowe. Massachusetts: Harvard University Graduate School of Design 1998, 31-41.

Cohn, David. "Metro in Bilbao." *Bauwelt* 87, no. 5 (1996): 182-83.

Cohn, David. "Starparade: Verkehrsbauten in Bilbao." *Deutsche Bauzeitung* 133, no. 2 (1999): 54-59.

"Dos estaciones del Metro de Bilbao = Two Stations of Bilbao Metro Railway System." *A+T* no. 7 (1996): 64-79.

"Ferrocarril Metropolitano de Bilbao." *ON Diseño* no. 170 (1996): 162-77.

Mialet, Frederic. "Transports: le siècle de l'intermodalité." *d'Architectures* no. 92 (1999): 34-35.

Mistry, Mary. "Basque Underground." *Architectural Review* 201, no. 1203 (1997): 54-59.

"Norman Foster: Bilbao Metro, Bilbao, Spain." *GA document* no. 52 (1997): 98-101.

"Norman Foster: Ferrocarril metropolitano, Bilbao = Metropolitan Railway, Bilbao." *AV Monografías = AV Monographs* no. 57-58 (1996): 42-45.

"Norman Foster: Ferrocarril Metropolitano, Bilbao = Metropolitan Railway, Bilbao." *AV Monografías = AV Monographs* no. 79-80 (1999): 94-99.

"Stations chics pour métros de choc." *Architecture d'aujourd'hui* no. 267 (1990): 52-53.

"Unter Tage: Neugestaltung der Metro in Bilbao." *Architektur, Innenarchitektur, Technischer Ausbau* 105, no. 7-8 (1997): 72-75.

Houston MetroRail, Houston, Texas, USA (p. 30)

Barna, Joel Warren. "Rail Plans for Houston, Dallas." *Progressive Architecture* 71, no. 8 (1990): 32, 37.

Crossley, David. "Tracking Change: The Current Word on Houston's Transit Agenda." *Cite: The Architecture and Design Review of Houston* no. 72 (2007): 24-27.

Kwarter, Michael. "Just-in-time Planning: New York + Houston." *Architectural Design* 75, no. 6 (2005): 88-93.

Newberg, Sam. "Light Rail Comes to Minneapolis." *Planning* 70, no. 5 (2004): 6-11.

Spieler, Christof. "Down the Line: How Will Light Rail Change Houston?" *Cite: The Architecture and Design Review of Houston* no. 59 (2004): 14-19.

Spieler, Christof. "Houston Hitches a Ride on Light Rail." *Architecture* 93, no. 2 (2004): 35-36.

Spieler, Christof. "Trains of Thought: Six Cities, Six Light-Rail Systems, Six Visions." *Cite: The Architecture and Design Review of Houston* no. 58 (2003): 18-25.

Spieler, Christof. "METRO: What's Next?: Planned Extensions Will Connect Neighborhoods to Rail, But Will the Neighbors Want It?' *Cite: The Architecture and Design Review of Houston* no. 61 (2004): 14-19.

Thompson, Gregory L., and Thomas G. Matoff. "Keeping Up with the Joneses: Radial vs. Multidestinational Transit in Decentralizing Regions." *Journal of the American Planning Association* 69, no. 3 (2003): 296-312.

Curitiba Bus System, Curitiba, Brazil (p. 32)

Ceccarelli, Nicolo. "Curitiba, una città 'sostenibile' = Curitiba, a Sustainable City." *Spazio e società* 18, no. 70 (1994): 66-81.

"Curitiba: um sistema visual urbano." *Projeto* no. 177 (1994): 73-77.

Di Giulio, Susan. "Architect, Mayor, Environmentalist: An Interview with Jaime Lerner." *Progressive Architecture* 75, no. 7 (1994): 84-85, 110.

Frausto, Martha E. "Planning Theories and Concepts, Implementation Strategies, and Integrated Transportation Network Elements in Curitiba." *Transportation Quarterly* 53, no. 1 (1999): 41-55.

Guillen, Carlos. "Solid Waste Management in Curitiba, Brazil." *Ekistics* 60, no. 358-359 (1993): 85-91.

Hunt, Julian. "The Urban Believer: A Report on Jaime Lerner and the Rise of Curitiba, Brazil." *Metropolis* 13, no. 8 (1994): 66-67, 74-77, 79.

Kroll, Lucien. "Creative Curitiba." *Architectural Review* 205, no. 1227 (1999): 92-95.

Lerner, Jaime. "Brasil Curitiba: un sistema de transporte urbano integrado." *CA: revista oficial del Colegio de Arquitectos de Chile* no. 58 (1989): 44-51.

Lerner, Jaime. "Daadkracht: Curitiba en de potenties van de stad = Making It Happen: Curitiba and the Potentials of the City." *Archis* no. 12 (2000): 18-23.

Macedo, Joseli. "City Profile: Curitiba." *Cities* 21, no. 6 (2004): 537-49.

Meurs, Paul. "Een ecologische metropool in Brazilië: Curitiba." *de Architect* 25, no. 2 (1994): 52-59.

Leidsche Rijn Bridges, Utrecht, the Netherlands (p. 34)

Corbellini, Giovanni. "Pragmatismo, sperimentazione, ironia: strategie recenti fra progetto e infrastrutture nei Paesi Bassi." *Paesaggio urbano* no. 4 (2004): 24-31.

Havik, Klaske. "De kunst van het construeren: bruggen van Max.1, West 8 en Marijke de Goey." *de Architect* 32, no. 5 (2001): 70-73, 105.

"I ponti di Leidsche Rijn'. *Lotus Navigator* no. 7 (2003): 74-77.

Speaks, Michael. "Gran naranja blanda = Big Soft Orange." *AV Monografías = AV Monographs* no. 73 (1998): 34-42.

Speaks, Michael. "Design Intelligence. Part 7: Maxwan." *a+u: Architecture and Urbanism* no. 393 (2003): 140-47.

Tilman, Harm. "'We willen ieder plan laten lukken': Max.1 en de weerbarstige praktijk." *de Architect* 29, no. 5 (1998): 52-65, 116-17.

International Airport, Singapore, Singapore (p. 36)

"Aéroport Changi = Changi Airport, Singapour – Singapour: Skidmore Owings +." *Moniteur architecture AMC*, special issue (2009): 122-23.

"Skidmore, Owings & Merrill: Changi International Airport Terminal 3." *Architecture* 90, no. 4 (2001): 88-91.

"Terminal 3 Building, Changi International Airport, Singapore." *SOM Journal* 1 (2001): 104-19.

"Three Projects at Changi International Airport, Changi, Singapore 1998–2001." *a+u: Architecture and Urbanism* no. 386 (2002): 74-93.

Weathersby, William et al. "Lighting." *Architectural Record* 191, no. 11 (2003): 227-32, 234, 239-44, 246, 249, 251-52, 254.

Sepulveda and Century Boulevards, Los Angeles, USA (p. 37)

Choi, Wonsun. "Dance of Light." *L.A. Architect*, March-April 2001: 38-39.

Currimbhoy, Nayana. "Lighting." *Architectural Record* 189, no. 2 (2001): 177.

Hammatt, Heather. "Auto focus: The Approach to Los Angeles International Airport is Seen in a New Light." *Landscape Architecture* 90, no. 10 (2000): 34, 36.

Linn, Charles et al. "Lighting…" *Architectural Record* 189, no. 2 (2001): 175-201.

"Nuovo landmark per Los Angeles = A New Landmark for Los Angeles." *Domus* no. 832 (2000): 28-29.

Pedersen, Martin C. "City High Lights: Outdoor Lighting Design Has the Power to Transform Urban Landmarks – and Even Create New Ones." *Metropolis* 21, no. 9 (2002): 88-91.

Russell, James S., ed. *The Mayor's Institute: Excellence in City Design.* New York: Princeton Architectural Press, 2002, 68-69.

Trauthwein, Christina. "Dusk 'til Dawn." *Architectural Lighting* 16, no. 1 (2001): 24-27.

International Airport, Seville, Spain (p. 37)

"De la tierra al cielo: nueva terminal del aeropuerto de San Pablo, Sevilla, 1987–1991." *AV Monografías = AV Monographs* no. 36 (1992): 52-60.

Dixon, John Morris. "Welcome to Seville." *Progressive Architecture* 73, no. 7 (1992): 82-85.

Hessel, Andrea. "Sevilla: Wo, bitte, geht's zur EXPO?' *Baumeister* 89, no. 8 (1992): 35-39.

"Il nuovo aeroporto di Siviglia di Rafael Moneo." *Casabella* 56, no. 590 (1992): 23.

Irace, Fulvio et al. "Le nuove porte della città = The New Gates of the City: Barcellona, Siviglia, Londra, Osaka." *Abitare* no. 305 (1992): 210-11, 218-19, 308.

Moneo Valles, Rafael. "Flughafengebäude in Sevilla." *Deutsche Bauzeitschrift* 40, no. 8 (1992): 1129-38.

Pink, John. "Flight and the Souk." *Architectural Review* 190, no. 1144 (1992): 69-74.

"Rafael Moneo: Branch Office, Bank of Spain and New San Pablo Airport Terminal l." *a+u: Architecture and Urbanism* no. 274 (1993): 65-80.

"Rafael Moneo: terminal de Séville." *Techniques et Architecture* no. 401 (1992): 127-31.

Rodermond, Janny. "Sevilla Airport: de hof van Moneo." *de Architect thema* no. 46 (1992): 56-59.

Sainz, Jorge. "Una mezquita aérea: nuevo aeropuerto en Sevilla." *Arquitectura Viva* no. 22 (1992): 14-21.

Ustarroz, Alberto. "Rafael Moneo: il nuovo aeroporto di Siviglia." *Domus* no. 736 (1992): 36-47.

Metro, Porto, Spain (p. 38)

Cannatà, Michele; Fernandes, Fátima. "Territorio compartido: la nueva red de metro de Oporto." *Arquitectura Viva* no. 109 (2006): 34-37.

Confurius, Gerrit. "Diskret, unauffällig, bürgerlich: Neubau einer Metro in Porto: Architekt, Eduardo Souto de Moura, Porto." *Bauwelt* 96, no. 21 (2005): 44-47.

Machabert, Dominique. "Re-designing the Town: Subway, Porto." *Techniques & Architecture* no. 466 (2003): 55-57.

Ménard, Jean-Pierre. "Flux mécaniques: stations de metro, Porto, Portugal." *Moniteur architecture AMC* no. 173 (2007): 144-46.

"Metro de Porto, Portugal = Porto Metropolitan Train, Portugal: Eduardo Souto de Moura, arquitecto." *ON Diseño* no. 276 (2006): 268-77.

Solà, Manuel de. "Estaciones del metro a Porto i Copenhague: criptes publiques." *Quaderns d'arquitectura i urbanisme* no. 252 (2006): 64-65.

Souto de Moura, Eduardo. "Unter Grund und über Brücken: Metro für Porto = Below the Earth and over Bridges: A Metro for Porto." *Topos: European Landscape Magazine* no. 24 (1998): 32-35.

Souto de Moura, Eduardo, Jacques Lucan, and Eduard Bru. "Eduardo Souto de Moura: obra reciente = Recent Work." *2G: revista internacional de arquitectura = International Architecture Review* no. 5 (1998): 84-89.

Souto de Moura, Eduardo, Luis Rojo de Castro. "Eduardo Souto de Moura 1995– 2005." *El Croquis* no. 124 (2005): 136-45.

Souto de Moura, Eduardo. "Porto: Edouardo Souto de Moura's Stations for the City's New Metro Dystem." *Architecture Today* no. 168 (2006): 18-20, 23.

Souto de Moura, Eduardo, Cornelia Tapparelli, and Marco Mulazzani. "Eduardo Souto de Moura: metropolitana, Porto, Portogallo." *Casabella* 70, no. 740 (2005): 112-31.

Ferry Terminal, Mihonoseki, Japan (p. 39)

Chow, Phoeve. "Meteoric Rise." *Architectural Review* 201, no. 1203 (1997): 44-48.

Gubitosi, Alessandro. "Ferry Terminal at Mihonoseki, Japan." *l'Arca* no. 100 (1996): 42-47.

Hein, Carola. 'Prestige en vermaak: grands projets in Japan = Prestige and Diversion: Grands Projets in Japan." *Archis* no. 2 (1998): 48-61.

"Meteor Plaza." *Kenchiku bunka* 51, no. 595 (1996): 57-64.

"Mihonoseki Terminal: Shin Takamatsu Architect & Associates." *Japan Architect* no. 14 (1994): 100-103.

"Schlagkräftig: zwei Fährterminals in Japan: Mihonoseki." *Architektur, Innenarchitektur, Technischer Ausbau* 105, no. 7-8 (1997): 42-45.

"Shin Takamatsu Architect & Associates: Meteor Plaza." *Japan Architect* no. 24 (1996): 138-39.

"Shin Takamatsu Architect & Associates: Meteor Plaza, Shimane, 1994–95." *GA Japan: environmental design* no. 20 (1996): 16-33.

"Shin Takamatsu: Shichinuiko Terminal, Nima-cho, Shimane Prefecture." *Architectural Design* 64, no. 5-6 (1994): 86-87.

Denver International Airport, Denver, Colorado, USA (p. 40)

Barreneche, Raul A. "Denver's Tensile Roof." *Architecture* 83, no. 8 (1994): 89-97.

Berger, Alan. "Screening Junkspace: Is Denver Squandering its Opportunity to Build a World-class Airport Landscape?" *Landscape Architecture* 93, no. 1 (2003): 36, 38-40.

Betsky, Aaron. "Denver International Airport door Fentress Bradburn Architects: de architectuur van de jet lag." *de Architect Dossier* no. 7 (1998): 34-37.

Blake, Edward. "Peak Condition." *Architectural Review* 197, no. 1176 (1995): 60-63.

Cattaneo, Renato. "Il grande terminal di Denver: A Canopied Air Terminal." *l'Arca* no. 73 (1993): 18-23.

Drewes, Frank F. "Denver International Airport." *Deutsche Bauzeitschrift* 43, no. 7 (1995): 97-102.

Fisher, Thomas. "Projects: Flights of Fantasy." *Progressive Architecture* 73, no. 3 (1992): 105-107.

Landecker, Heide. "Peak Performance: Elrey Jeppensen Terminal, Denver International Airport, Denver, Colorado, C.W. Fentress, J.H. Bradburn and Associates, Architect." *Architecture* 83, no. 8 (1994): 44-53.

Pavarini, Stefano. "Trentaquattro cime: Denver International Airport." *l'Arca* no.

87 (1994): 18-29.

Russell, James S. "Is This Any Way to Build an Airport?' *Architectural Record* 182, no. 11 (1994): 30-37, 97.

Stein, Karen D. "'Snow-capped' Symbol: Landside Terminal, Denver International Airport." *Architectural Record* 181, no. 6 (1993): 106-7.

Waldheim, Charles. "Airport Landscape." *Log* no. 8 (2006): 120-30.

TGV Méditerranée, Aix-en-Provence, Avignon and Valence, France (p. 42)

Bucci, Federico. "Le architetture del viaggiatore = Architectures for Travellers." *Ottagono* 34, no. 132 (1999): 46-51.

Caille, Emmanuel. "AREP-RFR: gare TGV Méditerranée, Avignon." *Moniteur architecture AMC* no. 120 (2001): 78-85.

Cardani, Elena. "Le nuove tappe della velocità: New TGV Stations." *l'Arca* no. 162 (2001): 54-61.

Duthilleul, Jean Marie, and Florence Michel. "La reconquête du sens." *Architecture intérieure créé* no. 262 (1994): 72-75.

Fontana, Jacopo della. "Accessibilità e intermodalità: Three TGV stations." *l'Arca* no. 130 (1998): 18-25.

Friedrich, Jan. "7.24 Uhr ab Gare de Lyon: drei Bahnhöfe für den TGV in Südfrankreich." *Bauwelt* 92, no. 37 (2001): 12-19.

"Gare TGV Méditerranée, Avignon." *Moniteur architecture AMC* no. 121 (2002): 88-89.

Klauser, Wilhelm. "Coherente strategie van landschap tot detail: drie TGV stations in Zuid-Frankrijk van AREP." *de Architect* 32, no. 11 (2001): 74-79.

"Le tre stazioni del TGV mediterraneo: Valence, Avignon, Aix-en-Provence = The Three Stations of the Mediterranean TGV." *Industria delle costruzioni* no. 367 (2002): 54-67.

Libois, Brigitte. "Knooppunten en hun landschappen: TGV Mediterranée, Frankrijk." *A+* no. 175 (2002): 98-105.

"Méditerranée: TGV, des gares hors la ville." *Connaissance des arts* no. 584 (2001): 32.

Mialet, Frederic. "Three New Stations for the TGV Méditerranée." *d'Architectures* no. 92 (1999): 41-43.

Schneider, Sabine. "Schnell wie der Mistral: drei neue TGV-Bahnhöfe eingeweiht." *Baumeister* 98, no. 8 (2001): 11.

Slessor, Catherine. "French Lessons: TGV stations, Provence, France, Valence station/ Avignon Station/Aix Station." *Architectural Review* 213, no. 1274 (2003): 44-51.

"SNCF – AREP: Valence TGV Station, Valence, France." *GA document* no. 69 (2002): 42-49.

"Territoires d'intermodalité." *Techniques & Architecture* no. 455 (2001): 54-67.

"TGV – Méditerranée." *Architecture intérieure créé* no. 263 (1994): 86-91.

Van Acker, Maarten. "Infrastructurele landschappen met een publieke horizon: vijf projecten van Michel Desvigne Paysagiste." *de Architect* 39, no. 6 (2008): 40-47.

A16 Service Station, Bay of Somme, France (p. 44)

Gauzin-Muller, Dominique. "One Programme, Three Sites: Autoroute Service Points for the Somme, the Lot and the Correze." *d'Architectures* no. 133 (2003): 24-27.

Laforge, Christophe, Arnaud Yver, and Hannetel & Associés. "Pascale Hannetel." *Studies in the History of Gardens & Designed Landscapes* 23, no. 2 (2003): 152-68.

Pousse, Jean François. "Immersion: aire de la baie de Somme." *Techniques et Architecture* no. 441 (1999): 28-33.

"Réalisations 1998: Equipements." *Moniteur architecture AMC* no. 94 (1998): 155.

IJburg Bridges, Amsterdam, the Netherlands (p. 46)

Pieters, Dominique. "Bruggen slaan voor de toekomst: nieuwe realisaties van Wilkinson Eyre, Foster and Partners, Birds Portchmouth Russum, Grimshaw and Partners en Venhoeven c.s." *de Architect* 33, no. 4 (2002): 76-81.

Russell, James S. "Lacy Struts That Promise in a New City's Greatness." *Architectural Record* 190, no. 1 (2002): 59-61.

Humber River Bridge, Toronto, Canada (p. 48)

Carter, Brian. "Thunderbirds are go." *Architectural Review* 199, no. 1189 (1996): 58-59.

"Connections: Flight of the Thunderbird." *Canadian Architect* 41, no. 2 (1996): 12-13.

"Fahrrad- und Fussgängerbrücke über den Fluss Humber in Toronto, Kanada = The Humber River Bicycle Pedestrian Bridge in Toronto, Canada." *Architektur + Wettbewerbe* no. 168 (1996): 24-25.

CHAPTER 2
Central Artery/Tunnel, Boston, USA (p. 57)

Bowen, Ted Smalley. "New Plans Forming above and around Boston's 'Big Dig'." *Architectural Record* 192, no. 6 (2004): 54.

Bowen, Ted Smalley. "Big Dig Snafu Delays Boston Greenway Projects." *Architectural Record* 194, no. 10 (2006): 29.

Brown, Robert A. "Filling the Cut: After Years of Planning, the Rose Kennedy Greenway is Finally Taking Shape in Boston." *Urban Land* 65, no. 3 (2006): 65-68.

Campbell, Robert. "A Walk in Progress: A Tour of the (More or Less) Finished Sections of the New Rose Kennedy Greenway Reveals That Intentions Have Been Met – and Missed." *Landscape Architecture* 98, no. 3 (2008): 28-30, 32, 34.

Campbell, Robert, and Charles Lockwood. "The Big Dig: What's Up under Boston?" *Architectural Record* 190, no. 3 (2002): 84-86, 88.

Di Mambro, Antonio. "Il grande scavo di Boston = Boston's Big Dig." *Spazio e società* 14, no. 54 (1991): 24-51.

Faga, Barbara. "Boston's Big Dig." *Topos: European Landscape Magazine* no. 51 (2005): 86-92.

Freeman, Allen. "Above the Cut: The Big Dig Selects Landscape Teams for Three New Parks in Downtown Boston." *Landscape Architecture* 93, no. 3 (2003): 62-67.

Gisolfi, Peter. "Accidental Parks: Cities are Creating Open Space from Urban Remnants – But Can Remnants Effectively Bind the City Together?" *Landscape Architecture* 97, no. 8 (2007): 74-76.

Greenberg, Ken. "A Good Time for Cities." *Places* 19, no. 2 (2007): 4-11.

Murray, Hubert. "Il grande scavo continua = The Big Dig Continues: Central Artery/Tunnel, Boston." *Spazio e società* 18, no. 73 (1996): 32-49.

Murray, Hubert. "Paved with Good Intentions: Boston's Central Artery Project and a Failure of City Building." *Harvard Design Magazine* no. 22 (2005): 74-82.

Roy, Tamara, and Kelly Shannon. "Wanted: Visionary Landscape Designer: Boston's 'Big Dig'." *Archis* no. 5 (2003): 112-15.

Shaw, Barry. "Hiding the Highway." *Architectural Review* 190, no. 1141 (1992): 68-71.

Wallace Floyd Associates. "Grand Unifiers: The Central-Artery Tunnel Project, Boston, MA." *Harvard Architecture Review* 10 (1998): 24-29.

A5 National Road, Yverdon-les-Bains/Biel, Switzerland (p. 58)

Laimberger, Raoul. "Siedlung entlasten – Natur belasten? = L'intégration de l'A5 dans le paysage." *Anthos* 36, no. 1 (1997): 8-13.

HST Tunnel, Leiderdorp/Hazerswoude, the Netherlands (p. 59)

Bakker, Gemma. "De aanleg van de HSL: een rapportage = Building the HSL: A Report." *Archis* no. 5 (2000): 66-75.

Bosma, Koos. "Escapades in het Groene Hart: de HSL in een dwangbuis = Adventures in the Green Heart: High-speed Line in a Straightjacket." *Archis* no. 8 (1996): 18-25.

Bosma, Koos. "Gerommel in de marge of nieuwe aanpak? Parallelstudie HSL-Zuid = Borderline or Break-through? Parallel Study HSL-South." *Archis* no. 4 (1998): 56-57.

Jardins Wilson, Plaine Saint-Denis, France (p. 60)

Courajoud, Michel, and Benoît Scribe. "Jardins Wilson." *AA Files* no. 38 (1999): 2-9.

"Couverture et jardins de l'A1 a Saint Denis." *Moniteur architecture AMC* no. 90 (1998): 14.

"L'espace public ou la naissance d'une ville." *Moniteur architecture AMC* no. 104 (2000): 126-27.

Lortie, André. "Paris-phèrie: Plaine Saint-Denis e il 'Grand axe'." *Casabella* 56, no. 596 (1992): 32-43, 69-70.

Place des Célestins, Lyon, France (p. 62)

Charbonneau, Jean-Pierre. "Grand Lyon: samenhangende aanpak voor de hele agglomeratie." *de Architect* 27, no. 11 (1996): 48-61.

Chaslin, Francois. "Gli spazi publici della grande Lione." *Domus* no. 784 (1996): 7-13.

Danner, Dietmar. "Helix: das Parkhaus Célestins in Lyon." *Architektur, Innenarchitektur, Technischer Ausbau* 103, no. 7-8 (1995): 32-35.

"Erlebnisparkomanie." *Werk, Bauen + Wohnen* no. 10 (1995): 71.

"Essential Geometry: Restructuring of the Place des Celestins." *Techniques & Architecture* no. 419 (1995): 43-45.

Ménard, Jean-Pierre. "Details: Les parcs de stationnement entre urbanisme et urbanité." *Moniteur architecture AMC* no. 77 (1997): 62-79.

"Place des Célestins." *Bauwelt* 86, no. 25 (1995): 1436-37.

Tårnby Station, Tårnby, Denmark (p. 64)

"Tårnby Station." *Arkitektur DK* 43, no. 1 (1999): 50-55.

Silicon Graphics North Charleston Campus, Mountain View, California, USA (p. 66)

Betsky, Aaron. "Agile Architecture." *Architectural Record* 184, no. 5 (1996): 72-79.

Callaway, William. "A Secret Ingredient?" *Urban Land* 58, no. 11-12 (1999): 96-99.

Cohen, Edie Lee. "Silicon Graphics." *Interior Design* 61, no. 6 (1990): 166-71.

Drewes, Frank F. "Freigelegt – Büro in Kalifornien = Exposed – The Office in California." *Deutsche Bauzeitschrift* 44 (1996), special edition, 12.

Gillette, Jane Brown. "Parking at Its Best." *Landscape Architecture* 88, no. 2 (1998): 26, 28-31.

Lang Ho, Cathy. "Silicon Graphics, Mountain View, California." *Architectural Record* 186, no. 6 (1998): 154-58.

Martin, Michelle. "An Instant Landmark in Silicon Valley.' *World Architecture* no. 68 (1998): 64-69.

"Silicon Graphics Inc., Amphitheater, Technology Center and North Charleston Park, Mountain View, California." *Land Forum Special issue. The SWA Group: Recent Projects* no. 14 (2002): 107-10.

"Studios Architecture: North Charleston Campus, Silicon Graphics Computer Systems, Mountain View, California, U.S.A." *GA document* no. 53 (1997): 106-17.

Port Terminal, Nice, France (p. 69)

Boudet, Dominique. "La mise en valeur des grands espaces publiques: le port." *Moniteur architecture AMC* no. 163 (2006): 168, 172-73.

"De nouvelles entrées de ville." *Moniteur architecture AMC* no. 120 (2001): 170-75.

Channel Tunnel Rail Link, Kent, UK (p. 69)

Armour, Tom. "Channel Tunnel Rail Link, Kent, UK: Project Profile." *Landscape Design* no. 321 (2003): 26-27.

"En Route: A Round-up of News and Views of Some Current Transport Schemes." *Landscape Design* no. 320 (2003): 19-22.

Gibb, Richard, and David M. Smith. "BR Would Like to Apologize for the 14-Year Delay." *Town and Country Planning* 60, no. 11-12 (1991): 346-48.

Lloyd, Jiggy. "The Channel Tunnel Rail link." *Landscape Design* no. 190 (1990): 14-16.

Moor, Nigel. "South East Looks to East Thames Corridor for Rescue." *Building* 257, no. 5 (1992): 37.

Schiphol Airport Plantation, Amsterdam, the Netherlands (p. 70)

"Adriaan Geuze – West 8: urbanidad y paisaje = Urbanity and Landscape." *AV Monografías = AV Monographs* no. 73 (1998): 92-101.

"Aménagement paysagers, aéroport de Schiphol, Amsterdam, Pays-Bas: West 8." *Architecture d'aujourd'hui* no. 363 (2006): 68-69.

Andela, Gerrie. "Uitdagende landschappen voor ontdekkingsreizigers: vervreemding en verzoening in het werk van West 8 = Challenging Landscape for Explorers: Estrangement and Reconciliation the Work of West 8." *Archis* no. 2 (1994): 40-41.

Bosma Koos, and Martijn Vos. "Het einde van de dinosaurus?: Overwegingen bij de uitbreiding van Schiphol." *Archis* no. 2 (1998): 8-17.

"Flughafengärten: Landschaftsarchitektur in Amsterdam-Schiphol." *Bauwelt* 90, no. 39 (1999): 2204-5.

Geuze, Adriaan. *West 8: Mosaics*, Ludion, 2006.

Graaf, Jan de. "Die Gärten von West 8 = The Gardens of West 8." *Topos: European Landscape Magazine* no. 11 (1995): 115-23.

"Landscaping Schiphol, Amsterdam, The Netherlands 1992–1996." *a+u: Architecture and Urbanism* no. 313 (1996): 66-69.

Primas, Urs. "Das bearbeitete Territorium." *Werk, Bauen + Wohnen* no. 10 (1997): 12.

Righetti, Paolo. "Schiphol in Progress." *l'Arca* no. 79 (1994): 26-31.

Rodermond, Janny. "De poëzie van het pretentieloze: werk van West 8." *de Architect* 24, no. 3 (1993): 45.

Rodermond, Janny, and Harm Tilman. "Holland: Remade oder Ready-made? = Holland: Re-made or Ready-made?' *Topos: European Landscape Magazine* no. 31 (2000): 32-40.

Van Dijk, Hans. "West 8: Landscape Design for an Airport." *Domus* no. 815 (1999): 18-19.

M6 Service Station, Tebay, UK (p. 70)

Dawson, Susan. "Motorway Services with a Touch of Wordsworth." *Architects' Journal* 200, no. 20 (1994): 28.

Transit Station, Everett, Washington, USA (p. 71)

MacLeod, Leo. "University at the Station." *Urban Land* 61, no. 7 (2002): 33.

Oslo Airport, Gardermoen, Norway (p. 72)

Affentranger, Christoph. "Neue Ära: Flughafen Gardermoein Oslo." *Deutsche Bauzeitung* 133, no. 2 (1999): 60-69.

Arosio, Enrico. "Aviaplan a Oslo: Aeroporto Gardermoen = Gardermoen Airport." *Abitare* no. 380 (1999): 118-23.

Bakken, Anton A. "Adkomstsonen: Oslo lufthavn Gardermoen adkomstsonen." *Byggekunst: the Norwegian Review of Architecture* 77, no. 1 (1995): 30-35, 52.

Davey, Peter. "Moving Places." *Architectural Review* 205, no. 1227 (1999): 42-43.

Erlien, Gisle. "Oslo Airport, Gardermoen: Planning." *Byggekunst: The Norwegian Review of Architecture* 81, no. 1 (1999): 16-19.

Feste, Jan. "Norwegen: die Nähe zur Natur = Norway: An Affinity for Nature." *Topos: European Landscape Magazine* no. 27 (1999): 56-62.

Gronvold, Ulf. "Oslo International Airport, Gardermoen." *Arkitektur, Arkitektur i Norge* 98, no. 8 (1998): 24-27.

Katborg, Peter. "Helhetsplan: Oslo lufthavn Gardermoen helhetspan." *Byggekunst: The Norwegian Review of Architecture* 77, no. 1 (1995): 24-29, 52.

Lund, Nils-Ole. "Oslo Airport at Gardermoen." *Byggekunst: The Norwegian Review of Architecture* 81, no. 1 (1999): 20-23.

Miles, Henry. "The Flying Norsemen: Airport, Gardermoen, Oslo, Norway." *Architectural Review* 205, no. 1227 (1999): 44-53.

Mulazzani, Marco. "Aviaplan: nuovo aeroporto Gardermoen. 1998. Oslo, Norvegia." *Casabella* 65, no. 695-696 (2001): 46-53.

"Overordnet landskapsplan: Aviaplan AS." *Byggekunst: The Norwegian Review of Architecture* 81, no. 6 (1999): 24-29.

Paganelli, Carlo. "Un frammento di ala: Oslo International Airport." *l'Arca* no. 130 (1998): 46-51.

Stokke, Gudmund. "Aviaplan AS: Gardermoen, Oslo, Norway." *Arkitektur: The Swedish Review of Architecture* 101, no. 5 (2001): 22-25.

Stokke, Gudmund. "Oslo Airport, Gardermoen: Masterplan", "Terminal Building." *Byggekunst: The Norwegian Review of Architecture* 81, no. 1 (1999): 12-15, 26-41.

Vedal, Terje. "Adkomstsonen: 13.3 Landskapsarkitekter AS." *Byggekunst: The Norwegian Review of Architecture* 81, no. 6 (1999): 30-35.

Parc de la Gare d'Issy-Val de Seine, Issy-les-Moulineaux, France (p. 74)

Ménard, Jean-Pierre. "Details: les parcs de stationnement entre urbanisme et urbanité." *Moniteur architecture AMC* no. 77 (1997): 61-68.

Plateau de Kirchberg, Luxembourg (p. 76)

Fonds Kirchberg. "Evolutionary Phases in the Urbanization of the Kirchberg Plateau." *a+u: Architecture and Urbanism* no. 433 (2006): 56-59.

Latz, Peter. "Die Grünflächen auf dem Plateau de Kirchberg in Luxembourg." *Gartenkunst* 8, no. 1 (1996): 153-60.

Latz, Peter. "Reclaiming Public Open Space, Avenue John F Kennedy, Kirchberg, Luxembourg." *Topos: European Landscape Magazine* no. 41 (2002): 87.

Latz, Peter. "The Idea of Making Time Visible." In *About Landscape: Essays on Design, Style, Time and Space*. Edition Topos (European Landscape Magazine). Basel: Birkhäuser, 2003, 77-82.

Nottrot, Ina. "The Development of the Kirchberg District." *a+u: Architecture and Urbanism* no. 433 (2006): 94-102.

Ballet Valet Parking Garage, Miami Beach, Florida, USA (p. 78)

Barreneche, Raul A. "Miami Beach Comes of Age." *Architecture* 85, no. 4 (1996): 98-107.

Dunlop, Beth. *Arquitectonica*. New York: Rizzoli, 2004.

Kasdin, Neisen. "Preserving a Sense of Place: Public-private Projects in Miami Beach Stand Up to the Challenge." *Urban Land* 59, no. 4 (2000): 18, 20.

Takesuye, David. "ULI Awards Profile: Ballet Valet: Miami's South Beach Public Parking: Retail Facility." *Urban Land* 59, no. 4 (2000): 124-25.

Zunino, Maria Giulia. "La Miami che sarà = Miami: The Shape of Things to Come." *Abitare* no. 395 (2000): 156-62.

Interchange Park, Barcelona, Spain (p. 80)

Ceccaroni, Marco. "Parc Trinitat tracce lineari: a Barcelona, Spagna." *Abitare* no. 331 (1994): 134-37.

"Freizeitanlage im Autobahnkreisel 'La Trinitat', Barcelona, 1990–1993." *Werk, Bauen + Wohnen* no. 6 (1995): 14-17.

"Parc de la Trinitat." *Garten + Landschaft* 104, no. 1 (1994): 27-31.

"Parks im Abseits der Städte." *Bauwelt* 87, no. 37 (1996): 2142-45.

"Parque del nudo de la Trinitat. Barcelona: Enric Batlle y Joan Roig, arquitectos." *ON Diseño* no. 153 (1994): 93-97.

Salazar, Jaime. "Knooppunt La Trinitat in Barcelona door Roig en Battle: begrip voor stedelijke wanorde." *de Architect Dossier* no. 10 (1999): 60-67.

Parkway, Sant Cugat del Vallès, Spain (p. 81)

Batlle Durany, Enric. "Linien im Raster = Grids and Lines." *Topos: European Landscape Magazine* no. 29 (1999): 46-49.

"Bridge in Collfava, Sant Cugat del Valles (Batlle & Roig)." *Architecti* 10, no. 45 (1999): 63-65.

Ceccaroni, Marco. "E. Batlle e J. Roig in Catalogna: Parc Central de Sant Cugat." *Abitare* no. 354 (1996): 154-57.

"Enric Batlle & Joan Roig, Parque central, Sant Cugat (Barcelona) = Central Park, Sant Cugat (Barcelona)." *AV Monografías = AV Monographs* no. 51-52 (1995): 122-24.

"Espacios libres del Plan Parcial Coll Favà, Sant Cugat del Vallés = Open Spaces of the Coll Favà Partial Plan, Sant Cugat des Vallés." *On Diseño* no. 176 (1996): 176-81.

"Parque central de Sant Cugat del Vallès: Enric Batlle y Joan Roig, arquitectos." *ON Diseño* no. 157 (1994): 112-17.

RN170, Saint-Gratien, France (p. 81)

"Boulevard Intercommunal du Parisis." *Lotus Navigator* no. 7 (2003): 61-64.

Smets, Marcel. "The Contemporary Landscape of Europe's Infrastructures = Il nuovo paesaggio delle infrastrutture in Europa.' *Lotus international* no. 110 (2001): 116-43.

Bus Terminal, Baden-Rütihof, Switzerland (p. 82)

Remmele, Mathias. "Ortsbezogen, spannungsvoll, bildhaft: Knapkiewicz & Fickert, Busterminal Baden-Rütihof und Siedlung Lokomitive Winterthur." *Archithese* 37, no. 1 (2007): 38-45.

Simon, Axel. "Coach Terminal, Baden-Rütihof: Knapkiewicz & Fickert." *A10: New European Architecture* no. 11 (2006): 38-39.

Von Fischer, Sabine. "Reiselust: Busterminal für Twerenbold Reisein Rütihof bei Baden, von Knapkiewicz & Fickert Architekten, Zürich." *Werk, Bauen + Wohnen* no. 10 (2006): 34-39.

Riverfront Park, Pittsburg, USA (p. 83)

"Allegheny Riverfront Park, Lower Level, Pittsburgh, PA: Architects: Michael Van Valkenburgh Associates." *Land Forum* no. 5 (2000): 70-73.

Bullivant, Lucy. "New Relationship between Landscape Architecture and Urban Design: 5. Landscape as a Living Medium: Michael Van Valkenburgh Associates." *a+u, Architecture and Urbanism* no. 430 (2006): 130-35.

Freeman, Allen. "Going to the Edge: With the Linear Allegheny Riverfront Park, Pittsburgh Starts Weaving Together its Downtown and Rivers." *Landscape Architecture* 93, no. 7 (2003): 86-91, 106-7.

Hasbrouck, Hope, and Jason Sowell. "Urbanism und Landschaftsarchitektur = Cities Revamping Waterfronts." *Garten + Landschaft* 117, no. 4 (2007): 20-22.

"Michael Van Valkenburgh Associates: Allegheny Riverfront Park." *Architecture* 86, no. 1 (1997): 92-93.

Moffat, David. "Allegheny Riverfront Park, Pittsburgh, Pennsylvania." *Places* 15, no. 1 (2002): 10-13.

Nyren, Ron. "Top Ten Urban Parks." *Urban Land* 65, no. 10 (2006): 58-62.

Pearson, Clifford A. "Michael Van Valkenburgh Takes People for a Walk over the Water's Edge in his Design for Pittsburgh's Allegheny Riverfront Park." *Architectural Record* 188, no. 3 (2000): 102-5.

Thompson, Ian. "The Pittsburgh Weddings." *Landscape Design* no. 298 (2001): 13-15.

Weller, Richard. "Michael Van Valkenburgh Associates: Allegheny Riverfront Park [ed.] by Jane Amidon." *Landscape Australia* 28, no. 109 (2006): 72.

Louisville Waterfront Park, Louisville, Kentucky, USA (p. 84)

Calkins, Meg. "Return of the River: Hargreaves Associates Redefines the American Park to Heal an Urban Waterfront and Help the People of Louisville Regain Their River." *Landscape Architecture* 91, no. 7 (2001): 74-83.

Hargreaves, George. "Surcos: las formas del paisaje reciclado = Furrows: The Shapes of Recycled Landscape." *Quaderns d'arquitectura i urbanisme* no. 217 (1998): 162-69.

Hasbrouck, Hope, and Jason Sowell. "Urbanism und Landschaftsarchitektur = Cities Revamping Waterfronts." *Garten + Landschaft* 117, no. 4 (2007): 20-22.

Hasegawa, Hiroki. "Louisville Waterfront, Louisville." *Process* no. 128 (1996): 102-7.

Hudnut, William H. "Reclaiming Waterfronts." *Urban Land* 58, no. 7 (1999): 50-55.

Nyren, Ron. "Top Ten Urban Parks." *Urban Land* 65, no. 10 (2006): 58-62.

Thompson, J. William. "Rethinking River City." *Landscape Architecture* 86, no. 8 (1996): 70-77, 83.

Vaccarino, Rossana. "I paesaggi ri-fatti = Re-made Landscapes." *Lotus international* no. 87 (1995): 82-107.

Faliron Coast, Athens, Greece (p. 86)

Fragonas, Panos. "Regenerating Faliron Bay and Reconnecting the City with the Sea." *Architecture in Greece, E arhitektonike tou demosiou horou sten Europe* 37 (2003): 112-15.

Ingersoll, Richard. "My Big, Fat, Greek Olympics." *Architecture* 93, no. 7 (2004): 29-30.

Kalandides, Ares. "Olympia in der Stadt: die innerstädtischen Wettkampfstätten." *Bauwelt* 95, no. 29 (2004): 30-31.

Papayannis, Thymio. "Sanierung der Bucht von Faleron, Athen = Faleron Bay: Large-scale Restoration of the Athens Seafront." *Topos: European Landscape Magazine* no. 38 (2002): 55-59.

Rambert, Francis. "Revitalisation of the Falaire Coast by the Olympic Games." *d'Architectures* no. 112 (2004): 38-39.

Reichen, Bernard. "Neuordnung der Faliro-Küste in Athen." *Garten + Landschaft* 114, no. 8 (2004): 13-15.

Reichen, Bernard, and Philippe Robert. *Reichen and Robert*. Basel: Birkhäuser, 2003, 58-61.

Hoenheim-Nord Terminus, Strasbourg, France (p. 88)

Adam, Hubertus. "Magnetfeld am Stadtrand: Zaha Hadid, Interchange Terminal Hoenheim-Nord, Strasbourg, 1999–2001 = Champ magnétique en bordure de ville: Zaha Hadid, terminus de transbordement Hoenheim nord, Strasbourg 1999–2001." *Archithese* 31, no. 4 (2002): 56-61.

Ascher, Francois et al. "Tramway terminus Line B, Hoenheim, Strasbourg (Zaha Hadid)." *Techniques & Architecture* no. 455 (2001): 24-29.

Davoine, Gilles. "Zaha Hadid: parking et terminus de tramway, Strasbourg-Hoenheim." *Moniteur architecture AMC* no. 116 (2001): 52-56.

Egg, Anne Laure. "Station multimodale: terminus land art, Hoenheim." *Architecture intérieure créé* no. 299 (2000): 90-95.

Fairs, Marcus. "Zaha's Park-and-Ride: Hoenheim Traffic Interchange, Strasbourg; Architects." *Building* 266, no. 8185 (2001): 40-47.

Fernández-Galiano, Luis. "Mayo: paisajes de pasión = May: Landscapes of Passion." *AV Monografías = AV Monographs* no. 99-100 (2003): 170-73.

Giovannini, Joseph. "Field of Motion." *Architecture* 90, no. 9 (2001): 136-42.

Hadid, Zaha, Walter Nägeli, and Mohsen Mostafavi. "Zaha Hadid 1996–2001. Beginnings and Ends." *El Croquis* no. 103 (2000): 140-47.

Höhl, Wolfgang. "Voorbij betekenis en object: Tramterminal in Hoenheim-Nord door Zaha Hadid." *de Architect* 32, no. 11 (2001): 70-73.

"Intercambiador, Estrasburgo (Francia) = Intermodal Transportation Terminal, Strasbourg (France)." *AV Monografías = AV Monographs* no. 91 (2001): 98-103.

Kimmel, Laurence. "Plan, masse – Zaha Hadid à Hoenheim: L'architecture-paysage." *Faces* no. 55 (2004): 18-22.

"Parking et terminus de tramway, Strasbourg-Hoenheim." *Moniteur architecture AMC* no. 121 (2002): 80-83.

Paschini, Luca. "Zaha Hadid: parcheggio, Strasburgo 2001." *Casabella* 66, no. 702 (2002): 78-87.

Pavarini, Stefano. "Terminal multinodale: Honenheim-Nord, Strasbourg." *l'Arca* no. 145 (2000): 4-7.

Pavarini, Stefano. "Transport Junction, Strasbourg. 1999." *Arca plus* 7, no. 25 (2000): 68-71.

Ruby, Ilka, and Andreas Ruby. "Landed Square." *Architectural Design* 74, no. 4 (2004): 76-79.

"Terminus Hoenheim-Nord, Strasbourg, Strasbourg, France 1999–2001." *a+u: Architecture and Urbanism* no. 374 (2001): 44-51.

Trasi, Nicoletta. "Mies van der Rohe Awards 2003." *l'Arca* no. 185 (2003): 56-59.

"Zaha Hadid: visionnaire et/ou réaliste?" *Architecture d'aujourd'hui* no. 324 (1999): 108-9.

"Zaha M. Hadid: Car Park and Terminus Hoenheim-Nord, Strasbourg, France." *GA document* no. 66 (2001): 102-7.

Verneda Parking Lot, Barcelona, Spain (p. 90)

"Organisation of an Interior Block Space, Barcelona." *ON Diseño* no. 212 (2000): 154-61.

Toledo Escalators and Car Park, Toledo, Spain (p. 92)

Acuña, Paloma. "José Antonio Martínez Lapeña & Elías Torres Tur, Architects: La Granja Escalator, Toledo, Spain." *Architecture* 89, no. 10 (2000): 130-35.

Bertolucci, Carla. "Spanish Steps: External Staircase, Toledo, Spain." *Architectural Review* 211, no. 1260 (2002): 52-55.

"Escalera de La Granja = La Granja escalator." *Via arquitectura* 9 (2001): 92-97.

"Escalera de la Granja, Toledo = La Granja Escalators, Toledo." *AV Monografías = AV Monographs* no. 87-88 (2001): 92-96.

"Escaleras de la Granja en Toledo." *Arquitectura* no. 325 (2001): 6.01-6.17.

"Escaleras de la Granja, Toledo = Escalators of la Granja, Toledo." *ON Diseño* no. 224 (2001): 216-25.

Fernández-Galiano, Luis. "2000 En Doce Edificios = 2000 in Twelve Buildings." *AV Monografías = AV Monographs* no. 87-88 (2001): 218-25.

Jakob, Markus. "Das rollende Stadttor." *Werk, Bauen + Wohnen* no. 6 (2005): 12-13.

"José Antonio Martínez Lapeña & Elias Torres Tur, Architects:La Granja Escalator, Toledo, Spain 1997–2000." *a+u: Architecture and Urbanism* no. 375 (2001): 116-23.

"La Granja escaleros = La Granja Stairs." *Quaderns d'arquitectura i urbanisme* no. 231 (2001): 76-83.

"La herida leve: escaleras de la Granja, Toledo." *Arquitectura Viva* no. 75 (2000): 92-95.

Martínez Lapeña, Jose Antonio, and Elías Torres Tur. "Im Zickzack nach ober =The Great Escalator of Toledo." *Topos: European Landscape Magazine* no. 36 (2001): 64-66.

"Rolltreppe in Toledo = Escalator in Toledo = Scala mobile a Toledo = Escalier roulant à Tolède = Escalera mecánica e Toledo." *Detail* 42, no. 4 (2002): 420-23.

"Rolltreppe in Toledo." *Bauwelt* 92, no. 19 (2001): 24-25.

"S.L.: Escalier mécanique, Tolède, Espagne = Mechanical Stairs, Toledo, Spain: Lapena-Torres arquitectos." *Architecture d'aujourd'hui* no. 340 (2002): 72.

Séron-Pierre, Catherine. "Martinez Lapeña & Torres Tur: escalier mécanique urbain, Tolède." *Moniteur architecture AMC* no. 118 (2001): 64-67.

Villari, Alessandro. "José Antonio Martínez Lapeña, Elias Torres Tur – incisioni: risalita a Toledo = Incisions: Climbing Toledo." *Spazio e società* 22, no. 92 (2000): 12-21.

Highway Coverage, the Hague, the Netherlands (p. 95)

Boekraad, Cees, and Wilfried van Winden. "Een plaza op de highway: Grotius-plaats in Den Haag." *de Architect* 24, no. 10 (1993): 55-57.

Van Rossem, Vincent. "Stadträume mit konträrem Gesicht: drei Sanierungs-projekte in Den Haag." *Bauwelt* 88, no. 43-44 (1997): 2450-57.

Railway Station, Frankfurt, Germany (p. 95)

Bodenbach, Christof. "ICE, BRT und FRA: Fernbahnhof Flughafen Frankfurt von Bothe Richter Teherani." *Baumeister* 96, no. 8 (1999): 6.

Bothe, Jens. "Zukunftsweisend: ICE-Bahnhof Frankfurt Airport." *Architektur, Innenarchitektur, Technischer Ausbau* no. 10 (1997): 32.

Dawson, Layla. "Frankfurt Gateway: Station, Frankfurt Airport, Germany." *Architectural Review* 205, no. 1227 (1999): 78-81.

"Fernbahnhof Flughafen Frankfurt am Main." *Bauwelt* 90, no. 24 (1999): 1310.

Russell, James S. "ICE Station, Frankfurt, Germany." *Architectural Record* 190, no. 1 (2002): 120-23.

Thorne, Martha, ed. *Modern Trains and Splendid Stations: Architecture, Design, and Rail Travel for the Twenty-first Century*, London: Merrel, 2001, 87-88.

Highway Control Center, Nanterre, France (p. 96)

"Autobahnviadukt: Autobahnbrücke mit Betriebsgebaude in Nanterre." *Architektur, Innenarchitektur, Technischer Ausbau* 105, no. 7-8 (1997): 56-61.

Bennett, David. *The Architecture of Bridge Design*. London: Telford, 1997, 134-37.

Cardani, Elena. "Motorways Control Centre, Nanterre (1999). (Odile Decq and Benoit Cornette)." *Arca plus* 7, no. 25 (2000): 78-83.

Cardani, Elena. 'Un'agenda di idee: For Motorway Services.' *l'Arca* no. 145 (2000): 64-69.

Gubitosi, Alessandro. "Un'agenda di idee: A Motorway Centre in Nanterre." *l'Arca* no. 90 (1995): 44-47.

Mialet, Frederic. "L2, A14." *d'Architectures* no. 83 (1998): 30.

"Odile Decq and Benoît Cornette." *Architectural Design* 64, no. 5-6 (1994): 42-49.

"Odile Decq, Benoît Cornette: ponte autostradale e centro di controllo, Nanterre = Highway Bridge and Highway Control Center, Nanterre." *Domus* no. 791 (1997): 24-27.

Ruby, Andreas. "Abgehängt: Autobahnkontrollzentrum und Hochstrasse A14 in Nanterre." *Bauwelt* 86, no. 31 (1995): 1690-93.

Slessor, Catherine. "Highway Patrol: Motorway Control Centre, Nanterre, France." *Architectural Review* 205, no. 1227 (1999): 82-84.

Such, Robert. "Space for Change." *Architectural Design* 70, no. 3 (2000): 94-97.

"Translation: viaduc et centre d'exploitation des autoroutes." *Techniques et Architecture* no. 422 (1995): 88-91.

"Viadotto e centro di gestione delle autostrade a Nanterre = Viaduct and the Motorway Management Centre in Nanterre." *Industria delle costruzioni* no. 367 (2002): 20-25.

Chassé Site, Breda, the Netherlands (p. 98)

Borasi, Giovanna. "OMA – West 8 – Petra Blaisse/Inside Out – Xaveer de Geyter: Chassé Terrain, Breda." *Lotus international* no. 120 (2004): 88-111.

"OMA: Chassé, Breda." *Quaderns d'arquitectura i urbanisme* no. 238 (2003): 162-87.

"OMA: Chassé Terrain, Breda: aparcamiento = Parking." *a+t* no. 20 (2002): 24-29.

"Tiefgarage." *Bauwelt* 94, no. 14 (2003): 22-23.

Gran Via de les Corts Catalanes, Barcelona, Spain (p. 100)

"Gran Via, Barcelone, Espagne – parc et couverture partielle = 'Gran Via', Barcelona, Spain – Park and Partial Covering: Arriola & Fiol arquitectes." *Architecture d'aujourd'hui* special issue no. 363 (2006): 84-895.

Rieder, Max. "The Gran Via in Barcelona." *Topos: European Landscape Magazine* no. 53 (2005): 94-97.

Porta Susa TGV Station, Turin, Italy (p. 102)

Foppiano, Anna. "Torino Porta Susa = New H-S station: Torino Porta Susa." *Abitare* no. 453 (2005): 202-5.

"Gare de Turin, Porta Susa, Italie." *Architecture méditerranéenne* no. 59 (2003): 74-76.

"Grandi eventi, grandi opere = Major Events, Major Works." *Domus* no. 850 (2002): 26.

Guarnieri, Marco. "Torino Porta Susa: Illustrations of Competition Entries Including that of Winners AREP." *Parametro* 35, no. 258-259 (2005): 114-23.

"Progetto vincitore: Arep." *l'Arca* no. 187 (2003): 22-35.

Baveno Bridge, Baveno, Italy (p. 104)

Zunino, Maria Giulia. "Il ponte di Baveno (Novara) = Bridge, Baveno (Novara)." *Abitare* no. 389 (1999): 172-73.

Highway Bridge, Klosters, Switzerland (p. 107)

"An Klosters vorbei: die Sunnibergbrück bei Klosters, Graubünden, CH." *Deutsche Bauzeitung* 132, no. 5 (1998): 78-83.

"Hänger." *Werk, Bauen + Wohnen* no. 9 (1997): 9-12.

Menn, Christian. "L'art de combiner l'impératif économique à l'esthétique = Nice Price … Good Looks." *Architecture d'aujourd'hui* no. 335 (2001): 62-63.

Schregenberger, Thomas. "Tre ponti recenti in Svizzera e Germania = Three Recent Bridges in Switzerland and Germany." *Domus* no. 827 (2000): 18-19, 24.

"Sunnibergbrücke, Schweiz = Sunniberg Bridge, Switzerland = Pont Sunnibergen en Suisse." *Detail* 39, no. 8 (1999): 1450-51.

HST Bridge, Dordrecht, the Netherlands (p. 107)

Bakker, Gemma. "Brug over het Hollandsch Diep = Bridge over Hollandsch Diep." *Archis* no. 11 (2000): 42-49.

Kloos, Maarten. *Benthem Crouwel: 1980–2000.* Rotterdam: 010 Publishers, 1999, 226-29.

Maes, Ann. "HSL-Zuid = HSL in the Netherlands." *Abitare* no. 453 (2005): 208-11.

International Airport, Bilbao, Spain (p. 108)

"Aeropuerto de Bilbao = Bilbao Airport." *ON Diseño* no. 221 (2001): 356-79.

"Aeropuerto de Sondica, Bilbao = Sondica Airport, Bilbao." *AV Monografías = AV Monographs* no. 87-88 (2001): 26-33.

"Aeropuerto y torre de control de Sondica = Sondica Airport and Control Tower, 1990 & 1993, Bilbao (Spain)." *AV Monografías = AV Monographs* no. 61 (1996): 84-87.

"Bauen für den Aufschwung." *Werk, Bauen + Wohnen* no. 12 (1996): 34-35.

Dal Co, Francesco. "Santiago Calatrava: aeroporto Sondica e torre di controllo = Sondica Airport and Control Tower, Bilbao 2000." *Casabella* 65, no. 686 (2001): 18-37, 88-89.

"Santiago Calatrava." *a+u: Architecture and Urbanism* no. 305 (1996): 118-19.

"Santiago Calatrava 1989–1992." *El Croquis* 11, no. 57 (1992): 78-83.

"Santiago Calatrava: Aeropuerto Sondica, Bilbao, España, 1990–2000." *Lotus international* no. 108 (2001): 84-91.

Sicignano, Enrico. "Santiago Calatrava: la poesia della struttura e della materia = Santiago Calatrava: The Poetry of the Structure and of Matter." *Industria delle costruzioni* 30, no. 299 (1996): 4-54, cover.

"Un atto sublime: New Sondica Airport, Bilbao." *l'Arca* no. 152 (2000): 4-17.

Wohlin, Rasmus. "Fågel, fisk eller terminal?" *Arkitektur: The Swedish Review of Architecture* 101, no. 5 (2001): 44-49.

Railway Station Shanghai, China (p. 108)

Arnaboldi, Mario Antonio. "Una poetica spaziale: Shanghai-South Rail Station." *l'Arca* no. 221 (2007): 8-17.

Bussel, Abby. "Big Wheel Keep on Turning: A Massive Intermodal Station Helps Mobilize Shanghai's Burgeonning Population." *Architecture* 95, no. 7 (2006): 46-49.

Mascaro, Florian. "La gestion de projet: partage des données et travail collaboratif." *Architecture intérieure créé* no. 313 (2004): 130-31.

Ménard, Jean-Pierre. "Chantier: Shanghai Express." *Moniteur architecture AMC* no. 153 (2005): 36-38.

Vogliazzo, Maurizio. "Arep in China: in Shanghai and Beijing." *l'Arca* no. 190 (2004): 56-61.

Millau Viaduct, Millau, France (p. 110)

Bennett, David. *The Architecture of Bridge Design.* London: Telford, 1997, 116-33.

Buonomo, Marc, and Lionel Blaisse. "Entre ciel et terre: Viaduc, Millau, France." *Architecture intérieure créé* no. 312 (2003): 108-17.

Cardani, Elena. "Discreto ma calibrato: Millau Viaduct." *l'Arca* no. 172 (2002): 89.

Dubois, Marc. "Flinterdunne messtreep." *de Architect* 36, no. 3 (2005): 80-83.

"Europe: Millau Viaduct, France." *Architects' Journal* 221, no. 24 (2005): 80-86.

Futagawa, Yoshio. "Two Bridges: Millau Viaduct, Millau, Averyon, France, and Millennium Bridge, London." *GA document* no. 12 (1999): 138-43.

Hunt, Anthony. "Delight: Millau Bridge Joins the Lineage of Awesome European Viaducts." *Architectural Review* 217, no. 1300 (2005): 98.

Irace, Fulvio. "Sul Grand Canyon d'Europa = Over the Grand Canyon of Europe." *Abitare* no. 447 (2005): 91-97, 158.

Lane, Thomas. "C'est magnifique: Architects: Foster & Partners." *Building* 269, no. 8350 (2004): 46-52.

Martin, Jean-Marie. "La strada sospesa più alta del mondo: Foster and Partners: Viadotto Millau, Millau, Averyon, Francia = Foster and Partners, Millau Viaduct, Averyon, France: A Work Spanning Two Centuries." *Casabella* 69, no. 734 (2005): 80-91.

Mead, Andrew. "Foster's French Flying Lesson." *Architects' Journal* 220, no. 23 (2004): 6-7.

"Millau Viaduct (Grand Viaduc de Millau)." *Kenchiku bunka* 51, no. 601 (1996): 30-34.

"Norman Foster: Millau Viaduct, Millau, Aveyron, France." *GA document* no. 86 (2005): 108-11.

"Spectacle in Southern France: The Millau Viaduct." *Space Design* no. 387 (1996): 98-99.

Stephens, Suzanne. "Bridges That Seem to Float on Air Illustrate Feats of Architecture and Engineering." *Architectural Record* 195, no. 8 (2007): 78-79.

"Viadotto di Millau, Aveyron, Francia = Millau Viaduct, Averyon, France." *Industria delle costruzioni* 42, no. 399 (2008): 34-39.

Walther, René. "Harfenreihe über dem Tarn: le Grand Viaduc de Millau, Südfrankreich – Entwurf, Michel Virlogeux, Architekt, Norman Foster." *Deutsche Bauzeitung* 140, no. 2 (2006): 28-35.

Walther, René. "Schrägseilbrücke = Cable-stayed Bridge: le Grand Viaduc de Millau, Frankreich – Entwurf/Design, Michel Virlogeux, Architekt/Architect, Lord Norman Foster." *Deutsche Bauzeitung* 140, no. 6 (2006): 50-53.

Oriente Station, Lisbon, Portugal (p. 112)

Amoretti, Aldo et al. "Esposizione universale di Lisbona: l'oceano, un patrimonio per il futuro = Lisbon World Exposition: The Oceans, A Heritage for the Future." *Abitare* no. 370 (1998): 184-97.

Arnaboldi, Mario Antonio. "Il disegno della stazione: 'Do Oriente' stazione in Lisbon." *l'Arca* no. 96 (1995): 22-25.

Arnaboldi, Mario Antonio. "Estacao do Oriente, Lisbon (Santiago Calatrava)." *l'Arca plus* 4, no. 12 (1997): 104-7.

Barata, Paulo Martins. "Uno shed sopra il ponte = Shed over the Bridge." *Lotus international* no. 99 (1998): 82-91.

Binney, Marcus. *Architecture of Rail: The Way Ahead,* Academy Editions. London, 1995, 84-91.

Calatrava, Santiago. "Estação do Oriente: der Bahnhof von Santiago Calatrava." *Bauwelt* 89, no. 26 (1998): 1514-17.

Cohn, David. "Arboleda frente al mar: estación intermodal de Lisboa." *Arquitectura Viva* no. 38 (1994): 102-7.

"Do Oriente railway station, Lisbon; Architects: Santiago Calatrava." *GA document* no. 43 (1995): 16-19.

"Estacao do Oriente, Lisboa 1993." *Architecti* 7, no. 31 (1995): 60-69.

"Estación de Oriente = Oriente Station, 1993, Lisbon (Portugal)." *AV Monografías = AV Monographs* no. 61 (1996): 102-3.

"Gare de l'Orient, Expo'98 Lisbonne." *Architecture méditerranéenne* no. 52 (1999): 145-52.

Jodidio, Philip. *Building a New Millennium*. Cologne and London: Taschen, 1999.

Jodidio, Philip. *Santiago Calatrava*. Cologne and London: Taschen, 2001.

Lemoine, Bertrand. "Gare d'Oriente: gare ferroviaire et routière, Lisbonne." *Acier pour construire* no. 59 (1998): 8-15.

Mialet, Frédéric. "Dossier. Transports: Le siècle de l'intermodalité." *d'Architectures* no. 92 (1999): 44-45.

Molinari, Luca. "Segnali sul territorio: le stazioni di Calatrava = New Landmarks: Calatrava's Stations." *Ottagono* 34, no. 132 (1999): 52-59.

Rambert, Francis. "Interview with Santiago Caltrava about the Orient Railway Station." *d'Architectures* no. 84 (1998): 42-43.

"Santiago Calatrava: Competition Project for the Orient Station, Lisbon, Lisbon, Portugal 1994." *a+u: Architecture and Urbanism* no. 298 (1995): 26-33.

"Santiago Calatrava: Orient Station, Lisbon, Portugal." *GA document* no. 56 (1998): 84-97.

Sat, Claudio, and Luis Vassalo Fossa. "Expo Lisbona 98." *Casabella* 62, no. 654 (1998): 66-85.

Sharp, Dennis et al. "Orient station, Lisbon." *Architectural Monographs, Santiago Calatrava* no. 46 (1996): 98-103.

Sicignano, Enrico. "Santiago Calatrava: la poesia della struttura e della materia = Santiago Calatrava: The Poetry of the Structure and of Matter." *Industria delle costruzioni* 30, no. 299 (1996): 4-54.

Spier, Steven. "Orient Express." *Architectural Review* 204, no. 1217 (1998): 34-35.

Thorne, Martha, ed. *Modern Trains and Splendid Stations: Architecture, Design, and Rail Travel for the Twenty-first Century*. London: Merrel, 2001, 20-23, 120-25.

Casar de Cáceres Bus Station, Casar de Cáceres, Spain (p. 114)

"Bus Station, Casar de Caceres, Spain: Justo García Rubio, 2003." *Architecture of Israel* no. 68 (2007): 12-13.

Daguerre, Mercedes. "Justo García Rubio: stazione di autobus, Casar de Cáceres, Spagna." *Casabella* 70, no. 740 (2005): 154-61.

"Estación de autobuses del Casar de Cáceres = Bus Station Casar de Cáceres: Justo García Rubio, arquitecto." *ON Diseño* no. 252 (2004): 296-305.

"Justo García Rubio: Casar de Cáceres Sub-regional Bus Station, Casar de Cáceres, Spain." *GA document* no. 95 (2007): 94-99.

"Justo Garcia Rubio: estación de autobuses, Casar (Cáceres) = Bus Station, Casar de Cáceres (Cáceres)." *AV Monografías = AV Monographs* no. 105-106 (2004): 64-67.

"Justo García Rubio Arquitecto: Casar de Cáceres Subregional Bus Station, Cáceres, Spain 2003." *a+u: Architecture and Urbanism* no. 245 (2006): 78-85.

Pisani, Mario. "Stazione per autobus a Casar, Cáceres = Bus Station Casar, Cáceres." *Industria delle costruzioni* 39, no. 384 (2005): 26-27.

Spencer, Ingrid. "This Stop: Curvy Concrete for a Bus Station Spain." *Architectural Record* 193, no. 11 (2005): 75-76.

North Terminal, Washington National Airport, Washington, DC, USA (p. 116)

"Cesar Pelli wins AIA Gold Medal." *Progressive Architecture* 76, no. 2 (1995): 31, 36.

Guiraldes, Pablo. "El arte de volar." *Summa+* no. 34 (1998): 66-79.

Linn, Charles. "Cesar Pelli's New Passenger Terminal at National Airport in Washington, D.C., Eases the Life of the World-Weary Traveller." *Architectural Record* 185, no. 10 (1997): 88-95.

Riera Ojeda, Oscar, ed. *National Airport Terminal: Cesar Pelli*. Gloucester, Mass.: Rockport, 2000.

Schwartz, Adele C. "Washington National to Get a New Terminal – at Last." *Airport Forum* 25, no. 5 (1995): 16-19.

Vitta, Maurizio. "Architettura, funzione e storia: A New Terminal in Washington." *l'Arca* no. 103 (1996): 28-31.

Vitta, Maurizio. "Pragmatismo e funzionalismo: New Terminal at Washington National Airport." *l'Arca* no. 124 (1998): 28-35.

CHAPTER 3
Tunnel and Ferry Terminal, Mannheller, Norway (p. 127)

Bjørbekk, Jostein. "Warten auf die Fähre = Waiting for the Ferry." *Topos: European Landscape Magazine* no. 24 (1998): 83-87.

"Bjørbekk & Lindheim, Ferry Terminal di Mannheller." *Lotus Navigator* 7 (2002): 128-32.

"Mannheller fergekai, Sogndal." *Byggekunst: The Norwegian Review of Architecture* 80, no. 6 (1998): 28-31.

Footbridge, Rapperswil/Hurden, Switzerland (p. 128)

Bieler, Walter. "Wood Construction in Bridge Building." *Archithese* 32, no. 6 (2002): 30-33.

Viaduct Promenade, Paris, France (p. 128)

Amelar, Sarah. "From Railway to Greenway." *Architecture* 86, no. 4 (1997): 138-42.

Attias, Laurie. "Building." *Metropolis* 16, no. 4 (1996): 66, 99-101.

Berger, Patrick, and Jacques Lucan. "Patrick Berger." *a+u: Architecture and Urbanism* no. 11 (1999): 70-79.

Garcias, Jean-Claude. "Il percorso degli animali = The Parade of Animals." *Lotus international* no. 97 (1998): 82-88.

Lucan, Jacques. "Au risque de la banalité." *Moniteur architecture AMC* no. 64 (1995): 56-57.

Meade, Martin. "Parisian Promenade." *Architectural Review* 200, no. 1195 (1996): 52-55.

"Viaduc de la Bastille in Paris = 'De la Bastille' Viaduct in Paris." *Detail* 36, no. 5 (1996): 829-34.

A837 Rest Stop, Crazannes, France (p. 129)

"Area di Crazannes." *Lotus Navigator* no. 7 (2003): 113-17.

Bann, Stephen, Michel Conan, and John Dixon Hunt. "Bernard Lassus." *Studies in the History of Gardens & Designed Landscapes* 23, no. 2 (2003): 169-74.

Conan, Michel. "The Quarries of Crazannes: Bernard Lassus's Landscape Approach to Cultural Diversity." *Studies in the History of Gardens & Designed Landscapes* 23, no. 4 (2003): 347-65.

"Intervenciones en autopistas, Francia." *Escala* 40, no. 199 (2004): 74-75.

"Intervenciones en autopistas (Francia) = Interventions in the Highway (France)." *AV Monografías = AV Monographs* no. 91 (2001): 94-97.

Lassus, Bernard. "Landschaft als Lehre." *Werk, Bauen + Wohnen* no. 10 (1997): 24-27.

Lassus, Bernard. "Steinbruch-Skulptur an der Autobahn = A Rest Area with a Difference." *Topos: European Landscape Magazine* no. 24 (1998): 88-93.

Lassus, Bernard. "Dynamite with Design in Mind." *Landscape Design* no. 288 (2000): 19-20.

Lassus, Bernard. "Histoires pour demain." *Gartenkunst* 12, no. 2 (2000): 227-48.

Oneto, Gilberto. "Paesaggio ri-cavato." *Ville giardini* no. 342 (1998): 54-57.

National Routes Project, Norway (p. 130)

Berre, Nina, ed. *Detour. Architecture and Design along 18 National Tourist Routes*, Oslo: Statens Vegvesen and Nasjonale Turistvegar, 2007.

Garabit Highway Rest Area, Garabit, France (p. 132)

Vexlard, Giles. "Motorway Service Station Garabit, France." *Topos: European Landscape Magazine* no. 53 (2005): 86-89.

Mont Saint-Michel Jetty, Mont Saint-Michel, France (p. 134)

"Der Weg ist das Ziel: Feichtinger Architectes." *Architektur & Bauforum* no. 221 (2002): 81-85.

"La quête de l'île: projet maritime du Mont Saint-Michel = The Island's Guest: Restoration of the Maritime Character of Mont St.-Michel." *Techniques et Architecture* no. 487 (2006): 80-85.

Manet, Marie-Claude. "Mont-Saint-Michel: son caractère maritime sera-t-il enfin rétabli?" *Sites et monuments* no. 156 (1997): 12-15.

Trasi, Nicoletta. "Mont-Saint-Michel: un paesaggio marittimo ritrovato = Mont-Saint-Michel: A Rediscovered Maritime Landscape." *Metamorfosi* no. 47 (2003): 8-11.

Walch, Dorothea. "Mont-Saint-Michel, Frankreich = Mont-Saint-Michel, France." *Topos: European Landscape Magazine* no. 48 (2004): 94-101.

High Line Park, New York City, New York, USA (p. 136)

Chamberlain, Lisa. "Open space overhead." *Planning* 72, no. 3 (2006): 10-11.

Epple, Eva-Maria. "High Line Park in New York." *Garten + Landschaft* 114, no. 3 (2004): 26-27.

Feldman, Cassi. "Friends in High Places: In the Shadow of the High-Line, Other Open-space Efforts Wither." *City Limits* 29, no. 1 (2004): 8-9.

"Field Operations, New York, USA." *a+t* no. 25 (2005): 98-117.

Gisolfi, Peter. "Accidental Parks: Cities are Creating Open Space from Urban Remnants – But Can Remnants Effectively Bind the City Together?" *Landscape Architecture* 97, no. 8 (2007): 74-76.

Hardy, Hugh. "The Romance of Abandonment: Industrial Parks." *Places* 17, no. 3, (2005): 32-37.

Kayatsky, Ilan. "New York's High Line Reveals First Look at its New Plans." *Architectural Record* 193, no. 5 (2005): 60.

Kayatsky, Ilan. "High Line Finalists Unveil Imaginative Designs." *Architectural Record* 192, no. 8 (2004): 36.

Keeney, Gavin. "The Highline and the Return of the Irreal." *Competitions* 14, no. 4 (2004): 12-19.

"La coltre sopra i binari: Field Operations, Diller and Scofidio + Renfro sovrappongono a una linea ferroviaria di Manhattan un parco lineare = The Blanket over the Tracks: Field Operations, Diller and Scofidio + Renfro Lay Out a Linear Park on Top of a Railroad Line in Manhattan." *Lotus international* no. 126 (2005): 106-11.

Lang Ho, Cathy. "Walking the High Line." *Architecture* 91, no. 9 (2002): 120.

Nicolin, Paola. "Diller Scofidio – Ed Ruscha." *Abitare* no. 453 (2005): 122.

Richardson, Tim. "Elevated NY Landscapes." *Domus* no. 884 (2005): 20-29.

Steen, Karen E. "Friends in High Places: How a Pair of Self-proclaimed 'Neighborhood Nobodies' Saw an Abandoned Elevated Railway and Envisioned a New Park." *Metropolis* 25, no. 4 (2005): 118-23, 149, 151, 153, 155, 157.

Stegner, Peter. "High Line in the Museum of Modern Art." *Topos: European Landscape Magazine* no. 51 (2005): 6.

Ulam, Alex. "New York's High Line Spurring Innovative Buildings and Planning." *Architectural Record* 194, no. 6 (2006): 54.

Ulam, Alex. "Taking the High Road: New York City's Defunct High Line Rail Trestle is Ready to Be Reinvented." *Landscape Architecture* 94, no. 12 (2004): 62, 64-69.

"Umnutzung der Highline, New York." *Bauwelt* 95, no. 39 (2004): 8.

Widder, Lynnette. "The Central Park of Our Century: Entwicklungsprojekte um die stillgelegte Bahnstrasse 'Highline' in New York." *Bauwelt* 97, no. 19 (2006): 46-49.

Bibliothèque François Mitterrand Station, Paris, France (p. 138)

"Atmosfere metropolitane: BNF Underground Station, Paris." *l'Arca* no. 145 (2000): 89.

"Connexions: transports publics à Paris." *Techniques et Architecture* no. 412 (1994): 50-57.

Footbridge, Boudry, Switzerland (p. 140)

Amelar, Sarah. "Passerelle on the Areuse, Boudry, Switzerland." *Architectural Record* 192, no. 6 (2004): 252-53.

Baus, Ursula. "Verdichteter Weg: Brücke über die Areuse bei Boudry." *Deutsche Bauzeitung* 137, no. 5 (2003): 62-67.

Cètre, Jean-Pierre. "Cadre pittoresque – passerelle sur l'Areuse: Geninasca Delefortrie, architectes." *Faces* no. 53 (2003): 53-57.

"Fussgängerbrücke in Boudry = Pedestrian Bridge in Boudry = Ponte pedonale a Boudry = Passerelle piétonne à Boudry = Puente peatonal en Boudry." *Detail* 43, no. 6 (2003): 608-9.

Quinton, Maryse. "Laurent Geninasca et Bernard Delefortrie: passerelle en forêt, Boudry, Suisse." *Moniteur architecture AMC* no. 141 (2004): 58-61.

Tower Lighting, La Courneuve, France (p. 141)

Vitta, Maurizio. "La torre della luce = A Lighting Tower in La Courneuve." *l'Arca* no. 104 (1996): 76-79.

Escalator, Elevator and Bridge, Lérida, Spain (p. 142)

Busquets, Joan, and Luis Domènech Girbau. "Dalla città alla cittadella: un piano per Lérida." *Casabella* 49, no. 514 (1985): 16-27.

Gregotti, Vittorio. "Amadó e Domènech a Lérida: l'architetto e la città." *Abitare* no. 349 (1996): 155-61.

Hernandez, Juan M. "Nuove strutture di transizione a Lerida: un progetto di Amadò, Busquets, Domènech, Puig = New Transitional Structures at Lerida." *Lotus international* no. 59 (1989): 62-73.

"Neugestaltung des historischen Zentrums von Lérida, E = Redesigning the Historical Centre of Lérida." *Detail* 27, no. 5 (1987): 483-88.

"Neuordung des Stadtquartiers Canyeret, Lerida/Spanien = Rehabilitation of the District Canyeret, Lerida/Spain." *Architektur + Wettbewerbe* no. 148 (1991): 8-9.

Solà-Morales Rubió, Ignasi. "Murallas que no separan: Amadó y Domènech en Lérida." *Arquitectura Viva* no. 15 (1990): 16-20.

Metrocable Line, Medellín, Spain (p. 142)

"Metro de Medellín, Medellín, Colombia." *Escala* 39, no. 188 (2001): 38-42.

Viviescas, Fernando M. "La institución de la ciudad por el espacio público: el complejo metropolitano Tren-Boulevar-Río Medellín." *Escala* 30, no. 176 (1997): 31-37.

Ferry Terminal, Naoshima, Japan (p. 143)

"Kazuyo Sejima + Ryue Nishizawa (SANAA): Marine Station Naoshima, Kagawa, 2003–06." *GA Japan: environmental design* no. 83 (2006): 52-61.

"Marine Station Naoshima, Kagawa Pref. 2003–06." *Japan Architect* no. 64 (2007): 40-41, 128.

Sejima, Kazuyo, Ryue Nishizawa, and Juan Antonio Cortes. "SANAA Kazuyo Sejima Ryue Nishzawa, 2004–2008." *El Croquis* no. 139 (2008): 102-19.

Sejima, Kazuyo et al. "SANAA: Kazuyo Sejima + Ryue Nishizawa 1998–2004." *El Croquis* no. 121-122 (2004): 222-27.

"Terminal de Ferries Naoshima, Japón = Naoshima Ferry Terminal, Japan: Architects, Kazuo Sejima, Ruye Nishizawa, Rikiya Yamamoto, Erica Hidaka." *Via arquitectura* 17, Summer (2007): 94-99.

"Terminal de Transbordadores de Naoshima = Naoshima Ferry Terminal, 2003–2006, Kagawa (Japón = Japan)." *AV Monografías = AV Monographs* no. 121 (2006): 100-105.

Rijeka Memorial Bridge, Rijeka, Croatia (p. 144)

"3LHD: Memorial Bridge, Rijeka, City of Rijeka, Croatia 2001." *a+u: Architecture and Urbanism* no. 390 (2003): 92-97.

"3LHD: ponte monumento a Rijeka, Croazia = Bridge-Monument at Rijeka, Croatia – Memorial Bridge, Rijeka, Croatia, 1997–2001." *Lotus international* no. 130 (2007): 91-94.

Amelar, Sarah. "Mememorial Bridge, Rijeka, Croatia." *Architectural Record* 192, no. 6 (2004): 258-59.

"Brückenmahnmal in Rijeka = Bridge Memorial in Rijeka = Ponte commemorativo a Rijeka = Pont commémoratif à Rijeka = Puente commemorativo en Rijeka." *Detail* 44, no. 6 (2004): 647-51.

"Memorial Span: Mahnmalsteg in Rijeka: architekten, 3LHD." *Deutsche Bauzeitung* 137, no. 5 (2003): 38-45.

"Memory Span: Memorial Bridge, Rijeka, Croatia." *Architectural Review* 212, no. 1270 (2002): 45-47.

A16 Highway, Bienne (Switzerland) to Belfort (France) (p. 146)

Davoine, Gilles. "Autoroute transjurane." *Moniteur architecture AMC* no. 97 (1999): 68-73.

Geissbühler, Dieter. "Bad in Bellinzona, Transjurane und AlpTransit Gotthard: die Landschaft in der Arbeit Flora Ruchat-Roncatis." *Archithese* 27, no. 4 (1997): 44-47.

Gresleri, Glauco. "La Transjurane/architettura per l'autostrada." *Parametro* no. 191 (1992): 90-93.

Pelzel, Traudy. "Flora Ruchat Roncati: nuova trasversale ferroviaria del gottardo, Svizzera 1993–2015." *Casabella* 69, no. 732 (2005): 20-23.

Craigieburn Bypass, Melbourne, Australia (p. 148)

Adams, Scott. "Craigieburn Bypass in Melbourne." *Topos: European Landscape Magazine* no. 54 (2006): 71-73.

Beza, Beau. "Benchmark Bypass." *Landscape Australia* 28, no. 109 (2006): 16-18, 20-22.

Broome, Beth. "A Souped-up Bypass is a Destination in Its Own Right." *Architectural Record* 193, no. 8 (2005): 55-56.

Capezzuto, Rita. "Australian Bypass." *Domus* no. 882 (2005): 118-21.

Van Schaik, Leon. "Craigieburn Bypass." *Architecture Australia* 94, no. 4 (2005): 60-67.

Portland Aerial Tram, Portland, Oregon, USA (p. 150)

Brake, Alan G. "Architecture on the Go." *Architecture* 92, no. 12 (2003): 73-74.

Cava, John. "Urban High Eire: Portland's Aerial Tram." *l'Arcade* 21, no. 4 (2003): 47-48.

"Direkte Verbindung: agps architecture, Portland Aerial Tram." *Archithese* 38, no. 1 (2008): 8-11.

Gragg, Randy. "Portland, AGPS Architecture and Arup Tease Drama out of the Aerial Tram, a Landmark of Engineering Bravado." *Architectural Record* 195, no. 8 (2007): 126-32.

Libby, Brian. "L.A. Firm Wins Competition for Portland Aerial Tram." *Architectural Record* 191, no. 5 (2003): 50.

Robben Island Ferry Terminal, Cape Town, South Africa (p. 152)

Barac, Matthew. "The Stuff of Legend." *World Architecture* no. 108 (2002): 62-66.

"The Clock Tower Precinct." *Architect & Builder* 53, no. 1 (2002): 42-67.

"Nelson Mandela Gateway to Robben Island Building." *South African Architect* no. 3-4 (2002): 30-36.

"Robben Island Ferry Terminal Building, Victoria & Alfred Waterfront, Cape Town." *South African Architect* no. 7-8 (2000): 30-31.

E4 Highway Sections, Sundsvall, Sweden (p. 157)

Schibbye, Bengt. "Högt spel vid Höga Kusten." *Arkitektur: The Swedish Review of Architecture* 97, no. 2 (1997): 14-17.

Suneson, Torbjörn. "Sweden: Top Managers for Open Spaces." *Topos: European Landscape Magazine* no. 27 (1999): 50-55.

Wingren, Carola. "The City's Threshold." *Topos: European Landscape Magazine* no. 24 (1998): 94-100.

Rail and Bus Terminal, Santo André, Brazil (p. 158)

Corbioli, Nanci. "Obra premiada cria opções de transporte e ajuda a revitalizar região industrial." *Projeto* no. 250 (2000): 46-51.

"Em busca da integração do transporte público." *Projeto* no. 251 (2001): 72-73.

Normandy Bridge and Viaduc, Le Havre/Honfleur, France (p. 158)

Asensio Cerver, Francisco. *New Architecture. II: Recent works*, Barcelona: Arco, 1997: 234-45.

"Le pont de Normandie." *Deutsche Bauzeitschrift* 43, no. 10 (1995): 149-54.

Strasbourg Tram (Line A), Strasbourg, France (p. 160)

Belmessous, Hacène. "L'effet tramway: premier bilan d'une renaissance." *Architecture intérieure créé* no. 286 (1998): 74-76, 79.

Diedrich, Lisa. "Strassburg: Comeback der Trambahn = Strasbourg: The Tram's Comeback." *Topos: European Landscape Magazine* no. 15 (1996): 110-16.

Garnier, Juliette. "Le Tramway de Strasbourg." *Moniteur architecture AMC* no. 61 (1995): 32-37.

"Le renouvellement Strasbourgeois." *Techniques et Architecture* no. 400 (1992): 40-43.

Mialet, Frédéric. "Dossier. Le tramway: des coutures dans le bâti." *d'Architectures* no. 97 (1999): 25-27, 30-31.

Ruf, Janine. "Vom Münster zur Trabantenstadt: Seit 12 Jahren verändert die Tram das Gesicht von Strassburg." *Bauwelt* 97, no. 19 (2006): 30-35.

Scharf, Armin. "Stadtmobil: das Comeback der Strassenbahn." *Deutsche Bauzeitung* 129, no. 5 (1995): 120-21.

Thurn und Taxis, Lilli. "Trambahn für Strassburg." *Baumeister* 92, no. 9 (1995): 54-60.

"Tranvía = Tramway." *Quaderns d'arquitectura i urbanisme* no. 225 (2000): 102-5.

Douro Promenade, Porto to Matosinhos, Portugal (p. 162)

Hauswald, Kerstin. "Porto 2002: Promenaden am Douro = Porto 2002: promenades on the Douro." *Topos: European Landscape Magazine* no. 41 (2002): 39-45.

Kjoerulff-Schmidt, Arendse. "Paseio Marítimo strandpark." *Landskab* 86, no. 2 (2005): 52-53.

Palazzo, Elisa. "La forma dell'acqua. Il margine atlantico e fluviale a Porto." In *Passeggiate luno molti mari*, ed. Marco Massa. Florence: Artout Maschietto, 2005.

"Passeio Atlántico." *Arquitectura*. no. 335 (2004): 76-79.

Øresund Bridge and Tunnel, Copenhagen (Denmark) to Malmö (Sweden) (p. 164)

"Broens portraet." *Arkitektur DK* 44, no. 6 (2000): 304-11.

"Building Bridges." *Architectural Review* 207, no. 12 (2000): 78-79.

"Missing link: Halbzeit für die Öresundbrücke." *Deutsche Bauzeitung* 132, no. 11 (1998): 14.

"Øresund Verbindung zwischen Dänemark und Schweden = Øresund Link between Denmark and Sweden." *Architektur + Wettbewerbe* no. 168 (1996): 37.

Falbe-Hansen, Klaus, and Örjan Larsson. "Die Brücke über den Öresund." *Bauwelt* 92, no. 12 (2001): 40-47.

Hultin, Olof. "Bro till himmelen? = A Bridge to Heaven?" *Arkitektur: The Swedish Review of Architecture* 100, no. 2 (2000): 4-15.

Melvin, Jeremy. "Building Profile: The Øresund Link." *Architectural Design* 71, no. 3 (2001): 99-103.

Møller, Pouli, and Roger Svanberg,. "Øresundsforbindelsen, kyst til kyst = The Oresund Link, Coast to Coast." *Landskab* 80, no. 3-4 (1999): 58-65.

Müller, Robert. "Lichtspiele: nur mit einer passenden Beleuchtung lässt sich der Charakter einer Brücke auch bei Dunkelheit ablesen." *Deutsche Bauzeitung* 132, no. 5 (1998): 145, 148-49.

"Øresundsbroen = The Øresund Bridge." *Arkitektur DK* 40, no. 4-5 (1996): 330-33.

Rotne, Georg Kristoffer Stürup. "Øresundsbroen = The Øresund Bridge." *Arkitektur DK* 44, no. 6 (2000): 312-29.

Williams, Austin. "Suspended Animation." *Architects' Journal* 212, no. 20 (2000): 34-36.

Bridge, Amsterdam, the Netherlands (p. 169)

Pieters, Dominique. "Bruggen slaan voor de toekomst: nieuwe realisaties van Wilkinson Eyre, Foster and Partners, Birds Portchmouth Russum, Grimshaw and Partners en Venhoeven c.s." *de Architect* 33, no. 4 (2002): 81.

Schoonderbeek, Mark. "Het vele moet je maken: werk van Ton Venhoeven C.S." *de Architect* 30, no. 9 (1999): 58-65, 113.

Wortmann, Arthur. "Het Oostelijke Havengebied in Amsterdam: drie ontwerpen voor de Javabrug = Amsterdam's Oostelijke Havengebied: Three Designs for the Java Bridge." *Archis* no. 12 (1996): 5-7.

Footbridge, Evry, France (p. 170)

Hespel, Christophe. "DVVD: passerelle piétonne, Evry." *Moniteur architecture AMC* no. 175 (2008): 153-55.

Footbridge, Paris, France (p. 170)

Arnaboldi, Mario Antonio. "Tra due sponde: New Bridges." *l'Arca* no. 133 (1999): 34-43.

"Dessin du mois: étude de Marc Mimram pour la nouvelle passerelle Solférino à Paris." *Architecture d'aujourd'hui* no. 282 (1992): 64-65.

"Garde-corps." *Moniteur architecture AMC* no. 118 (2001): 119.

"La liaison territoriale: entretien avec Marc Mimram." *Techniques et Architecture* no. 406 (1993): 74-79.

McGuire, Penny. "French Connection." *Architectural Review* 209, no. 1250 (2001): 32-33.

Ménard, Jacques-Pierre. "Marc Mimram, ingénieur: la passerelle Solférino, Paris."

Architecture d'aujourd'hui no. 326 (2000): 18-19.
Mimram, Marc. "Passerelle Solférino." *AA files* no. 31 (1996): 15-17.
Roulet, Sophie. "Traversées de Seine." *Architecture intérieure créé* no. 285 (1998): 6.
Such, Robert. "Redesigning the Seine." *Blueprint* no. 158 (1999): 13.

Mur Island, Graz, Austria (p. 172)

Acconci, Vito. "Mur Island, Graz, Austria." *Architectural Design* 78, no. 1 (2008): 100-101.
"Acconci Studio: The Island in the Mur, Graz, Austria 2001–2003." *a+u: Architecture and Urbanism* no. 396 (2003): 28-35.
Bossi, Laura. "L'isola che non c'era = The Island That Wasn't." *Domus* no. 860 (2003): 26-27.
Carlini, Elena. "Un teatro nell'acqua: Vito Acconci a Graz." *Parametro* no. 249 (2004): 72-73.
Gregory, Rob. "Island in the Stream: Artificial Island, Graz, Austria." *Architectural Review* 213, no. 1276 (2003): 36-37.
Gullbring, Leo. "Café H₂O, Graz, Autriche: Vito Acconci." *Architecture d'aujourd'hui* no. 356 (2005): 18-19.
Imperiale, Alicia. "Vito Acconci: le regole del gioco = Rules of the Game." *Ottagono* 37, no. 156 (2002): 52-59.
Lind, Dianna. "On the Shores of the Mur, a Steel and Glass Plaything." *Architectural Record* 191, no. 5 (2003): 123-25.
Ménard, Jean-Pierre. "Structures dynamiques: île sur la rivière Mur, Graz, Autriche." *Moniteur architecture AMC* no. 146 (2004): 127-29.
Roulet, Sophie. "Une île du troisième type: forum urbain, Graz, Autriche." *Architecture intérieure créé* no. 312 (2003): 62-65.
Vogliazzo, Maurizio. "Agora: Dreams and Visions: Acconci Studio." *l'Arca* no. 179 (2003): 28-29, 39.
Zunino, Maria Giulia. "Vito Acconci a Graz: isola sul Mur = Island in the Mur." *Abitare* no. 429 (2003): 148-51.

Simone de Beauvoir Footbridge, Paris, France (p. 174)

Baldassini, Niccoló. "Un segno come ponte: The Bercy Footbridge in Paris." *l'Arca* no. 139 (1999): 20-23.
Dana, Karine. "Paris-passerelle." *Moniteur architecture AMC* no. 98 (1999): 23-24.
Descombes, Arnaud. "Naissance d'un pont: mise en place nocturne de la lentille centrale de la passerelle reliant Bercy à la Bibliothèque François-Mitterrand." *Moniteur architecture AMC* no. 158 (2006): 20-22.
"Die letzte Pariser Brücke über die Seine: Dietmar Feichtinger." *Architektur & Bauforum* no. 200 (1999): 60-64.
"Fechtinger Architectes: Projekte." *Architektur & Bauforum* no. 208 (2000): 81-96.
Fromonot, Françoise. "Dietmar Feichtinger: ponte passerella Bercy-Tolbiac = Bercy-Tolbiac Footbridge, Parigi 1999." *Casabella* 64, no. 678 (2000): 44-47, 93.
Fuchs, Claudia. "Neues aus Paris-Bercy: Projekte und Wettbewerbe." *Garten + Landschaft* 109, no. 12 (1999): 18-21.
"Fussgängerbrücke Bercy-Tolbiac, Paris = Bercy-Tolbiac Pedestrian Bridge, Paris = Passerelle Bercy-Tolbiac, Paris." *Detail* 39, no. 8 (1999): 1445.
Lemoine, Bertrand. "Ein schwebender Spazierweg: die Fussgängerbrücke Simone de Beauvoir in Paris von Dietmar Feichtinger." *Werk, Bauen + Wohnen* no. 3 (2007): 40-45.
Loyer, Béatrice. "Effort discret: la passerelle Bercy-Tolbiac, Paris = Discreet Effort: Bercy-Tolbiac Footbridge, Paris." *Techniques et Architecture* no. 445 (1999): 34-35.
Niemann, Sebastian. "Nachgefragt in Paris: ein Österreicher an der Seine: Dietmar Feichtinger, seit 1989 in Paris." *Deutsche Bauzeitung* 141, no. 4 (2007): 56-60.
Pagès, Yves. "Feichtinger architectes, RFR ingénieurs: passerelle de Bercy-Tolbiac sur la Seine à Paris." *Moniteur architecture AMC* no. 132 (2003): 98-99.
"Projekt: Fussgängerbrücke Bercy-Tolbiac in Paris = Project: Footbridge Bercy-Tolbiac in Paris." *Architektur + Wettbewerbe* no. 185 (2001): 54-55.
Slessor, Catherine. "New Seine Crossing." *Architectural Review* 206, no. 1229 (1999): 20, 23.
Sowa, Axel, and Sebastian Niemann. "Passerelle Simone-de-Beauvoir, Paris: Feichtinger Architectes, RFR ingénieurs." *Architecture d'aujourd'hui* no. 367 (2006): 30-32.

Tonon, Carlotta, and Françoise Fromonot. "Cecil Balmond, Dietmar Feichtinger: nuove esperienze della progettazione strutturale." *Casabella* 71, no. 757 (2007): 76-85, 93-94.

Salerno Maritime Terminal, Salerno, Italy (p. 176)

Burdett, Richard. "Un futuro per Salerno = A Future for Salerno." *Domus* no. 829 (2000): 104-5.
"Concorsi per Salerno." *Casabella* 64, no. 683 (2000): 17-19.
"Ferry Terminal in Salerno, Salerno, Italy 1999." *a+u: Architecture and Urbanism* no. 374 (2001): 96-100.
Hadid, Zaha, Walter Nägeli, and Mohsen Mostafavi. "Zaha Hadid 1996–2001. Beginnings and Ends." *El Croquis* no. 103 (2000): 190-93.
"Maritime Terminal Salerno, Salerno, Italy." *GA document* no. 99 (2007): 30-33.

Arnhem Central Station, Arnhem, the Netherlands (p. 178)

"Architectuur opgelost in infrastructuur: het Arnhemse stationscomplex van UN Studio = Architecture Dissolved in Infrastructure: The Arnhem Station Complex by UN Studio." *Archis* no. 11 (2000): 10-21.
"Architettura di flussi: il diagramma dei flussi come origine della forma in un progetto di UN Studio = Flow Architecture: The Flowchart as Source of the Form in a Project by UN Studio." *Lotus international* no. 127 (2006): 78-81.
"Ben van Berkel: Arnhem Station Area (Masterplan, Transfer Hall, Bus Terminal, Willems Tunnel, Parking). 1996–2020." *Lotus international* no. 108 (2001): 76-79.
Bokern, Anneke. "Architektur gewordene Bewegungsflüsse: Arnhem Centraal von UN Studio, 1996–2007." *Werk, Bauen + Wohnen* no. 12 (2003): 18-25.
Brensing, Christian. "Stahlgeflecht und V-Stützen: Tunneleinfahrt und Parkdeck beim Bahnhof in Arnheim." *Bauwelt* 93, no. 42 (2002): 30-31.
Ibelings, Hans. "Flow: UN Studio's New Transit Hub Tries to Eliminate Signs by Using Light and Space as Wayfinding Devices." *Metropolis* 23, no. 5 (2004): 70-71.
"Ontwerp stationsgebied Arnhem, Van Berkel & Bos." *de Architect* 28, no. 7-8 (1997): 21-23, 68.
Rodermond, Janny, Caroline Bos, and Ben van Berkel. "Op weg naar een inclusieve ontwerpstrategie: in gesprek met Caroline Bos en Ben van Berkel." *de Architect* 29, no. 6 (1998): 60-65, 105.
Tiry, Corinne, and Christophe Hespel. "Parking, gare centrale d'Arnhem, Pays-Bas." *Moniteur architecture AMC* no. 158 (2006): 90-91.
Trelcat, Sophie. "Parking et tunnel, Arnhem, Pays-Bas = Garage & Tunnel, Arnhem, NL: UN Studio." *Architecture d'aujourd'hui* no. 340 (2002): 106-11.
Van Berkel. "Arnhem." *Daidalos* no. 69-70 (1998): 130-33.
Van Berkel, Ben, and Caroline Bos. "Arnhem, Pays-Bas: plan d'aménagement pour la gare centrale, projet en cours." *Architecture d'aujourd'hui* no. 321 (1999): 58-63.
Van Berkel, Ben, and Caroline Bos. "UN Studio: Arnhem Central." *AA files* no. 38 (1999): 23-31.
"Van Berkel & Bos: el músculo formal = The Formal Muscle." *AV Monografias = AV Monographs* no. 73 (1998): 64-71.
"Van Berkel & Bos: Infrastructural Project, Arnhem, The Netherlands." *Architectural Design* 69, no. 3-4 (1999): 66-69.
"UN Studio: Arnhem Central, Arnhem, the Netherlands." *GA document* no. 91 (2006): 44-47.
"UN Studio van Berkel & Bos: Arnhem Central, Arnhem, the Netherlands 1996–2007." *a+u: Architecture and Urbanism* no. 405 (2004): 88-95.

Incheon International Airport, Seoul, South Korea (p. 180)

Dawson, Susan. "Metal Works: Transport." *Architects' Journal* 215, no. 25 (2002): 1-16
Farrells, FTP. *UK>HK: Farrells Placemaking from London to Hong Kong and Beyond*, Hong Kong: MCCM Creations, 2008, 130-35.
Levinson, Nancy. "Transportation Centre, Incheon International Airport, Incheon, South Korea." *Architectural Record* 191, no. 8 (2003): 120-25.
Melvin, Jeremy. "Transportation Centre for Incheon Airport, Seoul." *Architectural Design* 72, no. 5 (2002): 115-19.
Melvin, Jeremy. "Under One Roof." *Blueprint* no. 196 (2002): 38-42.
Thomas, Ralph. "Space Station: Transportation Centre, Inchon International Airport, South Korea." *World Architecture* no. 103 (2002): 34-40.

"Transportation Centre, Inchon International Airport." *Architecture Today* AT profile supplement no. 1 (2002): 2-15.

Williams, Austin. "Terminal Triumphs." *Architects' Journal* 213, no. 12 (2001): 6-7.

CHAPTER 4

Transport Node, Nantes, France (p. 189)

Cardani, Elena. "Stazione e mercato: Place Pirmil in Nantes." *l'Arca* no. 88 (1994): 84-85.

"Mise en tension: station de tramway et marché couvert, Nantes." *Techniques et Architecture* no. 420 (1995): 92-93.

"Petites constructions: histoire(s) du kiosque." *Moniteur architecture* AMC no. 98 (1999): 72-73.

Stürzebecher, Peter. "Eine Erfolgsgeschichte: die Strassenbahn in Nantes." *Bauwelt* 91, no. 39 (2000): 36-39.

"Tranvía = Tramway." *Quaderns d'arquitectura i urbanisme* no. 225 (2000): 105.

Pedestrian Mall, Lund, Sweden (p. 190)

Andersson, Sven-Ingvar. "Sienapris 1998: Lunds stationsområde." *Landskab* 79, no. 6 (1998): 130-35, 144.

The Embarcadero, San Francisco, California, USA (p. 196)

Betsky, Aaron. "The City by the Bay Goes from Port to Sport." *Architectural Record* 184, no. 3 (1996): 13.

"The Embarcadero, San Francisco, California." *Land Forum* no. 1 (1999): 60-63.

Fisher, Bonnie. "From the Water's Edge." *Urban Land* 58, no. 1 (1999): 72-77.

Fisher, Bonnie. "Closeup: The Embarcadero." *Planning* 71, no. 1 (2005): 16-17.

Hinshaw, Mark. "Free from the Freeway – But Does the New Embarcadero Really Connect San Francisco to Its Waterfront?' *Landscape Architecture* 92, no. 5 (2002): 132, 131.

Hinshaw, Mark, Bonnie Fisher, and Boris Dramov. "[San Francisco's Embarcadero]." *Landscape Architecture* 92, no. 7 (2002): 9.

Lockwood, Charles. "San Francisco Reclaims its Downtown Waterfront." *Urban Land* 55, no. 10 (1996): 63-67.

Lockwood, Charles. "On the Waterfront: San Francisco Embarcadero Waterfront." *World Architecture* no. 58 (1997): 128-31.

Lockwood, Charles. "On the Waterfront." *Grid* 3, no. 3 (2001): 84-88.

Thompson, J. William. "Embarcadero: Free from the Freeway." *Landscape Architecture* 83, no. 6 (1993): 60-61.

Alicante Tram Stop, Alicante, Spain (p. 198)

Cohn, David. "Geheimnisvolle Architektur – hohe Ingenieurkunst: Strassenbahn-haltestelle 'Sergio Cardell' in Alicante (E) – Architekten, Subarquitectura." *Deutsche Bauzeitung* 141, no. 11 (2007): 30-34.

Cohn, David. "A Traffic-stopping Tram Stop Floats on Air." *Architectural Record* 195, no. 12 (2007): 63.

Cohn, David. "Strassenbahnhaltestelle 'Sergio Cardell' in Alicante (E) = Tram Stop 'Sergio Cardell' in Alicante (E): Architekten/Architects: Subarquitectura." *Deutsche Bauzeitung* 142, no. 6 (2008): 56-59.

Herrero, Gonzalo. "Tram Stop, Alicante: Subarquitectura." *A10: New European Architecture* no. 17 (2007): 24-26.

"Subarquitectura: parada del tram = Tram Stop, Alicante." *Via arquitectura* Winter special issue (2007): 49-57.

"Subarquitectura: Tram Stop, Serigo Cardell Plaza, Alicante, Spain 2005." *a+u: Architecture and Urbanism* no. 441 (2007): 48-53.

Westend City Center, Budapest, Hungary (p. 201)

Slatin, Peter. "From Hollywood to Frankfurt." *Grid* 2, no. 1 (2000): 38.

Warson, Albert. "Trizec Hahn Launch Massive Central European Retail Drive." *World Architecture* no. 70 (1998): 31.

Bus and Rail Transit Station, San Francisco, USA (p. 201)

Collyer, Stanley. "Shifting the Center of Activity: San Francisco's Transbay Transit Center." *Competitions* 18, no. 1 (2008): 16-27, 64.

Evitts, Elizabeth A. "Three Proposals for San Francisco's Transbay Neighbourhood." *Architect* 96, no. 10 (2007): 22.

King, John. "Pelli-Hines Team Picked for Transbay." *Architectural Record* 195, no. 11 (2007): 35.

Krueger, Robert. "New San Francisco Transbay Transit Center Expected to Unite City's Transportation System." *Urban Land* 67, no. 3 (2008): 26-28.

LeTourneur, Chris, and Kieron Hunt. "Travel Retail: Transportation Hub Retail is Spurring Mixed-use Town Centers and Transit-oriented Development." *Urban Land* 62, no. 2 (2003): 52-59.

Lou, Ellen. "The Transbay Plan." *Urban Land* 63, no. 5 (2004): 98-99.

"Transbay May Lead to New San Francisco Skyline." *Architect* 97, no. 8 (2008): 23.

Redevelopment Charing Cross Station, London, UK (p. 202)

Binney, Marcus. "Über den Gleisen von Charing Cross: 'Embankment Place' in London." *Bauwelt* 83, no. 46 (1992): 2596-2601.

Davies, Colin, and Terry Farrell. "Underneath the Arches." *Architects' Journal* 193, no. 21 (1991): 30-39, 43-45.

Davies, Colin. "For Appearance's Sake: Embankment Place." *Architects' Journal* 193, no. 25 (1991): 66-67.

"Embankment Place." *Architectural Record* 175, no. 10 (1987): 132-33.

"Fitting Out a Gigantic Floorplate." *Architects' Journal* 198, no. 11 (1993): 47-55.

Ibelings, Hans. "Terry Farrell a Londra: Charing Cross nodo urbana." *Abitare* no. 313 (1992): 162-65.

Lueder, Christoph. "Embankment Place." *Deutsche Bauzeitschrift* 40, no. 8 (1992): 1139-47.

Moore, Rowan, and Terry Farrell. "Special Feature: Terry Farrell & Company." *a+u: Architecture and Urbanism* no. 231 (1989): 37-132.

Spring, Martin. "Vaulting Ambition." *Building* 253, no. 36 (1988): 40-45.

Spring, Martin. "Triumphal Arch." *Building* 256, no. 4 (1991): 45-90.

"Terry Farrell Partnership: Lee House & Embankment Place, London." *Architectural Design* 57 (1987): 50-54.

Welsh, John. "High & Mightly." *Building Design* no. 1034 (1991): 30-32.

Railway Station, Dortmund, Germany (p. 202)

Brinkmann, Ulrich. "Hauptbahnhof Dortmund." *Bauwelt* 88, no. 34 (1997): 1828-29.

Gubitosi, Alessandro. "Significante a 360: Dortmund Central Station." *l'Arca* no. 145 (2000): 12-19.

Heindl, Franziska. "Neue Bahnhöfe: Leipzig eröffnet, Wettbewerbe Stuttgart und Dortmund." *Baumeister* 95, no. 1 (1998): 12.

Kähler, Gert. "Architectural Encounters of the Fourth Kind: het werk van = Work by Bothe, Richter, Teherani." *Archis* no. 7 (1999): 60-71.

Müller, Sebastian. "Ein Ufo in Dortmund." *Bauwelt* 91, no. 48 (2000): 60-61.

Schiphol Airport Plaza, Amsterdam, the Netherlands (p. 203)

"Einer von fünf: Flughafenerweiterung Schiphol/Amsterdam." *Architektur, Innenarchitektur, Technischer Ausbau* 99, no. 7-8 (1991): 24-26.

"Flughafengebäude 'Schiphol Plaza', Amsterdam = 'Schiphol Plaza' Airport Building, Amsterdam = 'Schiphol Plaza', édifice de liaison de l'aéroport d'Amsterdam." *Detail* 37, no. 4 (1997): 570-76.

Gubitosi, Alessandro. "Le 'stazioni' per volare: Schiphol Plaza, Amsterdam." *l'Arca* no. 125 (1998): 40-45.

Máčel, Otakar. "Construir el futuro: ampliacíon del aeropuerto de Amsterdam." *Arquitectura Viva* no. 29 (1993): 28-33.

Melet, Ed. "De ingetogen machine: Terminal-West van Benthem Crouwel NACO architecten." *de Architect* 24, no. 9 (1993): 110-15.

Slawik, Han. "Schiphol 2000: der Ausbau der Amsterdamer Flughafens Schiphol (Benthem, Crouwel mit Netherlands Airport Consults)." *Deutsche Bauzeitung* 124, no. 11 (1990): 128-32.

Stungo, Naomi. "Air Extensions." *RIBA Journal* 100, no. 8 (1993): 36-39.

Tilman, Harm. "Terminal 3 op Schiphol van Benthem Crouwel NACO: machine of huiskamer." *de Architect Dossier* no. 7 (1998): 42-47.

Van Deelen, Paul. "Ambitie: Uitgroeien tot Mainport." *Bouw* 48, no. 12-13 (1993):

18-23.

Van Dijk, Hans. "Onderbroken probleemoplossing: Stationsgebouw West van Schiphol = Interrupted Problem-solving: West Terminal at Schiphol Airport." *Archis* no. 9 (1993): 35-45.

Van Dijk, Hans. "Benthem Crouwel NACO: aeroporto internazionale Schiphol, Amsterdam = Schiphol International Airport, Amsterdam." *Domus* no. 815 (1999): 8-19.

Wendt, Dave. "Springlevend zonder praatjes: Benthem Crouwel Architekten." *de Architect* 27, no. 1 (1996): 18-37.

Wortmann, Arthur. "Leerer Raum für Schiphol: Flughafenerweiterung in Amsterdam." *Bauwelt* 84, no. 31 (1993): 1610-11.

Leipzig Central Station, Leipzig, Germany (p. 204)

Bauer, Matthias. "Triumph des Kommerz: die 'Promenaden' im Leipziger Hauptbahnhof." *Deutsche Bauzeitung* 131, no. 12 (1997): 28.

"Flächen wecken im Stadtfoyer." *Deutsche Bauzeitung* 129, no. 5 (1995): 32-33.

Heindl, Franziska. "Neue Bahnhöfe: Leipzig eröffnet, Wettbewerbe in Stuttgart und Dortmund." *Baumeister* 95, no. 1 (1998): 12.

Hocquél, Wolfgang. "Bahnanlagen der Zukunft, II: Hauptbahnhof Leipzig." *Bauwelt* 85, no. 34 (1994): 1800-1801.

Hofmann, Helga. "Shop and go: die Renaissance der Bahnhöfe: Deutschlands grösste Marktplätze." *Architektur, Innenarchitektur, Technischer Ausbau* no. 3 (1998): 52-55.

"Pilotprojekt: Shopping-Mall im Leipziger Hauptbahnhof." *Architektur, Innenarchitektur, Technischer Ausbau* no. 3 (1998): 56-63.

"Promenaden Hauptbahnhof Leipzig, Leipzig, Germany." *Urban Land* 64, no. 2 (2005): 56-57.

Nordseepassage, Wilhelmshaven, Germany (p. 206)

Paganelli, Carlo. "Contrapposizioni: Nordseepassage, Wilhelmshaven." *l'Arca* no. 136 (1999): 12-19.

Kyoto Station, Kyoto, Japan (p. 208)

Binney, Marcus. *Architecture of Rail: The Way Ahead*, London: Academy Editions, 1995, 135-45.

Futagawa, Yukio, and Hiroshi Hara. "Hiroshi Hara." *GA document* no. 47 (1996): 20-23.

Hara, Hiroshi. "Hiroshi Hara: Kyoto Station Building, Kyoto-shi, Kyoto, Japan." *GA document* no. 52 (1997): 76-97.

Hein, Carola. "Prestige and Diversion: Grands Projets in Japan." *Archis* no. 2 (1998): 48-61.

Hein, Carola. "Shopping-Schlund: der neue Bahnhof von Kyoto und die Überlagerung von Verkehr und Kommerz." *Architektur, Innenarchitektur, Technischer Ausbau* no. 3 (1998): 41-51.

"Hiroshi Hara + Atelier Ø: Kyoto Station Building." *Japan Architect* no. 28 (1998): 72-75.

"Hiroshi Hara + Atelier Ø: Kyoto Station Building, Kyoto, 1991–97." *GA Japan: environmental design* no. 28 (1997): 12-37.

"JR Kyoto Station: Hiroshi Hara and Atelier Ø." *Japan Architect* no. 7 (1992): 200-207.

"JR Kyoto Station (Reconstruction Proposal): Design Competition." *Japan Architect* no. 5 (1992): 236-37.

"Kyoto Station Building." *Kenchiku bunka* 52, no. 611 (1997): 25-32, 36-56, 57-64.

Mancke, Carol, and Michael Bade. "Kyoto's Latest Controversy." *World Architecture* no. 61 (1997): 40-44.

Noennig, Jörg Rainer. "Stad op doorreis: het Centraal Station van Kyoto van Hiroshi Hara." *de Architect* 31, no. 4 (2000): 38-43.

Thorne, Martha, ed. *Modern Trains and Splendid Stations: Architecture, Design, and Rail Travel for the Twenty-first Century*, London: Merrel, 2001, 99-101.

Dubai International Airport, Dubai, United Arab Emirates (p. 210)

Mirti, Stefano. "Contract = Custom: Dubai International Airport." *Abitare* no. 476 (2007): 243-44.

"Project Profile: Dubai Airport, Dubai." *Landscape Design* no. 320 (2003): 34.

Airport Terminal, Paris, France (p. 213)

Betsky, Aaron. "An Airport is not a Monument: Charles de Gaulle's Terminal 2E." *Deutsche Bauzeitung* 142, no. 6 (2008): 14-15.

"Equipements." *Moniteur architecture AMC* no. 139 (2003): 62-83.

Foges, Chris. "Pier Review: Charles de Gaulle Airport's Ill-fated Terminal 2E has been Reconstructed with Impressive Precision." *Architecture Today* no. 187 (2008): 72-74.

Guardigli, Decio. "Una Versailles per aerei: New Terminal E at the Paris Airport." *l'Arca* no. 179 (2003): 4-11.

"Modules en ligne à CdG2." *Moniteur architecture AMC* no. 130 (2003): 212-15.

Phillips, Ian. "Design par excellence." *Interior Design* 75, no. 3 (2004): 85-86, 88, 90.

Reina, Petger. "Investigation into Collapse of Terminal 2E Continues." *Architectural Record* 192, no. 7 (2004): 163-64.

Footbridge, London, UK (p. 214)

"'Blade of Steel' May be New London Bridge." *Architect & Builder* (1997): 20.

Davey, Peter. "Delight." *Architectural Review* 207, no. 1238 (2000): 106.

Hagen Hodgson, Petra. "Transformation zur Jahrtausendwende." *Werk, Bauen + Wohnen* no. 6 (1998): 6-19.

Hagen-Hodgson, Petra. "Neue Vernetzungen: Millennium- und Aufbruchstimmung in London." *Deutsche Bauzeitung* 134, no. 6 (2000): 71-81.

Hart, Sara. "Troubled Bridge over Water: Arup & Partners Takes the Bounce Out of the Footsteps." *Architectural Record* 189, no. 3 (2001): 157.

"Il nuovo ponte sul Tamigi." *Industria delle costruzioni* 31, no. 312 (1997): 68-69.

"Millennium Bridge, London." *Detail* 39, no. 8 (1999): 1444.

"Norman Foster: Millennium Bridge, London, England." *GA document* no. 58 (1999): 20-23.

"Norman Foster: Millennium Bridge, London, U.K." *GA document* no. 69 (2002): 100-105.

Pavarini, Stefano. "Millennium Bridge." *l'Arca* no. 113 (1997): 4-7.

Pieters, Dominique. "Bruggen slaan voor de toekomst: nieuwe realisaties van Wilkinson Eyre, Foster and Partners, Birds Portchmouth Russum, Grimshaw and Partners en Venhoeven c. s." *de Architect* 33 (2002): 76-81.

Ridsdill Smith, Roger. "Foster and Partners, Ove Arup & Partners, Sir Anthony Caro: Millennium Bridge, Londra, Gran Bretagna 2002." *Casabella* 67, no. 709 (2003): 64-69.

Slavid, Ruth. "In the News." *Architects' Journal* 207, no. 10 (1998): 22-23.

Slavid, Ruth. "Foster and Caro Win with 'Simple' Bankside Bridge." *Architects' Journal* 204, no. 22 (1996): 10.

Sudjic, Deyan. "The Bridge that Wobbled." *Domus* no. 847 (2002): 92-103.

A77 Toll Station, Melun, France (p. 214)

Baldassini, Niccolò. "La geometria di Mimram: Structural Architecture." *l'Arca* no. 96 (1995): 26-33.

"Gare de péage autoroutier, Melun." *Moniteur architecture AMC* no. 67 (1995): 100-101.

"La liaison territoriale: entretien avec Marc Mimram." *Techniques et Architecture* no. 406 (1993): 74-79.

Picon, Antoine. *Marc Mimram*, Gollion: Infolio Editions, 2007, 166, 172-77.

Intermodal Terminal, Rochelle, Illinois, USA (p. 215)

Szatan, Jerry W. "On Track: Two New Developments are Helping Bolster the Chicago Region's Historic Role as a Freight Transportation and Distribution Center." *Urban land* 62, no. 6 (2003): 65-69.

Waldheim, Charles, and Alan Berger. "Logistics Landscape." *Landscape Journal* 27, no. 2 (2008): 219-46.

Suvarnabhumi Airport, Bangkok, Thailand (p. 216)

"Displacement Ventilation: Second Bangkok International Airport, Bangkok, Thailand." *World Architecture* no. 50 (1996): 140-41.

Dixon, John Morris. "Murphy-Jahn Joins Engineers Werner Sobek and Matthias Schuler to Bring Suvarnabhumi Airport, Bangkok's Sleek New Air Terminal, in for a Landing." *Architectural Record* 195, no. 8 (2007): 108-17, 132.

Heeg, Manfred. "Suvarnabhumi International Airport, Bangkok: Engineering, Konfektion und Montage des Membrandachs = Engineering, Manufacturing and Installing the Membrane Roof." *Detail* 46, no. 7-8 (2006): 824-25.

Holst, Stephan. "Suvarnabhumi International Airport, Bangkok: innovative Klimakonzeption = Innovative Climate Concept." *Detail* 46, no. 7-8 (2006): 820, 822.

"Internationaler Flughafen Bangkok: Suvarnabhumi Airport." *Intelligente Architektur* no. 57 (2006): 30-47.

"Passagier-Terminal-Komplex, Suvarnabhumi International Airport, Bangkok = Passenger Terminal Complex, Suvarnabhumi International Airport, Bangkok." *Detail* 46, no. 7-8 (2006): 810-14.

Pavarini, Stefano. "Forma e dimensione: Suvarnabhumi International Airport, Bangkok." *l'Arca* no. 225 (2007): 2-15.

Sobek, Werner. "Suvarnabhumi International Airport, Bangkok: Tragwerk und Formfindung= Structure and Form-finding." *Detail* 46, no. 7-8 (2006): 818-19.

Webb Bridge, Melbourne, Australia (p. 218)

Bowtell, Peter. "Webb Bridge, Melbourne." *Topos: European Landscape Magazine* no. 53 (2005): 26-27.

"Denton Corker Marshall in Collaboration with Robert Owen: Webb Bridge, Melbourne, Australia 2003." *a+u: Architecture and Urbanism* no. 412 (2005): 134-39.

"El ejemplo de Melbourne: nuevos bordes en común = Melbourne's E(i)xample: New Water's Edge in Common." *a+t* no. 26 (2005): 144-57.

Hart, Sara. "Architects Discover Bridge Design Can Be the Perfect Union of Art and Science." *Architectural Record* 192, no. 6 (2004): 279-84, 286.

Hénard, Jean-Pierre. "Structures dynamiques: Webb Dock Bridge, Melbourne, Australie." *Moniteur architecture AMC* no. 146 (2004): 130-31.

"Ponte d'arte = The Art Bridge." *Domus* no. 863 (2003): 110-15.

"Ponte pedonale e ciclabile a Melbourne, Australia = Webb Bridge, Melbourne, Australia." *Industria delle costruzioni* 42, no. 399 (2008): 52-57.

Reboli, Michele. "Denton Corker Marshall: Webb Bridge, Melbourne, Australia." *Casabella* 70, no. 740 (2005): 52-55.

Stephens, Suzanne. "Webb Bridge, Melbourne, Australia." *Architectural Record* 192, no. 6 (2004): 248-51.

Orival Service Station and Restaurants, Nivelles, Belgium (p. 220)

Calcagno, Benedetto. "Nivelles: area di servizio Totalfinaelf Europe = Nivelles: Total-Fina-Elf Europe Service Station." *Abitare* no. 428 (2003): 170-71.

Dubois, Marc. "Herwaardering van de automobiliteit." *de Architect interieur* no. 1 (2000): 48-51.

Dubois, Marc. "Un ponte sull'autostrada: Samyn and Partners, area di sevizio 'Aire de Nivelles'. 2001. Belgio." *Casabella* 65, no. 695-696 (2001): 74-81.

Fontana, Jacopo della. "Segno e servizi: Two Petrol Stations." *l'Arca* no. 145 (2000): 50-53.

Pieters, Dominique. "Dynamiek van beweging en demping: restaurantbrug en servicehaven 'Orival' door Philippe Samyn te Nijvel (B)." *de Architect* 32, no. 10 (2001): 90-93.

Quaquaro, Benedetto. "Sensibilità e misura: Along the Highway." *l'Arca* no. 188 (2004): 76-81.

Van Synghel, Koen, Dominique Pieters, and Marc Dubois. *Samyn & Partners, architecten en ingenieurs*. Gent and Amsterdam: Ludion Publishers, 2005, 48-51.

Railway and Bus Station, Lausanne, Switzerland (p. 225)

"Bernard Tschumi: Interface Flon Railway and Bus Station, Lausanne, Switzerland." *GA document* no. 67 (2001): 84-91.

"Bernard Tschumi: Interface Flon Station, Lausanne, Suisse, 1988–2001." *Lotus international* no. 108 (2001): 92-95.

"Bernard Tschumi: Ponts-Villes Projects, Lausanne, Switzerland." *Architectural Design* 64, no. 3-4 (1994): 64-69.

Davoine, Gilles. "Bernard Tschumi, Luca Merlini et Emmanuel Ventura: gare d'interconnexion, Lausanne." *Moniteur architecture AMC* no. 123 (2002): 42-46.

"Gare du Flon, Lausanne." *Werk, Bauen + Wohnen* no. 12 (2000): 1-6.

"'Gare du Flon' in Lausanne, Schweiz." *Architektur + Wettbewerbe* no. 140 (1989): 42-48.

Giovannini, Joseph. "Lines of Desire." *Architecture* 90, no. 7 (2001): 74-79.

Merlini, Luca, and Bernard Tschumi. "Ponts-Villes: Ideenwettbewerb für die Gare du Flon, Lausanne = Ponts-Villes concours d'ideés pour l'aménagement de la Gare du Flon, Lausanne." *Archithese* 19, no. 1 (1989): 45-49.

"Métropont, ponte e nodo di scambio a Losanna = Interface Flon Railway and Bus Station, Lausanne." *Industria delle costruzioni* no. 367 (2002): 38-45.

Peverelli, Diego. "Interface des transports publics à Lausanne: architectes, Bernard Tschumi, Luca Merlini." *Faces* no. 54 (2004): 2962-63.

Tschumi, Bernard. "[Three Competition Entries]." *AA files* no. 18 (1989): 30-42.

Wieser, Christoph, and Martin Josephy. "Architektonische Verknüpfung von Stadtetagen." *Werk, Bauen + Wohnen* no. 12 (2000): 54-57.

Ferry Terminal, Tromsø, Norway (p. 225)

Pavarini, Stefano. "Splendido isolamento': Tromsø Terminal." *l'Arca* no. 189 (2004): 66-69.

Bicycle Storage, Amsterdam, the Netherlands (p. 226)

Betsky, Aaron. "Built Experiments." *Ottagono* 37, no. 154 (2002): 94-101.

Oosterman, Arjen. "A Bicycle Shed is a Building (Lincoln Cathedral is a Piece of Architecture): Amsterdam." *Archis* no. 2 (2001): 77-79.

"Results of Redesign Competition for Bicycle Shed at Amsterdam's Central Station: VMX Architects." *Archis* no. 4 (2001): 116-19.

Seidel, Florian. "Fünf Jahre lang neben Centraal: temporäre Fahrradgarage am Hauptbahnhof in Amsterdam." *Bauwelt* 92, no. 37 (2001): 32-33.

"VMX: Bicycle Park, Amsterdam." *Quaderns d'arquitectura i urbanisme* no. 239 (2003): 72-77.

"VMX Architects: Bicycle Storage, Amsterdam, the Netherlands 1998–2001; Apartment Block at Sarphatistraat, Amsterdam, the Netherlands 1998–2002." *a+u: Architecture and Urbanism* no. 403 (2004): 134-37.

Berlin Central Station, Berlin, Germany (p. 228)

Arnaboldi, Mario Antonio. "L'idiosincrasia di Eiffel: Lehrter Station, Berlin." *l'Arca* no. 139 (1999): 36-43.

Bachmann, Wolfgang. "Unterwegs im Berliner Hauptbahnhof." *Baumeister* 104, no. 1 (2007): 10.

"Berlin Hauptbahnhof: Lehrter Bahnhof." *Detail* 45, no. 12 (2005): 1449-55.

Brensing, Christian. "Tunnel Vision: Railway Station, Berlin, Germany." *Architectural Review* 220, no. 1313 (2006): 52-59.

Brinkmann, Ulrich. "Pragmatisches Monument: der Berliner Hauptbahnhof in Betrieb: Architekten, gmp, Hamburg." *Bauwelt* 97, no. 26 (2006): 8-17.

Bund Deutscher Architekten BDA et al. with Meinhard von Gerkan, eds. *Renaissance of Railway Stations: The City in the 21st century*, in Stuttgart: BDA, 1996, 110-21, 250-257.

Caviezel, Nott. "Bahnhofbaustelle gigantisch: der neue Lehrter Bahnhof in Berlin von gmp von Gerkan, Marg und Partner Architekten." *Werk, Bauen + Wohnen* no. 12 (2003): 46-49.

Gerfen, Katie. "Glass Ceiling." *Architecture* 94, no. 2 (2005): 51-52.

Gerkan, Meinhard von. "The New Berlin's Infrastructure." *Domus* no. 770 (1995): 111-14.

Hamm, Oliver G. "Vom Kopf, über den Umsteige, zum Zentralbahnhof: der Lehrter Bahnhof in Berlin-Moabit." *Bauwelt* 84, no. 26 (1993): 1424-31.

Hettlage, Bernd. "Grosser Bahnhof: Eröffnung des Berliner Hauptbahnhofs." *Deutsche Bauzeitung* 140, no. 6 (2006): 20-22.

"Lehrter Bahnhof: Hauptbahnhof Berlin: Alles was Stahl mit Glas kann." *Intelligente Architektur* no. 57 (2006): 48-59.

"Lehrter Main Station in Berlin." *Detail* 1 (2006): 59-65.

"Linked in Lattice: Berlin Central Station." *Architecture + Design* 25, no. 1 (2008): 96-100, 102, 104.

Mazzoni, Cristiana. *Stazioni: architetture 1990–2010*. Milan: Federico Motta Editore, 2001, 250-53.

Mialet, Frédéric. "Dossier. Transports: le siècle de l'intermodalité." *d'Architectures* no. 92 (1999): 36-38.

Thorne, Martha, ed. *Modern Trains and Splendid Stations: Architecture, Design, and*

Rail Travel for the Twenty-First Century. London: Merrel, 2001, 78-81.

Vyne, Anne. "Grand Central." *Architectural Review* 205, no. 1223 (1999): 47-49.

Waiss, Klaus-Dieter, Masahiko Yamashita, and Meinhard von Gerkan. "Architecture of Diversity and Harmony: Recent Works of von Gerkan, Marg and Partner." *Space Design* no. 380 (1996): 5-72.

"Zentralbahnhof Berlin: Lehrter Bahnhof." *Architektur + Wettbewerbe* no. 178 (1999): 38-39.

Yokohama Port Terminal, Yokohama, Japan (p. 230)

Alford, Simon. "Ticket to Ride." *Architects' Journal* 216, no. 9 (2002): 24-31.

Bideau, André. "Raumhaltiges Relief: Osanbashi Pier, FOA's real existierende Datscape." *Werk, Bauen + Wohnen* no. 11 (2002): 30-38.

Black, Stuart. "Foreign Office's Origami Adds Wow Factor to Yokohama Ferry Terminal." *RIBA Journal* 109, no. 7 (2002): 14-15.

Bullivant, Lucy. "Yokohama's Custom-made Ferry Terminal: Two Young Architects Pull Off the Commission of a Lifetime." *Metropolis* 22, no. 3 (2002): 100-105.

Buntrock, Diana. "The New Wave: Ferry Terminal, Yokohama." *World Architecture* no. 109 (2002): 52-60.

Daniell, Thomas. "Strange Attractor: The Yokohama International Port Terminal." *Archis* no. 5 (2002): 105-9.

Desmoulin, Christine. "Origamimétisme: Terminal Maritime International, Yokohama, Japon." *Architecture intérieure créé* no. 307 (2003): 78-83.

Dubbeldam, Winka. "Fluid Topologies: Archi-Tectonics: Dis-A-Pier: Fährterminal Yokohama, 1994." *Archithese* 30, no. 3 (2000): 32-34.

"F.A.O. Architects Limited: Yokohama International Passenger Terminal." *Japan architect* no. 45 (2002): 118-21.

Fernández-Galiano, Luis. "Summer: Roller Coaster Origami." *AV Monografías = AV Monographs* no. 99-100 (2003): 208-11.

"Foreign Office Architects." *AA files* no. 29 (1995): 7-21.

"Foreign Office Architects: International Ferry Terminal, Yokohama." *Quaderns d'arquitectura i urbanisme* no. 236 (2003): 172-86.

"Foreign Office Architects: plate-formes nouvelles." *Architecture d'aujourd'hui* no. 324 (1999): 75-88.

"Foreign Office Architects: Yokohama International Passenger Terminal." *Japan Architect* no. 48 (2003): 62-63.

"Foreign Office Architects: Yokohama International Passenger Terminal, Kanagawa, 2002-02." *GA Japan: environmental design* no. 57 (2002): 64-73.

"Foreign Office Architects: Yokohama International Port Terminal, Japan." *Architectural Design* 65, no. 5-6 (1995): xviii-xix.

"Foreign Office Architects: Yokohama International Port Terminal, Yokohama, Japan." *Architectural Design* 67, no. 9-10 (1997): 68-73.

"Foreign Office Architects: Yokohama International Port Terminal, Yokohama, Japan 2002." *a+u: Architecture and Urbanism* no. 370 (2001): 52-53.

"Foreign Office Architects: Yokohama Port Terminal, 1995–2002." *Lotus international* no. 108 (2001): 80-83.

Hays, Michael K., and Lauren Kogod. "Twenty Projects at the Boundaries of the Architectural Discipline Examined in Relation to the Historical and Contemporary Debates over Autonomy." *Perspecta* no. 33 (2002): 54-71.

Ibelings, Hans. "Pretty, But a Bit Dull, Too: Yokohama International Ferry Terminal." *Archis* no. 4 (2002): 92-93.

Kipnis, Jeffrey, Ciro Najle, and Toyo Ito. "Foreign Office Architects: Works and Projects." *2G: International Architecture Review* no. 16 (2000): 1-144.

Klauser, Wilhelm. "Fährterminal Yokohama: Konstruktion einer Plattform aus Stahl." *Bauwelt* 93, no. 26 (2002): 22-27.

Klauser, Wilhelm. "Kruising tussen scheepsbouw en origami: internationale haven-terminal von Foreign Office Architects in Yokohama." *de Architect* 33 (2002): 72-77.

Klauser, Wilhelm. "Zaera & Moussavi: Harbor Waves: Maritime Terminal, Yokohama." *AV Monografías = AV Monographs* no. 96 (2002): 110-23.

Klauser, Wilhelm. "Japanese Theme Parks: Occupying Home Base." *Architecture d'aujourd'hui* no. 348 (2003): 66-73.

Marzot, Nicola. "FOA, terminal passeggeri del porto di Yokohama." *Paesaggio urbano* no. 2 (2004): 16-33.

Meyer, Ulf. "New Non-Cartesian Geometry: Foreign Office Architects, Fährterminal Yokohama, 1995–2002." *Archithese* 32, no. 4 (2002): 46-51.

Meyer, Ulf. "Parque de pasajeros: Zaera y Moussavi, terminal marítima de Yokohama." *Arquitectura Viva* no. 84 (2002): 96-103.

Moore, Rowan. "Point of Departure." *Domus* no. 851 (2002): 64-75.

Moussavi, Farshid, and Alejandro Zaera Polo. "Exploiting Foreignness: A Conversation with Farshid Moussavi & Alejandro Zaera Polo." *El Croquis* no. 76 (1995): 18-43.

Moussavi, Farshid, and Alejandro Zaera Polo,. "Yokohama International Port Terminal." *Byggekunst: The Norwegian Review of Architecture* 79, no. 4 (1997): 46-53.

Moussavi, Farshid, and Alejandro Zaera Polo. "Foreign Office Architects Ltd: Terminal passeggeri del porto di Yokohama (2002), Osanbashi Pier, Giappone." *Casabella* 65, no. 695-696 (2001): 108-15.

Moussavi, Farshid et al. "Yokohama International Passenger Terminal." *Kenchiku bunka* 57, no. 660 (2002): 17-58.

Moussavi, Farshid et al. "Foreign Office Architects 1996–2003." *El Croquis* no. 115-116 (2003): 1-124.

Noennig, Jörg Raider, and Yoco Fukuda. "Alles fliesst: das Internationale Fährterminal in Yokohama: Architekten, Foreign Office Architects." *Deutsche Bauzeitung* 137, no. 4 (2003): 54-61.

Pollock, Naomi. "Foreign Office Architects Blurs the Line between Landscape and Building in Its Undulant Dunelike Yokohama Port Terminal." *Architectural Record* 190, no. 11 (2002): 142-49.

"Power Made Pliable." *Techniques et Architecture* no. 463 (2003): 79-83.

Righetti, Paolo. "Un molo internazionale: A Terminal for Yokohama." *l'Arca* no. 94 (1995): 34-47.

Scalbert, Irénée. "Foreign Office Architects: Yokohama International Port Terminal." *AA files* no. 30 (1995): 86-87.

Scalbert, Irénée. "Foreign Office Architects Ltd.: terminal passeggeri del porto di Yokohama, Yakohama, Giappone 2002." *Casabella* 67, no. 708 (2003): 30-41.

Slatin, Peter. "Origami Experience." *Architecture* 92, no. 2 (2003): 68-73.

Teague, Matthew, Susan Dawson, and Ruth Slavid. "Metal Works: Major Structures." *Architects' Journal* 215, no. 12, suppl. (2002): 1-16.

"Terminal in Yokohama." *Detail* 44, no. 11 (2004): 1312-16.

Tiry, Corinne, and Christophe Hespel. "Terminal Maritime International, Port de Yokohama, Japon." *Moniteur architecture AMC* no. 158 (2006): 100-101.

"United Kingdom: Foreign Office Architects." *Architectural Design* 66, no. 7-8 (1996): 76-79.

Van den Heuvel, Dirk. "Architectuur als een tautologische machine." *de Architect* 27, no. 3 (1996): 52-61.

Webb, Michael. "Cruise Control: International Port Terminal, Yokohama, Japan." *Architectural Review* 213, no. 1271 (2003): 26-35.

"Yokohama International Port Terminal." *Industria delle costruzioni* no. 367 (2002): 68-81.

"Yokohama International Port Terminal, Kanagawa, 1994–, Glass Center, Newcastle, England, 1994–." *GA Japan: environmental design* no. 14 (1995): 60-64.

Zaera Polo, Alejandro, and Farshid Moussavi. "Zaera-Polo and Moussavi: Young Dark Horses Win Yokohama Port Terminal Competition." *Kenchiku bunka* 50, no. 584 (1995): 73-110.

Zaera-Polo, Alejandro. "Roller-coaster Construction." *Architectural Design* 72, no. 1 (2002): 84-92.

Seattle Olympic Sculpture Park, Seattle, Washington, USA (p. 232)

Carter, Brian. "Art in the Park: Sculpture Park, Seattle, USA." *Architectural Review* no. 1332 (2008): 44-49.

Casciani, Stefano. "Il cimento di natura e artificio = The Trial of Nature and Artefact." *Domus* no. 908 (2007): 42-49.

Deitz, Paula. "Landform Future." *Architectural Record* 193, no. 10 (2005): 94-96, 98.

Enlow, Claire. "Zig Zag, Art on a Green Carpet: A Sculpture Park to Unfold on the Seattle Waterfront." *Landscape Architecture* 92, no. 8 (2002): 22-23.

Enlow, Claire, and Charles Anderson. "Art in the Open: Architecture and

Infrastructure Support a Living Landscape in Seattle." *Landscape Architecture* 97, no. 8 (2007): 2, 100-109.

Gonchar, Joann. "Former Brownfield Site Reinvented as a Connection between the City and the Water's Edge." *Architectural Record* 195, no. 7 (2007): 159-60.

Gordon, Alastair. "Site Specific: Rejecting Object-driven Architecture, Weiss-Manfredi Create Functional Work of Great Beauty." *Metropolis* 23, no. 6 (2004): 82-87, 106-7.

Moffat, Sallie. "Shore Thing." *Architectural Lighting* 21, no. 6 (2007): 34-38.

Olson, Sheri. "Weiss-Manfredi Develops Plans for Seattle Sculpture Park." *Architectural Record* 190, no. 7 (2002): 36.

"Olympic Sculpture Park, 2901 Western Avenue, Seattle, Washington, USA." *a+t* no. 29 (2007): 138-45.

"Olympic Sculpture Park, Seattle, USA." *Topos: European Landscape Magazine* no. 60 (2007): 112-13.

Pastier, John. "Zorro-like Audacity: Weiss-Manfredi's Olympic Sculpture Park Boldly Reconnects Seattle to its Long-neglected Waterfront." *Metropolis* 26, no. 10 (2007): 176, 178, 180-81.

Pearson, Clifford A. "Weiss-Manfredi Weaves the Olympic Sculpture Park and its Mix of Art and Design into the Urban Fabric of Seattle." *Architectural Record* 195, no. 7 (2007): 110-17, 124.

Reeser, Amanda. "Weiss-Manfredi Architects: Olympic Sculpture Park." *Praxis: journal of writing + building* no. 4 (2002): 66-69.

Sokol, David. "Art Parks: Art Blended with Green Space." *Urban Land* 66, no. 11-12 (2007): 160-63.

"Weiss/Manfredi: Olympic Sculpture Park, Seattle Art Museum, Seattle, Washington, U.S.A." *GA document* no. 102 (2008): 98-107.

Weiss, Marion Gail, and Michael A. Manfredi. "Olympic Sculpture Park in Seattle." *Topos: European Landscape Magazine* no. 59 (2007): 38-44.

Weiss Manfredi Architects. "Olympic Sculpture Park." *Space* no. 480 (2007): 70-77.

Souterrain Tunnel Complex, The Hague, the Netherlands (p. 234)

Boudet, Dominique. "Galerie souterraine." *Moniteur architecture AMC* no. 149 (2005): 82-84.

De Mos, Pieter. "Verlicht Haags souterrain." *Bouw* 46, no. 14-15 (1991): 17-18.

Dijkstra, Rients. "Stedebouw achteraf: het Souterrain van OMA." *de Architect* 24, no. 10 (1993): 42-51.

"OMA: Souterrain, The Hague, The Hague, the Netherlands." *GA document* no. 84 (2005): 50-63.

Poli, Matteo. "OMA, deep down…" *Domus* no. 877 (2005): 64-69.

"Souterrain Den Haag." *Arch plus* no. 174 (2005): 22-25.

"Souterrain, The Hague, the Netherlands." *Industria delle costruzioni* 40, no. 388 (2006): 50-57.

"Souterrain, The Hague: Two Tram Stations and a Car Park, 1994–2004." *El Croquis* no. 134-135 (2007): 44-61.

Ter Borch, Ine. "Ondergrondse ruimtelijkheid: ondergrondse tramstations en parkeergarage in Den Haag." *de Architect* 35, no. 12 (2004): 66-71.

Railway Station, Seville, Spain (p. 237)

"Antonio Cruz & Antonio Ortiz: Santa Justa Railway Station, Seville." *AV Monografías = AV Monographs* no. 79-80 (1999): 34.

Binney, Marcus. *Architecture of Rail: The Way Ahead.* London: Academy Editions, 1995, 98-105.

Bottero, Maria. "Cruz e Ortis a Siviglia: Santa Justa, stazione di Luce." *Abitare* no. 313 (1992): 144-49.

Cenicacelaya, Javier. "Cruz & Ortiz: Stazione di Santa Justa, Siviglia." *Domus* no. 739 (1992): 29-37.

"Cruz et Ortiz: Gare Santa Justa, Séville." *Techniques et Architecture* no. 401 (1992): 98-103.

Cruz Villalón, Antonio, and Antonio Ortiz Garcia. "Antonio Cruz y Antonio Ortiz." *El Croquis* 10, no. 48 (1991): 4-76.

Cruz Villalón, Antonio, Antonio Ortiz Garcia, and Michel Toussaint. "Estación de Santa Justa, Sevilha." *Architécti* no. 10 (1991): 60-70.

Domínguez Ruz, Martín. "Das Objekt im städtischen Umfeld." *Archithese* 21, no. 5

(1991): 39-55.

"Estación de ferrocarriles Santa Justa, Sevilla." *ON Diseño* no. 139 (1992): 104-17.

"Estação ferroviária de Santa Justa." *Projeto* no. 156 (1992): 106-11.

Fernández-Galiano, Luis. "Five Stars: The Shapes of Social Opulence." *AV Monografías = AV Monographs* no. 51-52 (1995): 6-7.

Hamm, Oliver G. "Anschluss an Europa: Bahnhof Santa Justa, Sevilla." *Deutsche Bauzeitung* 126, no. 6 (1992): 50-55.

Hessel, Andrea. "Sevilla: Wo, bitte, geht's zur EXPO?' *Baumeister* 89, no. 8 (1992): 24-39.

Kusch, Clemens F. "Bahnhof Santa Justa in Sevilla/Spanien." *Deutsche Bauzeitschrift* 40, no. 3 (1992): 311-20.

Lahuerta, Juan-José. "The New Station of Seville: An Underground Movement." *Lotus international* no. 70 (1991): 6-22.

Russell, James S., and David Cohn. "Expo '92 Seville." *Architectural Record* 180, no. 8 (1992): 114-25.

Sainz, Jorge. "La escala justa: Cruz y Ortiz, nueva estación en Sevilla." *Arquitectura Viva* no. 20 (1991): 16-27.

"Santa Justa Railway Station, 1988–1991, Seville (Spain)." *AV Monografías = AV Monographs* no. 85 (2000): 42-49.

Slessor, Catherine. "Traveler's Jog." *Architectural Review* 190, no. 1144 (1992): 63-68.

Tilman, Harm. "Station Santa Justa Sevilla: Cruz en Ortiz versterken stedelijke structuur." *de Architect thema* 22, no. 9 (1991): 53-57.

"Vaults of Transit." *AV Monografías = AV Monographs* no. 51-52 (1995): 14-15.

Railway Station, Madrid, Spain (p. 238)

"Atocha." *El Croquis* 4, no. 19 (1985): 53-65.

"Atocha: nueva estación de ferrocarril, Madrid, 1985–1988." *El Croquis* 7, no. 36 (1988): 64-83.

Binney, Marcus. *Architecture of Rail: The Way Ahead*, London: Academy Editions, 1995, 92-97.

Capitel, Antón. "The Urbanized Station." *Lotus international* no. 86 (1995): 68-79.

Catalano, Patrizia. "Das Tor zur Innenstadt: der neue Atocha Bahnhof in Madrid." *Architektur, Innenarchitektur, Technischer Ausbau* 98, no. 7-8 (1990): 54-55.

Cohn, David. "Monument to mobility: Atocha Station, Madrid, Spain: Jose Rafael Moneo, Architect." *Architectural Record* 179, no. 7 (1991): 222-29.

Draaijer, Paul. "Het gebouw, niet de architect: het Atocha station in Madrid van Rafael Moneo." *Archis* no. 7 (1991): 12-20.

Frampton, Kenneth. "Rafael Moneo." *Architecture* 83, no. 1 (1994): 45-85.

Gazzaniga, Luca. "Rafael Moneo: Stazione di Atocha, Madrid." *Domus* no. 748 (1993): 29-39.

"J.R. Moneo: progetto per la Stazione di Atocha a Madrid." *Industria delle costruzioni* 24, no. 219 (1990): 64-65.

Kusch, Clemens F. "Bahnhof 'Atocha' in Madrid." *Deutsche Bauzeitschrift* 39, no. 6 (1991): 819-26.

Moneo, José Rafael, and Francesco Dal Co. "Special Feature: Rafael Moneo." *Architecture and urbanism* no. 227 (1989): 27-134.

"Rafael Moneo: Extension of Atocha Station, Madrid." In *Anuario 1993: Arquitectura espanola = Yearbook 1991: Spanish Architecture*, ed. A. Garcia-Herrera, Madrid, 1993, 42-49.

"Rafael Moneo a Madrid: Atocha, Nuclei di città." *Abitare* no. 313 (1992): 150-53, 220.

"Sobre las vías oblicuas: ampliación de la Estación de Atocha, Madrid, 1984–1992." *A & V* no. 36 (1992): 42-51.

Zardini, Mirko. "New Railway Constructions: Rafael Moneo: Renovation of the Atocha in Madrid." *Lotus international* no. 59 (1988): 100-113.

Zimmermann, Annie. "Rafael Moneo." *Techniques et Architecture* no. 382 (1989): 102-7.

Airport Parking, Nice, France (p. 238)

Cardani, Elena. "Un parcheggio-giardino: For Nice Airport." *l'Arca* no. 190 (2004): 91.

Tiry, Corinne, and Christophe Hespel. "Parking, aéroport de Nice." *Moniteur architecture AMC* no. 158 (2006): 92-93.

Metro, Copenhagen, Denmark (p. 239)

"Copenhagen Metro: KHR Architects." *C3 Korea* no. 246 (2005): 98-111.

Erlandsen, Helge, and Hans Trier. "Metroens forløb = The Metro Story." *Arkitektur DK* 47, no. 1 (2003): 36-43.

Keiding, Martin. "Metroens diskrete charme = The Metro's Discreet Charm." *Arkitektur DK* 47, no. 1 (2003): 2-7.

"Københavns Metro stationer under jorden = The Metro's Subterrainean Stations: arkitekt, KHR AS Arkitekter." *Arkitektur DK* 47, no. 1 (2003): 9-25.

"Københavns minimetro = Copenhagen minimetro." *Arkitektur DK* 40, no. 4-5 (1996): 266-71.

Kural, René. "The metro." *Quaderns d'arquitectura i urbanisme* no. 252 (2006): 74-79.

Liese, Julia. "Licht im Tunnel: die neue Metro in Kopenhagen = Light in the Tunnel: The New Metro in Copenhagen = Luce in galleria: la nuova metropolitana di Copenhaghen = Lunière dans le tunnel: le nouveau métro de Copenhague = Una luz en el túnel: el nuevo metro de Copenhague." *Detail* 44, no. 6 (2004): 628-32.

"Metro: die U-Bahn von Kopenhagen." *Bauwelt* 94, no. 22 (2003): 18-23.

"Metroens visuelle identitet = The Metro's Visual Identity Program: arkitekt, Mollerup Designlab A-S." *Arkitektur DK* 47, no. 1 (2003): 48-51.

"Seeing the Light: Metro System, Copenhagen, Denmark." *Architectural Review* 212, no. 1270 (2002): 70-71.

Solà, Manuel de. "Estaciones del metro a Porto i Copenhague: criptes publiques." *Quaderns d'arquitectura i urbanisme* no. 252 (2006): 64-65.

Steffensen, Erik. "H.C. Andersen ville have elsket Metroen = H.C. Andersen Would Have Loved the Metro." *Arkitektur DK* 47, no. 1 (2003): 44-47.

Barajas Airport Extension, Madrid, Spain (p. 240)

"Airport Terminal in Madrid." *Detail* 1 (2006): 66-72.

Cohen, David. "Madrid Barajas Airport, Madrid, Spain." *Architectural Record* 193, no. 10 (2005): 150-57.

"Flughafenterminal in Madrid = Airport Terminal in Madrid = Terminal aeroporto di Madrid = Terminal aéroportuaire à Madrid = Terminal del aeropuerto Madrid-Barajas." *Detail* 45, no. 12 (2005): 1456-62.

Ibelings, Hans. "Richard Rogers: Estudio Lamela: New Airport Terminal Barajas, Madrid." *A10: New European Architecture* no. 8 (2006): 62.

Kockelkorn, Anne. "Neuer Terminal am Flughafen Barajas, Madrid." *Bauwelt* 97, no. 8 (2006): 2.

Manterola Armisén, Javier. "Técnicas de vuelo: ampliación del aeropuerto de Barajas." *Arquitectura Viva* no. 107-108 (2006): 52-57.

"Nueva área terminal del Aeropuerto Madrid-Barajas = New Madrid-Barajas Airport Terminal Area: Richard Rogers & Partnership, Estudio Lamela, INITEC y TPS." *ON Diseño* no. 273 (2006): 112-45.

"Nueva área terminal del Aeropuerto Madrid-Barajas = New Madrid-Barajas Airport Terminal Area: Richard Rogers & Partnership, Estudio Lamela, INITEC y TPS." *ON Diseño* no. 276 (2006): 242-45.

Powell, Ken. "Madrid Airport." *Architects' Journal* 223, no. 16 (2006): 27-39.

Powell, Ken; Dawson, Susan. "Flight Fantastic." *Architects' Journal* 217, no. 21 (2003): 28-43.

"Richard Rogers: NAT New Terminal Building, Barajas Airport, Madrid, Spain." *GA document* no. 79 (2004): 70-73.

"Richard Rogers: New Area Terminal, Madrid Barajas Airport, Madirid [sic], Spain." *GA document* no. 90 (2006): 70-83.

"Richard Rogers: Barajas International Airport, Madrid, Spain." *GA document* no. 58 (1999): 88-91.

"Richard Rogers & Estudio Lamela: ampliación del aeropuerto, Barajas (Madrid) = Airport Extension, Barajas (Madrid)." *AV Monografías = AV Monographs* no. 111-112 (2005): 24-35.

Slessor, Catherine. "Spanish Soft Machine: Airport Terminal, Madrid, Spain." *Architectural Review* 220, no. 1313 (2006): 34-45.

Solomon, Nancy B. "Flights of Fancy in Long-span Design." *Architectural Record* 193, no. 10 (2005): 181-84, 186, 188.

Vogliazzo, Maurizio. "Luxe, calme et volupté: New Barajas Air Terminal, Madrid." *l'Arca* no. 214 (2006): 2-13.

Wall Street Ferry Terminal, New York City, New York, USA (p. 242)

"Smith-Miller – Hawkinson: Pier 11." *Quaderns d'arquitectura i urbanisme* no. 232 (2002): 146-57.

Stephens, Suzanne. "Smith-Miller + Hawkinson Architects Brings Architecture to the Public Realm with a Small Ferry Terminal on Pier 11 near Wall Street." *Architectural Record* 189, no. 5 (2001): 220-23.

Mamihara Bridge, Kumamoto, Japan (p. 244)

Aoki, Jun. "Mamihara Bridge: Jun Aoki & Associates." *Japan Architect* no. 14 (1994): 226-27.

"Jun Aoki & Associates, Mamihara Bridge, Kumamoto, 1994-95." *GA Japan: environmental design* no. 16 (1995): 140-43.

"Mamihara Bridge: Jun Aoki & Associates." *Japan Architect* no. 20 (1995): 138-39.

"Mamihara Bridge in Soyo, Japan." *Architektur + Wettbewerbe* no. 168 (1996): 28-29.

Intermodal Station Square, Louvain, Belgium (p. 246)

Capitanucci, Maria Vittoria. "Leuven: Station Square." *Abitare* no. 428 (2003): 192-93.

De Bruyn, Joeri. "A Passenger Centre in the Station Surroundings, Leuven (Manuel de Sola-Morales)." *A plus* no. 175 (2002): 74-81.

Montaner, Jose Maria. "Remodelling of Stationsplein, Louvain, Belgium." *Arquitectura.* no. 335 (2004): 72-75.

"Remodelacao da Praca da Estacao do Lovaina: Architects: Manuel de Solà-Morales." *Architecti* 15, no. 61 (2003): 22-29.

Smets, Marcel, ed. *Melding Town and Track: The Railway Area Project at Leuven,* Ghent and Amsterdam: Ludion, 2002, 176.

Taverne, Ed, and Marijke Martin. "The Railway Area in Leuven." *Archis* no. 9 (1993): 22-28.

CREDITS

t=top, m=middle, b=bottom, l=left, r=right,
numeration from top to bottom

3LHD 144, 145tl, 145r1

Hervé Abbadie 45
Claude Abron 23tl, 23ml, 23mr
Acconci Studio 169t, 172, 173tr, 173mr, 173bl, 173br
agps architecture 150t
Luis Ferreira Alves 163l1, 163l3, 163l4
Sven-Ingar Andersson 190tl, 190tr
AREP Group 42l, 42br, 43tl, 43tr, 43ml, 43mr, 102, 103, 108b
Arriola & Fiol Arquitectes 100, 101
Atelier de Midi 74, 75
Erieta Attali 243m, 243bl, 243br
Gerhard Aumer 207tl

Iwan Baan 137ml, 137mr, 137br
Lodewijk Baljon 154l, 155bl, 155mr, 155br
Zsolt Batár 200t
Alain Baudry 170t
Cyril Becquart / Altivue 42tr
Javier Belzunce 238t
Benjamin Benschneider 233tl, 233mr, 233bl
Alan Berger cover, 215
Leif Bergum 127b
Hélène Binet 89t, 89bl
Bjørbekk & Lindheim 72
David Boureau 175tl, 175m
Jacques Boyer / Roger-Viollet 184l
Aljosa Brajdic 145bl, 145r2, 145r3, 145r4
Brasil Arquitetura 158m
Marcus Bredt 229
Robert Burley / Design Archive 49ml
Joan Busquets 95t

Santiago Calatrava 112, 113b
David Cardelús 93
Tristan Chapuis / Number 6 Factory 109
Young Chea 181ml
China Photos / Getty Images 222r, 223b
Cancan Chu / Getty Images 223t
City of Curitiba / PMC/IPPUC 33tl, 33r1
City of Louisville, Kentucky 85tl
Colegio Oficial de Arquitectos de Madrid 15
Paul Chemetov / Alexandre Chemetoff 24bl, 24br
Jean-Louis Cohen 236, 240, 241
Collectie Spaarnestad Photo 187b
Collectie Spaarnestad Photo/ANP 187t
Atelier Michel Corajoud 60, 61r
Stéphane Couturier / Artedia 63bl, 63br

Nikos Danielidis 87t, 87br
Richard Davies 29br
Michel Denancé 43br
Denton Corker Marshall 218, 219bl
Jan Derwig 47
Manuel de Solà-Morales 246
Michel Desvigne / Christine Dalnoky 63tl, 63tr, 63m
Dietmar Feichtinger Architectes 134, 135tr, 135ml, 135mr, 135bl, 135br, 174
Ramon Domènech / B01 arquitectes 142t
Patrick Duguet 81b

ECE Projektmanagement 205tl

Lina Faria 33r2, 33r3, 33r4, 33bl
Rosa Feliu 163m5
Fentress Architects 40t, 40bl
Jacques Ferrier Architectures 69t
Magne Flemsæter 131tr, 131ml, 131mr
Daniel Fondimare 135tl
Fonds d'Urbanisation Luxembourg 77m
Foreign Office Architects 230, 231b
Dan Forer 79tl, 79b
Foster + Partners 28, 29bl, 110-111
Klaus Frahm 207tr, 207ml, 207mr
Matthias Friedel 95b
David Frutos 199ml, 199bl
Octavio Frutos 193tl, 193tr, 193m

Justo Garciá Rubio 114, 115l
Jean-Pierre Gardet / POMA 142ml, 142mr, 142b
Antonio Gaudério 186r
Dennis Gilbert / VIEW 19
Jeff Goldberg / Esto 117tr, 117m, 117mr
Goldman Properties 78, 79tr, 79mr
John Gollings 84tl, 84tr, 85ml2, 85mr1, 85b, 148tr, 148br, 149b, 219ml, 219br
Grimshaw Architects 46
Antoine Grumbach 138b, 139

Hiroshi Hara + Atelier Phi 208, 209
Roland Halbe 89m, 89br
Hargreaves Associates 84b, 85tr, 86ml1, 85m, 85mr2
Andrea Helbling 151t
Herzog + Partner 26
HOK (Hellmuth Obata Kassabaum) 30, 31tl, 31ml, 31mr, 31br
HPP Architects 204, 205b
Timothy Hursley 41br
Peter Hyatt 148l, 149tr

Ingenhoven Architects 20

James Corner Field Operations 136, 137tr, 137bl
Thomas Jantscher 140, 147t
Ellen Jaskol 41t
JLAA (Jaime Lerner Arquitetos Associados) 32
Ben Johnson 110t, 111mr
Adam Jones 195tl, 195tr, 195b
Jones & Jones 194, 195m
Jun Aoki Associates 244

KHR arkitekter AS 64
M. Klein 61tr, 61ml, 61bl
Bernard Kohn 24tr
Nelson Kon 158t
Jørgen Koopmanschap 169b
Paul Kozlowksi 23tr
KuiperCompagnons 118, 119

Klaas Laan 155t

Luis Lamich 91tl, 91tr
Luis Lamich, Carlos Sanfeliu, Bernat Martorell 90, 91b
Bernard Lassus 129
Latitude Nord 132, 132-133
Michael Latz 77tl
Latz + Partner 76-77, 77b
Fondation Le Corbusier 213t
Ronnie Levitan 153tl, 153tr, 153mr
Library of Congress 185, 186l
Janners Linders 107b, 203
London & Continental Railways (LCR) 69b
London Transport Museum Collection 161l
Stéphan Lucas 43bl
Lucien le Grange Architects & Urban Planners 152, 153bl, 153br
Luftbildverslag Hans Bertram 27r2

Bruno Mader Architectes 44, 133tl, 133tr, 133mr
Walter Mair 83b
Duccio Malagamba 37b
Mitsuo Manno 39t
Martinez Lapeña-Torres Arquitectes 92
Massachusetts Institute of Technology 122
Ed Massery 83tr
Peter Mauss / Esto 224
Maxwan 34br, 35l1, 35l2, 35l4, 35r3, 57m, 57b
Shannon McGrath 219t
Nick Merrick / Hedrich Blessing 40br, 41bl
Ole Meyer 65tr, 65m
Michelin et C(ie) 124
Satoru Mishima 231tl, 231tr, 231ml, 231mr
Vegar Moen 131b
Adam Mørk 239
Montgomery Sisam Architects 48
Jean-Marie Monthiers 141b, 214m, 214b
Jacques Mossot 158b
MOW AOSO-ATO 247bl, 247br
Stefan Müller-Naumann 27
Murphy/Jahn Architects / Werner Sobek 216
Jeroen Musch 34l, 34tr, 35l3, 35r1, 35r2, 226t
Museum of Finnish Architecture / Kari Hakli 257t

Håkan Nordlöf 157

Odile Decq Benoît Cornette architectes urbanistes 96t
Office for Metropolitan Architecture (OMA) 234
OKRA 189m, 189b

Hans Pattist 25
Pelli Clarke Pelli Architects 116, 116-117, 117tl, 117ml, 201m, 201b
Atelier Alfred Peter 160, 161
Marie-Françoise Plissart 247t, 247ml, 247mr
Attila Polgár 200b
Robert Polidori 243t
Aldo Enrico Ponis 104

Rabier / EPGD/EPAD 16r
RATP 24tl, 138tl, 138tr
Erik Recke / Datenland 202m, 202b
Reichen et Robert Associés 86, 87m1, 87m2, 87m3, 87b
Christian Richters 170b, 221tl, 221m, 221bl, 221bm, 221br

ABOUT THE AUTHORS

Kelly Shannon is Professor of Landscape Urbanism at the University of Leuven. She received her degree in architecture from Carnegie-Mellon University in Pittsburgh (1988) and postgraduate degree from the Berlage Institute in Amsterdam (1994). She is a registered architect in New York and has worked for several international offices, including Mitchell Giurgola Architects (New York), Hunt Thompson (London), Renzo Piano Building Workshop (Genoa), and Gigantes Zenghelis Architects (Athens). In 2004 Shannon obtained her PhD, entitled 'Rhetorics & Realities: Addressing Landscape Urbanism, Three Cities in Vietnam,' from the University of Leuven. She has been a visiting professor at the University of Colorado in Denver, the University of Catalonia in Barcelona, and the AHO School of Architecture in Oslo. She contributes to a number of European periodicals and regularly participates in international design competitions. She is co-editor (with Bruno De Meulder) of *Explorations of/in Urbanism* and *Urban Fascicles OSA*, two book series from SUN publishers in Amsterdam. Her research is at the intersection of urban analysis, mapping and new cartographies, design, and landscape urbanism. Most of her work focuses on the evolving relation between landscape, infrastructure, and urbanization in south and southeast Asia (Vietnam, Sri Lanka, Bangladesh, and India). More specifically, her work focuses on the development of landscape urbanism strategies that work with water and topography.

Marcel Smets, Professor of Urbanism at the University of Leuven and Flemish State Architect (2005-2010), has long been fascinated by the increasingly complex relationship between infrastructure, urban development, urbanization, and landscape. Smets studied architecture (Ghent University, 1970) and urban design (Delft University of Technology, 1974). He obtained his PhD from the University of Leuven (1976), where he was appointed to the Chair of Urbanism in 1978. He was a founding member of ILAUD (1976), and a visiting faculty member at University of Thessaloniki (1985) and at Harvard Graduate School of Design (2002-04). He has been active in the field of theory and history with books on Huib Hoste, Charles Buls, the Belgian garden city movement, and the reconstruction of Belgium after 1914. He served as critic for *Archis, Topos, Lotus, Casabella* and has been juror for many competitions. From 1989 to 2002 Smets was director of Projectteam Stadsontwerp, a research and design group specialized in the urban redevelopment of abandoned industrial and infrastructural areas. In this capacity he was chief urban designer of projects in Leuven, Antwerp, Hoeilaart, Rouen, Genoa, and Conegliano. The award-winning transformation of the Leuven station area has been widely published. Through numerous research projects, published articles, and his own urban design practice, Smets has explored both the theoretical and practical relations between urbanism, mobility, and landscape.

ACKNOWLEDGEMENTS

The authors wish to thank the Netherlands Architecture Fund, the EFL Foundation, and the Vlaamse Commissie voor Architectuur en Beeldende Kunst for their funding; the Belgian Fund for Scientific Research for its grant that helped to finance Smets's sabbatical leave; and the Department of Architecture, Urbanism and Planning at KU Leuven for its financial and logistical support.

More particularly, the authors wish to thank a number of individuals who have been instrumental in making this book possible. Eelco van Welie and Caroline Gautier of NAi Publishers for making their belief in the significance of this publication so clearly evident; Maud van Rossum and Piet Gerards for their illuminated graphic design; Billy Nolan for his meticulous text editing. Assistance with the research, the bibliography, and the gathering of images from Jean-Louis Cohen, Greet De Block, Ellen Braae, Annelies De Nijs, Jillian Farris, Vasudha Gupta, Espen Hauglin, Janike Larsen, Nathan Ooms, Maarten Van Acker, Ward Verbakel, Laura Vescina, Catherine Vilquin and Xiang Zeng was very proficient and greatly appreciated. Annie Collaer, Greet De Block, and Veronique Patteeuw are thanked for their efforts in drafting and following up funding applications. Moreover, Pan Haixiao and Jean-François Doulet are thanked for providing some hard-to-find images and information related to Chinese projects.

Smets's interest in the topic was triggered by an article for *Lotus* (commissioned by Alessandro Rocca), while Shannon's was prompted by her doctoral research on landscape urbanism. Alex Krieger made his office at the Harvard GSD available to Smets for the fall semester of 2004, and in addition to the amazing collection and services of the Frances Loeb and Widener libraries, this quiet workplace in Gund Hall provided the necessary focus to see the first results of the research and exchanges between the authors take form. Discussions with Alan Berger, Joan Busquets, Bruno De Meulder, Alexander D'Hooghe, Kenneth Frampton, André Loeckx, Didier Rebois, Eduardo Rico, Manuel de Solà-Morales, Richard Sommer, Charles Waldheim, and Mirco Zardini worked as a major intellectual incentive for the authors.

Above all, however, the inexorable, systematic, and enthusiastic work of Nele Plevoets, and the unfailing assistance she received from Toon Quanten in collecting the extensive set of images, is impossible to evaluate. Without it, this book would never have been possible.

COLOPHON

Concept Marcel Smets, Kelly Shannon
Text Kelly Shannon, Marcel Smets
Image research Nele Plevoets
Copy editing Billy Nolan
Design Piet Gerards Ontwerpers (Piet Gerards, Maud van Rossum)
Printing NPN drukkers
Production Caroline Gautier (NAi Publishers)
Publisher Eelco van Welie (NAi Publishers)

This publication was made possible, in part, by the Netherlands Architecture Fund, the EFL Foundation and the Vlaamse Commissie voor Architectuur en Beeldende Kunst.

Although every effort was made to find the copyright holders for the illustrations used, it has not been possible to trace them all. Interested parties are requested to contact NAi Publishers, Mauritsweg 23, 3012 JR Rotterdam, the Netherlands, info@naipublishers.nl

NAi Publishers is an internationally orientated publisher specialized in developing, producing and distributing books on architecture, visual arts and related disciplines.
www.naipublishers.nl

Available in North, South and Central America through D.A.P./Distributed Art Publishers Inc, 155 Sixth Avenue 2nd Floor, New York, NY 10013-1507, tel +1 212 627 1999, fax +1 212 627 9484, dap@dapinc.com

Available in the United Kingdom and Ireland through Art Data, 12 Bell Industrial Estate, 50 Cunnington Street, London W4 5HB, tel +44 208 747 1061, fax +44 208 742 2319, orders@artdata.co.uk

Printed and bound in the Netherlands

ISBN 978 90 5662 720 1